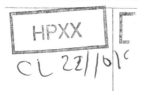

DAVID LIVINGSTONE
THE DARK INTERIOR

David Livingstone
THE DARK INTERIOR

Oliver Ransford

JOHN MURRAY

Printed and bound in Great Britain at
The Camelot Press Ltd, Southampton
0 7195 3492 5

42

Contents

Contents

Illustrations

Illustrations

ACKNOWLEDGEMENTS

The author is most grateful to John Murray (Publishers), Allan Hendry, the School of Oriental and African Studies, the Livingstone Memorial, Blantyre and the National Archives of Rhodesia for permission to reproduce these illustrations.

Acknowledgements

It is a pleasure to acknowledge help from many quarters in writing this book. Some of my largest debts are owed to Professor George Shepperson, Professor R. S. Roberts, Rev Dr W. F. Rea, S.J., and to Professor M. Gelfand, who have all encouraged me in this task.

Special thanks too are owed to Mr R. W. Stacey, and the staff of the Bulawayo Public Library, Mr N. Johnson and his staff, Dr A. Duggan, Mr A. Harrison, Miss S. Loseby, Mr I. Cunningham, Mr G. Dugdale, Mrs R. Kelly, Mr D. H. Simpson, and to Mr E. E. Burke and the staff of that remarkable institution, the National Archives of Rhodesia.

I am also glad to have the opportunity of recording my appreciation of help provided to me by Mr G. Clendennan, Mr P. Cole-King, Mr R. Cunningham, Dr and Mrs Hubert Wilson, Mr Barry Mortimer, Mr L. H. Gann, Mr D. D. Yonge, Dr Flora Macdonald, Mr G. Guy, Mrs C. Rheinallt Jones, Mr R. Stuttaford, Mr Sandilands, Mr V. S. Bosazza, Mr D. H. Harries and Dr A. C. Ross.

It is also gratifying to mention the names of my colleagues who helped me to unravel the complexities of Dr Livingstone's medical history and of some of his associates. These include Dr P. Baker, Professor P. Deighton, the late Dr L. W. Thompson, Dr J. C. Shee, the late Dr J. Kingsley, and Dr P. A. Evans.

I was very fortunate in having been guided through the wilds of Botswana by Mr and Mrs Alan Henderson, Mr D. Blackbeard and Mr R. Gilbert. Throughout the writing of this book Mr John R. Murray has given me far more assistance than any writer is entitled to expect from his publisher. Mr Peter Gibbs kindly corrected the proofs.

For permission to see and use unpublished material in their possession I am especially grateful to Mrs E. M. Healey, Mr Harry Oppenheimer and Mr A. O. Ransford. I have been faithfully sustained in my work by Mr Dick Haiza and Miss Maria Dube. Endless patience with my script was displayed by Mrs Hill-Jowett, Mrs P. Nel and Miss Burns.

Acknowledgements

Finally, as always, my wife has been my greatest ally in writing this account. She has shared all my journeys in Africa to sites associated with Dr Livingstone, and to her go my deepest thanks of all.

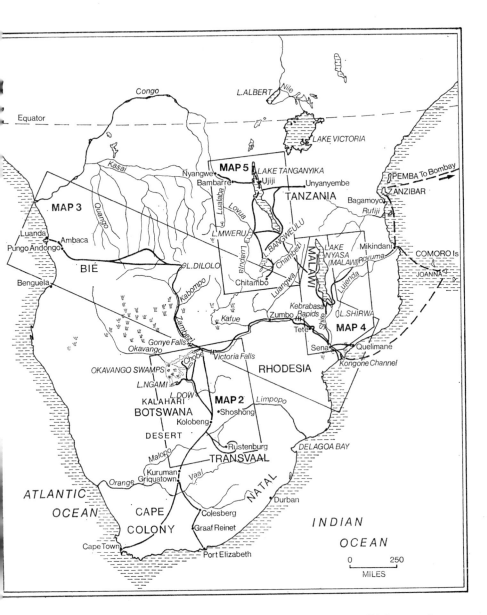

Map 1. General Map of Sub-Saharan Africa to illustrate Livingstone's
Journeys, 1841–1873

The Psychological Background

Despite the profusion of books which have been written on Dr Livingstone, much about him remains obscure; students of his career are puzzled by the inconsistencies and flaws in his character—the difficulty he experienced in working harmoniously with European colleagues, the tireless persecution of those he believed were enemies, his occasional deliberate distortion of the truth, the lack of charity for those martyred for the Christian cause in Africa, the spells of apathy which followed months of intense activity.

A fresh examination of the ambiguity displayed by this remarkable man, does, I hope, justify the publication of yet another biography of Livingstone. In it I have tried to find some logic and coherence in his aberrant conduct, and to make it intelligible to the general reader. My qualifications for this presumption include a life-long interest in Livingstone, a medical training and practice, a Non-Conformist missionary background which allowed insight into the particular strains to which such circles are subject, a long residence in Central Africa (longer even than Livingstone's) which allowed me to visit nearly every place associated with him, discussions with authorities on his life—like Professor Shepperson and General Smuts—and access to new material.*

Livingstone was a many-sided genius who is still revered as a missionary and emancipator. He was also one of the great explorers of history (who traversed a prodigious thirty thousand miles of unknown Africa), but unlike so many others he travelled peacefully and he extended his

* Unpublished Livingstone papers from the National Library of Scotland, National Archives of Rhodesia, the Archives of the United Society for the Propagation of the Gospel, The School of Oriental and African Studies, and The University of Witwatersrand; the Moffat papers, Baines papers, Stewart Papers, U.M.C.A. papers, and Helmore Papers all held in the National Archives of Rhodesia; Livingstone's extensive correspondence with his publisher, John Murray; his letters to Miss Burdett-Coutts, the Brenthurst Papers belonging to Mr H. Oppenheimer (which include the journals of Baines and Hardisty); and the Charles and David Livingstone Papers held at the Livingstone Museum, Zambia.

explorations into the realms of the intellect and spirit. Livingstone, too, was among the earliest in the fields of Bantu linguistics, tropical medicine, African botany, zoology, anthropology and geology. He pioneered new missionary methods which are now regarded as axiomatic, and he wrote one of the most influential books in the English language, *Missionary Travels and Researches in South Africa.*

Fortunately Livingstone was a compulsive correspondent, and for many years maintained an explicit diary. This enormous output of written words provides a unique record of a man's day-to-day mood, and I confidently expected to elucidate the cause of his contrariety from it. Certainly these writings showed that during his adult years, Livingstone experienced a very wide range of emotional life, which moved rhythmically between one pole of delusional exaltation, and a 'down' of bleak depression. His wife put it this way: Livingstone, she said, was 'a mixture of the sanguine and the nervous'.

But my first tangible clue to David Livingstone's character came, ironically, from a study of his brother Charles, who accompanied him on the Zambezi Expedition of 1858-64. In letters to his wife, Charles was then forever sighing that 'my nervous system can never again endure hard study', that 'my mental anxiety induces the old nervous, sleepless difficulty at once', that his 'health would break down permanently', and preaching will lead to 'my end in the madhouse'; Charles feared too that he had experienced 'a narrow escape . . . from insanity', and explained that his 'nervous difficulty does make me peevish and irascible'. The other members of the expedition often referred darkly to Charles's 'condition', and we know that he was subsequently treated for mental difficulties.

Charles's correspondence also makes it clear that he often lapsed into depression and hypochondriacal sullenness, awakening then 'to grief and loneliness'. Sometimes, too, his behaviour was overtly psychotic, leading Dr Kirk to comment that Charles 'acted before the men in such a way as to make them look on him as mad', and that 'his conduct upcountry was that of a madman'. During 1860, Charles's anomalous behaviour was climaxed by attacks of frank mania, as when he physically assaulted his brother, 'tearing with nails so as to draw blood'.

These symptoms are typical of Manic Depressive Disorder, an illness also known as Manic Depressive Insanity, Cyclothymia, and *Folie Circulaire*, due to its phasic character. The complaint is hereditary, and

2

several members of a family may be affected. (Livingstone himself described one of his sisters as 'dottie' and Janet, the other, as 'daft', while Charles explained that the latter was 'nervous and almost an invalid'.) But not all relatives may necessarily be deemed psychotic: in some siblings the responsible gene is of such 'diminished penetrance' that their symptoms are attenuated, showing merely an unstable mood, irascibility and rigidity alternating with periods of mild depression.

In this study of Livingstone I have suggested that his intrinsic ambivalence, his follies and his sublimities, were manifestations too of a manic depressive disorder, and that sometimes they verged on the psychotic.

The symptoms of the inherited malady are therefore important to this work, and can be briefly considered here. The patients are generally well-endowed intellectually, and are often deeply religious, though without bigotry; they show alternating phases of depression and hypomania (excitable exuberance) each phase averaging six months, and sometimes separated by periods of complete normality (but occasionally the cycle is rapidly accelerated, a phenomenon known as the 'switch process'); it is a common condition—statistics suggest that over six per cent of a European community are, in some degree, cyclothymic, and that the figure is especially high among Jews and Scots; the symptoms may become noticeable at puberty, but more commonly appear during the thirties (often being initiated by stress and enforced celibacy); they tend to be most florid after forty; in Europe the highest incidence of symptoms occurs during spring and early summer, which has suggested some relationship between human cyclothymia and animal hibernation.

The manifestations of the depressed phase may be summarised as: gloom, feelings of guilt, pessimism, hypochondria, retardation of wealth of expression, misanthropy, inability to reach decisions, querulous anxiety, and periods of inertia.

Typical of the 'striving' periods of hypomania are: increased flight of ideas, enterprise, elation of mood, feeling of well-being, skill in dealing with people, unbalanced optimism, versatility, acceptance of undue risks, ruthlessness, self-assertion, easy irritation at non-conformance of plans, the kindling of violent likes and dislikes, lack of insight into people's minds, the passing of harsh judgements on others, childish lack of control, inability to master random impulses, exhilaration, euphoria, exaltation, aggression, suspicions which are trenchantly expressed, and

3

delusion that one stands in some special relationship with the Almighty—even to the extent of losing touch with reality.

The hypomanic phase of the malady may shade off into attacks of overt mania; but when the condition stops short of this, cyclothymia is a creative illness which often leads to great achievement, and those who suffer from it may be most valuable members of society. Indeed many of the great 'achievers' in history have been cyclothymic—Cromwell being a good instance.* In other patients, descent into a pathological state is prevented through discipline, dedication to some over-riding cause and through rationalisation of errant emotions—as by attributing apparent set-backs to the intervention of Providence.

Livingstone, especially after forty, provides a classical demonstration of the symptom-complex of cyclothymia, and recognition of this allows the paradoxes in his career to fall into place like pieces of a jig-saw puzzle. Many of the manifestations of the illness are cited in the following pages, particularly in the later chapters. It is enough here to note that during a depressed phase, Livingstone showed apathy (by neglect of the Journal and passive acceptance of immobilisation), meekness, feelings of guilt ('my desperately wicked heart'), avoidance of criticism of others, and bleak misanthropy. Hypomania in his case was manifest by dynamism (enviable periods of well-directed energy carried him through the great trans-African journey of 1853–56), restlessness, facile optimisim and obduracy (Kirk considered him 'one of those sanguine enthusiasts . . . whose reason and better judgement is blinded by headstrong passion'), frenzy of thought ('ideas flow through my mind with rapidity and vividness'), small intense hatreds, a bolder signature, truculence, disregard of others' feelings, and a conviction that he was the designed and designated instrument of the Almighty ('I have been the channel of the Divine Power').

Dr Kirk was several times appalled by Livingstone when he was hypomanic, and once wrote, 'I can come to no other conclusion than that Dr Livingstone is out of his mind'. He also mentions Livingstone's use of 'filthy abusive language', which led Charles to style his brother 'the

* John Sell Cotman was a notable contemporary example of cyclothymia, who alternated between moods of extravagant hope with which went vivid activity, and periods of utter gloom during which he neither painted nor—although a prolific correspondent—wrote letters. The illness, in some degree, was transmitted to all his five children, their symptoms ranging from eccentricity to mania requiring confinement in an asylum. Mary Lamb, too, was a typical cyclothymic who stabbed her mother to death during one 'fury'. Her brother, Charles, was only mildly affected.

cursing consul of Quillimane'. Kirk summed him up thus: 'I can only say that his head is not of the ordinary construction, but what is termed "cracked".'

But if a cyclothymic temperament governed Livingstone's behaviour, it also fathered his achievements. Without it Livingstone would not have been the great man he was. A proper insight into his psyche therefore allows us to see him, not as the saintly figure of his earlier adulatory biographers, but as a man essentially human, and therefore of even greater stature than they delineated.

The peaks and troughs of Livingstone's emotional life can be well demonstrated on a graph. Its shape excludes the possibility of the depression being of a reactive type, as does the family history, and the failure of pleasant circumstances to alleviate the gloom. And although the swings of Livingstone's moods were undoubtedly sometimes conditioned by his health and environment, their influence was far less than in an unaffected person—for Livingstone's exultant buoyancy would be maintained through periods of disabling illness and extravagant hardship.

To enter properly into the role of Livingstone's biographer, one must become both a psycho-detective and a pilgrim through Africa. For only by following the courses that Livingstone took and only by seeing the sights he saw, may one gain that proper intimacy with the man who was aptly named the 'moral giant' of the Victorian Age. But once this rare intimacy is attained, one turns disciple, and becomes aware that if the problems presently besetting Africa are to be solved, the enlightened lines that Livingstone laid down must be constantly reviewed and followed.

I

The Formative Years

After Livingstone became famous a number of romantic accounts were published concerning his ancestry. They lack authenticity, and much of our knowledge of his forebears is contained in the précis which, at the express wish of his publisher, he included in the opening chapter of his first book, *Missionary Travels and Researches in South Africa.**

The family claimed descent from a physician companion of St Columba, whose posterity continued to practise medicine on Iona lying off the west coast of Scotland. They bore the name of Mac en Leigh—sons of the Physician—which was subsequently modified to MacLeay and finally anglicised to Livingstone. During the seventeenth century one branch of the family moved to Ulva, so wild an island as to be certain to breed rugged, tenacious people. Livingstone's great-grandfather, a Catholic belonging to a sept of the Stewarts of Appin, fell fighting for Prince Charlie's cause in 1746, and his widow was subsequently turned out of her cottage during a snow-storm by the soldiers of 'bloody Cumberland'. Thereafter the family was converted to protestantism 'by the Laird coming round with a man having a yellow staff'—a reference to the pastoral staff of St Moluag which is now once more held by the family who were its hereditary keepers in mediaeval days, the Livingstones of Lismore.

The remains of the cottage where Livingstone's grandfather, Neil, lived can still be seen on Ulva, and here Livingstone's father, also called Neil, was born in 1789. Towards the end of the eighteenth century, 'the failure of kelp and potatoes'[1] led most of Ulva's six hundred inhabitants to emigrate to Canada, but Livingstone's grandfather sought employment instead at Blantyre, one of the new industrial centres springing up in Scotland.† Neil, his son, after working in the Blantyre cotton factory,

* Hereafter referred to as *Missionary Travels.*

† There persists a Livingstone family legend, however, that Neil senior quit Ulva because he had been pilloried unjustly for some alleged misdemeanour and made to sit each Sunday on a penitent stool before the congregation.[2]

apprenticed himself to a tailor, David Hunter, a lowlander of covenanting stock, whose daughter Agnes he married in 1810. Finding tailoring uncongenial, Neil Livingstone became an itinerant tea-pedlar in the adjoining rural areas. The work was badly paid and Neil had difficulty in supporting a growing family. His seven children* accordingly grew up in poor circumstances. But David, the second son, never regarded this as hardship: the physical discomforts of poverty and inequality were no less valid 150 years ago than they are today, but their psychological impact was far less wounding, and certainly they were not resented as they would be now. Rather it was recognised that hard work, self-denial and thrift could lead to better days. Indeed Livingstone later insisted that 'were it possible, I should like to begin life over again in the same lowly style'.

He was, in fact, fortunate in having been born at a time which was rich in opportunity for the commoners of Britain. The slump which followed the Napoleonic Wars was succeeded by a period enormous with British energy, while in Scotland universities flourished and provided opportunities denied in England to the lowly born. The horizons of Livingstone's 'humble poor' were constantly widening as he grew up; private enterprise coupled with practical idealism carried the British to all parts of the globe and endowed them with an influence in world affairs out of all proportion to their numbers. A talented new generation was growing up. The four years preceding 1813 alone saw the births of Gladstone, Darwin, Thackeray, Liddell, Bright, Pusey and Browning.

Britain changed in other ways during David Livingstone's childhood and youth. Parliament passed the Reform Act and outlawed the slave trade, Oxford became a centre for intellectual renewal, and a wave of evangelicalism swept through the country which set men searching for means to spread the Christian gospel. The middle classes suddenly found their voice, and improving economic circumstances allowed them to interest themselves in foreign missions. Devout eyes were even turning to Africa, the least known continent.

Its Mediterranean littoral had played an early and distinguished part in the story of human progress, and the Dutch had more recently settled the southern tip of the continent, but the core of Africa, that part lying between the Sahara and the Limpopo River, remained shut off by nature from the rest of the globe. There existed few natural harbours, most of

* Five boys and two girls; two of the sons died in infancy.

7

the rivers were unnavigable because of the sand bars at their mouths or cataracts upstream, and the climate was desperately unhealthy. Moreover there was little in the continent to tempt adventurers: neither great cities nor gathered wealth lay there to be easily plundered. So gradually the conviction grew in Europe that the only commerce that paid its way in Africa was in slaves.

The Arabs had early discovered the potential of the African slave trade, and during the sixteenth century the Portuguese, followed by other maritime powers, joined in the man-hunt from the west coast, to supply the new world's demand for labour. Gradually the English won the largest interest in the trade, which shipped more than 14 million Negroes across the Atlantic, while many more died in the pandemonium which raged inland as war parties hunted down their victims. The intrusion of Europe into the dark continent had brought no benefits.

The Livingstones* lived quietly in the top apartment of a high tenement building named Shuttle Row in Blantyre where David was born on 19 March 1813. The three-storey building has happily been preserved as a memorial to him, and we see it today very much as it was then. It consisted of twenty-four single-room apartments overlooking a curve in the River Clyde and the mill in which most of the tenants worked. The slums of Glasgow lay only eight miles away but the village of Blantyre stood in attractive rural surroundings. Shuttle Row itself was a wholly functional, angular building, although a pair of projecting spiral staircases lent to it surprising dignity. Water had to be carried up to the apartments, while waste was ejected through 'jaw-boxes' in the turret walls. The single room in which the Livingstone family lived, ate and slept, measured only fourteen by ten feet. Such accommodation would be accounted meagre by modern standards but 150 years ago it was considered to be perfectly adequate.

Close to the tenement stood the large cotton mill, now demolished. This pioneering building of the Scottish Industrial Revolution had been set up by David Dale. Dale was influenced by the social propaganda of his

---

* Although the family name was previously spelled Livingstone, the Doctor's father dropped the final 'e' until 1853 when he resumed the old spelling to conform with the title deeds of a newly-built cottage. Dr Livingstone had occasionally signed his name with the 'e' before this date and permanently followed his father's example during 1857 when being lionised in Britain. Some of Livingstone's correspondents, notably Mrs Moffat, regularly used the familiar form at an earlier date.

son-in-law, Robert Owen, and ran the factory in a cooperative manner, although demanding long hours of grinding work from his employees. The mill faced directly onto the Clyde, whose flowing beauty remained with David Livingstone for the whole of his life.

The village of Blantyre was itself carefully planned. Its buildings were surrounded by a wall whose single entrance was closed each night at 10 p.m. Within lived a genuine community, whose people were quick to help each other in times of illness or distress.

In these surroundings David passed the first impressionable years of his youth. The children held their parents in deep affection, and 'all felt that our happiness and well being was to each of them of the first importance'. Stern religious discipline pervaded the home; local Divines were held in reverent regard and Neil combined a pedlar's business with the distribution of Bibles to his clients. He left the 'auld kirk' for an Independent Congregational Chapel at nearby Hamilton and became a supporter of the newly formed missionary societies. Neil was well educated, and possessed the 'intense love of nature' and fiery temper which David inherited. The boy learned the three Rs in a lower apartment of Shuttle Row which served as a schoolroom. He became a great reader and soon showed evidence of insatible curiosity which was a hallmark of later life. But there was something vaguely disquieting about his self-sufficiency and a resident of old Blantyre remembered David as 'a sulky, quiet, feckless sort o' boy'. At the age of ten he was sent to work as a piecer in the Blantyre cotton factory where the majority of employees were children like himself. His work consisted of tying broken threads and tending a primitive loom, tasks which required him to walk up to twenty miles a day, yet even so he would place a book of Latin grammar, bought with his first week's wages, on the frame to study during a work stint which lasted from 6 a.m. to 8 p.m.

No doubt David was influenced by the Owenite socialism of his fellow workers, but what was already most singular about him was this obsession for educating himself and the grave abstraction of mind which allowed him to learn Latin grammar in the crowded clatter of a factory. This early habit of detachment remained.

He was an omnivorous student. After work he would hurry off to evening classes, and then pore late into the night over the books he borrowed from the village and Sabbath School libraries. Only at midnight did his scolding mother pack him off to bed for the bare five hours'

9

sleep that remained to him before breakfast and the next day's work. But weekends were his own to enjoy: 'We were taught by our confinement to rejoice in the beauties of nature', and he delighted in roaming through the lovely country around Blantyre clutching botanical and astronomical books, though the latter prompted 'deep and anxious' thoughts about the 'perplexing profundities of astrology'. He puzzled too over the fossil shells he found near Blantyre whose apparent age conflicted with the Pentateuch's account of the Creation. His younger brother, Charles, frequently accompanied him on these expeditions, and 'often came home full of complaints at being kept so long away and going so far',[3] tribulations which would be repeated thirty years later.

Neither were History or the Classics neglected. At fourteen David was deep in Weem's *Life of Washington* and *Pilgrim's Progress*; two years later he possessed a thorough knowledge of the works of Virgil and Horace. His father censored David's books, and was at pains to teach him the exact use of words ('awful' for instance was too strong an expression to be used for anything but a thunderstorm).[4] But the boy disliked 'dry doctrinal reading', and on one occasion when Neil asked him to read Wilberforce's *Practical View of Christianity* instead picked up a travel book. A moment later his father, losing his temper, 'seized a stick and was laying it on his shoulders'.

But before he was twenty, two events energised Livingstone in mind and body: one was employment in the more taxing (but better paid) work of spinner; the other was an introduction to the books of homespun philosophy written by Thomas Dick. Dr Dick devoted most of his life to proclaiming that science and religion, instead of being hostile to each other, were compatible. Through him Livingstone could understand that the God of Nature and the God of the Scriptures were one and the same, and like his father he abandoned the established church in favour of the chapel at Hamilton. Long afterwards he stated that he experienced 'no difficulty in understanding the theory of our free salvation by the atonement of our Saviour', but only now was he able to appreciate the personal obligation which devolved upon him in applying the provisions of that atonement. His objective was soon formulated: 'In the glow of love which Christianity inspires,' he was to explain, 'I soon resolved to devote my life to the alleviation of human misery.'

Already swayed by the Congregational precepts he heard each Sunday—the yearning love for humanity, shocked pity for its suffering, and the concern for human physical as well as spiritual welfare—David was further influenced by Karl Gützlaff, an Austrian medical missionary in China. During 1834 he came across tracts in which Gützlaff begged the British and Americans to send medical missionaries to China. The appeal was novel: little concern had been shown before for the heathen's health.

Not so for their spiritual welfare. Protestant zeal was reaching new heights during Livingstone's boyhood, and felt strong enough to heed the Biblical call to preach the Gospel to every creature. Following the lead of William Carey, the Baptist Missionary Society was founded in 1793. This was followed by the formation of the London Missionary Society in 1795, and four years later by the anglican Church Missionary Society. Within a century British societies alone were maintaining 2,750 men and 1,700 women workers in the field. The undenominational London Missionary Society, which Livingstone was to join, embraced an individualistic concept of Christianity, leaving its missionaries to choose whatever form of church government they held right. The Society was supported mainly by congregationalists belonging to the lower middle class, and its Directors took pride in being supported by their shillings rather than by the guineas of the rich. They emphasised, too, the importance of recruiting 'all rounders' (and even foreigners) instead of scholarly evangelists; when the Society sent thirty missionaries out to Tahiti in 1796, it especially sought 'godly men who understand the mechanic arts'.[5] This policy was again followed when the South African mission field was opened in 1799 and work there was steadily expanded.

Gützlaff's novel idea of medical missionary work crystallised Livingstone's aspirations: he decided to become both a doctor and a lay missionary, and it was only later at the instigation of his friends that he agreed to be ordained. In those days it was possible to obtain a medical qualification by attending college at Glasgow during the winter terms, and Livingstone was determined to pay for his education by working as a spinner in the summer months.

It was already a remarkable achievement for a working boy to have saved enough to enter college, and the translation from rural Blantyre to the grime of Glasgow marked a further breakaway from the narrower life of his youth. On a wintry day towards the end of 1836 he trudged with his father along the road leading to Glasgow. He came to a new world of tall chimneys and belching flames where the dull clang of factories mingled with the metallic clatter of winding gears. Father and son spent the remainder of the day seeking a lodging where David might board while attending college, and they found it in Rotten Row at two shillings a week.

Next morning Livingstone reported at Anderson's College, which stood at the north-east corner of George Street, and there he grimly expended his entire savings of £12 on tuition fees. The 'Andersonian' was the principal medical school in Glasgow at the time, and Livingstone immediately became so engrossed in his studies that he remembered being possessed by 'a sort of mania' (the phrase is significant) in his pursuit of knowledge. He set himself a wide-ranging curriculum, attending classes in theology under the noted abolitionist, Dr Ralph Wardlaw, in Greek and in Chemistry, where his teacher, James Young, later to make a fortune by inventing a process of distilling paraffin from shale, was to become a generous friend.

At first Livingstone felt very lonely in Glasgow, and positively refused to join the 'gaieties' of his fellow students. So weekends came as a relief. Every Saturday he would escape to Blantyre where his sisters were delighted to find him now 'so genial and pleasant'.[6] He attended service at Hamilton on Sunday and next day rose at 5 a.m., while his mother invariably cooked him some porridge and saw him off to Glasgow.

The diversities of college life made David less introverted. He was exposed at this time to the influence of Adam Smith, one of Glasgow's brightest *illuminati*. Livingstone's later belief that an 'invisible hand' was promoting the interests of humanity may have been owed to Smith, as was his more practical concern with communications which were to play such a large part in his plans for opening up Africa.

The first session at Anderson's college ended during April 1837 and next day Livingstone resumed work at the factory. It was now that he took an important step. Although inbred independence made him 'averse to being connected with any society, having a strong desire to serve Christ in circumstances which would free my service from all professional aspects',[7] he was persuaded to seek admission to the ecumenical London Missionary Society—for it sent 'neither episcopacy, nor presbyterianism, nor independency, but the gospel of Christ to the heathen'. On 12 August 1837 the pastor at Hamilton notified the Society of Livingstone's intentions and this was followed by a formal application for admission. Written in copperplate script, it is the first of many hundreds of Livingstone's letters which have survived. The free style that so characterised later writings had not yet developed; the prose is stilted, and badly spelled.* The L.M.S. Directors showed no haste in replying; only in January 1838 did Livingstone receive a series of questions designed to test his suitability for the mission field. These he duly answered and they were considered by the Directors of the Society on 23 July, together with a testimonial from Neil Livingstone which stressed his son's industry and informed them that he had turned down a well-paid teaching post for mission work. Probably Neil's letter exerted the larger influence, and Livingstone was invited to meet the Directors in London. Two Hamilton church deacons funded the journey, and on 20 August 1838 the Board accepted him on probation.

The aspiring missionary was despatched to Chipping Ongar in Essex for three months' training in Divinity and the Classics under the tutelage of the Reverend Richard Cecil. Livingstone's first weeks at Ongar were fretful and a candid friend remembered him as being 'ungainly in movement, slow and indistinct in speech'. Cecil soon had doubts about the new pupil: 'Mr Livingston will not do, I think, for a preacher. He is too heavy and has too little of the agreeable about him', he wrote, 'and as a pastor or evangelist I doubt if he could win those around him.'[8]

Nor were Livingstone's laboured attempts at extemporary public prayer appreciated and his tutor soon felt obliged to report unfavourably on his suitability. When the Directors met to consider this advice, Livingstone's fate (and that of Africa) hung briefly in the balance, for the majority in the selection committee had decided against him. But one member pleaded for an extension of his probation, and gained his point. Livingstone continued thereafter at Ongar (where one day he amazed his fellow-students by walking to London 'over hedge and ditch' on a compass bearing) until, in January 1839, Cecil grudgingly advised his acceptance by the Society, although admitting that the candidate's 'heaviness of manner, united as it is with a rusticity, not likely to be removed, still strikes me as having importance'. Two days later Livingstone was 'fully admitted under the patronage of the Society'.

His time at Ongar would have been even more disagreeable had Livingstone not enjoyed several friendships there and in London. His

---

* This poor spelling remained: some of the forms he habitually employed were *ajacent, ancle, bretheren, eiland* (for eland), *engenuity, Wedensday, boabab, Luetenant, poney, untill* and *vallies*. Where Livingstone's writings have been quoted in this book, his errant spellings have been retained without comment.

letters often refer nostalgically to 'our squad at Ongar' and the 'remembrance [of] my old fellow students'. Joseph Moore, later a missionary in Tahiti, was a particularly congenial friend; another was Thomas Prentice through whom he came to know the Ridley family at Felstead (and even indulged in a short romance with Catherine Ridley* until she rejected him for Prentice). But in 1839 he came under an even more important influence when he met Robert Moffat at the recently widowed Mrs Sewell's boarding house at 57 Aldersgate Street, where Livingstone lodged when in London. Their meeting resulted in a noble friendship which was sustained until Livingstone's death.

Moffat was a striking figure and greatly renowned in missionary circles. He was six feet tall, forty-four years old and at the height of his vigour. Like Livingstone, Moffat was a Scot who had been brought up in humble circumstances, and joined the L.M.S. He was sent to Africa in October 1816, and in 1824 began work at Kuruman, far to the north of the Society's other stations, turning it into a centre of Christian endeavour among the Bechuana people. In 1839 Moffat went on leave to England with his family, and so met Livingstone.

His importance to Livingstone's career can hardly be exaggerated, and even at this, the beginning of their relationship, Moffat directed the younger man's plans. Livingstone's heart had been first set on China, but that country was already embroiled in disturbances which culminated in the Opium War, and the Chinese mission field was closed. So now at the boarding house he shyly asked Moffat whether 'he would do for Africa?'. Moffat replied he would 'do' very well provided he 'would not go to an old station, but would advance to unoccupied ground'. Then Moffat stressed the opportunities for mission work beyond Kuruman in 'the vast plain to the north, where I had sometimes seen, in the morning sun, the smoke of a thousand villages, where no missionary had ever been'. Those grotesquely exaggerated words caught at Livingstone's imagination, and confirmed an earlier aspiration to make South Africa his field. During the previous July he had mentioned this to the Directors who at the time were considering sending him to the West Indies. His letter had also revealed his antipathy to the practice of medicine in any competitive form, and his sensitivity to criticism. 'In the event of being sent to the West Indies,' it read, ' I could not use the knowledge which I obtained

* She seemed an eminently suitable girl since she was descended from a brother of Nicholas Ridley, the Protestant Martyr.

without in all probability incurring the displeasure of medical men who have gone thither for the sake of gain, and it is well known how easily medical men can destroy each other's influence and usefulness, when an unsuccessful case occurs, as many hundreds of young men have experienced in this and other countries.' It ended with a plea to obtain further tuition in medicine.

The Directors accepted his points and agreed that he studied at Charing Cross Hospital and Moorfields Hospital for the Blind before proceeding to Africa. So 1840 found young Livingstone in London, 'very much pressed by the studies', delighted (as an ardent correspondent) by the introduction of penny postage, improving his acquaintances with the Moffat family, and making another friend in Reverend D. G. Watt. With 'my beloved Watt' Livingstone was to maintain a jovial correspondence over the next sixteen years which was sometimes positively roguish.

On a warm June morning that year, Livingstone attended a public meeting called by Mr Thomas Fowell Buxton and 'The Society for the Extinction of the Slave Trade and for the Civilisation of Africa', in Exeter Hall on the Strand. To reach it he had to force his way through a dense crowd which had gathered to watch the Queen's new husband come to perform his first public engagement in England.

Buxton was a well-known abolitionist who, when the Royal Naval patrols failed to render the slave trade unprofitable, made another attempt to eradicate the evil by proclaiming a new and positive policy for Africa. It reads today like an enlightened product of U.N.O. The continent must be explored, Buxton said, missionary enterprises stimulated, African languages studied, tropical diseases eliminated, sophisticated methods of agriculture introduced, engineering projects begun, and most important of all, legitimate commerce encouraged to exploit the continent's resources and thus undercut the trade in human beings.

Livingstone joined in the applause as Prince Albert climbed onto the platform followed by Buxton and a host of other notables. The Prince propped his carefully prepared notes on the brim of his upturned hat, and opened the proceedings in broken English; he had learnt the words by heart and was distracted only when his papers fell into the crown of his hat. After the Prince left, Buxton delivered his own speech. The meeting then not only endorsed Buxton's 'positive policy' but gave it substance by approving a plan to send a large expedition of technical experts up the Niger River.

Next year the Niger Expedition, carrying so many eager hopes for Africa, foundered in disaster. Its personnel was overwhelmed by malaria, and a third of the European staff perished within two months of entering the river. (Of the 158 black members only 11 sickened with malaria, and not one died. It was a clear demonstration of Negro immunity to malaria.) With them died Buxton's master plan for the continent. The upsurge of public zeal ebbed away in Britain as her people recoiled from a policy which involved such sacrifice, and it seemed that the long African nightmare would continue.

Soon after the famous Exeter Hall meeting, Livingstone went down with hepatitis which he ascribed to having 'inhaled too much of the effluvia of sick chambers, dissecting rooms &c during my stay in London'. He returned home to recuperate, but was back again in London by August secure in the knowledge he was appointed to Moffat's station at Kuruman. In November he sat his qualifying medical examination at Glasgow as he was unable to find the funds to take the more expensive English diploma. After being admitted as a licentiate of the Faculty of Physicians and Surgeons of Glasgow, there was just time to pay a hurried farewell visit to his parents. The family talked in the living room until midnight and then Mrs Livingstone once again packed her son off to bed. The following morning, 17 November, dawned bleak and cheerless. Family prayers were said and at his parents' request, David read to them from the 121st and 135th Psalms. Then father and son walked for the last time together to Glasgow where David caught the packet steamer for Liverpool.* He was in London next day and on 20 November 1840 was ordained for the Christian ministry at Albion Chapel, London Wall, a ceremony which would be recognised by all Non-conformist denominations although not by the Anglican and Catholic churches. With him as a fellow ordinand was the recently married William Ross who had also been appointed to Kuruman. On 8 December the two missionaries embarked on the sailing ship *George* for Cape Town. David Livingstone was on his way to his appointed field of labour.

In appearance Livingstone at this time was mildly unprepossessing. The face was determined and pugnacious. He was scarcely of middle height, and friends referred to him as a 'good and kind little fellow'. But

* The Livingstone family was now in the process of breaking up. The eldest son, John, had already emigrated to Canada and Charles would presently leave for the United States. The parents too were unsettled.

he was broad shouldered and sturdy. The hair was thick and dark brown, tinged with red. A minor mystery concerns the colour of his eyes: contemporary accounts speak of them as dark; Livingstone himself insisted they were blue, while both the Duke of Argyll and H. M. Stanley described them as hazel. Whatever their colour there was no doubt about the acuity of his vision: he himself once noted that with his naked eye he could readily pass the classical test of distinguishing Alcor, the small star in the Bear's tail. His manner was always to remain stiff and awkward, the articulation harsh and indistinct, the words often provocatively blunt.

But he was well fitted for a pioneering life in Africa. His knowledge of medicine was to gain him the friendship of tribesmen who would have regarded a clerical missionary with suspicion. His upbringing moreover had inured him to hardships, while a natural aptitude for handicraft allowed him to undertake tasks which would have daunted a less adaptable man. But always, as we shall see, his conduct lay at the mercy of a cyclothymic temperament which led to disturbing aberrances of mood.

2

Apprenticeship at Kuruman

Livingstone did not waste the thirteen-week voyage to South Africa. He learned the rudiments of Setswana, spoken in modern Botswana, and explored the mysteries of navigation with an obliging ship's captain. His enjoyment of the voyage was, however, marred by an absurd dispute with Ross. It illustrates some classical manifestations of cyclothymia— Livingstone's lack of proportion, easily aroused dislikes, and repeated reversion to an affront.

The voyage was rough and both the Rosses succumbed to sea sickness. Livingstone did everything he could for them—so much in fact that Ross accused him of being over-assiduous to his wife, and called him 'a liar' during the angry scene which followed.

'I suppose I did pay more attention to her than to him,' Livingstone wrote in bewilderment, 'But in the simplicity of my heart I never dreamed that this could be a possibility of offence.' It was all the more upsetting because the cause of the trouble was a lady whom Livingstone ungallantly described as 'a regular old maid', while for Ross he held 'no more regard to his opinions on the ground of his 9 years' education (his wife's boast) than if he were my Hottentot boy & could not read'. Five years later he was still grumbling that 'I feel strongly inclined to expose their conduct towards me. I believed he treated me most ungentlemanly.'

The feud continued. At Kuruman, Livingstone was made miserable by their 'inveterate enmity' and 'scandalising' while his feelings were not improved when Mrs Ross was confined at the station, for, although Livingstone was able to save the baby's life after the coloured midwife had bungled the delivery, he learned that Ross had criticised his handling of the case. When Mrs Ross later died of dysentery, Livingstone still felt bitter enough to inform a friend that she was 'no loss, certainly, not even to her own children'. Nor did he ever relent in his contempt for Ross: ten years afterwards he declined the L.M.S. Directors' suggestion that Ross

18

accompany him on an exploratory journey, with a curt intimation that 'the infirmities of his temper would spoil everything'.

Livingstone disembarked at Simonstown on 15 March 1841 and went to lodge with Reverend John Philip at 5 Church Square in Cape Town. The South Africa to which he had come was in a state of transition. European settlement had begun in 1652 and from Cape Town its more venturesome colonists had gradually spread out into the vast hinterland, dispossessing indigenous Hottentots of their country, and pegging out huge grazing farms. Towards the end of the eighteenth century these trekboers came into conflict with the massive southerly Bantu migration at the Great Fish River. This advance closed the Boers' expansion on the east, but the northern frontier towards the Orange River was still open. During the Napoleonic Wars Great Britain annexed the Cape in order to safeguard the sea route to India, and in the wake of annexation the L.M.S. set up stations in South Africa. The newly arrived missionaries, of whom John Philip was the most radical, sought to achieve equality between the colonials and the non-whites; in 1828 the pass system, which had immobilised the Hottentots, was abolished, and the emancipation of the country's slaves followed. The Afrikaans-speaking farmers—the Boers—greatly resented this direction of British policy, and to escape its restrictions increasing numbers quit the colony after 1835 and crossed the Orange River in an organised exodus. By the time Livingstone landed in Africa these emigrant Boers had gained control of what is now the Orange Free State and the Transvaal.

The Great Trek, the emigration of ten thousand whites from Cape Colony, allowed the Boers beyond the Orange to rule as they wished. They cherished an anglophobia and particularly disliked alleged misrepresentations made in missionary journals about their treatment of the country's native races.

Livingstone stayed for a month with John Philip in Cape Town, and these weeks must be counted among the most important of his life. Up to that time Livingstone's outlook on religious, social and political matters had been moulded by a Calvinistic upbringing, the tenets of Congregationalism, the philosophy of Adam Smith and the Owenite sentiment of the Blantyre factory workers. Now in Cape Town he fell under his host's influence and accepted his views without reservation.

Livingstone had arrived greatly prejudiced against John Philip, because Robert Moffat regarded him as a political agitator and an intolerably autocratic superintendent of the local L.M.S. stations. Moffat nicknamed Philip 'the Pope' and accused him of both assuming infallibility in doctrinal matters and subordinating his missionary duties to his love for disputation and the public eye.

Livingstone's conversion to Philip's views was rapid and easy—because there were remarkable parallels between their backgrounds. Both were Scots born in lowly circumstances, both became factory hands during childhood and both joined a Congregational Church. Like Livingstone, Philip fell under Buxton's spell and decided to study theology. Afterwards, becoming interested in science, Philip too sought to show that scientific discoveries demonstrated the truth of the Bible. Now, at the age of forty-two, John Philip was the London Missionary Society's Superintendent in South Africa, and also ministered to the Congregational community in Cape Town.

Philip was a forceful advocate for those he considered to be the oppressed sections of the South African community, and he agitated persistently for the Hottentots' rights. Philip also used his privileged position in government circles of South Africa and Britain to campaign for the creation of a belt of Bantu and Griqua* independent theocratic states around the borders of Cape Colony, which would curb colonial expansion. This policy was disrupted by the Great Trek, which Philip predictably regarded as rebellion against British authority leading to enslavement of Bantu people.

Dr Philip also held firm views about L.M.S. policy in Southern Africa. He regarded the Society as the disseminator of British civilisation which would best achieve its objects by improving the 'atmosphere' of the tribal milieu instead of seeking direct conversions. He emphasised the importance of associating secular education with evangelism, and as a disciple of the Clapham Sect, believed that through wide dissemination of education, the natives would attain equality with the white colonists. During his term of office he increased the number of mission stations in South Africa from five to eighteen, and looked forward to the further establishment of a chain of missions extending round the coast as far as Central Africa.

Philip insisted that the native tribes beyond the Cape's borders must be allowed to continue to govern themselves and defend their indepen-

* The Griqua or 'bastards' were of mixed Hottentot and European blood. Many of them had settled beyond the Orange River basing their power on the possession of guns and horses.

1. Shuttle Row, Blantyre

2. Robert Moffat as Livingstone knew him

dence, which in practice meant that they be permitted to import guns. This policy was anathema to the colony's Boer farmers and to the emigrants beyond the Orange, whose very lives depended on better arms than the natives' assegais and clubs. Philip faced their hostility resolutely with a sense of sacrificial acceptance which matched that later displayed by Livingstone. Indeed Philip's report to his Directors during 1837, which stated that 'the cause of God in Africa has always been dearer to me than my own temporal interests, than the concerns of my family and than life itself', might well have come from Livingstone's own pen.

At first Livingstone agreed with Philip's plan to create native theocracies beyond the South African borders, but subsequently their very defects led him to believe that the extension of British influence was the best method of reclaiming pagan Africa. But he never wavered in supporting Philip's hostility towards the Afrikaners. Even before leaving Cape Town he felt bitterly antagonistic towards the Boers of the interior, although he had not met them or heard their viewpoints. Yet seemingly more important at the time was his unfortunate involvement in the dissensions which had broken out among the members of Philip's Union Chapel, many of whom resented the attention their pastor was paying to the affairs of the L.M.S. When Philip invited his guest to preach in the Chapel, Livingstone took it upon himself to castigate his congregation for its lack of Christian feeling, and was genuinely surprised to discover that the church members thereafter looked on him as 'heterodox', and even preferred the despised William Ross as a possible candidate for their pulpit.

On 16 April 1841 Livingstone re-embarked in the *George* for Port Elizabeth. He remained in that town only long enough to antagonise its traders by his rudely opinionated behaviour when stocking up for the journey of five hundred and thirty miles by ox-wagon to Kuruman. Livingstone's initiation into African travel followed, and he enjoyed each moment of the ten weeks' trek. For there is a wonderful sense of liberty in the wide horizons of the high veld, and nothing compares with the excitement of the nightly camps when each star glitters with twice its usual brightness, and all is quiet except for the yelping calls of a distant animal.

'I like travelling very much indeed', Livingstone wrote enthusiastically when describing this 'prolonged system of picnicking', and he was particularly entranced by the enormous herds of antelope moving with tense vitality across the veld. He learned how to handle a gun and the span of oxen which drew the heavy wagon. Livingstone was to spend many months in these tilted wagons. A ton of goods could be squeezed into them and they provided comfortable sleeping quarters at night. Each wagon was drawn by fourteen oxen which were led by a small native voorlooper, while a driver walked beside his team, cracking a long whip over the backs of the straining beasts. Travel was confined to the cool hours of morning and evening, but in good conditions twenty miles were covered every day. Livingstone soon acquired a wagon of his own. Each was worth about £50, which represented a considerable outlay for a missionary whose annual salary as a bachelor was a mere £75. A good ox at the time cost about £4 and its loss was a serious blow.

On 31 July 1841 the wagon pulled into Kuruman, two hundred miles beyond the Colony's border, and there the newcomers were welcomed by Robert Hamilton and Rogers Edwards, both veteran artisans in the Society's service. The mission station lay in an oasis on the fringe of the Kalahari Desert. It had originally been established in 1816 at New Dithakong but a few years later Robert Moffat moved it to its present site. Livingstone's only instructions were to acquire the language at Kuruman until Mr Moffat's return from England.

He was surprised to discover that the missionaries had turned this corner of the wilds into a fair imitation of a comfortable English suburb. A street, quarter of a mile long and shaded by syringa trees, ran through the station, lined on one side by the walled gardens of the staff quarters. Opposite stood several school buildings, workshops, and a church capable of accommodating a thousand people. The building still stands, looking rather like an English tithe barn. It has a thatched roof and the walls were so thick, Livingstone considered, as to resemble a battery. He lodged with the Edwardses who proved 'kind to a fault', but he was presently to speak of them in different terms.

Moffat had placed the station close to the famous 'eye' of Kuruman, a fountain pouring out four million gallons of water a day which was led down a long irrigation trench lined with willows to a splendid orchard. But Livingstone was disappointed by the appearance of the surrounding expanse of barren plain. He grumbled to Watt that 'all around is a dreary desert for a great part of the year. . . . There is not a tree near the station which has not been planted by the missionaries. Low stunted scraggy bushes, many of them armed with bent thorns villainously sharp and strong are the chief objects which present themselves to the eye.'

Apprenticeship at Kuruman

Even more upsetting was Livingstone's discovery that the area was sparsely inhabited; in his first letter to his Directors he grumbled that 'the great desideratum is a want of population'. After taking a census he believed there to be less than one thousand inhabitants within a ten-mile radius of the station: it was utterly unlike the scene conjured up by Moffat's striking description of 'the smoke of a thousand villages'.

Further investigation revealed that over three hundred men and women attended church services, but were so primitive that some reacted to the preacher's warnings about eternal damnation 'by creeping under the forms or hiding their heads with their Karosses', and Livingstone did not 'know half a dozen of whom I could say with confidence the man appears to have consecrated himself to the Redeemer'. Such tactless assertions did not endear the newcomer to the veterans of the Society's pet mission, for even in these early days few of them were spared his advice and guidance. Indeed Livingstone quickly made up his mind on controversial matters which had occupied his seniors' attention for years. They particularly resented his criticism of the policy of installing missionaries in comfortable 'civilised' stations instead of sending them 'forward' to propagate the gospel beyond, and his alternative advocacy of using trained Native Agents posted to distant tribes.

Livingstone had supposed that the missionaries, isolated here in the wilds, would have been at pains to live on good terms with each other, but this was far from being the case. Kuruman was a claustrophobic place, encased in absurd rigidities and bubbling with acrimony. Livingstone was despondent at the thought that this was all that had been accomplished, especially by the great Moffat. 'The missionaries in the interior', he sighed, 'are, I am grieved to say, a sorry set. I do not expect the Divine blessing in connection with them. I shall be glad when I get away into the region beyond—away from all their envy and back-biting,' and he informed a friend that 'The jealousies, heartburnings and open quarrels are enough to make the heart bleed.'* The constant 'jarring' upset him and later on he admitted that 'many a sleepless night I spent & wished I were not a missionary'. He complained that 'there is no more Christian affection between most if not all the "bretheren" & me than between my riding ox & his grandmother'. The missionaries were even on bad terms with the neighbouring station at Griquatown: Moffat

---

* Livingstone was himself an impenitent gossip and frequently treated his friends to highly spiced accounts of his colleagues' misdemeanours.

avoided calling there because it employed native teachers to spread the Gospel. Livingstone was also bitterly critical of the local traders claiming that David Hume, in particular, was 'a wicked man' who exploited the Africans.

The prospect of waiting for Moffat's arrival before he could escape from the station was irksome and Livingstone spent a good deal of time riding into the Kalahari which seemed to stretch endlessly from Kuruman to the north. It was a grey and sombre country, vast and tinder-dry, a blank on the map, where everything was hearsay and conjecture. For in 1841 the interior of South Central Africa was still a mystery. No European had penetrated far into what was quaintly termed 'the southern Sahara' since it was believed to correspond in size to that desert in the north, like a geographical mirror image. Yet for all its forbidding appearance and repute, the Kalahari beckoned to the explorer in Livingstone. And in a sense it made him.

The Africans living round Kuruman belonged to the Batlhaping tribe, a branch of the Tswana people. They were essentially cattle herders, and after twenty-five years' proselytisation formed a developing Christian community. Their relatively peaceful lives had been disastrously affected twenty years earlier by what is still spoken of with awe in Botswana as the *Mfecane*—the marauding. It was the central episode of recent Bantu history in Southern Africa.

The Mfecane had been sparked off by Shaka, king of the Zulus. He drove several neighbouring tribes over the Drakensberg to the high veld. They in turn fell on the peaceful Sotho people living there, who themselves became secondary agents of destruction as they fled through the modern Transvaal and Orange Free State. One branch of the Zulus, the Matabele, led by their warrior chief Mzilikazi, likewise escaped Shaka's wrath by crossing the Limpopo and establishing themselves in modern Rhodesia. From there they made frequent raids on the Tswana tribes living to the south-west, most of which were established in the comparatively fertile and tsetse-free country which separates the Kalahari from the high veld of the Transvaal. It was among these Tswana tribes that Livingstone passed his first years as a missionary.

He later became closely associated with a Sotho tribe called the Makololo. Similarly displaced by the *Mfecane*, the Makololo had fought their way across the Kalahari to the Chobe and Zambezi where they had imposed their rule on the indigenous Barotse. Their southern boundary

24

was protected from the Matabele by the virtually impassable Chobe swamps.

The influence of the Transvaal Boers was increasing in the Tswana country when Livingstone came to Kuruman. For the Boers laid claim to the tsetse-free corridor adjoining the Kalahari, although so far the Bakwena and Bangwaketsi tribesmen had resisted them. White traders, hunters and missionaries were accordingly still able to move into the interior along the disputed line of the so-called missionaries' road or 'English path' that passed through Kanye, Molepolole, Lephepe and Shoshong. By 1841 whoever dominated this 'road' held the key to the north, a fact which Livingstone and later Cecil Rhodes were quick to recognise.

Livingstone was to make many friends among the Bechuana tribesmen but his original impression of them was unflattering. 'The Bechuanas are great beggars', he gravely informed his parents, 'Indeed they seem to make it a matter of conscience to neglect no opportunity of asking.' Yet he soon began to appreciate their real qualities. They were cattle-herders, hunters and cultivators, living in stockaded villages, who grew crops where the rainfall permitted, but survived the droughts, which were distressingly frequent, through resort to desert succulents and even locusts as food. Initiation ceremonies played an important part in the lives of these people, and greatly offended the older missionaries who regarded them as manifestations of pagan evil: when they reached the age of puberty, boys went through arcane circumcision rites known as the *boguera*, before being admitted into an age-regiment in which they served during wars and on hunting expeditions.

Livingstone found that the tribes beyond Kuruman lived in an atmosphere of physical fear. The old menace of the Mantatees* had passed, but by 1841 it was replaced by an even more paralysing dread of the Matabele. It was this fear which made them welcome missionaries to their communities, not only for the protection which the Europeans' very presence afforded, but also for their ability to provide or mend muskets. Appreciating this, Livingstone told the Directors that the respect shown to him was not due to his character or teaching, but to 'a less lovely influence', the Europeans' superior arms.

* A section of the Sotho people who, fleeing before invaders from the east during the 1820s, harried the tribes living in what is now the Transvaal, Orange Free State and southern Botswana.

But he could do little for the Botswana until he had familiarised himself with their language; for this purpose (and to get away from Kuruman) he undertook a succession of lengthy journeys into the interior, which altogether occupied thirteen months of the two and half years that he spent based on Moffat's station. They were in fact journeys of exploration which carried him further north than white men had penetrated before. He heartily enjoyed the open-air life and the fascination of the unknown interior, immaculate and untouched, hostile yet enticing, a wilderness which developed acuity of mind and a sense of heightened living; long before it could have been anticipated, he was thus able to view the problems of Africa with keener eyes then his fellow missionaries, and to feel for the continent with a larger heart. These journeys strengthened his conviction that his brethren should no longer expend their energies on the stale pastures of evangelism round established mission stations. He asserted that from the moment a new church was viable, it should become self-governing and support its own resident minister, thus releasing the missionaries to carry the Gospel to those who had never heard it. The expeditions satisfied, too, a need to break away from Moffat's pervading influence at Kuruman: as he put it to Watt, he had 'not come to Africa to be suspended on the tail of anyone'. He intended instead to choose new ground for his work, and told his sisters, 'I would never build on another man's foundations. I shall preach the gospel beyond every other man's line of things.'

There is another aspect of Livingstone's wagon-journeys through Botswana on which sufficient emphasis has not been placed: far from being prodigious feats of endurance, they were pleasant and relaxed experiences. Although they entailed occasional anxiety about obtaining water, ox-wagon journeys were a great deal more comfortable than modern travel through the Kalahari by Land-Rover. They were in fact a repetition of the 'picnicking' he enjoyed so much, enlivened by excellent hunting and the excitement of seeing unexplored country. Certainly Livingstone found exploration preferable to the dull routine of Kuruman.

The first journey began on 18 October 1841. It was a tentative, testing affair made in company with Rogers Edwards. Livingstone implied in his correspondence that it was he who had initiated the expedition but here he was being less than frank; Edwards had planned it long before, and the newcomer volunteered to accompany him. They made first for Bakgatla country and from there trekked on to visit Bubi's branch of the Bakwena, and then Sechele's town, on the edge of the Kalahari Desert.

This was Livingstone's first intimate experience of the Kalahari, a sun-punished plateau larger than France. It is not a desert in the usual sense; only in its southern areas does one find the bare sand dunes which one associates with the word, and even parts of this arid country bear tufts of scorched grass which grow to knee height. Most of the huge plain is covered quite thickly with grass after the seasonal rains; its numerous 'pans' then fill with water, and in a favourable season there is a prodigious growth of melons named *tsama* which provides water for men and animals far into the winter. Even during the dry months, water can usually be obtained by digging in the sand. The rainfall increases as one travels north and here large areas are well wooded and park-like. The elevation of the Kalahari varies between two and four thousand feet, and although it can be ferociously hot by day the winter nights are often freezing cold.

In the Kalahari Livingstone developed a keen eye for the unexplored details of nature. The spell of this austere and silent land began to take a hold on him. For although the desert at first is seemingly a country of implacable indifference to man, gradually he perceived that there was nothing sterile about its aridity. For life continues to go on there, very quietly, but buoyantly and always fascinating in the way it renovates itself each season.

Livingstone caught this sense of hidden life in the Kalahari very well when he jotted down in his note-book, 'amid the apparent silence there is a stifled sound—murmurs—a continual hum of insects which fills the lower strata of air . . . myriads of insects crawl on the ground & flutter round the plants scorched by the heat of the sun. A confused noise issues from every bush, from the decayed trunks of the trees, the fissures of the rocks & from the ground . . . it is a voice that proclaims to us that all nature breathes—that in a thousand forms life is diffused in the dry & dusty soil.'

Primitive Bushmen and the related Bakgalagadi made a living from this bleached land of stunted trees, thorn bushes and succulents that draw sufficient moisture from the scorched sand to survive. And it was wonderful to see the great herds of game wandering over the dusty plains slaking their thirst on dew, or leaves and roots, since for months no surface water is to be found,* although men can draw it from the deep

* Livingstone noted with surprise that eland, gemsbok, duiker and stembok did not depend on open water for survival.

27

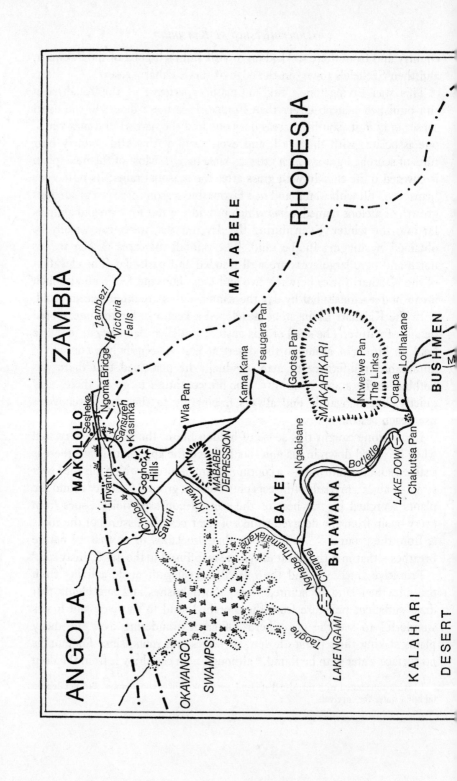

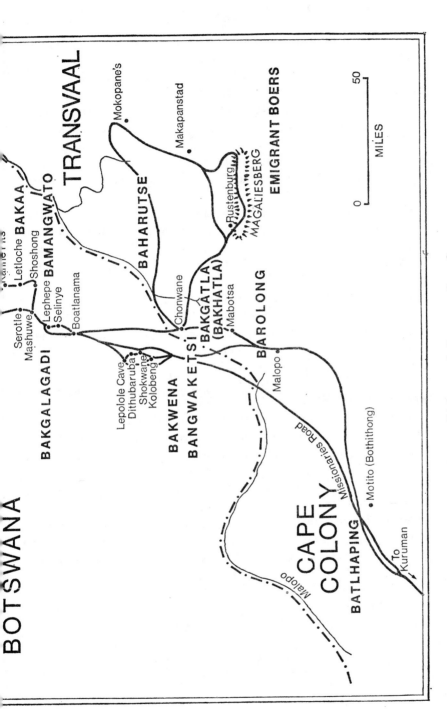

Map 2. Livingstone's Journeys 1841–1853

wells scattered through the wilderness. The courses which Livingstone took were dictated by these water-points, and they remain today exactly as he saw them. Like all travellers through the Kalahari he slowly forgot the harshness of the desert and became conscious instead of its beguiling serenity. At the end of each day in moments of especial grace the sun goes down like a molten ball in a translucent sky, and uncoils to form a brazen wall along the curved horizon, tinting each bush, every clump of grass, even the very sand with leaping colours of crimson, lavender and gilded purple before the sudden blackness of night embraces everything except the stars.

On returning to Kuruman, Livingstone wrote to London urging in almost peremptory terms that a new station be opened either among the Bakgatla or Bakwena; 'May I beg an early intimation', he wrote, 'empowering us to make an effort immediately in behalf of the poor heathen in the Interior.'

But three dreary months followed at Kuruman before he got away for a second journey during February 1842. The only doctor at the station, he signified his strange distaste for practising his profession by explaining that one reason he had trekked away was 'that I might for a season be freed from all attention to medicine'. The Directors were themselves inclined to give priority to conversion, and never appear to have commented on his curious attitude to medical work.

This time Livingstone travelled with four African companions and he remained away until June. The long absence allowed him to learn Setswana,* engage in direct evangelisation and fulfil a promise he had made to return to Bubi's Bakwena. He then moved on, forcing his wagons through the fringe of the desert until the combination of heavy sand and sickness among the oxen made him trudge on foot over the last forty miles to Shoshong, the Bamangwato capital ruled by chief Sekgoma, the great-great-grandfather of Sir Seretse Khama. Livingstone then courageously visited the nearby Bakaa who had recently murdered a white trader. His phlegm impressed the tribesmen and they even assembled to hear him preach.

Here Livingstone was only ten days' journey from the Botletle River which rumour said drained a great fresh water lake in the interior. But he

* Livingstone became highly proficient in the language and during 1852 published a Setswana dictionary. He was one of the first Europeans to appreciate that the various Bantu languages are cognate.

30

had not yet fully savoured the intoxication of discovery, and turned away to visit the Makalaka. Seven years were to elapse before he saw Lake Ngami.

The Doctor was strangely hooded in his references to the Makalaka, contenting himself with writing, 'I shall not however say anything more respecting them until I get better acquainted with their actual condition'. Possibly this wariness was owed to the Makalakas' possession of guns which he suspected were obtained from dealing in slaves. It was the first time he had been brought into contact with the curse of Africa.

From Shoshong Livingstone walked back to his wagons, accompanied by thirty tribesmen bearing Sekgoma's gifts. He revisited Bubi and was back at Kuruman in the June of 1842, after a lonely journey of a thousand miles. By now he had adapted himself to conditions of travel and had developed a certain expertise in dealing with them. He knew exactly what equipment and clothing suited him, and the familiar figure of the legendary explorer was already taking shape. An unclerical moustache prevented sunburn of the upper lip and he told his sister that 'A common midshipman's cap covers my head'.

Livingstone was confined to Kuruman for the next eight months, since Matabele raids to the north had so terrified the mission Africans that he was unable to recruit a single wagon driver for his next venture. But by February 1843 the turmoil had died down and Livingstone set off on his third journey of reconnaissance. He went straight to Sechele's who had been upset by his having paid more attention to Bubi. On hearing that the missionary intended to go further north, Sechele protested that no European could survive in the Kalahari, and matters were made worse when Livingstone's Kuruman servants refused to go any farther. But he pressed on over the next two hundred miles mounted on a riding ox with three Bakwena guides. He was now able to visit the isolated villages of the primitive Bakgalagadi and accounted his stay with them 'the happiest portion of my journey'. He also spent more time with the Bakaa, who refused him food lest they be accused of trying to poison him. Weak from fasting Livingstone fell one day from some rocks and suffered a compound fracture of a finger bone. A little later, awakened by a marauding lion, he rebroke the bone when he fired off his pistol. In his correspondence he makes light of the severe pain he suffered and only regretted that it prevented his shooting for the pot.

During this third journey from Kuruman, Livingstone became friendly with one of his Bakwena companions named Sehamy. Six months later, he learned that Sehamy had died and he fell into a sombre mood which, as we shall see, could wring out of him sepulchral soliloquies written in the archaic second person singular. This apostrophe reveals his feeling of guilt, so typical of the cyclothymic subject, at having failed to convert an intimate, whose soul would now inevitably be committed to Hell. 'Poor Sehamy', Livingstone lamented, 'where art thou now, Where lodges thy soul tonight? Didst thou think of what I told thee as thou turnedst from side to side in distress? I could now do anything for thee. I could weep for thy soul. But now nothing can be done. Thy fate is fixed. O, am I guilty of the blood of thy soul, my poor dear Sehamy? If so, how shall I look on thee in the Judgement? But I told thee of a saviour. O, didst thou think of Him, did He lead thee through the dark valley, did He comfort as only He can? Help me, O Lord Jesus, to be faithful to everyone. O remember me, & let me not be guilty of the blood of souls.' It was a pronouncement of the grim doctrine of conditional salvation which held that everyone who died 'in ignorance of the Saviour' was condemned to everlasting perdition. Livingstone would presently reject this hell-fire thesis for it could not be reconciled with his concept of a merciful God, and eight years later we find him writing that after a heathen's death assuredly the 'Judge of all the Earth will do right'.

At the end of this, the third Kalahari journey, Livingstone found good news awaiting him. Dr Moffat was on his way home to Kuruman and had sent on mail ahead. This included the Directors' anxiously awaited reply to Livingstone's request to branch out on his own. In it they pontificated, 'Nor do we hesitate to state our cordial concurrence in your sentiments as to the desirableness of undertaking the permanent operations of the Society among the tribes to whom your attention has been directed.' It was a cumbrously worded permission for him to break away from Kuruman. Livingstone immediately wrote back of the 'feelings of inexpressible delight with which I hail the decision of the Directors that we go forward to the dark interior', for it meant that his long apprenticeship was over.

3

Mabotsa and Chonwane

The Directors' letter was signed by Reverend Arthur Tidman, who shared with Reverend J. J. Freeman the joint post of Foreign Secretary for the Society, and it made some points which were less welcome to Dr Livingstone than permission to move north. For, after consulting Dr Moffat, the Society announced its resolve to divide the Colony into several administrative districts, each of which would be governed by a committee of missionaries.

Livingstone was now thirty, an important age in men searching for identity, and this decision seemed to establish that identity firmly; the wholeness of Livingstone's thinking, his innate rebelliousness, from this time begins to emerge. He feared that this step would diminish Philip's authority, and dreaded too that the local committee would behave like a 'presbitery'. Livingstone poured out his misgivings to Tidman, declaring that he reserved 'the power of withdrawing from that Committee if at any future time I feel that to be my duty'. He grumbled again that the population round Kuruman was far smaller than he had been led to expect, and then provided statistics to prove his point. In this exhausting letter he also brought up the thorny subject of overstaffing the South African missions when even more demanding fields existed in China and India, and regretted that still further missionaries were being sent out to the Colony. When they received this effusion, his Directors must have suspected that in Livingstone they had been saddled with a sadly opinionated and controversial agent.

As regards Livingstone's earlier plea to train Africans at Kuruman to act as native agents in new mission stations, the Directors' reply was dampening, saying that 'the matter should properly be considered by the newly-formed District Committee'. Knowing the colleagues who would form that committee, Livingstone felt unhappy.

Fortunately there was work to be done arranging his new mission

station, which he was to share with Edwards. They decided on settling at
Mabotsa among the Bakgatla, and early in August 1843 set off to prepare
their new site, travelling in the company of 'three Gentlemen from India',
who had come 'to this country in order to have their health restored by
the exercises of hunting and travelling'. Livingstone took a liking to one
of them; the future General Sir Thomas Steele, in turn was filled with
admiration for Livingstone, and years later acted as a pall-bearer at his
funeral.

Edwards and Livingstone took over ground at Mabotsa for the mission
after paying chief Mosielele a musket, gun-powder, lead and beads
worth £4. The ceremony subsequently featured in the Society's
Missionary Chronicle with an absurd sketch of the two Europeans formally
dressed in top hats and frock-coats instead of their rough working
clothes. Livingstone and Edwards then set about building 'a substantial
hut' as a nucleus for their station. They received little assistance from the
tribesmen, but one of the converts from Kuruman, named Mabalwe,
turned out to be unexpectedly helpful.

The two men returned to Kuruman on 27 September 1843. There
was still no news of Moffat's return, and Livingstone occupied his time
by composing an account of the establishment of the Mabotsa Mission.
In it he gave little credit to Edwards* and, most unfortunately, the Society
published an extract of his report which gushed over 'our intrepid
missionary, Mr Livingston', but said not a word about his colleague.
The omission did not go unnoticed by Rogers Edwards.

At the end of November, Kuruman at last heard that Moffat and his
family (including his grown-up daughter Mary whom Livingstone was
to marry) were approaching. Gladdened by the news Livingstone light-
heartedly rode one hundred and fifty miles to meet them near the Vaal
River, racing his horse up to the wagon as though 'at Ascot or the Derby'.
Moffat was delighted by the young man's attention. 'Such a visitant as
Mr Livingston in the wide wilderness', he announced, 'was to us a most
refreshing circumstance. Few can conceive of the hallowed feeling his
presence produced.' According to her father, the young man was at once
'smitten with Mary's charms'.[1]

Livingstone and Moffat so complement each other in the story of
Christian endeavour in South Central Africa that it is a little difficult to
recognise the differences between them. Livingstone without question

---

* It was a lapse which was repeated when Livingstone wrote *Missionary Travels*.

was the greater man, yet what a massive figure was Robert Moffat. He built up Kuruman into a flourishing station and then addressed himself to the tremendous task of translating the Scriptures into Setswana. Livingstone spoke of Moffat as 'the Apostle of the Bechuanas' and he was one of the few men from whom he would accept advice. But Moffat lacked Livingstone's power of inspiring others, and he was never fired by the great vision of redeeming Africa through Christianity and commerce. Yet more detrimental to the emergence of posthumous legend was the fact that Robert Moffat died peacefully in bed at an advanced age, and his splendid career was denied the final heart-rending tragedy of his son-in-law.

Already in 1841 the two men's thoughts were beginning to move along different lines. Moffat was essentially an evangelist: his ambition was to convert the Africans living round Kuruman and so save their souls from perdition. Livingstone, as in his lament for Sehamy, at first subscribed to the importance of this primary evangelical task and as late as 1847 declared that conversion was 'the great desideratum'. But he was also concerned with alleviating the Africans' barbarous environment and, under Philip's influence, with spreading the Christian ethic more widely, rather than identifying himself with a single mission station like Moffat. This change in attitude was effected by regarding himself as a missionary pathfinder and prospector, faced with the holy urgency of preparing millions of heathens living in distant lands to receive the Gospel. He believed that opening a way for conventional missionaries would do more to change the hearts and minds of Africans than any amount of preaching. With this wider interpretation of missionary duty in his mind, he proclaimed that 'the true and honest discharge of the common duties of every-day life is Divine service'. He similarly rationalised his concepts by assuring a correspondent, 'I am serving Christ when shooting a buffalo for my men or taking an observation' just as much as when evangelising. Yet Livingstone could never quite shrug off the fear that personal ambition rather than a convenient view of Christian service was the driving force which carried him so far beyond the normally accepted bounds of missionary activity. 'Some of the bretheren', he told his Directors, 'do not hesitate to tell the natives that my object is to obtain the applause of men. This bothers me, for I sometimes suspect my own motives.' But he comforted himself with a statement in the same letter that 'I am conscious that, though there is much impurity in my motives, they are in the main for the glory of Him to whom I have dedicated my all.'

Again unlike Livingstone, Moffat was not greatly interested in the Bantu way of life, many aspects of which were abhorrent to his Christian norms. Impressed by the apparent cultural poverty of tribalism, he never appreciated it as an ordered system of human relationships. He looked upon the Africans' interminable singing and dancing as a manifestation of Satan's work, and was much affronted by their scanty clothing. To him a man's moral worth could be measured by the number of garments he wore. Nor was Moffat much concerned with championing the rights of oppressed Africans. Livingstone in contrast displayed an indulgent interest in all forms of African culture. He respected its differences, and made no attempt at their elimination. Thus he regarded the *boguera* initiation ceremony (which Moffat condemned as an obscenity leading to sexual excess) as no more than 'a sanitary and political measure' that should not be discouraged. Later Livingstone differed even more sharply from his colleagues, not only by compiling geographical information and recording detailed observations of natural phenomena, but by following Philip's precept of striving to eliminate all the injustices to which the natives were subject. To attain this goal he was prepared to come to terms with anyone, even with the slavers whom he abhorred.

The first meeting of the controversial District Committee was held in the New Year. Immediately afterwards Livingstone and Edwards set off to start their mission at Mabotsa. Edwards in his fiftieth year suffered from an awkward complex. He longed to rise from artisan status to a full missionary, and now, associated with an ordained pastor brimming over with enterprise, he found himself resenting Livingstone's energy for the reflection it cast on his own. Trouble between them was inevitable.

Mabotsa is situated twenty-four miles north-west of modern Zeerust. The foundations of the house Livingstone built there—a pretentious one which included a bedroom, parlour and study with glass for the windows brought up from Kuruman—can still be traced at the foot of picturesque hills among fine wooded country. Livingstone was certain that the station would soon develop into a second Kuruman. But almost immediately a serious accident befell him—he was badly savaged by a lion.

The story of the encounter with the lion became the best known of all his adventures. He told Moffat of the mishap in a letter dated 15 February 1844, and in it suggests that it occurred either on 7 or 14 February

36

3. Mary Moffat Livingstone

4. David Livingstone, Cape Town, 1852. He described this photograph as follows: '. . . contains the sextant presented by Captain Steele and the watch chronometer presented by the Royal Geographical Society. It is a little pedantic. . . .'

1844.[2] The former date is most likely because on 16 February Edwards reported that the wound was 'very swollen and angry'.

Livingstone owed his life to the bravery of two Africans and also, he believed, to the thick tartan jacket he was wearing. But he sustained a compound fracture of the left humerus (the upper long bone of the arm) and many lacerations. He managed to walk home and was curiously diffident about the encounter, possibly because critics might suggest that a missionary's duties did not include engaging in a lion hunt. 'Had it been directly in the way of duty I should not have cared for the pains', he wrote, 'I don't know what they [the Directors] will think of me after this', and he advised his parents, 'I don't think you ought to make any talk of this to any one'. Long afterwards, when questioned by friends about his thoughts while in the lion's grasp, Livingstone put them off by saying he merely felt curiosity about 'what part of me he would eat first'.

What was far harder to bear than his injuries was the neglect shown him by Mr and Mrs Edwards when he lay in agony for weeks in a rough native hut. In fairness we must note that Edwards confessed that they felt 'much at a loss how to go to work' in treating the wound 'as neither of us [had] any skill in Surgery', while Livingstone refused their suggestion of moving to Kuruman.[3] But he was deeply hurt by their behaviour, complaining that 'I was without medical assistance, without house, and had very few attentions save *what the poor black fellows* about me could give. The lion left me with eleven ugly gashes and a shattered humerus, and these discharging excessively made me as weak as possible.' Years later the memory of the Edwards' indifference to his suffering rankled as fiercely as ever: 'Mrs E. scarcely ever looked near me after the first few days,' he wrote, '& to get my arm dressed even when crawling with maggots I had to send for Mr E. Occasionally he came of his own accord, but even when almost dead I would infinitely have preferred Bakhatla to dress it for me. It was evidently a grudge to him, & how could it be otherwise? He & she too were writing against me at the very time.'

For so serious a condition Livingstone should of course have obtained skilled surgical attention, but there was no doctor beside himself for hundreds of miles and 'it would have taken at least three months to reach Cape Town'. Obliged to treat himself, he 'fitted a screw to my arm, so as to produce pressure between the ends of the bones', and even considered inserting a seton between the two bony fragments but refrained from this excruciatingly painful measure because he was never 'able to plan a six weeks leisure'. A celebrated medical collegue, Sir Risdon Bennett, wrote afterwards that Livingstone had exhibited 'an amount of courage, sagacity, skill, and endurance that have scarcely been surpassed in the annals of heroism', and despite the difficulties, Livingstone's treatment produced a surprisingly good result. Although a false joint formed in the upper third of his humerus (an unusual condition which in 1874 allowed certain identification of the Doctor's corpse), he retained some use in the arm, but found it necessary to shoot from the left shoulder.

The injury delayed the construction of a proper house, but it was so well advanced by May that Livingstone felt justified in travelling to Kuruman for recuperative leave and, as Mrs Moffat announced, 'to pay his addresses to our eldest daughter'.[4] He had been contemplating matrimony for some time, and jokingly told Watt that he was thinking of advertising for 'some decent sort of widow' in the *Evangelical Magazine*. Yet he had nervously withdrawn when one of the Griquatown missionaries, considering his daughter suitable, sent her to Kuruman 'by way of an experiment'. But now he payed his court to Mary Moffat, for what more promising *parti* could be found than the daughter of 'The Apostle of the Bechuanas'. Rather bashfully he tells in one variant of *Missionary Travels** that during July he 'screwed up . . . courage to put a question beneath one of the fruit-trees' in the garden at Kuruman, and became formally engaged. A little later, Livingstone bleakly notified his Directors that 'Various considerations connected with this new sphere of labour, and which to you need not be specified in detail, having led me to the conclusion that it was my duty to enter into the marriage relation, I have made the necessary arrangements for union with Mary, the eldest daughter of Mr Moffat, in the beginning of January 1845. It was not without much serious consideration & earnest prayer I came to the above decision, and if I have not deceived myself I was in some measure guided by a desire that the Divine glory might be promoted in my increased usefulness.'

Mary Moffat was twenty-three at the time. She had been born at Griquatown in Cape Colony and completed her education in London where she had 'a narrow escape from marriage with a relation'.[5] Mary had few pretentions to good looks, nor was her suitor particularly flattering about her charms: he described his fiancée to Watt as 'not romantic but a matter-of-fact lady, a little black-haired girl, sturdy, and all that I want',

* There are eight known variants of the first edition of *Missionary Travels*.

and, less than two weeks before the appointed wedding day, he notified another friend a shade ungraciously that 'I am, it seems, after all to be hooked to Miss Moffat'.

Mary already exhibited a tendency to corpulence, and within two years her husband was remarking on her 'African' complexion and 'stout stumpy body'. Nor did her appearance improve with time; photographs in middle age suggest that she resembled an animated Queen of Spades.

They were married on 9 January 1845 at Kuruman by the neighbouring French missionary, Reverend Prosper Lemue.*[6]

Mrs Livingstone according to her husband was 'amiable and good tempered', and an accomplished housekeeper. Attending always to his comfort she became 'famous for roughing it in the bush'. After Mary's death her husband wrote, 'a right straight forward woman was she, no crooked way was ever hers & she could act with decision & energy when required'. 'In our intercourse in private', he declared on another occasion, 'there was more than what would be thought by some a decorous amount of merriment and play'. Livingstone indeed treated his wife with jocular affection, often referring to her as 'my dear rib', but his correspondence with her was far less demonstrative than that addressed to trusted friends. His selfishness, or what he considered duty, dominated their relationship. Thus he fretted over her 'frequent pregnancies', which he unkindly compared to the products of 'the great Irish manufactory', and when they endangered his plans, Livingstone shipped her off to Britain with the children. Yet when Mary died her husband's grief was genuine and overpowering.

At the time of his marriage Livingstone was already contemplating moving on from Mabotsa, although he had said nothing about this to Edwards. 'The sphere is too small for two missionaries', he told a friend, 'As I am the younger I purpose to go on to the Bakwains of either Bubi or Sechele'; and next month when the District Committee met for the second time Livingstone announced his desire 'to extend missionary labour to another tribe'. This meeting turned out to be an unhappy one for Livingstone: when he proposed his scheme for African teachers it was brusquely rejected by the committee's senior members, who resented the attempt to initiate policy, and there was even an unkind suggestion that he was seeking to create a seminary over which he might reign as Professor. He was particularly upset by the unexpected opposition of his

* In *Missionary Travels* Livingstone erroneously states that the wedding took place in 1844.

new father-in-law and felt 'very sorry afterwards that I had spoken so bitterly' in reply. Later on he confessed to the Directors that the incident 'caused me months of bitter grief'. It must then have been with relief that, early in March, Livingstone left Kuruman with his bride for Mabotsa. But there a worse blow awaited him: 'on the very day of our return', Livingstone told Tidman, Edwards flew at him with an accusation that his 'conduct has been dishonest, dishonourable and mischievous'. Edwards' attack was savage and unexpected. Among its causes were jealousy, offended dignity, the old-standing resentment at his own inferior position and realisation that the marriage meant a new and 'close connection with Kuruman'.

Livingstone never forgave Edwards for his outbursts, and drowned his indignation in a sea of correspondence. He rarely wrote with greater ease than when castigating a colleague, and for years his indefatigable pen ran tirades about Edwards' behaviour, each one a subtle manipulation of the facts, so that Moffat was left gasping 'Mr L. wants light'. Moffat was startled another day to receive from his son-in-law an incoherent report on Edwards' conduct running to 3,600 words; an even more tedious communication laid the case before the Directors, to whom Livingstone believed—wrongly as it turned out—Edwards had repeated his charges. The incident increased Livingstone's disgust for his colleagues, and he informed Watt that 'my desire is to have as little to do with the other missionaries as possible. I have had nought but . . . injury from them'. He subsequently suggested to the Directors that Edwards should be dismissed.

After delivering his accusations, Edwards took himself off to Kuruman leaving Livingstone miserable at Mabotsa, where he felt it his duty to remain until Edwards returned. But he began to prepare for a move to Sechele's Bakwena, commuting regularly to Chonwane, where he started to build another house.

The Bakwena received Livingstone kindly, and he believed he saw 'far greater prospects of usefulness here than at Mabotsa'. Ground for the new mission was bought for 'a gun, some ammunition, & beads', but when writing *Missionary Travels*, and remembering Boer accusations of supplying the Bakwena with muskets, he discreetly noted the price as about '£5 worth of goods'. The scanty remains of the house he built are still visible today in the Transvaal close to the Botswana border.

Livingstone was back at Mabotsa towards the end of the year to deliver his wife of their first child, a boy named Robert after her father.* By March 1846 the house at Chonwane was finished and the Livingstones moved there and began their long association with Sechele.

Sechele was in his middle thirties, a tall good-looking man who affected European clothes but wore his hair in long plaits. He was highly intelligent, mastered the alphabet within three days, and soon learned to read, being particularly enthralled by the travails of 'Johane Bunyana'. The chief became well versed in the Gospels too, but never quite brought himself to abandon pagan customs.

The Chonwane period of Livingstone's career lasted a mere eighteen months, and on the whole they were happy ones. He relished a woman's touch about the house and wrote that 'I have much cause for gratitude for comfort to which I was a stranger'. The move had brought him into closer proximity with the Transvaal Boers who were firmly established in the Magaliesberg and Marico valley, only thirty miles east of the station. They were deeply distrustful of their missionary neighbour, fearing that he would arm the independent tribes and threaten their new settlement. Accordingly the Boer Commandant at Marico, Gert Kruger,† warned Livingstone that they intended to deprive Sechele of the guns he already possessed. At about the same time another message arrived from a chief named Mokgatle, living four days journey to the east, requesting Livingstone to provide him with an African teacher.

Here was a golden opportunity to put the system of native agency into practice. During July 1846 Livingstone journeyed eastwards across the Marico River and through a dense African population to Mokgatle's kraal just north of Rustenburg where he hoped to leave an African evangelist. Then, crossing the headwaters of the Limpopo River to visit an isolated section of the Bakwena, he met Kruger and was able to dissuade the Boers from marching against Sechele.

Back at Chonwane he turned to building a school, until in November he undertook a second, longer journey into the infant Transvaal Republic and this time Mrs Livingstone and the baby went too. They trekked straight to the kraal of a chief named Seamogoe, some forty-five miles east of Rustenburg, and turned north to Makapanstad. Six days beyond they reached a cluster of Ndebele villages where Livingstone met the

---

* Thereafter, according to Tswana custom, Mrs Livingstone was known to them as 'Ma-Robert', i.e. Mother of Robert.

† Gerrit Johannes Kruger, uncle of the famous President Paul Kruger.

rival chiefs Mokopane and Mankopane, who seven years later were to lead a revolt against the Boers. Tradition asserts that his party camped under a group of Ana trees standing just outside Potgietersrus, before turning south for a second interview with Kruger. Kruger now regarded Livingstone as a British spy, so the project of leaving a native teacher among the Transvaal tribes was abandoned, and the family was back at Chonwane by the end of the year. The rains that season had been disappointing and Livingstone found that Sechele was proposing to move his tribe to Kolobeng, forty miles away, where the water supply was better. He knew the place well; as early as May 1846 he had begun to plant vegetables and corn along the banks of the Kolobeng River.

In March 1847 the Livingstones journeyed south to Dikgatlhong, a L.M.S. station south-east of Kuruman, to attend the third meeting of the District Committee. In committee Ross unkindly proposed 'That Mr Livingston be called upon to give his reasons why he left the Bakhatla station, to which he was appointed by the Directors, without the concurrence of the District Committee'. Moffat at once introduced a counter motion, approving of his son-in-laws' actions. This was seconded by the unrepentant Livingstone himself and carried.

After this unpleasantness the Livingstones moved on to Kuruman to await the birth of their second child. The Doctor found the delay 'rather trying', but his eldest daughter Agnes arrived safely in the May of 1847. Then they trekked slowly back to Chonwane, reaching the station in July. Almost immediately they removed to Kolobeng with the Bakwena.

When the Directors in London heard of this new step, they expressed the fond hope that 'we may now regard you as permanently settled'. This piece of wishful thinking was soon to be disappointed.

4

Kolobeng and Ngami

The new station at Kolobeng, about two hundred and seventy miles north-north-east of Kuruman, was named after its river which in Livingstone's time was fully eighteen feet across and three feet deep. Today the Kolobeng is a mere stream whose depth after sundown mysteriously increases. Sechele's great nephew who lives there today accounts for the phenomenon by suggesting that the rocks contract in the cold and 'squeeze out the water'.

The remains of Livingstone's house can still be seen, almost lost among flowering mimosa on a small eminence of volcanic rock, over which frowns a long red iron-stone ridge. The house measured fifty feet long by twenty feet wide; its size amazed the Africans who called it 'a mountain with several caves in it'. The approach road cleared by the Doctor (*ngaka* in Setswana)* is plainly visible. In front of the house, beyond the flat stone which was Livingstone's dental chair, the ground drops away quite steeply to the syringa-lined stream flowing through a meadow-like flood-plain, part of which Livingstone cultivated as a vegetable garden. The scanty remains of a workshop survive while a large anthill nearby was clearly used as a forge. There was no church, for the *Ngaka*'s congregations rarely numbered more than a dozen; Livingstone would address them from the rocky platform before the house in a manner which must have reminded him of an illustration from his childhood's Bible.

Until the house was completed in the July of 1848 the Livingstone family made do with a mud hut; but when once installed, and until 1851, it represented the nearest thing to a home that the family was to know. Its situation is attractive, one of the most pleasant to be found in Botswana. Game abounded in the vicinity, and Livingstone recalled shooting buffalo from his front door.

It was during the period of his residence there that Livingstone's work

* Rendered by many variants: nyaka, nasik, nake, narki, etc.

came nearest to that of an established missionary, and here he passed 'some of the happiest years of my life'. Perhaps his contentment etched itself onto the rocks of Kolobeng for it is one of those places where a curious sense of intimacy is felt with an era now past and a man long since dead.

One might have imagined that Sechele's Bakwena people would have been eager for conversion to the Christian faith: after all they were easygoing, they liked and admired Dr Livingstone, they wanted to imitate the procedures as well as the clothes of Europeans, and the very authority of the missionaries' precepts in the midst of so much laxity and uncertainty gave them an aura of superiority. Yet Livingstone was disappointed by the Bakwena's response to his preaching, and he did not find it amusing when the chief offered to convert them by judicious use of a rhinoceros whip. Sechele became his especial spiritual quarry but unhappily the chief was so fond of his five wives as to feel 'incapable of putting them away'.[1] At the end of July 1848, however, Sechele suddenly decided to dismiss four of them and, despite the unanimous disapproval of his people, applied to Livingstone for baptism.

On the first sabbath of October Sechele was duly baptised. In the following March, however, a stern entry appears in the observant Doctor's Journal: 'symptoms of pregnancy observed in Mokokon', one of the wives recently 'put away'. An even more damning note followed: 'Confessed he had been twice with her about the beginning of January 1849. . . . He shews much sorrow for his sin. Cut him off for a season.'

Sechele was the only convert Livingstone ever made, and his grief at the chief's backsliding was extravagant: its 'lancinating pangs', he wrote, 'fell on the soul like drops of aqua fortis on an ulcerated surface'. He had felt uneasy about whether 'Christianity gives any licence for assaulting the civil institutions of man (slavery?)' and was mindful too that by Divine command Hagar had resumed a polygamous state. But now he had made his mind up on the latter point and later would assault the institution of slavery with all his vigour. Yet Livingstone's ridigity in excommunicating his only convert for having resumed relations with an ex-wife would strike most people today as absurd. He was, however, adamant that the apostate be denied communion for the next two years, although as a great concession the bewildered Sechele was allowed 'to remain as a spectator of the ordinance'.

Before this blighting of his hopes, Livingstone felt that 'no portion of our lives ever seemed to glide more swiftly past than the year which has elapsed since our location on the Kolobeng'. Nor had the blow fallen, when, on 7 March 1849, the Journal noted with satisfaction 'Mrs L. delivered of a son, Thomas Steele—quick recovery. May God accept & save him.' It had been a happy year: both Mary and David had settled down extremely well at Kolobeng and their only regret was the lack of evangelical success. 'The Livingstones are in excellent spirits', Mrs Moffat reported, 'They are all in good health and things are very encouraging there.'[2]

Livingstone's descriptions of his life at Kolobeng are valuable contributions to our knowledge of missionary activities in South Central Africa last century. The *ngaka* was an all-rounder who could turn easily from being a farmer to a gunsmith, physician or builder; indeed he enjoyed comparing his activities to those of Alexander Selkirk. His wife occupied herself with domestic chores like cooking and making bread, butter and soap. Their stipend allowed the employment of three servants about the house as well as a labourer for outside work.

The Livingstones rose with the sun at Kolobeng, and attended a short family service. Then husband and wife went off to their classes. From eleven Livingstone addressed himself to manual labour. After midday dinner and an hour's rest Mrs Livingstone attended her flourishing infant school, while her husband returned to his heavier tasks until sunset when he would stroll over to the African town to engage in religious talks. With justification he said of missionaries that 'the wife must be the maid-of-all-work within while the husband must be the jack-of-all-trades without'.

In the evenings Livingstone attended the sick who came up to the house. It was a life of service and not without its rewards, although later on he would often bemoan the fact that he spent so little time playing with his children. But there were no more applicants for baptism; Livingstone was never to enjoy the missionary thrill of exhibiting a convert to the world or of building up a thriving centre of Christian endeavour in the wilderness.

Provision of food for the family was a continual problem and when the rains failed, they became more and more dependent on Kuruman for corn and on Sechele's hunting parties for meat. Vegetables formed the staple diet, sometimes varied by a dish of roast locusts that, according to Livingstone, tasted very like shrimps, and 'enormous frogs which, when cooked, look like chickens'. Ten lean cows provided sufficient milk for the children, and after acquiring a horse, Livingstone went hunting himself so that often giraffe and eland steaks appeared on the table, and he recorded too that 'rhinoceros is our frequent fare'.

The success of Livingstone's ministry to the Bakwena was jeopardised, however, by a succession of droughts. The rains failed in 1847 and then successively over the following three years; presently the rushing river which had first attracted him to Kolobeng ran dry. Already at Chonwane the tribesmen had muttered that the Europeans' presence prevented rain, and now they attributed the drought to Livingstone's preaching of the Gospel, though, as he was careful to point out, they always treated his family with kindness and respect.

The drought seemed endless. The few clouds which appeared in the sky during the wet season were closely watched, but none of them held more than the faintest promise of rain, and all the time the heat pressed down on Sechele's gasping fields and the cattle grew thinner. At night the shrill whistle of a Bakwena rain 'doctor' would awaken Livingstone, and remind him of his failure to wean the tribesmen from their 'faith in nostrums & incantations'.

Over and over again Livingstone's correspondence refers to the failure of the rains at Kolobeng which he himself was half-inclined to ascribe to the devil's work, wondering 'has Satan power over the course of the winds & clouds?'. And he wrote now in a different vein to Tidman: 'The state of this Mission, which at the date of the last letter I had the pleasure of addressing you wore rather a pleasing aspect, has for the last few months assumed quite another phase.'

There was trouble, too, with the Boers. Late in 1848 Livingstone revisited the African tribes in the Transvaal and tried again to settle a black teacher with Mokgatle in December. But the Boers regarded the attempt as politically motivated; Kruger 'threatened in a most furious manner to send a commando against the tribe with which we meant to settle', and accused Livingstone of selling firearms to the subject tribes. Livingstone did manage to meet two Scots pastors representing the Synod of the Dutch Reformed Church, and afterwards had a stormy interview at Hekpoort with the two formidable Voortrekker leaders, Hendrik Potgieter and Andries Pretorius. But they declared themselves unable to guarantee the missionary's safety in the Transvaal, accused the Doctor of breaking an earlier promise to warn them of Sechele's intransigence, and forbade Livingstone to visit another Bakwena clan living nearby. Baffled by their attitude, Livingstone returned home. Soon afterwards Potgieter demanded that 'Leviston' be permanently withdrawn from Kolobeng, and added in an ingenuous postscript that the missionary had 'hastily fled' from their presence. To be misjudged and misspelt in a single letter was galling, and did nothing to improve Livingstone's opinion of the Boers.

Livingstone found the recurring droughts, Boer hostility, and the obstinate refusal of the Bakwena to accept conversion all bitterly frustrating; instead of becoming a second Kuruman, the mission station at Kolobeng seemed to imprison him.

For the Boers had closed the path of evangelisation to the east and he would never fall back on Kuruman. Only the country beyond the Kalahari offered an opening to missionary enterprise, and a key piece of the Livingstone saga fell into place when he apprehended that 'all my desires tend forwards, to the North. Why we have a world before us here.' Then, thinking of the white hunters pressing farther into the interior, he continued, 'We [missionaries] shall not we hope be outdone by a man of the world'.

For some time rumours of a large freshwater lake, named Ngami or Mokhoro, lying beyond the desert, had seeped down to Kuruman. They set Moffat hoping to visit 'a country far beyond us that contains an ocean, an inland sea'. In 1841 Livingstone learned that his future father-in-law 'has got £400 from some gent in England for the purpose' of reaching the lake. Next year, when within striking distance of the lake, the Doctor curbed his inclination to visit it. But Ngami continued to intrigue him and on 29 September 1847 he asked Moffat, 'When will you go to the Lake? If you don't next season I may as a relaxation take a trip in that direction.'

Two years earlier the Livingstones had provided hospitality at Mabotsa for two big game hunters, William Cotton Oswell and Mungo Murray. Both men had expressed a hope that he would join them on an expedition to Ngami, and afterwards Oswell made arrangements in the Cape to obtain the necessary servants and equipment.[3] Livingstone finally agreed to accompany them in April 1848.

It was one of the crucial decisions of his career, but his motives were varied: he wanted to carry the Gospel to unknown tribes, he hoped to find a better home than drought-stricken Kolobeng for the Bakwena, he was bored with sedentary life, disappointed with its evangelical results, and excited at the prospect of reaching country never seen before by Europeans.

Sechele was discouraging about the expedition's prospects, explaining that even Africans 'who are more accustomed to thirst than you are, cannot cross that desert'. Sekgoma, ruler of the Bamangwato, was actively obstructive, refusing to reveal a practical route lest his monopoly of a profitable ivory trade in the area was affected. In the end, Livingstone decided they must travel when surface water was most likely to be found, and to go around rather than through the worst part of the desert. Oswell presently informed him he would be at Kolobeng during May 1849. Livingstone therefore sent his family to Kuruman for fear of the Boers, where Mary was to fret so much that her mother concluded she 'needed sustaining grace'.[4] He then solemnly burned 350 letters to prevent them from falling into the Boers' hands and grudgingly agreed to a local trader named Wilson accompanying them. Wilson was unconcerned with exploration, but he was excited by the news that ivory was so plentiful in the lake country that cattle kraals were fenced with tusks.

Oswell and Murray reached Kolobeng punctually and moved on ahead. Livingstone himself left Kolobeng on 1 June 1849 to join them. The combined expedition now boasted five wagons, eighty trek oxen and twenty horses, nearly all supplied by Oswell. With them, beside drivers, travelled some thirty Bakwena, to buy ivory for Sechele.

The expedition to Lake Ngami was a splendid experience for Livingstone and resulted in a solid discovery which made his reputation as an explorer. It finally convinced him that his primary interest and ability lay in exploration rather than in the life of a settled missionary.

From the tree-covered hills of Shokwane the expedition followed the rough tracks of the 'high road' to Shoshong. It led them through Boatlanama, 'a lovely spot in the otherwise dry region', and beyond that to the water-point at Lephepe. It had been filled in on Sekgoma's orders, but today the pan is fenced off, bore-holes have been sunk nearby and it represents a considerable stretch of water. During the following miles to Mashuwe where water was obtained in a rocky sandstone hollow, two oxen were lost from thirst. The party now turned off the Shoshong 'road' and struck north-north-west across the Kalahari proper. Fascinated by the Bushmen who scratched a living from this arid country, they reached one of the driest parts of the desert at Serotle. Here they dug pits nine feet deep to water the horses but the oxen had to endure 'four full days of thirsting' before the wells refilled. A message from Sekgoma reached Livingstone here, warning him against penetrating farther into the desert. Wilson later impertinently claimed that only his persuasion prevented the expedition from turning back.

Beyond Serotle the going was even worse with the wagons sinking up to their felloes in the soft sand, and after two days the guide informed them that he doubted whether they would reach the next water hole alive. 'It will be long if I ever forget this night,' Oswell wrote later. Next day they managed to cover nineteen miles, but it seemed unlikely that the trek oxen, already bellowing from thirst, could survive the thirty miles that still separated them from the next known water. Providentially they came upon a small pool in the dry river-bed of the Mokoko which led them towards the squalid huts of Lotlhakane, a major cross-roads of the desert. The village stood beside an arena of caked mud the size of six rugby fields which contains several wells. Today one sees endless streams of cattle, oxen, donkeys and goats being driven to water by women, many of whom show signs of Bushman blood. In Livingstone's time the oasis was marked by twenty-six tall palmyra trees. These have gone and only a few stunted palms grow on the circumference of the pan.

Beyond Lotlhakane the guide lost his way. During the next two thirsty days they rode across the world's second largest diamond pipe at Orapa, totally unaware of the wealth which lay beneath their feet, and soon afterwards Oswell overtook a fleeing Bushwoman, whom he bribed to guide them to Chakutsa (Nchokotsa) pan, with its arabesque of mopani trees. The mirages of the Kalahari have a lucidity which can deceive the most experienced traveller and when he saw this saline pan, twenty miles in circumference, Oswell felt convinced it was Lake Ngami. But there was no mistaking distant columns of black smoke, made by the firing of reeds to flush out lions, and a sure indication of water.

On 4 July 1849 the party came upon the Botletle or Zouga River,* its course marked from afar by a frieze of tall trees, the water as blue as a roller's wing, except where tinted pink by masses of flamingoes resting on its surface. Now almost miraculously everything was changed. They had moved from a desert into a picturesque and well-populated region. Fish was plentiful, game was easily trapped in pitfalls, the local Africans were 'manly' and well nourished, while even the Bushmen had attained larger stature than their cousins in the desert.

* Pronounced Zowka. Livingstone always used the latter name.

From now on the journey became sheer enchantment. The expedition had travelled from one extreme of nature to another, from dreary vistas of scrub to glorious riverine scenery, and it must have been a splendid thing to come upon this river which had never before been visited by civilised men. The party passed up the Botletle's bank, following its course first in a northerly direction and then curving round to the west, enraptured all the time by the unexpected colour and beauty.

Livingstone always enjoyed an opportunity of detecting resemblances between one place and another, and the memory of this first journey up the river was still warm enough eight years later for him to write that the banks 'are very beautiful, resembling closely many parts of the river Clyde above Glasgow'.

The excitement of finding this sudden burst of colour in the midst of a shrivelled desert aroused Livingstone to a fuller appreciation of the wonders and beauties of nature. From now on, as his travels were extended through tropical Africa, he wrote copious notes about the continent's flora and fauna.

Almost immediately he recorded the lechwe, puku and sitatunga as new species of antelope; and he carefully described the grotesque baobab trees, measured their enormous girths and wondered at their oddly shaped branches which seem as though they are only waiting for a witch's touch to set them writhing and gesticulating.*

In particular his interest quickened in the bird life around him, and the pioneering ornithological work which followed has not yet received proper recognition. During the next eight years, Livingstone reported the presence and habits of no less than ninety-one different birds in Africa, and his descriptions remain a remarkable testimony to his powers of observation. He was particularly interested in avian migration, often recognising birds he had known in Scotland. He was the first to report the residence of swallows in Central Africa during its winter months; he described the Penduline tit which was unknown to official science until 1871, vividly detailed the strange nesting habits and 'conjugal devotion' of hornbills, and the curious behaviour of oxpeckers 'which attach themselves to buffaloes and rhinoceros with the same instinct that dogs attach themselves to man'; he recorded the use of spiders' webs by the tawny-flanked

* His descriptions of these individual giants of the Kalahari are so precise that each can still be recognised. It is interesting to note that their girths measure less today than in his time, possibly because his calculations erred, but more probably because the reduced amount of water now available has caused them to shrink.

prinia for nesting, was confounded by the polygamous male ostrich which feigned lameness to distract attention from its latest mate's nest, noted that an ostrich's 'roar is almost exactly like a lion' and its running speed between twenty-six and forty miles an hour.* Several times he recorded his amazement at the honey-guides whose persistent calls lead men to bee-hives so that they—the avian guides—might claim the discarded comb, and refuted the common belief that the honey-guide often treacherously directed people instead to a snake or dangerous animal. ('This', he says of the Bantu, 'is in accordance with their way of talking of all good as if it were evil. Pain, guilt, hunger, &c, are called God.')

Livingstone was dazzled by the beauty of the carmine bee-eater, and wondered whether the presence of the sacred Ibis on the Zambezi suggested a possible association with the Nile. He disposed of the fable that certain birds pick the teeth of crocodiles although allowing that the *Ibix religiosa*, spoonbill and maraboo often roost at mid-day near these reptiles. And he announced that the Africans named one bird 'the son-in-law of God' since it proclaimed the onset of the wet season by calling 'pula pula', their word for rain.

Now on the Botletle Livingstone also noted that ten different kinds of fish were taken from the river by natives using nets and spears. He admired these 'inland sailors' and preferred to leave his wagon and travel up-river in their canoes which he discovered were hollowed out of a single trunk so that 'if the tree has a bend, so has the canoe'. Game abounded on both banks of the river. They watched kudu, buffalo, black and white rhinoceros and 'elephants in prodigous numbers'. The Botletle swarmed with crocodiles† and everywhere hippopotamuses raised their antique heads from the water to watch the white men go by. At Ngabisane, where the bush thickened, they temporarily abandoned all but one wagon and pressed on with the horses. It was puzzling to find that the higher they ascended the Botletle, the broader it became. The explanation lies in the fact that, as it flows, the Botletle loses much of its water by evaporation, and literally dies in the desert.

The experience of travelling along this immense river in the middle of the Kalahari aroused many reflections in Livingstone's mind: 'I could not help feeling sad', he informed Tidman, 'as I looked down on the steady flowing waters of the Zouga (exactly like the Clyde just above Bothwell

* In fact an ostrich can exceed forty m.p.h.
† Though Livingstone for long believed the crocodiles of Central Africa to be alligators.

bridge), and thought of the thousands who have paddled over them in total ignorance of Him who bore our sins on his own body on a tree'. And even more exalted thoughts were kindled after the explorers passed down a small descent at the edge of the sand veld, and saw still larger trees lining the banks of another river, the Thamalakane* which joins the Botletle. The mopane forest along its banks was filled with wild life and even today thousands of impala and lechwe roam its sunlit glades, together with innumerable gnu, tsessebe, waterbuck and warthog.

From local natives the travellers learned with growing excitement that the Thamalakane flowed from 'a country full of rivers—so many no one can tell their numbers'. 'Is this not a highway into the Interior?' Livingstone enquired in his Journal, 'Is it not the Niger of this part of Africa?' he asked Watt, and informed Tidman 'The fact that the Zouga is connected with large rivers coming from the North awakens emotions on my mind which make the discovery of the Lake dwindle out of sight.' From this moment Livingstone would always be 'water conscious' and hopeful that the African interior might be laid open by using navigable rivers.

The waters of the Botletle had been somewhat oily, but those of the Thamalakane were 'so clear, cold, and soft . . . that the idea of melted snow was suggested', and he told the Directors that according to local Africans 'the water came from a mountainous region'.

From the rivers' confluence, Oswell and Livingstone rode for many miles down the sluggish Nghabe channel, racing each other up hillocks for the first view of the lake. They reached it on 1 August 1849. Lechulatebe, chief of the Batawana living there, extended only a tepid welcome, and they were disappointed to find the lake was so shallow that it could 'never be of much value as a commerical highway'. Livingstone ascertained it was 'about 70 miles in length', but during his next visit noticed that the lake had shrunk due, he believed, to a continuing desiccation of Africa, a subject on which he frequently expounded.

The changing size of Lake Ngami is due to its being part of a freakish river system. Livingstone never properly appreciated the complexities of its intricate drainage which turns the north-western corner of modern Botswana into a watery paradise.

* Livingstone, whose ear was usually well attuned to African intonations, inexplicably spelt it Tamunak'le.

Kolobeng and Ngami

The vast Okavango swamp lying north of Ngami represents the dammed-up delta of a large river rising in the highlands of Angola. It discharges water through several competing channels, the amount each carries depending on their degree of blockage by floating islands of sudd. One of these channels—the Taoghe—feeds Lake Ngami directly and the lake's extent is determined not so much by the rainfall as by the quantity of sudd on its course. Another channel runs into a ridge of Kalahari sand which deflects its water southwards as the Thamalakane river, and then eastwards as the Botletle. The Thamalakane at their confluence is joined to Lake Ngami by the Nghabe channel, which may run in either direction according to which competing channel has captured most of the swamp water.

In 1849 the lake was a noble sheet of water. Thirteen years later Baines found it no more than a pan. In 1925 it again covered an extensive area, but in 1950 was quite dry. During 1951 it had increased to five miles of water but when the author visited the lake twenty years later it was represented by a star-shaped pond, only fifty yards across.

Livingstone had already heard rumours of a warrior chief named Sebetwane, ruler of the Makololo, who lived beside a great river still farther away to the north, and at Ngami these were confirmed by more factual information. The Doctor hoped to press on and make contact with these Makololo, but Lechulatebe was concerned lest he opened a road north by which the Makololo could obtain muskets to use against his tribe. So he closed the fords to the white men and refused them guides to the north. Livingstone made a brave attempt to cross the Botletle on a home-made raft, and when it sank Oswell volunteered to bring up a boat from Cape Town. Mollified by this promise, and because the season was now dangerously advanced, Livingstone reluctantly agreed to turn back, though not without affirming that 'most sorely do I dislike to be beat'. The little party accordingly returned along their wagon spoor and Livingstone, trailing Oswell to conserve water, reached Kolobeng on 9 October.

Oswell's share in the discovery of Ngami went practically unnoticed. This was mainly due to self-effacement, but Livingstone has been criticised for monopolising the limelight. It is only fair therefore to note that although Oswell financed the expedition, Livingstone was its real leader, and it would never have succeeded but for his command of Setswana and the ascendency he established over the Africans they met. Oswell contented himself with reporting the journey only to friends, though one of his letters was read out at a meeting of the Royal Geographical Society. Livingstone communicated the discovery to Moffat who promptly publicised it in the Cape press. Sir Roderick Murchison, President of the Royal Geographical Society, was sufficiently impressed to make a grant of £25 to Livingstone who spent it on a chronometer. Clearly he intended to chart future journeys more exactly.

Wilson profited, too, by buying ivory and according to Livingstone 'made £500 clear gain by the trip'. Tidman in London was delighted by the splendid publicity which Livingstone's exploits had given his Society, for the Doctor, still less an explorer than missionary, urged that the credit for the venture should go to the L.M.S., insisting that 'the lake belongs to missionary enterprise'.

But the most important result of the expedition to Ngami was the authentic information Livingstone had obtained about the Makololo and the other tribes living beside great rivers far away to the north. It determined him to quit the Bakwena and move to this more populous region. This would inevitably require more journeys of discovery. He came to regard Kolobeng as no more than a springboard from which he would launch himself further into the interior. The prospect of leaving the Bakwena seemed no great hardship, for his failure in proselytisation had not escaped the notice of his superiors: when Mr Freeman visited Kolobeng towards the end of 1849 he reported bleakly that 'the apparent results' from Livingstone's labours 'are very limited'. The Doctor's colleagues' antagonism continued to be a running sore, and he longed to be independent of them. In his dark moments he even regretted the grinding poverty of a missionary's life, and grumbled to his parents that if he took up trading he would make as good a living as Wilson. But this was a passing phase and Livingstone soon recovered his true voice, when at the end of 1849 he vowed to the Directors that he intended to 'plant the seed of the gospel where others have not planted'. To accomplish this, in the April of 1850 he set off to find Sebetwane.

5

The Zambezi

On 26 April 1850 Livingstone with his entire family set out from Kolobeng to reach the Makololo. Taking three young children and a pregnant wife into malarial country was risky, but Mary would not hear of sitting out another long separation at Kuruman. Oswell hoped that, after refitting in Cape Town, he too would join the expedition, but Livingstone refused to wait for him. He had temporarily lost interest in his friend because, as Oswell's biographer has pointed out, Livingstone 'had been unable to resist the desire and opportunity of being the first to visit Sebotoané'.

'Oswell was excessively anxious that I should promise to accompany him', Livingstone told Moffat, 'but I declined, yet I don't know how to get quit of him.' It is our first intimation of the Doctor's jealousy for rival explorers.

So now the Livingstones rumbled off in their wagon along the road to Shoshong and visited Sekgoma; in consequence their route lay farther to the east than in 1849 and they ascended the northern bank of the Botletle until the unexpected presence of tsetse drove them to the other side. The Thamalakane also was fly-infested and Livingstone knew that the trek oxen would perish if they pressed on. So he decided to leave his wife at Lechulatebe's kraal to have her baby while he went northwards on foot with only two men. Mary was beginning to learn that her comfort came second in her husband's order of priorities.

Lechulatebe, after the gift of a much-prized gun, agreed to Livingstone crossing the Botletle, but before leaving, Livingstone consoled Mary with a 'peep' at Lake Ngami. The strange scene of the Livingstone family at the lake has come down to posterity as an illustration in *Missionary Travels*. In it we see Robert and Agnes dressed in hot, incongruous clothes beside the water. To the left stands the Doctor, recognisable by the heavy moustache and midshipman's cap; he is pointing out something to an indifferent Mrs Livingstone who wears a Victorian bonnet, and nurses baby Thomas. An African servant brews up some tea while beyond is parked their tilted trek-wagon. The drawing, according to the Doctor, was begun by 'Mr Alfred Rider, an enterprising young artist who had come to make sketches of the country and of the lake immediately after its discovery [and who] had died of fever before our arrival'. Rider's bereaved mother subsequently lent the unfinished sketch to Livingstone, who employed another artist to work up the picture and add the figures of his family.*

On the very next day the two older children went down with fever. It was Livingstone's first experience of malaria in Europeans, and he was shaken by its virulence. Fortunately he had read McWilliam's account of the efficacy of quinine in fever, and had some with him. He administered it in larger doses than those advocated by McWilliam and combined with calomel. The children quickly recovered: he had hit upon the prescription of the famous 'Livingstone Rousers'† which were to play such a large part in opening up tropical Africa to white men.

The first prescription he used was: calomel gr 3, Quinine Hydrochloride gr 3, Rhubarb gr 10, Resin of Jalap gr 4, mixed with a little spirit. By 1855 he had replaced the rhubarb with tincture of cardamons 'to form a bolus' and added a flavouring of ginger or cinnamon. In 1860 he preferred to use double the doses of Jalap and calomel and again prescribed the drugs in pill form.

But the children's illness, and Mrs Livingstone's expressed anxiety to be confined at Kolobeng, decided Livingstone to give up his plan of visiting the Makololo that year, and so the wagons rumbled slowly back along their tracks. They met Oswell hunting on the Botletle, and were back at Kolobeng before the end of July 1850.

Despite this failure, another idea which would drive him across Africa was evolving in Livingstone's mind: not only must he find the Makololo but also seek an easier route to their country than the long vulnerable haul from the Cape. On the way back to Kolobeng he mentioned to Moffat his hope of finding 'a passage to the sea for supplies. A great and difficult undertaking, but my ambition mounts thus far, though I tell it to few';

* Most copies of the book's first edition show the scene as a woodcut by J. H. Whymper. But variants substitute a tinted lithograph by W. West or one by T. Picken, or a chromolith in four colours by West in which the Doctor's figure is unaccountably omitted.

† The name was inspired by the Doctor's remark that 'two ordinary sized pills would be a rousing dose for a woman'.

1   Livingstone and his family at Lake Ngami

he realised, however, that the proposal would cause criticism from his missionary colleagues, and grumbled 'had it been possible to foresee the state of feeling now existing I should never have joined the mission'.[1] Six weeks later he also informed Tidman that 'we must have a passage to the sea, on either the eastern or western coasts. I have hitherto been afraid to broach the project on which my, perhaps dreamy, imagination dwells'. His plan was given fresh impetus a little later when messengers arrived at Kolobeng with an invitation from Sebetwane to visit him.

It was all the more distressing that, at this time of expanding vision, tragedy befell the Livingstone family. On 1 August 1850, Mrs Livingstone was safely delivered of a little girl who was christened Elizabeth, but the infant contracted pneumonia and, after six agonising weeks, died. 'Have just returned from burying our youngest child', the bereaved father wrote on 18 September. 'Never concieved before how fast a little stranger can twine round the affections. She was just six weeks old when called away to see the King in his beauty. I have not the slightest doubt but that she is saved by one whom she could not know. She is home now, yet it was like tearing out one's bowels to see her in the embrace of the King of Terrors. . . . Wish we were all as safe as she is now.' They buried her in a grove of mimosa trees near the Kolobeng house, and Livingstone set up a board with a Setswana inscription which read: 'When men die they are not annihilated. Jesus will raise and judge them all.' Elizabeth's grave is still to be seen some three hundred yards down the slope from the ruined Kolobeng house. Beside its pathetic little heap of rough stones, Sechele later buried one of his sons.

At the time of the baby's death Mrs Livingstone had succumbed to a debilitating attack of Bell's Palsy, a paralysis of one side of the face. Her recovery was slow, so the following months were depressing ones at Kolobeng, and not improved by a visit from a reproachful Mrs Moffat. Hearing of the family's distress she had undertaken the long journey from Kuruman, filled with 'gloomy forebodings' about the Livingstones' future, but beguiled by 'that work of thrilling interest, Anderson's *Annalls of the English Bible*'.[2] She found her daughter prostrated with 'nervous headaches', and did not conceal her opinion that Livingstone's rashness in taking his family into pestilential regions was responsible for both his daughter's death and Mary's illness. It was about this time that Sechele announced that he intended moving his tribe to a better rainfall area, and Livingstone's heart sank at the prospect of building yet another house. To reduce his spirits further a report reached Kolobeng that Oswell had forestalled him by travelling alone to the Makololo, and indeed, after Livingstone had left him on the Botletle in the June of 1850, Oswell had contacted messengers from Sebetwane to Livingstone, hoping they would guide him to the Chobe; fortunately for Livingstone the messengers refused and went on to Kolobeng. But the fear of being forestalled, combined with his other troubles, caused a note of hopelessness to creep into Livingstone's correspondence: 'We had a hailstorm some nights ago which broke about 16 panes of glass. I have no heart to mend them,' he wrote at this time, 'Never felt so little inclination to exert myself.' Still in this depressed mood Livingstone took the family down to Kuruman in October hoping that the change would improve Mary's health. But he thought his colleagues seemed 'never sunk so low before' while relations with the Moffats again became strained when they learned that, despite her having fallen pregnant, Livingstone still intended to carry his wife and the children off on another attempt to reach Makolololand.

After they left Kuruman in February 1851 to prepare for the next journey, an admonitory letter from Mrs Moffat followed. It was written in April 1851 but did not catch up with Livingstone until five months later at Orapa when he was returning from the Zambezi. Livingstone was infuriated when he read, 'Before you left the Kuruman I did all I dared to do to broach the subject of your intended journey, and thus bring on a candid discussion, more especially with regard to Mary's accompanying you with those dear children. But seeing how averse you and Father were to speak about it, and the hope that you would never be guilty of such temerity (after the dangers they escaped last year), I too timidly shrunk from what I ought to have had the courage to do. Mary had told me all along that should she be pregnant you would not take her, but let her come out here after you were fairly off. Though I suspected at the end that she began to falter in this resolution, still I hoped it would never take place, i.e. *her going with you*, and looked and longed for things transpiring to prevent it. But to my dismay I now get a letter, in which she writes, "I must again wend my weary way into the far Interior, perhaps to be confined in the field?" O Livingstone, what do you mean? Was it not enough that you lost one lovely babe, and scarcely saved the others, while the mother came home threatened with Paralysis? And will you again expose her & them in those sickly regions on an *exploring* expedition? All the world would condemn the *cruelty* of the thing to say nothing of the

59

indecorousness of it. A pregnant woman with three little children trailing about with a company of the other sex, through the wilds of Africa, among savage men and beasts! Had you *found a place* to which you wished to go and commence missionary operations, the case would be altered. Not one word would I say, were it to the mountains of the moon. But to go with an exploring party, the thing is preposterous. I remain yours in great perturbation. M. Moffat.'

This letter persuaded Livingstone that to free himself for further exploration he would have to send Mary away and 'orphanise' the children.

While Mrs Moffat was composing her hurtful letter, Oswell was making his way back to Kolobeng, and presently smoothed over his relations with Livingstone by presenting a new wagon to him and by going on ahead to open up the wells along their intended route.

The Livingstones themselves left Kolobeng on 24 April 1851. That night they slept near Molepolole under a feature which is still known as 'Livingstone's cave'. Opening out on a steep rocky slope, it was held in great awe by the Bakwena, for witches were put to death inside, and it was believed that anyone who entered it died. Livingstone decided to break the taboo. He scrambled up to the cave, explored it thoroughly and found that inside it divided into two decked channels. As a curious memento the Doctor 'left at the end of the upper branch one of Father Mathew's leaden teatotal tickets'.* Years afterwards his grandson, Dr Hubert Wilson, tried in vain to retrieve the medal, and in 1972 the author was no more successful.

Further on Livingstone allayed his conscience in a letter which read 'Mosquitoes and fever, aye African fever, make it a venture to take in wife and children thither', but continued, 'I should think myself a sorry caitif if unwilling to make a venture for his glory. . . . I am happy to say Mary reciprocates these sentiments.' At the end of April the wagons rolled expectantly up to the familiar water-point at Boatlanama. The wells were almost dry. This renewed Livingstone's anxiety, and he used matching prose to explain his feelings to Tidman: 'It is a venture to take wife & children into a country where fever, African fever, prevails. But who that believes in Jesus would refuse to make a venture for such a Captain?'

* Father Mathew, the canny Roman Catholic apostle of temperance, sold over two million medals in Ireland for a shilling each to persons he had persuaded to take the pledge. He was less successful when he extended his crusade to Britain and the United States.

The Zambezi

They joined up with Oswell at Mashuwe and trekked on to Shoshong. Sekgoma, more friendly now, provided a guide for the next stage through the desert. After enduring three anxious days without water they came to Chakutsa Pan. From there Livingstone intended to continue along the Botletle and Thamalakane, but by a lucky chance Oswell performed a small service for an African who responded by offering to lead them north by a shorter route.

The change of plan permitted the party to gain a headstart on three traders, who were also making for Sebetwane's country. Livingstone had no hesitation in attributing this advantage to the intervention of Divine Providence, an early manifestation of the teleological doctrine that would give structure to his later life. His activities, he was coming to believe, were willed and blessed by God.

They now entered new country, traversing the western edge of the parched Makarikari Depression, a sinister arid landscape. But presently they came to a chain of springs called 'the links', and at Tsaugara pan engaged a Bushman guide. He led them almost due west to Kama Kama. From there the party began the most hazardous part of the journey.

To Livingstone this was 'the worst piece of country in Africa for sand, drought and dreariness'. It led to the immense Mababe Depression, an ancient lake bed covered with scrubby bushes about six feet high on which were festooned masses of brown creeper grass so that each one looked like a miniature haystack. Quite 'destitute of water', its huge emptiness and immense silence oppressed the party. 'Not a bird or an insect could be seen,' Livingstone wrote, 'the stillness of death reigned over the scene.'[3] Days passed without finding water, but not for a moment did Livingstone consider turning back. On 11 June they noticed birds in the sky and soon afterwards saw rhinoceros spoor, a sure sign that they were approaching water. Since the oxen were now too weak to pull the wagons, they were unyoked and stumbled off, led by instinct towards water and followed by two of Livingstone's men, leaving the wagons marooned for four anxious days in the vast plain. It was now that the bush assumed its most menacing aspect, and when a servant spilled some of the remaining water Livingstone envisaged the children 'perishing before our eyes'. Afterwards, recollecting their plight, he paid one of his rare compliments to his wife; 'It would almost have been a relief to me to have been reproached with being the entire cause of the catastrophe, but not one syllable of upbraiding was uttered by their mother, though the tearful eye told the

61

agony within.' On the fifth day, to their 'inexpressible relief', one of the servants returned with water.

Going forward again they came to the small river Mababe, probably the headwaters of the Khwai. Beyond lay an extensive marsh and they were aware of having reached a frontier of a sort. Now because of tsetse, stores could be carried only on men's heads, while instead of water being scarce, it became embarrassingly plentiful.

Trekking on along a watercourse dotted with pans, today the haunt of many elephants, they came to the Sonta or Savuti channel which they crossed by night to avoid fly, and on the 19th unyoked the oxen on the banks of the Chobe. They had come at last to 'the country full of rivers'.

Sebetwane had already heard of their approach and was waiting for them nearby at his southern capital of Linyanti. Swimming their oxen to Kasu island, reputedly free of tsetse, Livingstone and Oswell then paddled off in a canoe to greet the chief. They met him on 21 June 1851.

The first encounter passed off very well. After shaking hands Livingstone told Sebetwane about his hope of being allowed to preach to his people. Sebetwane readily agreed, then led them to clean sleeping quarters. They did not rest for long. 'In the dead of night', writes Oswell, Sebetwane 'paid us a visit alone, and sat down very quiet and mournfully at our fire. Livingstone and I woke up and greeted him, and then he dreamily recounted the history of his life, his wars, escapes, successes and conquests, and the far-distant wandering in his raids.' Livingstone felt as though he was listening to the commentaries of Caesar. Afterwards he would frequently describe the 'weird scene': the savage warrior and the gaunt Europeans crouched together over a fire, their faces lit up by the flames, with Sebetwane talking 'with subdued manner and voice . . . through the live-long night'. Livingstone interrupted him occasionally with a question, and all the time he scribbled down everything the chief told them about leading his tribe's fighting march from its homeland to the Zambezi. After defeating the Barotse living there, Sebetwane set up his people as overlords among them in a domain comprising most of modern Barotseland. Now the Makololo formed a ruling aristocracy in the midst of riverine tribes on whom they had imposed knowledge of Setswana.

The Doctor was delighted with Sebetwane: the texture of his mind and the weave of his intellect more closely resembled those of a European than of any other African he had known. Oswell was no less impressed, finding Sebetwane 'far and away the finest kafir I ever met'. The Makololo likewise aroused Livingstone's enthusiasm and he came to regard them as appointed leaders for African progress. His approval was returned and their descendants still remember the Doctor's *butu* or human kindness. Yet he never made a convert among them.

Livingstone was surprised to find some of the Makololo wearing European clothes, one man even flaunting 'a gaudily flowered dressing gown', but it was distressing to discover that this finery was obtained by selling captured enemies to slave traders. The realisation of the slave trade's extent fell on him like a hammer blow.

For the present the Makololo were at peace, having established a well defined hierarchical system. The Sotho, whom Sebetwane had led from beyond the Vaal, formed its elite; the Bakwena and Bamangwato who joined their northern migration were of slightly inferior status, while the mass of subject Barotse formed a helot class. But they were possessed by a consuming fear of the Matabele who had recently driven Makololo outposts from the healthy Batoka Highlands; Sebetwane at once appreciated that a resident missionary, particularly the son-in-law of Mzilikazi's admired friend, Robert Moffat, would be a 'shield against Moselekatze' and might even allow the Makololo to resettle the highlands, so he happily accepted Livingstone's suggestion of living with them.

Everything now looked most promising; Livingstone had gained the friendship of a powerful chief who could be relied upon to assist his plans for evangelising the Makololo, and might even become the Constantine of Central Africa. But the unexpected occurred: Sebetwane contracted pneumonia, and died on 7 July 1851, less than three weeks after their first meeting. A Zambezi tradition insists that the fatal illness was brought about by a fall from Livingstone's horse, which opened an old wound and infected the lungs.

Sebetwane's death was a heavy blow, and it prompted Livingstone to compose a second soliloquy over the loss of an African friend which typifies the guilt-laden feelings of cyclothymic depression. It is similar in style to that which lamented Sehamy's death, but reveals a lessening fear that heathens who had not heard the Christian message were doomed to eternal damnation, and were instead 'greater objects of compassion than those who . . . rejected it'. 'Poor Sebitoane,' * it ran, 'my heart bleeds for thee, and what would I not do for thee now that nothing can be done.

* Livingstone variously spelled the chief's name as Sebituane and Sebitoane(é).

63

Where art thou now? I will weep for thee till the day of my death. Little didst thou think, when in the visit of the white man thou sawest the long cherished desires of years accomplished, that the sentence of death had gone forth. Thou thoughtest that thou shouldst procure a weapon from the white man which would be a shield from the attacks of the fierce Matibele; but a more deadly dart than theirs was aimed at thee, and though thou couldst well ward off a dart, none better, thou didst not see that of the King of Terrors. I will weep for thee, my brother, and I would cast forth my sorrows in despair for thy condition, but I know that thou wilt recieve no injustice whither thou art gone; shall not the judge of all the earth do right? I leave thee to him. Alas! Alas! Sebitoane! I might have said more to him. God forgive me. Free me from bloodguiltiness. If I had said more of death I might have been suspected as having forseen the event and guilty of bewitching him. I might have recommended Jesus and his great atonement more. It is however very difficult to break through the thick crust of ignorance which envelopes their minds.'

The little party of Europeans on the Chobe was now placed in a position of potential peril, for the Makololo could be expected to attribute Sebetwane's death to their influence; instead the tribesmen's friendly attitude did not change. There was, however, a nagging delay before Livingstone could obtain permission from the dead chief's successor, his daughter Mamochisane (who soon afterwards surrendered the chieftainship to her brother Sekeletu), to visit the great river which Sebetwane had told him lay to the north. Then, while Mary and the children remained on the Chobe, Livingstone and Oswell rode a zigzag course across what is now the point of the Caprivi strip. On 4 August 1851 they 'came to the beautiful river Sesheke,* and thanked God for permitting us first to see this glorious river'. It was the Upper Zambezi, five hundred yards across, and 'mightier' than any river Oswell had known in India. Livingstone later noted that the 'river was not previously known to exist there at all. The Portuguese maps all represent it as rising far to the east of where we were.'

The Zambezi is divided into three sections, the lower extending from the coast to Cabora Bassa (in Livingstone's time the gorge was usually spelt Kebrabasa), the middle to the Victoria Falls, and the upper to its source. The lower Zambezi had of course been known to the Portuguese

* This part of the Zambezi was known to the Africans as the Leeambye; Livingstone called it after a town on its bank.

for over three centuries, but Livingstone knew perfectly well that Silva Porto, a Portuguese trader, had visited the upper river in 1847–48. It has often been pointed out that all Livingstone's 'discoveries' were well known to the Africans living in the interior, and indeed that they often guided him to them; it is less well appreciated that the honour of reaching the upper Zambezi belongs to the Portuguese. Livingstone's real accomplishment was to reveal the entire course of the Zambezi to the world, describe it and provide observations of latitude, longitude and altitude which enabled maps of the area to be drawn. But African chauvinism is justified in emphasising that the rivers, lakes, flora and fauna had all been there before, bearing native names, though the suggestion that Livingstone was no more than 'a tourist' cannot be accepted.

He and Oswell stared long at the river and could do no more than exclaim 'How glorious! How magnificent! How beautiful!' In Livingstone it inevitably awakened memories of 'the long-lost scenes of the Firths of Clyde and Forth which came back so vividly, I might have cried', but he restrained his tears lest the African guide ascribed them to fear of the crocodiles basking along the river banks.

His arrival at the upper Zambezi was a tremendous moment in Livingstone's life and a cardinal breakthrough in the history of African discovery. It revealed that, instead of being a 'second Sahara', the continental interior was a land of great rivers and lush fertility inhabited by an immense population. After dismissing the temptation to make a four-day march eastwards to see the great waterfall of Mosi-oa-Tunya, perhaps because subconsciously he refused to face up to the existence of an obstruction to the river's navigation, Livingstone searched up the Zambezi for a place salubrious enough to establish a mission among the Makololo.

On his return to the Chobe, Livingstone became preoccupied by the realisation that he had penetrated the fringe of the slave trade. With singular credulity he accepted Makololo protestations that they abhorred the trade and had only been involved in it for a year. This piece of disingenuous information made him smart with indignation; but for Lechulatebe's wilful obstruction on the Botletle during 1849, he would have prevented the Makololo becoming entangled in the abomination. However Oswell was less gullible, and noted that Sebetwane 'has had traffic for the last three or four years'.

Livingstone learned that the man-hunt along the upper Zambezi had been initiated by half-caste Luanda slavers and their Mambari levies,* while Arab slavers were also now approaching from the east coast. The Portuguese had bartered printed cottons, variously coloured baize and muskets for a number of captives and incited Sebetwane into making more raids. At the end of their last visit, the Mambari drove away two hundred captives carrying elephant tusks, for the slave trade was only profitable if combined with the sale of ivory at the coast; moreover they left an assurance they would be back to conduct more business the following year.

The revelation of the extent of the poisonous slave trade made Livingstone determined to provide the antidote. He had already hinted at pioneering a missionary path from the coast to Linyanti and now the plan was elaborated by invoking Buxton's 'positive policy' of carrying commerce as well as Christianity to the interior. For Livingstone was certain that the bartering of industrial goods for local products instead of captives would undercut the slave trade. This note, which marked the change from missionary to African statesman, sounded with growing clarity through the next twenty years.

We catch it first at Linyanti when he startled Oswell by announcing that he intended marching to the west coast, more than a thousand miles away. Then, realising perhaps that this would mean marooning his family on the Chobe, he suggested instead that Oswell made an 'open manly attempt to make a path patent for future use', and thus render 'important service to both commerce and Christianity'. Oswell demurred on the ground that wagon travel was impossible in this country.

Although the Doctor still adhered to his scheme of settling among the Makololo, this seemed of secondary importance to these new responsibilities and would have to be delayed. Pondering over his policy, he mused 'Pity the market is not supplied with English manufacture in exchange for the legitimate products of the country. If English merchants would come up the Zambezi during the months of June, July and August the slave trade would very soon be driven out of the market' by the purchase of all available ivory. Unwittingly he had enunciated the Victorian goal of 'philanthropy plus five per cent'.

But his thoughts ranged farther: to free himself for the task of revealing an economic route for traders to the interior, he must send his family to Britain and devote himself for two years to exploration. The more

* Who came from Bié.

obvious course of sending them to Kuruman was impractical, he said darkly, since Mary had been unhappy there, and more 'reports made & circulated by the natives would render my wife miserable'.

The earliest reference to the decision appears on 8 October 1851, when, ignoring Mary's plight, Livingstone wrote, 'I shall feel parting with the children much. It will be like tearing out my entrails. But more is done every day for Queen Victoria and no boohoo about it. I hope I am not such a sorry sojer to our Captain as to fail in any duty.' A few days later he informed Tidman of his intentions.

Livingstone cannot be acclaimed a model husband and father, though his attitude to domestic duties can be understood. Beginning to think of himself as divinely chosen to open up Africa, he regarded the task from which so much good would flow as taking precedence over family responsibilities. Once revealed he would never deviate from the appointed 'line of duty'. 'I shall try to come and fetch you soon,' from Kuruman, he told Mary when at Linyanti during 1853, 'but I must see it [my] duty first.'[4]

His mind made up, the wagons on the Chobe were packed and the party began the long journey back to Kolobeng. The route they had taken from Chakutsa was impractical in dry weather, and they travelled down the Thamalakane. Having reached the Botletle they crossed to its southern bank,* and here under a camel thorn bush on 15 September 1851 Mrs Livingstone, as her husband noted nonchalantly in his Journal, was delivered of a baby boy, whom he named Oswell but nicknamed Zouga after the unlikely birth place.

Livingstone was even reticent on the subject of his wife's travail to his companion. When Oswell objected to camping in a grassless spot for eight days and asked what the matter was, Livingstone was silent for a long time before coming out with 'Oh nothing . . . Mrs L. had a little son last night.' This exhibition of heartlessness moved even his eulogistic biographer, Dr Blaikie, to protest his hero's lack of feeling.

A week afterwards Livingstone received Mrs Moffat's unkind letter written the previous April. Five days later, he wrote a biting reply: 'What you say about difference of opinion is true. In my past life I have always managed to think for myself and act accordingly. I have

---

* In his journal Livingstone noted that here he mended a wagon wheel for 'Mrss Bushe & Shelley'. The entry led Dr Blaikie, Livingstone's first biographer, to make a curious mistake by writing that the service was rendered to 'Mrs Bysshe Shelley'!

occasionally met with people who took it on themselves to think for me, and they have offered their thoughts with an emphatic "*I think*". But I have generally excused them on the score of being a little soft-headed in believing they could think for me and themselves.' It was a charmless reiteration of his stubborn sense of independence. Mrs Moffat's words rankled, for next month he grumbled to Tidman that 'the death [of] the child and complaint of the mother have both been charged to my account, and I have been asked if the "loss of one child, &c &c, was not enough to satisfy me." This & other severe expressions have been used even by those whom I esteem.' By November, however, Livingstone's anger cooled, and although barbed, the tone of his next letter was more jocular: 'From the way Mrs M. has written to us for some time past, I expect to be obliged to pull down my breeches as soon as we reach Kuruman and get my bottom warmed with the "taws". I can't please everyone, and least of all those who know not the objects I have in view.'

As they continued their homeward journey Mrs Livingstone cannot have relished the prospect of being packed off to England with the children. Accordingly, although she 'never had an easier nor better' confinement, her spirits sank and she complained of severe pains down the right side of the body. Her facial palsy recurred and as late as March 1852 she was still 'threatened by symptoms of paralysis in the whole right side and extremities'. Her condition can be confidently attributed to hysteria induced by Livingstone's decision to send her home, and she became 'difficult': the Doctor later told his brother that Mary's 'mind has been a little affected ever since she had a stroke of paralysis.'[5]

For his part Livingstone was deeply grieved too by the price he would pay for freeing himself to work on his master plan: 'To orphanize my children will be like tearing out my bowels', he lamented to Tidman, and two weeks afterwards wrote again begging the Directors to support his family in England during his absence.* If they declined, he continued, he would continue working with the Bakwena. Then suddenly he shifted his ground, using words that shouted out from the paper: 'But stay, I am not sure. So powerfully convinced am I that this is the will of the Lord I should, I will go, no matter who opposes,' and in fact he sent his family to England before the Directors replied.

On 27 November 1851 the Livingstones reached Kolobeng after an easy journey. During their absence Sechele had moved the Bakwena to

* They accepted the charge, and paid Mary a generous £120 a year during the separation.

Dimawe seven miles upstream. But Livingstone was unconcerned. The uncertain years were over. His way was opened before him.

He said good-bye to Sechele without regret, for the Bakwena had failed him by their 'determined hostility to the requirements of the gospel'. In the end his attempt to recruit them to the Christian faith had been less effective than their own objective of enmeshing him in the web of tribal politics. Only Mrs Moffat felt grieved at the abandonment of Kolobeng, which she wrote later, 'is a wreck . . . verily we have to mourn for we cannot now say that any good has been done'.[6] She saw Mary 'as a sacrifice ready to be offered up'.[7] She could not know that her son-in-law's new venture would open half a continent to missionaries.

The Livingstones arrived at Cape Town on 16 March feeling 'an odd-looking squad' in their old fashioned clothes, and the Doctor was so unaccustomed to civilisation as to be inclined to climb downstairs backward. While they waited dismally for a boat to convey Mary and the children to England, Oswell fitted them out with a new wardrobe though 'in a way rather too splendid for a poor missionary family'. Livingstone's nerves were on edge at the prospect ahead and when one of the children asked how long it would be before they would be at home together again, he exclaimed melodramatically 'Never! the mark of Cain is on your foreheads: your father is a missionary.' Nor were his spirits improved by the painful surgical removal of his uvula—the little tongue at the back of the throat—in the hope that this would improve his wayward articulation.

Not until 23 April 1852 did Livingstone wave a sad farewell to his family in the *Trafalgar*. 'It was only with the greatest difficulty I could restrain my sorrow in parting,' he told Oswell, 'Had I given way in the least, I should have burst into a regular roar.' But he was free now to begin his appointed crusade, and all Africa lay open.

6

On the Threshold

When Livingstone bade farewell to his 'dearest earthly ties' he told Mary that the separation would last no more than two years. In fact five were to pass before she saw him again and by then he had become the most famous man in England.

For Mary Livingstone this was a time of misery and neglect: for her husband, years of wonderful achievement. Yet they started badly enough. After his family's departure, Livingstone's stay at 'this cold damp' Cape, instead of the anticipated ten days, dragged out to six full weeks. Mrs Livingstone, woman-like, suspected ulterior motives for the delay, but her husband assured her 'The repair of the wagon' was the 'source of attraction' in Cape Town, and the settlement of a libel case another.

There were many difficulties to contend with. When Livingstone applied for a permit to take ammunition beyond the Cape borders, the authorities hesitated to comply lest it reached hostile tribesmen. In the end he received all he asked for, but Cape Town's suspicions were justified: he gave a third of the powder and all the lead to the Makololo. He ran into trouble too by accusing the postmaster of Colesberg with over-charging for postage from Kuruman. The injured official retaliated with a threat of an action for defamation of character, and the miserable affair was only ended after Livingstone settled it out of court with the payment of £13 from his meagre capital.

The eighth Kafir war was raging at this time and the Society's Hottentot protégés were foremost in the fight against the colonials. It was whispered that Livingstone had sold them guns, and he met open hostility in the town, especially from members of Dr Philip's congregation who had not forgotten his tactless sermon eleven years earlier.

Livingstone, however, found a friend in the newly-appointed agent for the Society, the Reverend William Thompson, while another valuable contact was made with Mr (soon to be Sir Thomas) Maclear, the

On the Threshold

Astronomer Royal at Cape Town. Maclear gave Livingstone instruction in navigation and making dead reckonings, a kindness which led to the first attempt at scientific cartography in Central Africa.

Towards the end of May a letter from Tidman announced the Society was prepared to support his family during the separation. Yet, perhaps because he was wrapped in one of his depressed moods, Livingstone replied ungraciously. A suggestion that a missionary colleague named Ashton should accompany him across Africa was brusquely turned down with the intimation that he was both incompetent and cowardly. As for a further mild request to keep a regular journal during the coming journey, Livingstone returned only a curt 'I cannot promise to keep a journal', even though he had decided to write one up meticulously.

On 8 June 1852 he finally left Cape Town by wagon, and afterwards regarded this as the real beginning of his great trans-African journey which was to become part of the British heritage.

We are inclined to forget the leisurely manner in which the Victorians ordered their affairs, and somehow to think of the journey as being pursued at a tremendous pace, as though Livingstone was being driven by heavenly forces up to the Zambezi and across the continent. Nothing could be farther from the truth. This journey of six thousand miles occupied nearly four years. Livingstone reached Kuruman on 27 August 1852, and lingered there for fifteen weeks. He arrived at Linyanti on 23 May 1853 and only left it for the west coast during the following November. Luanda was reached on 31 May 1854 and he remained there until 20 September. It took almost a year to return to Linyanti, and he spent the next two months there. Only on 20 May 1856 did the Doctor arrive at Quelimane and the end of his epic journey.

He was delayed on the way to Kuruman by the collapse of a wheel of his overburdened wagon, an accident which he was later to regard as a bountiful disposition of Providence since it prevented his being at Kolobeng when the Boers attacked Sechele's tribe. He learned of this calamity three days after pulling into Kuruman.

A cloud of controversy envelops the battle of Dimawe and the looting of Livingstone's mission station, but some facts are undisputed: the Boers did attack Sechele, they killed more than sixty Bakwena and carried off a large number of children as 'apprentices', together with three thousand head of cattle. What remains doubtful is the truth of Livingstone's version of the affair to which he gave world-wide publicity.

71

He maintained that the Boer attack was unprovoked, cost the commando over thirty men killed, and that the burghers afterwards wantonly wrecked his house at Kolobeng, tore his library to pieces and went off with goods valued at £350*—accusations that have invariably been supported by Livingstone's biographers.

Bearing in mind that Livingstone was hopelessly prejudiced against the Boers (having already told his family that 'resistance to such tyrants and murderers is I think obedience to God'), it is important that his charges against them be reviewed in the light of evidence which has been largely ignored.

Although they had never occupied south-east Botswana, the Transvaal government claimed the territory by right of conquest. When Livingstone planted his mission at Kolobeng in the disputed territory, he not only enjoyed at least theoretical protection from the British government, but both blocked Boer expansion and kept the 'missionaries road' open. He had in short assumed a political role, though he never used it to mediate between Sechele and the Transvaalers; rather he encouraged the chief to defy them.

The Boers, with good reason, suspected Livingstone of supplying arms to Sechele and other independent chiefs on their western border. In 1849 the Transvaal government accordingly called for the missionary's removal from Kolobeng, and next year ordered Sechele to prevent Europeans from travelling north along the road. When in 1852, by the Sand River Convention, the British recognised the Transvaal's independence and renounced all jurisdiction north of the Vaal, the Boers decided to crush Sechele.

They were well aware that the Bakwena could muster six hundred fighting men, some of whom were armed with guns, and even possessed artillery. They accused Livingstone of supplying at least some of these guns—and it was a charge he had not bothered to contradict, possibly because he believed that it protected the tribesmen from aggression. But in 1852, when depressed at Cape Town, he altered his mind and wrote to

---

* The size of his loss elicited comment that a missionary with a family to support could scarcely accumulate such a sum on a meagre salary of £100 unless he indulged in trading and gun-running. But in fairness we must remember that Mrs Livingstone brought many articles of value to Kolobeng, and that he had been given gifts by hunters for whom he had provided hospitality. But one of his wagons was undoubtedly acquired through trading, and indeed Livingstone contended it was 'quite lawful', though perhaps not expedient, for missionaries to trade.[1]

the press that he would leave the Bakwena if it were proved that he had '*lent* or *sold* or *gave*' them a single gun.

Examination of Livingstone's correspondence reveals that not only did he act as Moffat's agent in selling guns and powder to the Bakwena,[2] but was prepared to repair their muskets for payment, and even sold them arms directly, although the actual quantity was insignificant.

In *Missionary Travels*, Livingstone suggests that the Bakwena possessed only five guns and scornfully rejected any suggestion that they were armed with cannon by declaring that the Boers had mistaken a cooking pot for one. Yet in 1847 the Doctor told Dr Moffat that the Bakwena possessed eighty muskets, and when the Boers finally attacked Sechele they were able to seize forty-eight of them. As for artillery Sechele himself boastingly wrote to the Boers 'I am myself possessed of cannon', and it is very difficult to believe that this was not known to Livingstone.

On 28 August 1852 a Boer commando of three hundred Europeans under Commandant Scholtz appeared before Dimawe. After attempting mediation, the burghers advanced on Sechele's 'battery' two days later, and stormed his entrenchments, losing three white men and a number of African auxiliaries killed. It is impossible to accept Livingstone's figure of over thirty-five Boers killed since the Transvaal government could not have concealed such heavy losses from a country that numbered only five thousand burgher families.

The rights and wrongs of this dispute between Sechele and the Boers do not concern us here, but we should examine the charge that the Boers sacked Livingstone's house at Kolobeng.

Scholtz places the blame squarely on the Bakwena. Two days after the fight he despatched a patrol to Kolobeng, which reported that Sechele's men had broken into the mission house some days earlier in search of guns and ammunition, although they had ignored Livingstone's workshop nearby. This the Boers now entered and removed two rifles and several half-finished guns on the ground that these represented a breach of the Sand River Convention. 'We found more guns and tools than Bibles', commented Scholtz, 'so that the place had more the appearance of a gunmaker's shop than a mission station, and more of a smuggling-shop than a school-place.' It may be that the Transvaalers then went on the rampage in the house and destroyed Livingstone's library, for the Doctor writes angrily of his books and Bibles being torn to pieces, but

73

such a sacrilege was less likely to have been committed by the God-fearing Boers than by Bakwena, who believed these same Bibles were used to bewitch Sechele. Moreover Scholtz had given strict orders that 'the missionaries' goods were not to be touched'.* Livingstone never visited Kolobeng to investigate the looting of his property, and evidence as to those responsible was lost when he gave instructions to burn down the house, lest it offered shelter to the Boers.[3] It is perhaps significant that the British authorities at the Cape refused to support his accusations against the commando. All in all it is difficult to avoid charging Livingstone, in his accounts of the battle of Dimawe and sack of Kolobeng, with deliberate distortion of facts to conform with his own prejudices, an exercise which he did not hesitate to adopt in the future.

Livingstone consoled himself for the destruction of his home and property at Kolobeng by stating that it freed him forever from sedentary mission work and the bondage of possessions. Over and over again he returned in his correspondence to this new sense of independence. Yet this did not prevent his denunciation of the Transvaal Boers rising to an almost hysterical pitch. 'Their conduct at Kolobeng', Livingstone announced a little incoherently, 'was like what we may suppose that of a gallant brigade of Satan's own, reeking red from pandemonium.' And three years later we find him rejoicing that 'malaria is not an unmitigated evil since it swept off many Boers in 1852'.

As for the Bakwena, they retired after their defeat to Dithubaruba but prevented the closure of the missionaries road, and its eventual annexation by the Transvaal. Livingstone's criticism of the Boers also had a long-term effect, for it so alienated British opinion from the Transvaalers that it became one of the factors responsible for the outbreak of two Boer Wars.

Livingstone anticipated spending only two weeks at Kuruman repairing his wagon before trekking north, but his stay was protracted to over three months, due perhaps to that lethargy typical of a depressive phase of cyclothymia. In *Missionary Travels* he blames the delay on difficulty in recruiting wagon-drivers, but here again he was being less than candid. In his journal, and to friends, he states that he was waiting for the Boers (whom he learned had threatened to kill him) to retire from the Kalahari and this was probably the true reason. It was not until 14 December 1852

* According to Pretorius's report, Edwards and Inglis, Livingstone's L.M.S. colleagues, volunteered that 'the house had been broken into by Sechele for powder and lead'.[4] This is supported by Livingstone's own intimation to his wife that their house was 'gutted' before the battle.[5]

that he escaped from 'durance vile' and headed north, with a single ox-wagon and several horses. He took six servants who turned out to be 'the worst possible specimens of those who imbibe the vices without the virtues of the Europeans'.* Also with him went a black trader from the West Indies named George Fleming, whom he believed to be an emancipated slave.

As he travelled northwards Livingstone's thoughts dwelt on the dangers ahead and revealed the mystical edge to his character: 'Am I on my way to die in Sebitoane's country?' he asked in the Journal, 'Have I seen the last of my wife & children? The breaking up of all my connections with earth, leaving this fair & beautiful world & knowing so little of it? I am only learning the Alphabet of it yet; and entering on an untried state of existence, following him who has entered in before me into the cloud, the veil, the Hades, is a serious prospect. Do we begin again in our new existence to learn much by experience, or have we full powers? My soul, whither wilt thou migrate to? Whither wilt thou lodge the first night after leaving this body? Will an angel soothe thy flutterings, for sadly flurried thou wilt be in entering on Eternity? O if Jesus speaks one word of peace that will establish in thy breast an everlasting calm. O Jesus, fill me with thy love now, and I beseach thee accept me & use me a little for thy glory. I have done nothing for thee yet, and I would like to do something. O do, do, I beseech thee, accept me and my service and take thou all the glory.'

To avoid Boer patrols, Livingstone kept well to the west of Kolobeng, though he would have dearly liked to visit Elizabeth's grave. At the turn of the year, after spending a few days at Dithubaruba, he pressed ahead to reach Boatlanama on 21 January 1853. But the wells were dry, nor was there water at Lephepe, though he found a little at Mashuwe.

He spent the last Sunday of January at Letloche water-hole. The scene there can hardly have altered over the last 120 years. A miniature canyon of pink granite descends in great steps to a well of clean water and a neighbouring muddy pool used by filth-caked cattle. The watering point is thronged with people and reminds the visitor of a Biblical scene. It was a favourite camping site for the European hunters of last century, but now is rarely visited; a middle-aged African told the author that he had never seen white men there before. Letloche is among the most evocative places

* He was even more scathing and 'Cromwellian' in his language when, after nursing these 'dregs' through fever, 'the first use the worthies made of their strength was whoredom'

75

in Botswana where the imaginative traveller feels very close to Livingstone. Next he came to Kanne, the last water for sixty miles.*

The jealousy of explorers is proverbial, and while trekking on to Lotlhakane Livingstone revealed this trait coupled with a sustaining belief that the trophies of exploration, in this case the Victoria Falls, were reserved for him by Divine providence. He explained to his brother Charles that a party of Europeans led by McCabe had recently reached Linyanti and managed to press on to 'within two days of the large Waterfall, yet it is left for me. I feel thankful to God, who, in permitting me to labour in his work, bestows tokens of the approbation of my fellow men by throwing discoveries in my way. . . . It is pleasant to recognize our Father's hands in all things.' Thus encouraged Livingstone reached the 'links' on 6 February and a fortnight later, when measuring a strangely shaped baobab, grasped that a tree's age can be estimated by counting its rings, a pioneering exercise in dendrochronology. He was at Gootsa pan on 22 February and beyond found that newly fallen rain had brought the arid land back to life again, and the country 'exceedingly lovely. All the ponds are full of water, the grass in seed, and the flowers of the forest in full blow.' From Kama Kama the party broke new ground to avoid tsetse and hacked a way through thick bush along the line of the magnetic meridian.[6] But it became necessary to make a ten-day halt when most of his companions went down with malaria. On 21 March they trekked on again with Livingstone's thoughts dwelling sadly on the separation from his family and his Journal entries are interrupted by a yearning cry 'I think much of my poor children', who, he says, 'are now the children of Jesus'. The going became very slow as they axed the way through acacia forest. With only Livingstone and one African still fit to work, he reflected 'I am spared in health while all the company have been attacked by the fever. If God has accepted my service then my life is charmed till my work is done.'[7] His sense of being a chosen servant of the Lord was growing.

Beyond Wia the scrub gives up and is replaced by serene grasslands with only the Gogha Hills standing out from the everlasting plain. Coming here today one can easily enter into Livingstone's lyrical mood when describing these 'scenes of perfect beauty', on which the ex-mill

* Many of the 1875 'thirstland trekkers'—five hundred Afrikaner men, women and children who were seeking new homes beyond the Okavango swamps—were to perish in the desert beyond.

76

boy bestowed the ultimate approbation as 'being equal to that of any gentleman's park in England'.

From the Gogha Hills a prominent sand ridge runs north east to the Chobe and had Livingstone taken this route he would have found an easy crossing place where the river is now straddled by the Ngoma Bridge. But his Bushman guides led him instead to the almost 'impassable barrier' of the Sansureh River beyond the water hole at Kasinka. He crossed it in a collapsible pontoon brought up from Cape Town. The distant Chobe beyond was widely flooded and he now entered a trackless swamp.

There is a sense of timeless claustrophobia about these swamps, through which for three days of prodigous effort Livingstone groped his way forward with a single companion. Sometimes he rode on horseback but for most of the way he was on foot and waist deep in water, carrying 'Aesop's burden', food, and a gun, while his companion bore the pontoon rolled into a bundle on his head.[8] This part of Livingstone's journey was so slow and so tortuous that one can only marvel at the man's physical endurance and moral resolution. In one letter he remarks in passing that the reeds and thick grass 'wore holes through strong moleskin "unmentionables" at the knees and the toes of the new shoes', and he devotes pages of the Journal to the passage through the swamp. It was typical that when he wrote *Missionary Travels*, he brushed aside his difficulties. They came at last to the Chobe and paddled twenty miles before descending as though from the sky upon a Makololo village, much to the wonderment of its inhabitants who considered the swamps to be their sure defence against Matabele raids. Livingstone waited there ten days while canoes were lashed together to ferry the wagon to the northern bank. During this time he considered devoting part of his life to the 'most honourable and holy work' of eradicating malaria. For he recognised the importance of the scourge and feared it 'seems destined to preserve intertropical Africa for the black races of mankind'. Moreover he knew that eradication of malaria was vital if missionary and commercial penetration of the continent were to be effected, and even remarked that the inventor of the mosquito net 'deserves a statue in Westminster Abbey'.

As we have seen, Livingstone's attitude to his proper duties as a doctor in Africa were curiously ambivalent. He accepted medicine as the noblest of professions, and appreciated that his good relations with tribesmen were owed to gratitude for medical treatment and a vain hope that this magician would provide 'gun-medicine' to improve their hunting. And he was careful to keep up with medical advances; within two years of the introduction of chloroform he made eager enquiries about the anaesthetic technique.

But Livingstone always regarded the practice of medicine as being of secondary importance to his work as a missionary. It is significant that he never established a hospital in Africa. Indeed, soon after arriving at

2 Livingstone's mosquito curtain

Kuruman, he told his old tutor Cecil, 'I feel it to be my duty to have as little to do with it [the treatment of disease] as possible', lest absorption in medicine turned him into 'a useless drone of a missionary'. Later he acknowledged that the drudgery of medical practice drove him to escape into the Kalahari, and informed his Directors that 'I believe the expenditure of such time and medicine [in therapy] is not the way in which in this country I can do most for the Redeemer's glory'. His attitude reminds us of that other great African explorer Mungo Park, who, despite a medical training, similarly neglected its practice.

But here on the Chobe in 1853 Livingstone toyed for a moment with the idea of investigating the cause of malaria. As it turned out he was diverted from the study of malarial aetiology not so much by conscience as by the success he achieved in preventing and curing its manifestations by quinine therapy. Accordingly his speculations about the causes of malaria remained as bizarre as those of his contemporaries.* He variously attributed it to exposure to an east wind, to 'miasmata' rising from swamps, and to the drinking of milk in the evening or of water that had flowed over granite. It was only during the course of the Zambezi Expedition that with a flash of inspiration he approached the truth and noted 'myriads of mosquitoes showed, as probably they always do, the presence of malaria'. Unfortunately he did not follow up this premise. Nor did he ever pay the detailed scientific attention to the study of mosquitoes which he did, for instance, to that of ants. It was one of Livingstone's traits subconsciously to ignore or reject any obstacle which might deter pioneering attempts to open up Central Africa, and it is tempting to attribute his failure to anticipate Ross's discovery of malaria transmission by forty years to this fixation.

In other areas of medicine, however, Livingstone was a notable pioneer. He listed more than fifty herbal remedies used by native 'doctors' and contributed many descriptions of tropical diseases before their manifestations were modified by the introduction of modern therapy. In a narrower field he was the first to record the association of the bites of a tampan (a type of tick) with the onset of Relapsing Fever, and to report the presence of haematuria (blood in the urine) among his carriers in an original reference to Central African Bilharzia. Livingstone could similarly claim to be the first man in modern times to provide authentic information about the tsetse fly,† and its carriage of Nagana to cattle. Whenever possible he took his trek oxen through fly country only by night, and casually noted that some tribesmen protected them from fly by smearing lion fat on their tails. During the last years of his life Livingstone achieved another 'first' when he described the presence of a filarial worm in the anterior chamber of the human eye, long before the condition of onchocerciasis was recognised.

Floods obliged Livingstone to make a long detour before he brought his wagon to the new site of Linyanti on 24 May 1853. There he was greeted by nearly seven thousand Makololo who were 'kind beyond all expectation'. Sekeletu, a youth of tired blood and 'coffee and milk' complexion was now chief. He greeted the Doctor affectionately, adopted him as a father, and presented him with twelve fine elephant tusks, while

* Richard Burton believed an attack of fever followed sleeping out in the moonlight while H. M. Stanley associated the disease with the presence of ozone in the air.
† There are several Biblical references.

his visitor, not to be outdone, gave the chief 'an improved breed of goats, fowls and a pair of cats' from the Cape.

Until mid-November Livingstone remained based on Linyanti. His first self-appointed task was to seek a healthy mission site, after which he intended to make the attempt to reach the coast. It seemed a bad omen that, within a week of his arrival, Livingstone went down with his first attack of malaria. It was the rather rare quartan form and he suffered relapses. Yet he remained on his feet: 'Never laid by', he boasted to his father-in-law, 'though much worse than some of our people who did', but he admitted to his wife that he had wished she had 'been there to make me warm and comfortable'.[9]

On 10 June Sekeletu announced that he was going to Sesheke and asked Livingstone to accompany him. But it was not until three weeks later that they set off on riding oxen. After travelling only thirty miles, an attempt was made on Sekeletu's life and, unnerved by his deliverance, he insisted on returning to Linyanti. Livingstone was detained there for another five weeks. During that time the Portuguese trader Silva Porto arrived in the town with a following of armed Mambari. Livingstone was vexed to find that Porto had reached the upper Zambezi before him, but he reduced the importance of the feat by suggesting that he was a half-caste. He suspected that another Portuguese traveller named Pereira had preceded them both to Linyanti, and was delighted to discover that although the Makololo had already given several newly born children the names of Ma-Robert, Nanes (Agnes), Monares (derived from the Dutch Mynheer), wagon, horse, gun and even Jesus, not one had been called Pereira.

Livingstone was still plagued by malarial relapses. He never scorned the nostrums of African 'doctors', explaining that 'I make it a rule to keep on good terms with my professional bretheren', so now he submitted to 'being stewed in their vapour baths', although without relief. 'This disease', he grumbled, 'takes the pluck out of one.'

Livingstone and Sekeletu set off again for Barotseland on 22 July, followed by a multitude of retainers, although Livingstone was mortified at being obliged to travel on the Sabbath. Again he declined the opportunity of visiting Mosi-oa-tunya; it was not his 'duty', he said, since the Makololo could never live there, so close to the Matabele.[10] Near Sesheke they embarked in a fleet of twenty-five canoes to ascend the river, a number which doubled from 'tribute' as they went. The river, here named the Leeambye, flowed through splendidly fertile country, and its beauty is vividly described in *Missionary Travels*. Ignoring Porto's visit, Livingstone added that 'I felt the pleasure of looking on lands which had never been seen by an European before'. But the loveliness was tainted: the Zambezi valley, which resembled the Nile in its inundations, was infested with tsetse. Landing at Imamongo the canoes were carried past Gonye Falls, and here Livingstone listened to the reactions of his companions to the rainbow arching over the falls: some said 'how grand the works of God are', but others 'washed their faces in the spray as a charm while those of the utilitarian school searched the holes in the rocks for round stones to grind snuff'.[11] Leaving Sekeletu at Naliele, Livingstone pushed farther up river with only a few companions, reaching the vast swamps of Lobale, the furthest limit of Barotseland.

Still disappointed in his quest for a suitable mission site, he determined now to put the second part of his plan—the finding of a way to the coast—into action. So they hurried downstream, meeting on the way an Arab slave-trader named Syde ben Habib who was to cross Livingstone's path several times during the coming years, and were back at Linyanti on 15 September 1853. Soon afterwards Livingstone's complacency was jolted by learning that a Hungarian traveller named Laszlo Magyar, after exploring in Zaire and Angola, had reached Linyanti the previous year, and now hoped to return and meet him. Livingstone declined to see Magyar and kept his feat to himself lest it damaged his own prestige.[12]

In Barotseland Livingstone's malaria had taken a more serious, cerebral form, and he suffered from symptoms of Menière's syndrome which is characterised by periods of vertigo. These triggered off a phase of acute depression which was reflected in his correspondence. 'I had perpetually to regret the absence of our friend Mr Oswell,' he wrote, 'and instead of pleasant conversations in the evenings I had to endure the everlasting ranting of the Makololo.'[13] He shrank from the interminable shouted conversations, squabbling and scolding, and the tuneless 'noise called singing' which was 'more like a severe penance than anything I had met before in the course of my missionary duties'. He bitterly deplored the degradation of the Zambezi Africans and their rigid conformity to the tribal *mores* which made them drive away or even destroy persons who were unorthodox in mind or deformed in body. 'They possess neither patriotism, courage, natural affection, honour nor honesty', he complained, 'They have no stimulus for any mental improvement. . . . The

81

idea of transgression has contributed to the lowest forms of barbarism. . . . Albinoes are shunned or killed. A child which cuts its upper front teeth first is also put to death in some tribes, and so are twins. The natural man presents few points of loveliness.' A final cavil in his Journal six days later reads, 'I have not yet met with a beautiful woman among the black people. . . . I cannot concieve of any European being so captivated by them as to covet criminal intercourse.'

But such querulous irascibility did not reflect Livingstone's real feelings towards the Africans. He could not wholeheartedly subscribe to the contemporary western belief that the races of mankind were unequally endowed. Heathen Africans to him were a 'fallen' people (as were, he said unflatteringly, the Boers and Irish); he believed them to be mere human constructs who would gain total humanity through education and conversion to Christianity. This, he conceived, could be best effected by European example and improvement of their socio-economic environment to that of western Europe, and he was to suggest practical ways of attaining this goal.

Having no fixed scale of racial characteristics, he rejected the idea of genetic inferiority. At the same time he did recognise a sliding scale of material and spiritual development which, for environmental reasons, the Africans had not yet managed to ascend. 'I have no prejudice against their colour,' Livingstone wrote towards the end of his life, 'Indeed anyone who lives long among them forgets they are black and feels they are just fellow men.' Yet the Doctor incredibly insisted that enslavement debased its victims physically and morally, and spoke knowingly of slaves' 'low retreating foreheads, prognathus jaws, lark heels and other physical peculiarities [which] always awakens the same feelings of aversion as those with which we view specimens of the "Bill Sykes" and "Bruiser" class in England'.[14] It was muddled thinking for a medical man, but we must remember that Livingstone was always looking out for evidence to belabour the slave trade, and to prove a point, favourably compared the appearances of free tribesmen with those of the pundits from the London Anthropological Society.

We must note too that Livingstone's enlightened racial views sometimes lapsed—as when he declared that 'each race is destined to perform its own part in one vast plan of creative Providence'.[15] But these were passing phases and his close association with Africans finally persuaded him that all men shared a common humanity, which could, through Grace, be perfectly realised. He once wrote, 'Genuine sympathy with human beings obliterates the distance of race and clime, rank and religion, and even of intellect.'[16] For him social backwardness elicited neither scorn nor disgust but a feeling of responsibility.

Livingstone could not begin his quest for a route to the sea until the cooling rains fell in November. Until then he busied himself with making acute observations of animal life for his Journal. He also conducted an extensive correspondence from Linyanti. In a single day this compulsive writer penned twenty-three letters which two traders carried back to civilisation. Then there was his destination to consider. Linyanti stood nearly midway between the Atlantic and the Indian Ocean, but as early as 19 July a note in his Journal shows that he had already decided to make first for the west coast, because if practical this route would mean a shorter sea passage for British trade to the interior. Probably he was influenced too by Porto and Magyar having passed safely through Angola, and he even briefly considered travelling in Porto's company but abandoned the idea since it risked his becoming associated by the Africans with slavers. He further decided to make for Luanda rather than the nearer port of Benguela, as it contained 'more English' and was 'more salubrious'; in any case he had already made a tentative arrangement to meet Oswell there.[17]

As the date of his departure approached, Livingstone's depression lifted and he felt glad to be going alone—he disliked the idea of a 'crusty companion'. He resolved to send back his unsatisfactory servants to Kuruman with Fleming, and engage porters at Linyanti. After long discussions with the tribal elders, twenty-seven men were selected while Sekeletu furnished a few beeves, four pack oxen, and some tusks to barter, hoping that Livingstone would open a profitable trade route to Angola and perhaps negotiate some non-aggression treaties to safeguard his flank during the struggle with the Matabele.

A thousand miles of country, most of it completely unknown, lay between Linyanti and Luanda, yet Livingstone's equipment for the journey was pitifully inadequate. He had two guns for himself and three muskets 'for my people', a small supply of biscuits, a few pounds of tea and sugar, twenty pounds of coffee, one small tin and a bag for spare clothing, a box of medicines, and another for his books (which included a Nautical Almanac, Thomson's Logarithm Tables, a Bible and a lined journal), a magic lantern with some slides of Biblical scenes, an artificial horizon, chronometer, thermometer and compass, beads worth £2 as 'journey money' for bartering, a small gypsy tent, a sheepskin mantle, and a horse rug to serve as a bed. His wagon he left in the care of Sekeletu.

On 8 November Livingstone wrote in his Journal, 'May God in mercy permit me to do something for the cause of Christ in these dark places of the earth'. He then in his Journal made certain dispositions of his property, and, voicing his fears, completed the entry with the supplication 'Be a father to the fatherless, and a husband to the widow for Jesus' sake'. For his objective was clear: in a letter to Robert Moffat he wrote it down in words which would be long remembered: 'I shall open a path into the Interior or perish'.[18]

5. First proof of illustration of Shinte's reception. Livingstone's annotation reads: 'Could the artist not make the sheaves of arrows on the boys' shoulders as a soldier carries his musket not on their backs? Many more rings on the legs and arms of Shinte would be an improvement.'

6. The engraver's sketch of one of the gorges cut by the Zambezi at the Victoria Falls, annotated by Livingstone

7

'A Man, an Ox or a Tusk'

Dr Livingstone's trans-African journey remains one of the great epics of human endurance. Few people, even today, would quarrel with Sir Roderick Murchison's appraisal of it as 'the greatest triumph in geographical research which has been effected in our times'.

The journey was saga-like in its indifference to death, and an extraordinary achievement on two other counts. Between November 1853 and May 1856 Livingstone passed through four thousand miles of largely unexplored country in what is today Angola, Zambia and Mozambique. It was an expedition into a vacuum, not only in the sense that it took him to places unknown to the civilised world, but also that it carried him backwards through time into a weirdly antique African scene.

In this period of solitary endeavour Livingstone encountered primitive tribesmen whose first interest was to rob or kill a stranger. Yet he emerged from the continent unscathed and was able to reveal both the country's high potential and the true character of its people for the first time.

During this journey Livingstone was mostly in an exultant phase, possessed by a mysterious flow of energy and resolution, and it is now that we see him at his best, with his special gifts of staunchness and courage so clearly demonstrated as to arm later generations against despondency and fear. In this period, Livingstone was resistant to fatigue, skilful in dealing with uncivilised people, always ready to take an optimistic view of dangerous situations. Yet he knew exactly when to be tough and when to gain his point through moderation. As H. M. Stanley noted long afterwards, 'mildness of speech was the great secret which had carried him successfully through'.

Although accompanied by only a handful of Makololo porters, and utterly isolated from the world, Livingstone, thanks to the inner harmony of his spirit, was unaffected by loneliness and he remained almost mystically happy because of the growing certainty that his endeavours were willed by God. The incredible physical hardships which he had to endure need to be constantly stressed. He was alternately scorched by a tropical sun, or soaked to the skin. For months he ate only the plainest native food, deficient in protein and vitamins alike. Rapacious chiefs harried him with demands for toll, yet he brushed them aside with fatherly calm and traversed a continent without firing a single shot in anger.

He followed the winding paths that knit Africa together, forced to rely on guides who vexed him greatly by their whims and treachery. Yet he was able to make rough notes about everything he saw of interest for transcription into a journal, and in such detail that later travellers in Africa complained that he had left them nothing to describe.

Other explorers who ventured into the unknown were almost invariably financed either by a scientific society, newspaper, or government, and were lavishly fitted out; Livingstone possessed the very minimum of equipment, travelled without a white companion and was backed only by Sekeletu. It was a modest power-base for all that followed. Fortunately his childhood had conditioned him to hardships and privation; as he noted, he could 'bear what other Europeans would consider hunger and thirst without any inconvenience', and made a virtue of poverty, explaining that 'a large array of baggage excited the cupidity of the tribes through whose country we wished to pass'.

Livingstone also differed greatly from contemporary explorers in his underlying motive for risking his life and turning away from civilisation. They were adventurers who were happiest when pitting themselves against unreasonable hazards, or were driven through the wilds by overwhelming intellectual curiosity; while some sought fame, perhaps the greatest number bowed to an inner insistence that they must conquer some physical obstacle simply 'because it's there'.

But no such forces were at work in Livingstone. He became an explorer because he felt increasingly that he was intended for the task of opening up Africa, and he accepted, even cherished, the charge without question or demur, hopeful that it would lead him to real holiness. This concept of his mandate grew stronger as the march proceeded until towards its end he felt assured he was an instrument of God, whose labours were essential for the ultimate triumph of Christianity in Africa. He believed he was working under a divine imperative to bring trade as well as Christian ethics and the Gospel to Africa, for he felt convinced that 'no permanent elevation of a people can be effected without commerce'.

'A Man, an Ox or a Tusk'

There were psychological compensations for accepting this arduous charge. Livingstone discovered delight in the very act of travel. He enjoyed the challenge of overcoming difficulties, as though success was a sort of alibi for his failure as an evangelist. Essentially a 'loner', Livingstone enjoyed solitude and was able to commit errors without risking comment or criticism. Instead he lived in an inner world of his own, walled off by his holy commission from contact with a far inferior outer existence.

Despite the lack of sophisticated instruments, Livingstone charted his course with a precision which also distinguished him from any previous explorer. He put into practice the teachings of Thomas Maclear and the obliging Captain of the *George*. At night, if the sky was clear, he would 'fix' his latitude by observing certain stars as they crossed the meridian, using a sextant and artificial horizon of mercury. He made the more difficult calculations of longitudes by measuring the angle between the moon and a given star at a specific time shown by his chronometer. Sometimes he would confirm this position by watching the occultations of stars by the moon through his telescope, or of Jupiter's moons by its disc. Then, by the light of the evening fire, he covered so many sheets of paper with intricate calculations that they filled a box which a man could only carry with difficulty. Once he amazed Sir Thomas Maclear by making 2,812 readings to fix a single position and his observations were so accurate as to draw from him the compliment that a traveller 'could go to any point across the entire continent along Livingstone's track and still feel certain of [his] position'.

Only a little less impressive than Livingstone's meticulous charting of the journey is the quality of his Journal. In its eight hundred pages he left a marvellous record of Bantu culture before it was eroded by outside influence. The Journal was written in elegant handwriting which only deteriorated when the Doctor was suffering from a particularly bad bout of fever. No other man had chronicled an expedition of this kind in such detail. It was an anthology of his daily experience and a tracing of the oscillations of an unusually active and subtle mind. Despite repeated illness, hardships and danger, he found the energy to record an array of random anecdotes, adventures, descriptions of people and places, the medicinal properties of plants (which he tried out on himself), the habits of animals, and his own communing with God that so refreshed his spirit. Some years later he relied heavily on the Journal when writing the text of

87

Missionary Travels, but in these first unedited notes we see Livingstone far more clearly than in the book. Thus the Journal provides additional evidence of his religious faith and dedication, of his illnesses and the participation of the Portuguese in the slave trade.

Sekeletu allotted twenty-seven porters to the expedition. Two of them, Pitsane and Mashawana, were true Makololo and acted as N.C.Os. The remainder were drawn from subject tribes, but Livingstone invariably referred to them all as Makololo. He found them 'a merry set of mortals'; the carriers in return served him with rare devotion. Inevitably occasional misunderstandings arose for the Makololo were subject to quaint fears and unreasonable suspicions, but in general they retained perfect confidence in their leader even though they never really fathomed the reason which drove him across Africa. Livingstone's account of the care the Makololo took of him remains one of the most moving tributes ever paid by a European to a primitive people.

He estimated that it would take one hundred and forty-eight days to reach Luanda; in fact two hundred and ten passed before he reached the west coast.

Livingstone travelled by canoe almost to the western limit of Makololo rule, while most of the porters marched along the river banks. They remained four days at Sesheke, and there Livingstone preached to large and attentive congregations. Beyond, the canoes were delayed only by the generosity lavished on them at successive villages. The Doctor was delighted by the graceful modesty of these people who when they bestowed the gift of an ox would say, 'Here is a little bit of bread for you', a manner which contrasted with that of the Batswana who, when presenting a goat, would exclaim 'Behold, an ox!'

Livingstone stayed at Naliele, where he restored to their homes twenty-four captives from a raid, this being the first occasion that he assumed the role of liberator. At Libonta, the last Makololo outpost, 'the people' felt uneasy at the prospect of leaving friendly country for the land of the Balonda which was a forested haunt of witchcraft and slavers. Beyond the confluence of the Zambezi and Kabompo (which Livingstone unaccountably believed to be the main stream so that from now on he referred to the Zambezi as the Leeba),* they quickly reached the first Balonda town.

Here its chief, a woman, refused them permission to travel any further

---

* Certainly today the Kabompo is smaller.

by canoe; she insisted instead that they leave the river and visit her brother Shinte, the paramount chief. In this she was supported by Manenko, her lusty daughter, who announced that she would accompany the white man to Shinte's town.

So Livingstone began the land journey with a thirty-mile trudge through flooded meadows and gloomy tropical forests to Shinte's, Manenko striding at the head of a remarkable procession, her sole clothing consisting of a tiny cloth covering her genitals. Behind came a boisterous drummer, then Livingstone with the Makololo and finally a crowd of Balonda 'loudly vociferating, whistling & using medicines to drive the rain away'. Manenko turned out to be a virago, whom the Doctor dubbed 'a black Mrs Caudle' after the nagging wife frequently portrayed at the time in *Punch*. He was shocked by Manenko's 'frightful nudity', amused by her antics, and admiring of 'her pedestrian powers'.

After four days they approached Shinte's town, but Livingstone refused to move next day as it was the Sabbath. Then on Monday 'Mrs Caudle' announced that she was menstruating and some time was wasted while she 'doctored' herself and (to Livingstone's relief) assumed more adequate clothing.

The Chief formally received Livingstone on 17 January 1854, together with a half-caste Portuguese who had turned up with a chain-gang of captives for sale. Shinte's display of barbaric grandeur seemed three-quarters fantasy and only a quarter real, and it became the subject of a well-known illustration in *Missionary Travels*. Shinte was seated on a makeshift throne placed in the centre of a large clearing. Under a leopard skin he wore a scarlet and green kilt, a check jacket topped by a head-dress of beads and feathers, and when he walked 'a profusion of iron & copper leglets gave him a peculiar waddling gait'. A thousand armed men squatted on the ground around the Chief with two hundred members of his 'outragious female establishment'. Livingstone seated himself in the shade of a tree forty yards away, with the apprehensive Makololo grouped behind. First a party of musicians capered about the arena performing 'various musical pieces'. The Balonda notables next delivered interminable speeches, punctuated by occasional crashes of musketry, as Shinte sat motionless on his throne, never shifting his gaze from Livingstone. Then three hundred soldiers, brandishing swords, suddenly made a mock attack on the white man, who, however, sat through the ordeal without flinching. More speeches concerning Livingstone's history and aspirations

89

were delivered by leather-lunged courtiers, after which Shinte's women entertained the gathering with songs. By now the sun was riding high and the clearing was filled with the hot uneasy smell of Africa. Suddenly Shinte stood up, the half-caste's Mambari followers fired off a ragged volley, and the spectacle was over. It had been a high moment of the glare and glitter of African history, a vivid demonstration of what a purely native culture could achieve.

This was only one of many occasions when Livingstone reported the contemporary scene in Africa, but his status as an African historian has not yet been sufficiently recognised.

So far the study of the Bantu past had been for him only of peripheral interest, but he was certainly impressed by the *mfecane*. Like many people in the mid-Victorian era, Livingstone believed that events were forged by conquering heroes and tyrants, and during his early missionary years he was more concerned with the careers of recent predatory chieftains than with the broader flows of tribal social history. He never fully perceived that unlike the individualistic Europeans, the Africans were essentially communalistic group-conformists.

But by the time he attended Shinte's reception, Livingstone was beginning to free himself from the parochial attitudes of Kuruman, and to seek a way through the labyrinthine threads of Central African history. He hoped to find tangible evidence to give coherence to traditional accounts. But this acute observer failed to recognise the Stone Age artifacts scattered through the sub-continent, and wondered whether the Bantu were sprung from an indigenous stock of high ability, or if they had been inspired by an alien people. After discovering traces of irrigation furrows near the Gonye Falls, Livingstone even suspected that 'superior minds must have risen at various times in this region'. But more generally he envisaged ancient Egyptian influence as spreading down from the north, and often drew attention to the similarity of Bantu and Egyptian customs. He found difficulty in accepting a Bantu origin for some of the more complex articles of their culture, and once suggested that these advances were the result of Divine intervention—though not in any derogatory sense, for he accepted that Noah's Ark had saved his own people.

Shinte, who regarded Livingstone as a valued human oddity, detained him in his town for ten days. The Doctor entertained the chief with a highly successful magic lantern show of Biblical scenes, and afterwards noted ruefully that this 'was the only mode of instruction I was ever pressed to repeat'. Shinte for his part presented his new friend with a curiously shaped sea-shell (held by the Balonda to be of immense value), and then further embarrassed him with the gift of a small slave girl. When Livingstone primly declined her, Shinte jumped to the natural conclusion and offered a more nubile maiden. Although the Doctor toyed with the idea of accepting her as a servant for Mary, he soon thought better of it.

Livingstone was fascinated by the Balonda way of life, although horrified by the women's indecent dress which made them 'obliged continually to thrust the hand between the thighs'. He decided that 'some of them might be good looking, but one cannot help feeling all is spoiled by their state of nudity. They cannot be viewed even with any degree of pleasure', an opinion with which the Makololo rather surprisingly agreed.

Shinte provided seven men to help carry the loads and a guide named Ntemese. He proved to be dishonest and Livingstone was delighted when 'our plague Ntemese' decided to desert. They marched on through a dense Balonda population, feeling vaguely uneasy among a people who mastered their fears by refracting them in a hundred narrow superstitions. Their villages, according to the Doctor (who disclaimed Rousseau's enchantment with the noble savage), were 'very pretty, being usually embowered in shrubs, bananas, manioc &c, but though apparently fitted to be the abodes of purity & love they are far from realising the poetic idea'. Presently they came to the land of the Balobale. No more gifts now came their way, there was nothing to shoot in this fly country and they were reduced to begging for their food.

On 20 February 1854 they reached Lake Dilolo, with Livingstone so ill with malaria as to be 'indifferent to the sight'. But beyond he noticed a change of direction in the flow of the rivers and realised they had passed the Central African watershed, fully five thousand feet above sea level. The thought of this proving to be a potential site for a mission station never entered his fevered mind as he stumbled on.

The rain fell in vindictive sheets when they approached the great Kasai River, which inevitably Livingstone found 'very much like the Clyde'. His real troubles now began. The country ahead was inhabited by the Bachokwe or Chiboque, a predatory and rapacious tribe. For the next five terrifying weeks the little party was threatened with repeated violence and subjected to impossible demands for hongo or toll. Any other man but Livingstone would have turned back, but, as Livingstone himself once

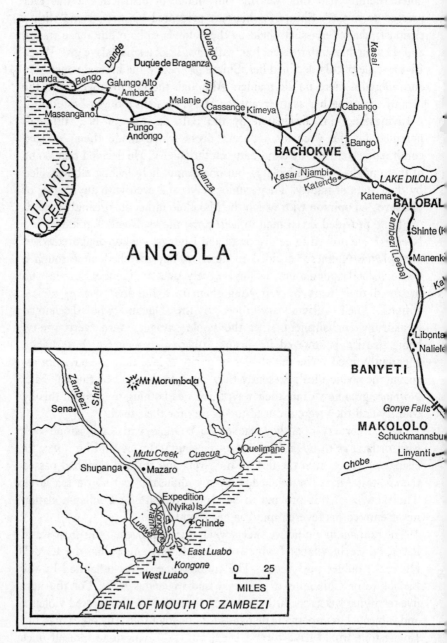

ANGOLA

Luanda
Bengo
Dande
Duque de Braganza
Galungo Alto
Ambaca
Massangano
Pungo Andongo
Malanje
Cassange
Kimeya
Quango
Lui
Cuanza
Kasai
Cabango
BACHOKWE
Bango
Kasai Njambi
Katende
Katema
LAKE DILOLO
BALOBA
Zambezi (Leeba)
Shinte (K
Manenk
Ka
Libonta
Naliele
BANYETI
Gonye Falls
MAKOLOLO
Schuckmannsbu
Linyanti
Chobe

ATLANTIC OCEAN

Zambezi
Shire
Mt Morumbala
Sena
Shupanga
Mazaro
Mutu Creek
Cuacua
Quelimane
Expedition (Nyika) Is
Chinde
Kongone
Chamo
Luawa
East Luabo
Kongone
West Luabo

0   25
MILES

DETAIL OF MOUTH OF ZAMBEZI

Map 3. Livingstone's Trans-A

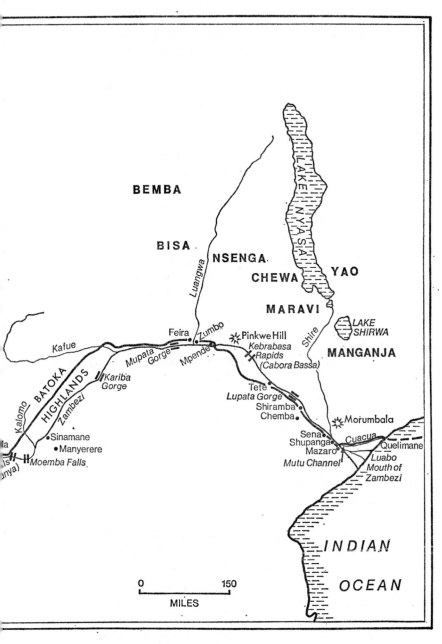

BEMBA

BISA

NSENGA

CHEWA

YAO

MARAVI

LAKE SHIRWA

MANGANJA

Feira
Zumbo
Pinkwe Hill
Kebrabasa
Rapids
(Cabora Bassa)

Kafue

Luangwa

Shire

LAKE NYASA

Mupata Gorge
Mpende

Kalomo
BATOKA HIGHLANDS
Zambezi

Kariba Gorge

Tete
Lupata Gorge
Shiramba
Chemba

Morumbala

Sinamane
Manyerere
Moemba Falls

Sena
Shupanga
Mazaro
Mutu Channel

Cuacua
Quelimane
Luabo
Mouth of Zambezi

INDIAN

OCEAN

0   150
MILES

ney November 1853–May 1856

explained, 'if I live I must succeed in what I have undertaken. Death alone will put a stop to my efforts.' He succeeded now through a combination of watchful pertinacity and adroit handling of childish minds which —through fear or misunderstanding—could very easily give way to rage and savagery.

The first act of brigandage, which became so hatefully familiar, befell the party at the crossing of the Kasai, when they were charged preposterous ferry fees. A chief named Katende soon afterwards made 'senseless demands' for hongo, and Livingstone had to part with a shirt. At the next river they were relieved of three copper armlets and soon afterwards gave a guide a length of cloth before he would show them the right path. Next morning the Bachokwe Chief Njambi accused one of the Makololo of a trivial crime and imposed a fine of 'a man, an ox, gun or other valuable article', threatening to storm Livingstone's camp if he refused to pay.

Everything hung in suspense next day as the Bachokwe surrounded the camp, grimacing to show their filed, cat-like teeth, brandishing their swords and pointing muskets at the solitary white man. But as the tension rose so did Livingstone's phlegm: he seated himself on a stool, placed a double-barrelled gun across his knees, and somehow persuaded Njambi to come and squat in front of him with his counsellors. Grudgingly, during the interminable discussion that followed, Livingstone handed over successively a shirt, beads and a white handkerchief; but the more he gave the more the demands increased, and Njambi shouted that he now would only be satisfied with a gun *and* an ox. Then one warrior charged right up to Livingstone from behind—and was stopped sharply when the Doctor turned round and put his gun to his face. Quite suddenly the tension snapped. The Bachokwe became conciliatory, and dropped their demands to a single ox. Thankful 'to avoid an effusion of blood', Livingstone agreed.

The demands went on thereafter, day after day, and it became evident that the expedition would soon be stripped of all its possessions. Yet even in these straits Livingstone found excuses for the tribesmen's extortions: this was slaving country, he reasoned, and the slavers could only pass their long coffles of captives through it provided they placated each successive chief with toll.

Going on through thick forests, with Livingstone mounted uncomfortably on the ox of vicious manners named Sinbad, the Makololo were so affected by the profound melancholy of African woodlands and by a growing belief they were lost, that they became sullen and finally mutinous. Livingstone, delirious with fever, rushed out of his gypsy tent brandishing a pistol, determined to show them who was master. The Doctor gratefully acknowledged that his followers 'never afterwards gave me any trouble'.

Livingstone was semi-comatose in his tent for the whole of 13 March; when he recovered he was touched to see that his men had built a protective stockade around him. It was a wise precaution, for soon another party of Bachokwe appeared with their demand for 'a man, an ox or a tusk'. 'We were determined to die for each other', wrote Livingstone, 'rather than deliver up one of our number' to slavery; and he prepared to fight off an attack. But African minds often work by contraries and they promptly presented him with three pigs.

Two weeks later another belligerent crowd of warriors gathered to bar their way, and Livingstone, weakened by malaria, was moved almost to despair by the injustice and wearisome inevitablity of their demands. 'The fever quite unmans me,' he wrote, 'yet I had to bear a day of torture by the people of this village.' It ended in a scuffle and finally Livingstone agreed to part with an ox and one tusk. By now the Makololo were cowed and determined to turn back. In the privacy of his tent that night their leader turned to his sure comforter, and in his Journal wrote: 'O Almighty God, help. Help & leave not this wretched people to the slave dealer and Satan.' Next morning it seemed that his prayers were answered, for the Makololos' spirits had revived and they went forward again. Going on they reached the precipitous drop into a valley of the Quango River (which reminded Livingstone of that part of the Clyde where the battle of Langside was fought). Another group of warriors now made ostentatious preparations to contest their path. Livingstone fully 'expected them to maul us'; but the attack never developed, thanks, he believed, to the depressing effect of persistent rain. The Makololo could scarcely believe their good fortune: 'We are the Children of Jesus', they shouted. Near the Quango, which marked the eastern border of Portuguese authority in Angola, the party stopped rather apprehensively at the village of Kimeya. Livingstone refused to give up his last blanket, and once again a fight seemed inevitable. But like an incident from a story book, relief was at hand. While the argument was going on, a half-caste Portuguese soldier suddenly appeared. His authority quietened the warriors, and the little party marched down to the river 'with light hearts', unconcerned by the few futile musket shots fired after it. Across the Quango, Livingstone saw a little group of square white houses through the gathering darkness. He had reached the furthest of the Portuguese outposts.

They were still three hundred miles from the sea, but from now on would be free from intimidation and extortion. On 12 April 1854 they arrived 'naked and famished' at Cassange (now Cassanza), then an important trading station but today no more than a decayed hamlet. There a Captain Neves provided generous hospitality, entertaining Livingstone at a banquet where he toyed unbelievingly with preserved fruit, American biscuits and Irish butter.

From Cassange they passed through country which looked as fertile as the Mississippi Valley. According to Livingstone's map, beyond Cassange they made a northerly diversion to visit the settlement of Duque de Braganza, but he had fever at the time and the Journal is silent about the place. He was received kindly at Ambaca, where Livingstone, a life-long abstainer, took a glass of wine as a remedy for his fever; thereafter he always carried a supply. Then they passed through mountainous country to Galungo Alto, which Livingstone accounted the most beautiful scenery he had seen in Africa. Here again he was so royally entertained that he prayed in his diary: 'May God abundantly reward and bless' his host.

They were nearing the sea now, and the Makololo, remembering the stories they had heard of white men fattening up Negroes at the coast for Cannibal feasts, became increasingly apprehensive, while Livingstone, weakened by malaria and dysentery, was only just alive and quite incapable of writing up the Journal. But he managed to keep going. The ground was ground no longer, but merely distance to be covered. All his energy was concentrated on reaching Luanda and he resented any other intrusion or call upon his energy. Dimly at last he saw a huddle of white houses in the distance, standing up against the sea. He stumbled on into Luanda on 31 May 1854. Only a single Englishman, a Mr Gabriel, lived there but his welcome was effusive. Yet it was the simplest thing which counted most for Livingstone: 'I shall never forget the delicious pleasure', he told Tidman, 'of tumbling into . . . bed after sleeping six months on the ground'.

8

'The Little Beginning'

Livingstone spent nearly four months at Luanda. For the first two weeks he rested in Mr Gabriel's house, thinking of nothing except his singular contentment at being where he was and his distress at finding no mail waiting for him at the port, nor even the aneroid barometer which he had specifically asked Steele to send out to him. A year later its absence led Livingstone to make an inaccurate calculation of the Zambezi's fall above Tete, which had serious consequences.

Only on 14 June 1854 did he feel sufficiently recovered to call on the Bishop of Angola with his Makololo, who presented a remarkably handsome appearance since Gabriel had fitted them out with striped cotton robes and red caps. The Makololo gazed in awe at the sea and were even more affected by the celebration of High Mass which they attended next day at the Cathedral. Livingstone was shocked by the frequent obeisances and genuflexions of the service, and inclined to applaud his 'people' when they decided that they had witnessed 'white men charming their demons'.

Several British warships were in harbour and the Makololo were vastly impressed by them too: 'it is not a canoe at all', they gasped on one man-o'-war, 'it is a town!'

Livingstone was delighted by the 'exhilarating presence of the warm-hearted naval officers', one of whom lent him a copy of Humbolt's *Cosmos* which afforded him 'happy reading' half way across the continent. Another, named Bedingfeld, offered Livingstone a free passage to St Helena, whence he could take ship to England, and when this was declined, agreed to carry his accounts of his journey to England. Only two years later Livingstone was fervently to wish he had never clapped eyes on Bedingfeld.

The Doctor next turned to writing or dictating reports for the L.M.S. and the Geographical Society, together with a sheaf of letters to friends

and relations. These completed, he examined the clandestine export of
slaves from Luanda and concerned himself with the administration of
Angola, commending the Portuguese for their lack of colour bigotry, and,
if critical of the accompanying miscegenation, allowed that they at least
recognised their half-caste children.

Livingstone declined other 'tempting offers' of passages to England for
several reasons: he believed his duty lay in returning the Makololo to
their homes and he was now sure that the Angolan route into the interior
was impossible for wagons because of tsetse fly. Accordingly his duty lay
in seeking an alternative route from Linyanti to the Indian Ocean. Far
away in Scotland, when he heard the decision, old Neil Livingstone
sighed 'Man David, I wish you [would] come now—for I don't think I'll
live to see you'.[1] He died at Hamilton just before his son came home.

So, as his strength increased, Livingstone began preparations for the
return march to Linyanti, drawing £70 of his salary on account for his
men's princely two shillings a month and to purchase 'journey money'.
The Bishop was more than helpful. He provided Livingstone with a
passport, on the back of which successive Portuguese officials would mark
the stages of the return journey. He gave clothes to the Makololo and for
Sekeletu provided a horse, a colonel's uniform and two donkeys which at
the time were believed to be immune to Nagana* but soon succumbed.
The local merchants were no less generous, presenting a musket to each of
the Makololo. They left on 20 September 1854 after the effusive Bishop
had tenderly embraced the Doctor which set him growling, 'I would have
preferred a kiss from my wife to a hug from this benevolent & kind-
hearted celibate in crimson silk gown & golden cross hung round his neck.'

It took Livingstone almost twelve months to reach Linyanti. Not
impelled by any urgency, he was occasionally apathetic and dispirited, and
prepared to relax for longer intervals with his Portuguese friends in the
Angolan hinterland. Though sometimes 'extremely wicked', the Makololo
were still 'the best sort of men I ever travelled with', and Livingstone
wrote in a final appreciation that 'the Argonauts were nothing to them'.

He had more time now to relish the beauty and fertility of Angola,
which mingles the flamboyant green of Assam with the dull metallic rust
of Southern Africa. His account provided the first clear spotlight that had
fallen on the country, and his remarkable faculty for picking up information was shown by a sketch map on which he scrawled 'petroleum

* The fatal disease of domestic animals transmitted by the tsetse fly.

reported', just north of the Icollo or Bengo River. It was our earliest intimation of that valuable commodity existing in Angola.

But it was the fertility which impressed Livingstone most: 'I never saw such luxuriant vegetation before', he wrote and observed that Angola enjoyed 'a perpetual harvest time'.[2] In his Journal, anticipating a more famous passage, he wrote that this 'land presents pictures of loveliness such as angels might enjoy'; and on another day: 'O, how often have I seen morning scenes the very essence of beauty and grace—flooded with still air of delicious warmth, yet the gentle zephyrs playing occasionally so as to give a sensation of coolness as of a fan; the still sun-shine before the heat has become trying; the grassy meadows, cattle feeding, goats & kids skipping or leaping & feeding, the rustling pines perched against the azure sky with its light fleecy clouds, the clumps of evergreen variously tinted trees; the fair sex of sooty black wending their way to the river with their watering pots poised on their heads, groups of herdboys with miniature bows, arrows and spears, men sewing under the shady banian, old men telling their deeds or repeating their wise saws, while others carry trees or branches to repair their hedges, and all flooded with delicious African air and African birds singing among the branches.' Consideration of Angola's prospects made such an impression on Livingstone that from now on he would examine plants not so much for their scientific interest as for their food potential; soils similarly were assessed for fertility, and geological features for mineral wealth. Africa had become his kingdom to develop.

But for all its advantages there was a great deal wrong with Angola. Fever was its 'great bugbear', while the 'inward gloom' of its dense rain forests, so evocative of invisible powers, turned its Negroid people* to innumerable superstitious observances. They suffered by having little need to work among such unrivalled fertility; they had not even invented any games, Livingstone observed, and he found it 'wonderful they don't go mad with ennui'.

Livingstone spent two months at Galungo Alto, delayed by illness among the Makololo. To pass the time, he visited the remains of several Jesuit stations in the neighbourhood, and his vaguely hostile attitude towards the Catholic Church relaxed. The Jesuits had been expelled from Angola in 1759 and their buildings now stood in ruins but he was fascinated by the faint holiness that lingered about their shrines; the air

* In Angola Livingstone for the first time met a people who were Negroid rather than Bantu.

there still seemed loud with muttered devotions and he marvelled at the old dormitories' nail-studded chests in which 'the bretheren stowed their grub'.[3] It seemed to him as though the Jesuits had only just left.

Still fretting at his failure to make any converts, Livingstone had comforted himself by reflecting that 'such was also the case with the Apostles', and that mere contact with Christianity was beneficial. This theory now seemed endorsed because the memory of the Jesuits was still kept warm in Galungo Alto; Negroes maintained the old churches in repair, and considered it a disgrace to be illiterate (though their books were no more than 'histories of saints, and miracles effected by the parings of saintly toe-nails and such like nonsense'). At funerals they even uttered 'a gibberish in imitation of the church service and words they never understood'. Livingstone went so far as to suggest that the monastical system practised by the Jesuits was the form best adapted to mission work in Africa, not least because it allowed lay auxiliaries to perform secular work, and left the priests free for the real task of evangelism.

Livingstone left Galungo Alto on 4 December for Pungo Andongo, an attractive village standing in the midst of an extraordinary group of gigantic rock columns fully three hundred feet high. There the Doctor learned from Gabriel that reports of his exploits had reached Britain; a *Times* cutting praised his work as 'one of the greatest geographical exploits of the age' while Glasgow University had conferred on him an honorary LL.D. (although his old Medical School declined a request for a M.D.),[4] and the Royal Geographical Society had awarded him its highest distinction, the Patron's Gold Medal. But there was bad news too: H.M.S. *Forerunner*, carrying the account of his Luanda journey, had foundered. This, he wrote, 'sent a pang to my heart until I read that Lieut. Bedingfeld was saved'. And now, in the residence of a merchant Prince overlooking the Cuanza River, he laboriously duplicated the despatches, although not without making a few mistakes which crept eventually into *Missionary Travels*.

Gabriel had suggested that he wrote personally to Lord Clarendon, the Foreign Secretary and to Sir Roderick Murchison, about his journey. Livingstone overcame his shyness and complied, though admitting that 'Having never written to a great Lord before I feel much tremor in attempting it. I would rather crawl a mile through the grass to slay a buffalo or a black rhinoceros.' He was even more bashful about sending his account to Murchison, enclosing in it a letter to Maclear with a request

7. The Kebrabasa Rapids from a sketch by John Kirk

8. The engraver's sketch of Mary Livingstone's grave based on a photograph by John Kirk. Livingstone's annotation reads: 'The Baobab tree on right is mentioned in text and in Commodore Evans' book as 60 feet in circumference—so must be made more like photo—Fig tree in centre is also peculiar in shape see photo—two [Bombax] trees behind house are also very characteristic which you will please observe.'

that he passed on whatever he thought suitable and explaining that he found it 'difficult to write to a stranger'. He and Murchison, however, soon became ardent correspondents, and were to play flint and tinder to each other's ideas for opening up Africa.

On New Year's Day 1855 Livingstone set out on the next stage to Cassange where he found a Portuguese-speaking African named Pascoal waiting with a gift of several oils by 'an embryo black painter' for the local paramount chief, together with two coffles of women for sale. His distress at the latter was somewhat alleviated by the thought that Naval patrols had at least made the slave trade 'turn back on itself' and away from the sea.

He was also shocked at Cassange to learn that two pombeiros or traders had crossed Africa between 1808 and 1811 and had thus forestalled any future claim to be the first man to accomplish the continental 'travessia'. But in those days it was accepted that the trophies of discovery could only be won by pure-bred Caucasians, and Livingstone was relieved to find that the pombeiros were merely 'trading blacks'. So his claims could be sustained. Ben Habib had also crossed the continent but, being an Arab, was similarly eliminated from the 'travessia' stakes.

They left Cassange on 17 February 1855 and plunged again into the wilds, taking an easterly route to avoid the most troublesome of the headmen they had encountered the previous year. Sickness was now the worst enemy. Near a village named Cabango the Doctor was laid up for twenty-five days with an illness which he first diagnosed as rheumatic fever and then as meningitis. It was in fact cerebral malaria that left him 'nearly deaf, half blind and miserably weak'. When he felt strong enough to move on, an ugly incident, reminiscent of the outward journey, developed. Shots were fired at the party and a rush of tribesmen threatened to overwhelm it. Livingstone staggered back along the path, grasping a six-barrelled revolver given to him by a Naval officer. He thrust it against the ringleader's stomach and to his relief thus resolved yet another crisis without bloodshed. But this was an isolated incident; generally the Bachokwe were less hostile than before, due, Livingstone believed, to his reputation as a man of peace and to the fact that now the Makololo were all armed with muskets.

While approaching Lake Dilolo through a complex of sluggish streams, Livingstone suffered his twenty-seventh bout of fever, and took such heavy doses of quinine as to cause vomiting of blood. He recovered

sufficiently to measure the lake and toyed with the idea of naming it after
Queen Victoria, but decided against this because it was 'too little',
though noting prophetically 'I may yet have an opportunity of offering a
tribute of respect to the Royal lady'.*⁵

From now on a more relaxed note appears in Livingstone's Journal as
they went leisurely down the Zambezi to an overwhelming welcome at
Sekeletu's towns. The Makololo carriers were regarded as heroes returned
from the dead, and strutted about in their European clothes assuring
their admirers that 'We have been to the end of the world'. Sesheke was
en fête and the 'people' were only faintly depressed at finding that several
of their women had remarried during their absence, but the sense of loss
was assuaged by their leader's assurance that they still had more wives than
he. Livingstone now learned that mail and bundles of gifts addressed to
him had come up from Kuruman and been left on an island just above
Mosi-oa-Tunya. On 6 September they were carried into Sesheke. 'A
whirl of thoughts rushed through my mind as I opened my letters', wrote
Livingstone, 'remembering that three years have elapsed since I heard
from my family.' But, inexplicably, there was only a single letter from
Mary.

After the second visit to Lake Dilolo, Livingstone had developed a
theory that the watershed of south-central Africa was a saucer-shaped
'watery plateau of less elevation than flanking hilly ranges', through which
rivers like the Zambezi broke in cascades; now he was 'struck all of a
heap' by finding in his mail a three-year-old paper by Murchison that
anticipated this important interpretation of African hydrography. The
gifts were disappointing too. Foodstuffs were weevily, two portraits of his
parents seemed bad likenesses, and he could think of nothing to do with his
sister Agnes's model of the Crystal Palace, until with a brain-wave he
despatched it to his kind host at Pungo Andongo.

From Sesheke Livingstone rode over to Linyanti which he had left
nearly two years before. But no thought of trekking to Kuruman for rest
entered his mind. He regarded the tremendous journey to the coast and
back as a failure and only 'the little beginning' of his task, since no wagon
path could be made from the Atlantic to the Makololo. And so he now
made preparations to march eastwards to the Indian Ocean in an attempt
to find a waterway into the African interior.

* He later considered calling the Zambezi after the Queen.

9

The Designated Instrument

He remained at Linyanti for seven weeks, overwhelmed by the affection of the chief who even attended his church services, though his presence, attired in the splendid Colonel's uniform, greatly distracted the congregation's attention. Livingstone devoted most of this time to writing despatches and bringing the Journal up to date with the usual miscellany of subjects. He noted that African women on the Zambezi menstruate more freely than their sisters in the south, reported that Negro grandmothers were capable of suckling orphaned infants, made one of the first references in modern times to the presence of ancient stone buildings in Rhodesia, pointed out the advantage in Africa of missionaries having a medical training, and had a good deal to say about the African character, summing it up as 'a strange mixture of good and evil, as everywhere else, the evil predominating'.

Syde ben Habib was again in Linyanti, having just completed a trading journey even more remarkable than Livingstone's, from Zanzibar to Benguela on the west coast and back to the Chobe. His route from Zanzibar had passed Lakes Tanganyika and Malawi, and now he suggested that Livingstone should reach the Indian Ocean along the path he had blazed. After a brief struggle with his conscience, the Doctor decided that his proper duty lay in finding a route to the sea 'admitting of water rather than land carriage', which meant following the Zambezi, and 'letting the éclat of discovering another lake alone'.[1] Had he followed ben Habib's advice in 1855, Livingstone would probably have solved the problem of the Central African watershed which engrossed his later years.

Ben Habib was on the point of leaving for the west coast again, and Sekeletu, delighted by the prospects for trade in Angola, organised a caravan of ninety-five Makololo to accompany him with forty tusks for sale.[2] Livingstone distrusted ben Habib. Instinctively he resented the Arabs' influence among the Africans, which he believed was due to the easily comprehensible tenets of Islam, the more relaxed relationship which allowed them to laugh at the Makololos' 'impure conversation' (while his own silence or reproach made them uneasy),[3] and their policy of cementing relations with tribal chiefs by marrying their daughters. The doubts about ben Habib were justified, for he took the Makololo off from Luanda to Zanzibar and 'sold the whole lot into slavery'. Livingstone subsequently used his influence at Whitehall to have the Makololo released, so that after 'a wonderful odessey' the survivors returned to their homes with some muskets as booty.[4]

Livingstone now had to decide along which side of the Zambezi to march. He chose the left bank because Bowdich's map erroneously placed Tete on it. There was no lack of volunteers to accompany him; eventually one hundred & eleven porters were chosen under three headmen named Sekwebu, Kanyata and Monaheng. The rank and file came from subject tribes, and Livingstone never had complete control of them because of difficulty in communication, but group loyalty and the weight of Sekeletu's orders kept them together. It was agreed that the Doctor would return them to Linyanti within two years; in fact five went by before he was able to lead them home.

Sekeletu was again generous, providing twelve beeves and three riding oxen for the journey and as much ivory as Livingstone could carry for buying provisions and goods for his own use. Sekeletu's shopping list included blue naval caps like Livingstone's, a sugar mill, several pairs of knives with ivory handles engraved 'S & D L', European suits, an iron rocking chair and green sun glasses, surely the first to find their way into Central Africa!

Sekeletu announced that he would accompany the Doctor as far as Mosi-oa-Tunya, from which point the expedition would temporarily leave the river to avoid rugged country and fly. They set off on 3 November 1855 and Livingstone passed into the third panel of the triptych of his trans-African journey through the heaviest storm he had known. That night he wakened in pouring rain to find that Sekeletu had covered him with his own blanket, a gesture which Livingstone treasured as proof of an untutored African's kindness. The incident set the Doctor musing in his Journal about the Negroes' chances of meeting the challenge of approaching civilisation. Sadly he decided that the race was doomed by the 'terrible necessity' of evolutionary advance.

On 12 November, Livingstone spent the night at Mparia Island near the confluence of Chobe and Zambezi, sleeping under a great tree which is still pointed out to tourists. Next day they reached Moleli Island near Katambora, at the head of the rapids leading to Mosi-oa-Tunya. They camped for the night of 14/15 November at Mamwe village opposite Chondo Island close to where the railway line on the northern bank now diverges from the road. Next night was spent on Kalai Island. From here Livingstone intended to strike off to the north, but almost casually next day, 16 November, he decided to take a canoe to Mosi-oa-Tunya, the smoke that thunders.

It was fitting that Livingstone should have come to the Falls by water, for it is by far the most dramatic approach to this scenic wonder of the world. He watched the distant spray looking exactly like moving columns of smoke from a grass fire, and then was expertly navigated to an island perched on the very brim of the great chasm. Crawling bravely to the brink and deafened by the everlasting thunder of the waters, he peered into the huge mist-filled rent in the earth's surface. Its 'opposite lip', he wrote, 'is ornamented with a large straight hedge of evergreen trees, whose leaves are constantly wet by the perpetual shower. Little streams run down from the hedge into the gulf, but never reach the bottom. The ascending mass of vapour blows them all aloft again.'[5] Yet Livingstone's Journal notes are oddly flat, although he worked them up into the only set piece of *Missionary Travels*, which included the famous passage that Mosi-oa-Tunya 'had never been seen before by European eyes, but scenes so lovely must have been gazed upon by angels in their flight'.

The Zambezi above the Falls is a serene river, fully a mile wide, passing through an archipelago of beautiful islands, until, after seeming hesitation, it precipitates its water into a great rift in the basalt rock, ninety feet across and twice as deep as Niagara. The water, falling sheer into the chasm, appears to explode at the bottom, breaking up into driving mist. The deluge carries down a strong draught which eddies through the canyon and at the points of greatest impact captures the spindrift spray, driving it up in five tremulous columns shot through with iridescence and fully six hundred feet high. In its ascent the mist catches at the light; on sunny days it forms a series of prismatic rainbows; in moonlight the bows are more muted in colour yet no less lovely.

Livingstone considered calling Mosi-oa-Tunya 'the smoke-sounding Falls of Victoria', but ultimately and happily settled for the simpler 'Victoria Falls'.

Next morning he went again to the island on the verge and busied himself in preparing a garden and planting seeds (from Kuruman) of peaches, apricots, cashew nuts, sweet-sop, cotton, onions, cress and coffee where they would be watered by the perpetual spray. Although stoutly fenced it was soon ruined by hippopotami. Rather shamefacedly Livingstone admits that he carved his initials on a tree, and they can still be discerned by the imaginative visitor. 'This was the only instance', he writes, 'in which I indulged in this piece of vanity,' but his memory appears faulty since the missionary John Mackenzie described an 'L' and an 'O' inscribed on the great baobab near the Ntwetwe pan, which had so impressed Livingstone early in 1853, and in the September of 1858 he was to cut his monogram on the inner bark of another baobab which stands beside the Zambezi.[6] It is still visible.

On 20 November Livingstone resumed his journey to the east coast and his 'labour of seeking out the lost thousands in the Interior'. It proved less arduous than the one to the Atlantic. Much of it passed through healthy upland country, where Livingstone was less plagued by malaria, and with such a large following there was little risk of being overwhelmed by a sudden attack.

His Journal now provides fresh evidence of his transition from a missionary labourer to an advocate for Africa who had assumed a states-manlike responsibility for the continent. Before he reached the coast this humble mill-hand from Blantyre felt it proper to address the King of Portugal at length on the policy that should be pursued in his African colonies. The document illustrates the tendency in cyclothymia to interfere, when self-assertive, in matters outside the subject's proper province and it never occurred to Livingstone that this unsolicited advice might risk incurring the king's resentment or fear that this meddling missionary would prefer to see his African colonies governed from Whitehall rather than Lisbon.

From Kalai, Livingstone directed his march almost due north. The first night was spent at the Dinde River which runs past the airport of the modern town named after him. Travelling on by moonlight to avoid tsetse he came presently to the Kalomo River which marked the end of Sekeletu's country. Beyond were degraded Batoka tribesmen, whose custom was to mutilate themselves by knocking out their upper incisor teeth so that they might look like their precious cattle. Even today in this primitive region one still hears the screams at night of girls subjected to this painful operation.

The Designated Instrument

Their route lay close to the line of the modern road across the Batoka Plateau whose undulating downs were splendidly suited for a healthy mission station. The crisp air revived Livingstone's energy and he was free from malaria thanks to avoidance of chills and the development of natural immunity. Progress too was assisted by his reputation; he was said to be 'the Son of God'; his smallest actions were seen as miracles; his possessions were considered objects touched by the supernatural. When using the sextant and artificial horizon the Batoka even believed him preparing 'to take the sun down from the heavens', while a distorted account of the attempt to measure the depth of Mosi-oa-Tunya with a line to which a weight and fluttering handkerchief were attached, suggested that this white wizard had himself flown into the gorge.

One day he was shocked by the squalid brutality of an African elephant hunt. Unlike his contemporaries Livingstone hated wanton killing of game. When he instructed his staff for the Zambezi Expedition two years later, he warned against 'the ferocious but child-like abuse of instruments of destruction', and imposed 'the duty of a sacred regard . . . to animal life'.

After crossing the Kafue the party turned back towards the Zambezi. Game was abundant, and Livingstone thought the country 'to be like what must have been seen by angels when megatheria fed undisturbed in primaeval forests'. Clearly a more famous phrase was still finding shape in his mind. They reached the Zambezi on 30 December 1855 just below the Kafue confluence.

The middle Zambezi is a six-hundred-mile stretch of slow-flowing water, beautifully fringed by a narrow belt of evergreen shade-trees. Its scattered people used canoes for travelling and Livingstone's party had to zigzag from one village to another along the few beaten tracks. At the Mupata Gorge they reached country which was periodically raided by Portuguese slavers, and found the Africans surly and suspicious. But Livingstone's faith in divine protection was growing: 'How precious to have an all-powerful Friend and Protector who can control the hearts and hands of men', he observed gratefully. The area had been abandoned by the Portuguese during 1836 in the face of threats from the south, and at Feira, Livingstone was moved to discover the ruins of a Christian Church, and its broken bell inscribed I.H.S. But there was little opportunity for indulging in regrets about the sad mutations of time: during that afternoon, 14 January 1856, he watched a threatening crowd gather on the path leading to the Luangwa. His mood was exalted; 'See, O Lord,' he wrote in his Journal, 'how the Heathen rise against me as they did to thy Son', yet he felt oppressed at the prospect of dying at random before he could broadcast his discoveries to the world, and considered turning back. In camp he extemporised a prayer for guidance, and that evening turned for added comfort to his Bible. It fell open at St Matthew's Gospel and its message confirmed his faith. As the light faded he wrote out this magnificent passage in the Journal: 'Felt much turmoil of spirit in having all my plans for the welfare of this great region and teeming population knocked on the head by savages tomorrow. But I read that Jesus came and said "All power is given unto me in Heaven and in Earth. Go ye therefore and teach all nations. And lo, I am with you always, even unto the end of the world." It's the word of a gentleman of the most sacred and strictest honour, and there's an end on't. I will not cross furtively by night as intended. It would appear as flight, and should such a man as I flee?'*

Early next morning, when he roused his men, Livingstone saw the warriors were preparing to launch an attack. Yet as the sky grew lighter, the Makololo carried the single canoe available for hire to the river unopposed. With the inevitably protracted crossing the greatest danger would come when the party was split up. Slowly batches of men were paddled safely to an island still to be seen in the middle of the Luangwa. Tension mounted as the morning dragged on until Livingstone was left with one or two companions on the bank, while a menacing ring of warriors pressed upon them. But the tribesmen were disarmed by his imperturbable courage as he 'amused' them with his watch and burning glass. Then he got into his canoe, and the mutter of hostility died away as he was paddled to safety.

This delivery made a profound impression on David Livingstone. From that moment he became finally convinced that he was an instrument designated by God to fulfil a part of His divine purpose. He saw himself, though humbly, as one of the Elect, as a man walking in light.

Livingstone had long harboured, albeit wistfully at first, the feeling that the Lord's finger was placed benignly upon him, that God guided his footsteps. The strange sense of being led through life by an over-ruling power had strengthened with the years. He accepted Heavenly 'tokens', 'indications' and 'providences' with increasing joy, so that the stream of providential inspiration flowed ever more strongly until now, when

* The quotation is from Nehemiah VI.11.

confronted by Mbaruma's warriors, it burst into a full flood of certainty that he had indeed been chosen as a channel for the Almighty's dispensations.

We have already noted a gleam of revelation in 1851, when Livingstone attributed to Providence the headstart he gained over two traders in reaching the Makololo. Then after surviving a dangerous encounter with an elephant, he commented 'I have had many escapes. We seem immortal till our work is done.' Three months afterwards he felt 'so powerfully convinced' that the task of finding a way to the sea was 'the will of God' that he would 'go no matter who opposes'. Later he accepted the use of Setswana by the Makololo as another manifestation of Heavenly purpose. Next year he felt no hesitation in ascribing his escape from the Boers at Kolobeng to the providential breakdown of his wagon. During 1853, when he alone among his party escaped malaria, Livingstone exulted 'if God has accepted my service then my life is charmed till my work is done'; afterwards he recognised 'our Father's Hand' in reserving for him the discovery of the Victoria Falls. It is interesting to note that all these expressions were recorded during hypomanic periods.

The sense of enjoying special protection was recently reinforced at Sesheke by a letter from Maclear which declared that Livingstone's survival from multitudinous perils 'can only be explained by Divine interference for a good purpose'.[7] A few days afterwards he told Mrs Moffat that he would be in no danger during the journey to Quelimane because of 'the fulfilment of the gracious promises of our Redeemer'. And now finally at the Luangwa confluence he had sought a sign of grace by opening his Bible at random and found Jesus's assurance of protection, after which he had passed safely through the gathering danger.

Such teleological interpretation of events was by no means uncommon in missionary circles at this time; occasionally it reached absurdity, as when some pious cleric suggested that the 'Higher Power' had instigated the Opium War in order to divert Livingstone from China to his appointed vocation in Africa.[8] But from now on Livingstone clung ever more firmly to the concept of providentialism. Only when morbidly depressed did his faith falter and he feared that Divine favour had been withdrawn from him—as at Kebrabasa in 1858 and during 1871 in Manyema.

The mandate from God, which he equated with his 'duty', became the foundation on which he built his later life. From this interpretation, that was both his refuge and his prison, Livingstone drew his strength. It was the core and kernel of his being, the Bethlehem-bright star of his vision, one of the keys to all that followed. Unless we appreciate this central facet of Livingstone's faith, which was modified by the ebb and flow of mood, he remains beyond the calipers of ordinary judgement.

Because he believed his life to be 'charmed', Livingstone was mantled against fear. When threatened again by hostile tribesmen, he did not flinch but instead looked 'up to that higher Power to influence their minds as He had often done before'. He thought of himself as a 'fellow worker with God', following a divine imperative whose dispensations would certainly prevail. Everything, he believed, was ordained; events followed a prescribed order, therefore all risks could be taken. 'There are no fortuities or chances', Livingstone noted later and added that God had bidden his people to 'be careful for nothing'.[9] He proclaimed his faith towards the end of *Missionary Travels* when referring to his manifold escapes by adding, 'I think that I see the operation of the unseen hand in all this'.

In England too he explained that his unexpected fame was due perforce to his having 'been the channel of the Divine Power', for it had come to him so miraculously that his life must indeed be charmed. He made God the author of all that he had accomplished when assuring Miss Coutts* that 'the notoriety which has attracted itself to me has been unsought. I did not pursue it. It followed me and great interest has been awakened in my sphere of labour. This seems to me so evidently the operation of a superior person surveying the minds of men towards long trodden down Africa that it inspires me with hope. . . . When it comes without effort it must be providential.'[10] Towards the end of his life he still remained confident of being in a state of grace, the designated human courier who would carry the benison of Western civilisation to Africa and shine his moral torch into the dark areas of brutality that excoriated the continent. He assured Stanley 'I feel as though appointed to this work and no other'.

The psychologically comforting doctrine of providentialism was accompanied by the conviction that a divine Intelligence had purposefully planned the whole future of the world and this allowed him to rationalise

---

* Angela Burdett-Coutts (1814–1906) was the daughter and heir of Sir Francis Burdett, who is remembered for his attempts to gain Parliamentary reform. Miss Coutts's mother was the enormously wealthy daughter of Thomas Coutts, the banker, whose name she added to her own. Miss Burdett-Coutts used her wealth in aiding many philanthropic causes, and she befriended Livingstone. She was created a Baroness in her own right in 1871.

his periodic indecision. 'There is a Governor among the nations', Livingstone wrote, 'who will bring all his plans with respect to our human family to a glorious consummation', in 'a golden age', when mankind could be equated with God's final design. This God was not the remote deity of the brimstone Calvinists, waiting for men's deaths to mete out judgement; the Almighty instead was a heavenly patron keeping a watchful eye on human frailty and willing to extend divine umpirage to all their disputes. As his 'fellow worker', Livingstone gladly accepted the particular mandate of carrying commerce to the interior. He was sure that this would destroy the slave trade and bring to its Africans social and economic prosperity which in their minds would be identified with Christianity and allow them to be welcomed 'into the body corporate of nations'.

Acceptance of a prescribed *ordo divinae* was facilitated by Livingstone's full comprehension of the benevolent interdependence of every living thing in the marvellous harmony of Nature. Long before he had told his brother Charles 'I admire the wonderful works of God, and the wisdom He has displayed in the animal kingdom'. Now the doctrine he developed allowed even the most savage acts of men and beasts to be bent into the purposeful framework of a beneficent interaction between all God's creatures and their environment.

Inherent in Livingstone's credo was the precept that the details of the sacred design might well be inscrutable to mere mortals, so should neither be judged nor condemned. This prescription transcended normal reason, and allowed Livingstone to display an unquenchable capacity for discovering a good purpose in every hindrance he met. He found it possible to accept even the worst setbacks as testing exercises or manifestations of the still incomprehensible workings of an indulgent Providence. 'Our mistakes even may be overruled for good', he wrote, 'and when we are left to suffer their effects it is only for necessary discipline and chastisement.'[11] Again in 1864, when he was brought down to earth by news of his eldest son's peril in the American Civil War, Livingstone could still reflect that 'the secret ballast is often applied by a kind hand above when to outsiders we appear to be sailing gloriously with the stream'.[12] And during his final weary journey he even decided that the loss of his vital medicine chest might be 'a blessing in disguise'.

But there lay dangers in Livingstone's certainty that it had been given to him to resolve the splendid dispensations of the Lord. For it led him to disregard unwelcome facts and to modify unacceptable evidence to fit in with the Holy purpose. As the corrosion of infallibility ate into his mind, especially during recognisable periods of hypomania, self-confidence turned into arrogance. He could make no allowance for the weaknesses of more ordinary men, and found it difficult to be gracious to his own assistants since they were merely carrying out the directions of the Almighty. He damned the opponents of his schemes as wicked men defying the holy imperative, as worldlings who jeopardised the work of a human instrument for whom the Lord himself had borne witness. Since the cause he represented was so clearly the cause of God, it followed that his adversaries were soldiers of Evil. This assurance bred in Livingstone vindictive dislike for anyone who did not share his vision or hindered its realisation. When his tolerance declined, the earlier difficulties he experienced in working harmoniously with European colleagues intensified, and this led to many misunderstandings and much unhappiness.

On the night of his delivery at the mouth of the Luangwa, Livingstone slept the exalted sleep of a man who believes he has experienced a miracle. In the morning he passed over to the left bank and inspected the line of ruined houses which was all that remained of the Portuguese settlement of Zumbo. Today a dusty cluster of new bungalows hide their decayed foundations, but the tired remains of the old fort the Doctor visited survive very much as he saw them.

Beyond Zumbo the going became difficult, and with some foreboding the procession approached the town of Chief Mpende who was known to be hostile to strangers; the anxiety was justified. At sunrise on 23 January 1856 Mpende's warriors threatened to attack the camp, but presently two old men approached, discovered that Livingstone was not a slaver, and then publicly announced that this stranger was 'one of that tribe that loves the black men'. (Livingstone savoured the phrase and recounted it later at many public meetings.) Mpende thereupon arranged for canoes to carry the whole party to the south bank of the Zambezi which he assured them would provide the shortest route to Tete.

Conditions there were still bad and on 9 February 1856, near the village of Pinkwe, Livingstone veered away from the river to cut across a great loop in its course. It was a disastrous decision for it meant that he missed seeing the Kebrabasa Rapids. But now he tended to brush aside anything that contradicted his belief that the Zambezi was the Lord's intended route to the interior. Unfortunately, at Tete, Livingstone, lacking an aneroid barometer, measured its altitude by the less accurate boiling point of water, and failed to appreciate that the Zambezi fell six hundred feet in the unexplored hundred mile gap of its course.

The last fifty miles to Tete were the hardest of all; the ground was covered with shingle and the exhausted men were so harried by henchmen of the 24th Emperor of Monomatapa, now a mere puppet of the Portuguese, that two tusks had to be surrendered 'to save the whole'. They went on 'skulking out of the way of villages' until, when only eight miles short of Tete, Livingstone could go no farther. He made camp, despatched his passport to the Commandant of Tete by runner, and slept. At 3 a.m. he was awakened by the arrival of two Portuguese officers who had brought out a 'civilised breakfast' for him. Thus refreshed he walked to the nearby settlement.

But he was close to physical collapse, passing brick dust urine (possibly a manifestation of a rare condition termed March Haemoglobinuria), and irritated by prolapsed piles. He therefore accepted a Major Tito Sicard's advice to rest for a month in his house until cooler weather allowed a safer passage through the pestilential Zambezi delta.

Despite fatigue, Livingstone at once wrote triumphant letters shouting of his success in finding a navigable river into the interior and a salubrious mission site in the Batoka Highlands. To Tidman he exulted, 'I can announce not only a shorter path for our use, but, if not eggregiously mistaken, a decidedly healthy locality' for a mission, and concluded by assuring him that 'the end of the geographical feat is but the beginning of the missionary enterprise'. Afterwards he poured out the story again to the Moffats, Thompson, Maclear, Gabriel and Moore, rejoicing that 'now I have the prospect of water carriage by the noble river to within 1 or 2° of the Makololo'.

Then, like a civil servant preparing a report on the area, Livingstone made a census of the population at Tete, scrutinised the local defences, inspected nearby coal-seams, examined the district's failing gold deposits, lamented that the officials' small salaries necessitated their setting up as part-time traders, enquired into the rebellions of the local half-caste bush-Caesars, and gathered medical and geographical information from a Senhor Candido. The Doctor did make a few enquiries about Kebrabasa, and learnt of the existence of 'one or two little rocky rapids'[13] that might hinder navigation but the report was dismissed as distasteful and therefore of little significance.

His activities were unhappily halted by a fresh attack of malaria, this time of the tertian type, and he did not get away from Tete until 2 April 1856, leaving most of the Makololo in Tito's care until he could return. Travelling by canoe with an escort to see him past the rebel forts, Livingstone was paddled with the current through the ancient cartographers' 'Spine of the world' at Lupata Gorge. He came to Sena on 27 April, and there, while recovering from another malarial relapse in a bat-infested house, characteristically bared his thigh and was positively disappointed when they showed no sign of being vampires. Soon a canoe carried him to Mazaro where the Mutu Channel, which contains water for only a few months of the year, connects the Zambezi to the Cuacua River and the sea. Weakness decided him against examining the Zambezi delta, since a naval officer had recently reported himself 'highly pleased' with its navigability, and instead he went to Quelimane, reaching it on 20 May 1856.

Mail was waiting for him but none unfortunately from his family. He learned that the Admiralty had ordered men-o'-war to call regularly at Quelimane to aid him on his arrival. Pleased by this attention, he was disconsolate to learn that, acting on these instructions, eight sailors had recently been lost on the bar. Livingstone repeatedly expressed his grief at having been unwittingly responsible for these men's deaths and later attempted to obtain pensions for their widows.

He had to wait six dreary weeks at Quelimane before the next ship came in. But some time in June he received a letter from Tidman dated 24 August 1855 whose contents included a brutally tactless notification that the Directors had no intention of providing financial support for opening up the Zambezi; though appreciative of his efforts they felt 'restricted in their power of aiding plans connected only remotely with the spread of the Gospel [while] the financial circumstances of the Society are not such as to afford any ground of hope that it would be in a position, within any definite period, to enter upon untried, remote, and difficult, fields of labour'. It was clear to Livingstone that the L.M.S. regarded his heroic journeys as an expensive waste of time, and this bitter pill was not sweetened by a reminder at the end of the letter that he was in debt to the Society. These ungracious comments, we know now, were inspired by a 'grumbling party' among the Directors which resented paying out money, intended for spreading the gospel, to support Mary Livingstone, especially at a time when the Society was showing a deficit of £13,000.

One can picture Livingstone sitting in his room, reading and re-reading Tidman's letter and repeating aloud the wounding words 'plans connected only remotely with the spread of the Gospel'. Although 'at a loss to understand the phraseology',[14] he feared that it might mean the Society intended to post him to China. Sixteen years earlier he would have rejoiced at the prospect, but now he knew Africa to be his appointed field. Rather than abandon it he would prefer to leave the L.M.S. and 'follow my own plans as a private Christian', and he told Gabriel 'If I cannot work for the good of this nation in connection with the same Society, I shall leave it and God will provide for my wants'.[15]

He put aside the despatch he had drafted for Tidman which described his scheme for exploiting the new 'providential opening for South African missionaries', and instead wrote a letter of mild remonstrances. His 'old love of independence' had already made him consider quitting the Society. As early as September 1853 Livingstone wrote that he would withdraw from the L.M.S. if it opposed his plans for the north; two years later he informed Mrs Moffat 'if it is decided that this field be left still and I must go to the south, my missionary career will be ended'. He was also uneasy to learn that the Directors had decided to cash in on his fame by sending him round Britain, appealing for mission funds like 'a public beggar'. This from a Society which had recently even refused his wife a £30 advance made him write 'Expect me to go begging money for them after that?', and he added 'sometimes I imagine a more extended mode of operation would be preferable to that of a mission station'.[16] Now the determination to leave the Society was strengthened, but he resolved to move cautiously lest the Directors stopped his salary or tarnished his reputation with a notice of dismissal. So he contented himself with pointing out to Tidman that they had expressly approved his plans to find a practical route to the Makololo, but to Murchison, Thompson, Gabriel and Maclear[17] he wrote frankly of his intention of pursuing his work alone, prophesying that 'means will be provided from other quarters'.

Soon after the receipt of Tidman's unfortunate letter, H.M. Brig *Frolic* put into Quelimane, and her Captain offered Livingstone a free passage to Mauritius, a step on the way home. He gratefully accepted. George Fleming was on board having been sent up by Thompson with supplies for his Society's wandering prodigy, and it seemed strange that this trader who had seen Livingstone off on his great adventure was there to greet him at its conclusion. Of the Makololo the Doctor decided to take only Sekwebu to England.* Fleming was to come in the brig too as the Captain's servant. They sailed thankfully from Quelimane on 12 July 1856.

It took Livingstone five months to reach England. The first lap ended at Mauritius where his undoubted charm comes out in a letter addressed to *Frolic*'s Officers:

'Gentlemen' [it reads] 'As my feelings seldom run readily to the surface and I might if trusted to verbal leave-taking appear stoical. I beg to return you all my sincere thanks on paper for the very kind and respectful treatment I received while a member of your mess. You will always occupy a warm corner in my memory and it will afford me the sincerest pleasure in future life to see notices of your advance in your profession. I pray that God may bless and preserve you and that we all by His mercy meet in His kingdom in happiness.

Believe me affectionately
your much obliged
David Livingston'[18]

He took passage on 22 October to Galle in S.S. *England*. From there the Doctor sailed in the *Nubia* to Suez, where he learned of his father's recent death. Proceeding overland to Alexandria he boarded the *Candia* whose passengers found the Doctor shy and uncommunicative. But he was far from reticent after finding an article in the ship reviewing W. D. Cooley's recently published book *Inner Africa Laid Open* which had described Livingstone's account of the Zambezi as 'nonsense'. The Doctor addressed a stern reply, accusing Cooley of 'running a muck' in his armchair when reporting the course of 'this River par excellance'. It was the beginning of a feud between the two men which only ended with the Doctor's death.

After the *Candia* narrowly escaped foundering in the Bay of Tunis, Livingstone changed to the *Elbeji* bound for Marseilles, where a waiting reporter described him as 'a rather short man with a pleasing and serious countenance which betokens the most determined resolution'. Passing through Paris and Dover he reached London on the evening of 9 December 1856, sixteen years and one day since he left England. News of

---

* Unhappily the experience was too much for Sekwebu and he committed suicide during the voyage.

his arrival next morning brought a flock of admirers descending upon the new celebrity whom they 'kept talking all next day'. Only on 11 December did Livingstone get away to Southampton where Mary, acting on erroneous information, had gone to meet him. The pilgrim was home at last, and Britain had found herself a genuine folk-hero.

'The Wonder of His Age'

A mood of fretful disenchantment lay over Great Britain at the time of Livingstone's homecoming. Revelations of the misdirection of the war in the Crimea had been so stunning that national purpose and sense of mission seemed to have disappeared, and people were submitting all their traditional standards to scrutiny and debate. Deep in their hearts they were searching for a man who would symbolise their real aspirations and point out a worthier cause to champion than material prosperity.

Such a man was David Livingstone. With him he carried an entirely new concept of the people of Central Africa, together with a practical formula for the redemption of their bodies and souls, which would permit Britain to expiate a century's accumulation of guilt for her share in the trans-Atlantic slave trade.

It was not surprising then that the nation found relief in welcoming this paragon who had lived on more intimate terms with primitive Africans than any other missionary and who combined a robust Christian faith with the old tried British virtues of fortitude in hardship and a will to win against all odds.

Livingstone was granted only three days with his family before pressing engagements called him back to London to face the full blast of Victorian adulation. Those three days were spent in getting to know the children again and bolstering his wife's morale. For Mary had passed through a harrowing time since parting with her husband. At first she lodged with her parents-in-law, but soon quarrelled with them, and because of her 'remarkably strange conduct' the old couple at Hamilton resolved to have nothing to do with her 'until there is evidence that she is a changed person'. Accordingly Mrs Livingstone moved on with her troublesome brood of children to poor lodgings in Manchester and Epsom.

There the combination of genteel poverty and loneliness led Mary to drown her misery in drink. This in turn made it impossible to live on the

L.M.S. allowance; unfortunately the Directors made her 'feel very uncomfortable' when she asked for more[1] and they refused a plea for enough to return to Africa. It was even whispered in the Mission House that Mrs Livingstone had lapsed into spiritual darkness, but all we can be certain about her feelings was a desperate longing to be reunited with her wandering husband.

Murchison, President of the Royal Geographical Society, publicly welcomed Livingstone home on 15 December 1856. One of those present at the meeting has left us a description of him at this time: 'his countenance is placid, but determined; and his eye at times betokens great vivacity. His accent is very much that of a foreigner.... His choice of expression, though sometimes rough, was generally picturesque and full of meaning'.[2]

For although Livingstone could apply his lucid vocabulary effortlessly in writing, the gift evaporated when called upon to face an audience. The spoken words did not flow; rather they were hewn out of his thoughts as though from wood, and the gruff voice was distinctly tinged with Gaelic and even Makololo cadences. Yet the broken delivery did nothing to detract from the force of his message; indeed the taciturnity which his wife regretted was highly regarded by his audience as the reserve of a man of action. The address at the R.G.S. was vociferously applauded and he was persuaded to speak again at length on Central African geography and to answer innumerable questions from the floor before the meeting closed.

Next day he was acclaimed again at a reception given by the L.M.S., whose Chairman embarrassed the guest of honour by comparing his sufferings during the trans-African journey to those of St Paul.[3] Livingstone again gave an unassuming account of his work in Africa, but was unable to refrain from stinging Tidman with a pointed reference to the 'utterances of the weaker brethren' who saw no connection between his travels and the propagation of the Gospel. That evening the Society entertained its prodigy at a grand banquet, but he received a more practical form of appreciation two weeks later when a meeting at the Mansion House raised an immediate £450 as a testimonial to the man whom Mrs Moffat now referred to as 'the wonder of his age'.

The lionising had begun. Comforted by the anticipated improvement of his financial position, Livingstone accepted his new-found fame as another manifestation of God's favour and intention, but he protested frequently that it was 'not of my seeking, nor was the éclat which greeted me at home a matter of my choice', especially since it flowed from no more than 'trying to do my duty'. Yet as his renown and prestige increased he took to worrying lest they be snatched away from him.

By now Livingstone was the man of the familiar portraits: the face lined by toil under a tropical sun, the chin stubborn, the moustache grizzled and the expression stern. A reporter described the Doctor as 'a foreign-looking person, plainly and rather carelessly dressed, of middle height, bony face and Gaelic countenance, with short-cropped hair and moustachios, and generally plain exterior. . . . He appears to be about forty years of age. His face is deeply furrowed and pretty well tanned. It indicates a man of quick and keen discernment, strong impulses, un-flexible resolution, and habitual self-command. Unanimated, its most characteristic expression is that of severity; when excited, a varied expression of earnest and benevolent feeling and remarkable enjoyment of the ludicrous in circumstances and character, passes over it. . . . When he speaks you think him at first to be a Frenchman; but as he tells a Scotch anecdote in true Glasgowegian dialect, you make up your mind that he must be, as his face indicates, a countryman from the north. His command of his mother tongue being imperfect, he apologises for his broken hesitating speech, by informing you that he has not spoken your language for nearly sixteen years; and then he tells you, as but a modest but earnest man can, concerning his travels. . . . His narrative is not very connected and his manner is awkward, excepting once when he . . . graphically describes the great cataract of Central Africa. He ends a speech of natural eloquence and witty simplicity by saying that he has "begun his work, and will carry it on".'

Livingstone carried the family off for Christmas to the cottage at Hamilton which his two sisters had built for their parents from the proceeds of a new millinery business. There he was honoured by being made a Freeman, a distinction which he told Maclear 'ensures the exemption from the payment of jail fees if put in prison'.

He was back in London with the New Year to stay with his medical friend Sir Risdon Bennett conveniently close to the Mission House, and was heard making enquiries about navigation through the Luabo mouth of the Zambezi with a view to returning to Africa. He had already agreed with the publisher John Murray to write an account of his travels and, having found suitable lodgings at 57 Sloane Street, shut himself up to turn his Journal into a book. There he remained until July, hard at the un-congenial task of writing *Missionary Travels* whose importance to any study of Livingstone is so far-reaching that it has been considered in a separate chapter. He rose at seven every morning and settled down to writing for the entire day and with such persistence that his massive manuscript was completed in an incredibly short time. The routine was rarely broken. But at the beginning of April he took time off to welcome his brother Charles home from America; he also visited the Zoo and then the British Museum, where he was greatly impressed by the antiquities from the Middle East, an interest that was later reflected in his acceptance of ancient Egypt as a diffusion nucleus which influenced the people of Central Africa. One day he was mobbed by admirers in Regent Street but escaped their attentions in a cab. And during this time, he was covertly making arrangements to leave the L.M.S., even though he sometimes still emerged from Sloane Street to discuss with the Directors his suggestion of despatching missions to the Makololo and the Matabele, so that peace might reign between the two tribes.

For some weeks the Directors remained ignorant of the intended resignation. Bathing in the reflected glory of their itinerant missionary, they were in a very different mood from that which had prompted the wounding words he read at Quelimane. Instead the Board was anxious to support Livingstone's new ideas of mission work, and only gradually did they realise that his feelings for the Society had altered.

The tortuous manner in which Livingstone severed his connection was motivated by his distress at the rebuff from Tidman at Quelimane, his wish to obtain more generous support for his next venture into Africa (from the Government if possible), by his fear of criticism for abandoning mission work for a better paid post, and finally, by his determination not to show his hand to the Society until better backing was secured.

So all seemed well at first in the Mission House. The Directors conferred with Livingstone on 12 January 1857 and tentatively agreed that missions should be sent to the Makololo and the Matabele, taking it for granted that Livingstone would lead the former. On 23 January a special committee appointed to study these projects reported favourably, recommending that a missionary be appointed 'to assist Dr Livingston' in organising 'the intended mission' to the Makololo, and that Moffat be invited to 'commence' a station among the Matabele. Three days later the full board of the Society confirmed these recommendations and the matter seemed settled. But that same day Livingstone wrote to Murchison repeating his intention of leaving the L.M.S. and his hope for a 'roving commission' from the Government. Next day Murchison forwarded Livingstone's view to the Foreign Secretary, Lord Clarendon.

The Directors got their first hint of trouble on 10 February 1857, when Livingstone notified them that he objected to the wording of the previous meeting's minutes; when challenged, however, he expressed his 'entire concurrence' with their plans.

This prudence was justified; no definite offer had been made by the Government and Livingstone was becoming so financially embarrassed that in March he sought an advance from the trustees of the London Testimonial and from John Murray too, 'though it is eating my book', he wryly explained, 'before it is made'. But gradually his irritation with the Directors increased as he discovered evidence of what he called Tidman's 'animus' towards him.

If Livingstone's account is reliable, after the Society had made him a special grant of £200 on account of his heavy expenses, Tidman kept it 'out of sight' for three months, and worse, 'strained every nerve to prevent my getting a farthing from the London Testimonial'. Evidently Tidman thought the money should go to the Society rather than to Livingstone.

Finally Tidman angered Livingstone again by declining to help him obtain a refund of his passage money from Galle, although this had been promised by the shipping company, and he concluded with some justification that 'this letting me alone looks like wishing me to feel the screw of want & then come humbly to them which, though I am as much a missionary as ever, I don't like to do'. So when the London Missionary Society grant of £200 was at last made available to him towards the end of March the Doctor was sufficiently aggrieved to refuse it since 'it will be considered a hold on me' and because he was also resolved on a line of action for the benefit of Africa that could not be approved by the Society. Then for good measure he announced that he would no longer draw his monthly salary from the Society,[4] and offered his resignation. On 20 April, however, immediately after attending his wife during a miscarriage, Livingstone met a judicious intermediary who persuaded him against quarrelling openly with the Society and conveyed a placatory offer from its Directors 'of entire freedom to follow my own plans as my severance would hurt them much'.

The rupture between Livingstone and the L.M.S. was thus apparently plastered over. The Board had capitulated and told him it would be ruined if he quit.[5] He, however, was 'not yet fairly on with the Government', and hoped to put off criticism about his leaving the Mission field for 'filthy lucre' as long as possible, and also had no wish to prejudice the appeal made by the Society for the two new missions. So at the Society's Annual General meeting on 14 May 1857, although he had again asked Clarendon for a salaried post, when the Directors tabled a report which included a reference to the station to be opened among the Makololo 'under the charge of Dr Livingston', he allowed the resolution to be moved without challenge and did not object to the wording when it appeared in the 'Chronicle' two months later.

But the truce was not genuine; Livingstone regarded himself as being 'only nominally connected with the Society'[6] and thereafter his contact with Tidman was minimal. Both became elaborately unapproachable, and only on 27 October 1857 did the Directors formally learn that Livingstone had left their Society. A fortnight later the matter was clinched with the publication of *Missionary Travels*, where its author announced speciously that financial responsibility for his ageing mother and the affliction of a 'clergyman's sore throat' had induced him to withdraw from the L.M.S.

These devious dealings reflected badly on Livingstone but they can be explained by his assurance that Divine intention, which conveniently fitted in with his own wish for independence, overrode considerations of loyalty and frankness. Livingstone was never able to fathom why his behaviour antagonised the Directors. 'They seem sore at my having left them', he told Mrs Moffat during 1862, 'it is a pity as I never felt a pang at parting.'[7]

Livingstone's manoeuvring to dissociate himself from the Society must be considered alongside his association with the Government. Among the first to greet the Doctor in Britain was Murchison, who was extremely flattering about his achievements in Africa and anxious that they be extended with Government support. In his private world of egomania, Livingstone was unable to brook a rival, but was prepared to accept a patron, and in the influential Murchison he had found the perfect intermediary to assist him in his tasks. He therefore agreed with Sir Roderick's proposition and, after lauding his protégé at the Mansion House meeting, on 5 January 1857, Murchison wrote to Lord Clarendon suggesting that the Government could make good use of a man of Livingstone's attainments in Africa. A week later he further proposed that the Foreign Secretary and Livingstone should meet to discuss his future employment.

In reply Clarendon intimated that he was interested in Murchison's recommendation and asked for Livingstone's views about how he might be best employed. The Doctor pondered over the matter for a few days, then on 26 January 1857 put down his proposals for Murchison, who forwarded them next day to the Foreign Secretary.

In this rather pompous memorandum, Livingstone began by stating that his ideas for the 'amelioration' of Africa differed from the policy 'followed by the Society'. He then announced his intention of returning to Africa to promote the special development of the Zambezi valley 'in a more secular capacity than before', being 'fully convinced that viewing the subject on a large scale I should be performing a work which would effect a much larger amount of good than I could do by settling down for the remaining portion of my life with any one of the small tribes which are dotted over the country'.

A little later, following a dampening meeting with the Prince Consort (who feared that a crusade in Mozambique might affect the interests of his cousin, King Pedro of Portugal) Livingstone provided Clarendon with a formal statement of his requirements for an expedition to Zambezia, which could be laid before the Cabinet. It advised the Foreign Secretary that he hoped to make the Zambezi a path for commerce into the interior, and assist the Africans living in the valley to grow crops for export by supplying them with '2 or 3 cotton gins of the simplest construction, 2 or 3 strong malleable iron ploughs, 2 presses for the extraction of oil from groundnuts, and 2 small pairs of rollers for extracting juice from sugar cane'. A week later Livingstone asked in addition for a copper boat. As we shall see these original modest proposals soon burgeoned into a costly expedition.

Clarendon, belatedly concerned about Portuguese reaction to the prospect of an official British expedition in Mozambique, was content to acknowledge this second memorandum and let the matter drop for the time being. He apparently even ignored a note from Murchison dated 17 April pressing again for Livingstone's employment because 'the poor man has cut his connection with the missionaries'. So the Doctor returned to his writing, irked by doubts but sure that his proper course would presently be made plain to him. On 2 May 1857, however, he decided to assure Clarendon that he was available for salaried appointment since he had left the L.M.S. Apparently Clarendon gave no definite reply for on 13 May Livingstone grumbled to Maclear about his uncertainty and was conciliatory next day at the Society's Annual General Meeting.

His vacillating conduct was to have serious repercussions on the fortunes of the infant Makololo Mission. But by now Livingstone found it natural to give precedence to his (and therefore the Lord's) designs rather than concern himself with a group of missionaries, even though he initiated their undertaking, and continued to give the impression that he would be its leader long after committing himself to a government-sponsored expedition to the Zambezi.

* * * * *

In the June of 1857 the Livingstones moved for the sake of increased quietness to a house at Hadley Green* and in the following month he completed the manuscript of *Missionary Travels*. Freed now from the burden of writing, Livingstone embarked on a triumphal tour of Britain, addressing crowded meetings in the principle cities of a country anxious to forget the shock of the Bengal Mutiny. His reception was enthusiastic. Not since the days of Wilberforce had public opinion been so galvanised by a single man or a nation's emotional need so fulfilled, as by the prospect of a civilising and sacred mission to Africa.

His touch was sure, his diagnosis apposite and his programme functional, for Livingstone appeared able to translate exalted ideas into practice. He was both a prophet and an executor of half-formulated aspirations. Sprinkled through his addresses were stubby homely words that made ordinary people as well as languid intellectuals warm to the speaker. Without his understanding why, this was oratory at its most effective.

Livingstone was to be seen everywhere that autumn, and the constant theme of his itinerant oratory was the need to carry into the African interior the twin agents of Christianity and commerce, which together would redeem the continent from both poverty and slavery. His pivotal phrase was 'civilisation and Christianity must go in together'. However, he was wise enough to know that he could do very little for Africa with his own resources and therefore he appealed to the business as well as to

* Where Mary's sister, Jane Moffat, kept house.

charitable instincts of his audiences. He assured them that in Zambezia he had come upon a bonanza of cotton wealth which would make Britain independent of the slave-grown product of the American southern states, and that in the Zambezi river he had discovered a water route which could carry mechanical transport cheaply into the interior. Thus by buying all available ivory, legitimate trade would destroy illicit slave dealing; at each meeting he defined an altruistic policy which happily appealed to British self interest.

In addition Livingstone proffered a new concept of the Africans to his gaping listeners. He revealed the Bantu as people of honesty and integrity, who should be encouraged to grow crops in their fertile pasturelands. European trade, he said, would turn them into wage earners and relieve their poverty, while their heathenism would be so enlightened by contact with western culture that conversion would follow and the promise of the brotherhood of man ultimately fulfilled. He was certain that such a social and economic revolution would be welcomed by its African beneficiaries. It was an expectation which failed to take into account the development of *Négritude*, and one which later critics condemned as overoptimistic.

The crusade began at Dublin where he addressed the British Association on his plans to lead a modest expedition back to the Zambezi, which clearly was Christianity's designated entry into Africa. Afterwards, the well-known General Sabine stood up to suggest that this splendid scheme be assisted by the provision of a steam launch, and the influential association went on to petition Government backing for Livingstone's venture. Livingstone must have regarded this appeal without enthusiasm. He wanted only financial support, but after extolling the navigability of the Zambezi, he could hardly refuse a steamer or admit that his examination of the river had been incomplete.

September saw Livingstone in Manchester, meeting the Chamber of Commerce and appealing to corporate cupidity rather than to altruism by emphasising the extent of the Zambezi cotton fields. He left behind him staring rows of export salesmen savouring the prospect of mantling regiments of pagans in Christian ethics and Manchester goods. At Glasgow he received a £2,000 testimonial, the freedom of the city, his honorary LL.D. and an honorary fellowship of the Faculty of Physicians and Surgeons. Dundee was his next stop, and then Edinburgh where he made the extraordinary announcement that the Zambezi rose in Central

Africa close to the source of the Nile.[8] There followed more gatherings in Leeds, Liverpool and Birmingham. And then only Cambridge remained, and 'farewell for ever', he rejoiced, 'to public spouting'.[9]

The tenor of his message had captured the attention of all sections of the British community. It attracted the bright-eyed abolitionists, it appealed to the merchants and the industrialists who scented profits to be made from the natural resources of Zambezia, and it enchanted churchmen anxious to evangelise the heathen. His speeches even caught the attention of statesmen who abhorred a political vacuum and were ready to be beguiled by these first whispers of Victorian imperialism.

But his accounts of the fertility of Central Africa sometimes sounded a little too ecstatic. For the sporadic patches of cotton he had seen were magnified into extensive fields; the seams of coal he inspected needed, he said, only the stimulus of European energy to furnish rich returns; the pastures he described were so rich that they ran cattle 'as heavy as prize beasts'.

Livingstone was indeed so dazzled by the dream of an enlightened Africa that he discounted its built-in pestilences and hazards. His speeches displayed the uncritical over-confidence of the cyclothymic subject. When describing his accomplishment of the 'travessia', its drudgery was forgotten and all difficulties ignored so that only the results stood out in bold relief. Despite an incomplete examination of the Zambezi, he told Murchison that steamers could pass from East to West Africa, and towards the end of *Missionary Travels* wrote that at low water for three hundred miles it would 'admit of navigation by launches, and would permit small vessels equal to Thames steamers to ply with ease in the deep channel'. It was no wonder that Murchison exulted that in the Zambezi Livingstone had revealed 'God's Highway' which would carry the Gospel into the interior.

The climax to Livingstone's exercise in 'public spouting' came at Cambridge, which 'beat Oxford hollow' in its reception. On 4 December 1857 the Doctor addressed a crowded assembly in the Senate House and no one who was present ever forgot the profound impression he made. 'Cambridge elevation and culture', glowed one admirer, 'came suddenly into contact with the mighty questions of African degradation and progress.'

His speech was virtually a summary of *Missionary Travels*, relieved occasionally by shafts of humour. Then he extolled the climate of the

Batoka highlands and again acclaimed the navigability of the Zambezi, before turning to his own plans for Central Africa. 'My desire', he said, 'is to open a path to this district that civilization, commerce and Christianity might find their way there.' To attain this he recommended that trade and mission work be encouraged. Then quite suddenly his appeal became more personal as he scanned the audience. 'The sort of men who are wanted for missionaries are such as I see before me', he said, 'I hope that many of those whom I now address will embrace that honourable career.'

As he went on to his peroration he touched the edge of true oratory. His voice gathered strength and with gloomy prescience he almost shouted the final words: 'I beg to direct your attention to Africa;—I know that in a few years I shall be cut off in that country, which is now open; do not let it be shut again! I go back to Africa to try to make an open path for commerce and Christianity; do you carry out the work which I have begun. I LEAVE IT WITH YOU.'

He looked up at the silent gallery filled with students; then the tension snapped and the hall filled with applause, louder even than that accorded to the victorious British generals at the end of the Napoleonic Wars. A public subscription was immediately raised to replace Livingstone's library at Kolobeng; the speech was published, widely studied and taken apart sentence by sentence; the last impassioned words continued to ring in the listeners' ears and directly inspired the universities of Oxford, Cambridge, Durham and Dublin to establish an anglican mission to Central Africa under the name first of the 'Oxford and Cambridge Mission' (O.C.M.) and subsequently as the 'Universities' Mission to Central Africa' or U.M.C.A.

By now Livingstone's Government appointment was virtually assured. For, despite opposition from the Prince Consort, the Cabinet could hardly resist the surge of public sympathy for his plans. After some discreet prodding, at the Doctor's instigation, by the Manchester Chamber of Commerce and the British Association, the Cabinet agreed in principle during October to support his expedition, and next month Livingstone met Captain Washington, the naval hydrographer, to discuss the part the Admiralty might play in its organisation. Then on 11 December, the Chancellor of the Exchequer unobtrusively announced a grant of £5,000 towards the venture. A few days later Lord Clarendon received Livingstone at the Foreign Office to discuss personnel and equipment.

'Just come here and tell me what you want,' he said amiably, 'and I will give it you.'

Captain Washington's logistics for the expedition were far too extravagant for Livingstone; he promptly drew up a more modest scale of requirements, and outlined his plan of campaign. It was simple but dependent on the Zambezi being the promised 'eligible path into the interior'. The expedition was to proceed from England in an ocean-going steamer of such light draught that it could proceed upriver to Tete. There the stores, including the three sections of a steam launch, would be unloaded. Depending on the difficulties found after reconnaissance of Kebrabasa, the launch was either to be assembled at Tete, or its sections carried past the rapids (which in fact would be impossible owing to the weight of its sections, but Livingstone omitted to mention this). The launch was then to bear the expedition in relays up river beyond the Kafue confluence, where a prefabricated iron house would be erected on or near the Batoka Plateau. Working from this base the expedition's staff, comprising a doctor, engineer, geologist, botanist, artist and cotton expert, would for two years devote themselves to exploration, research, evangelisation, instruction of the local Africans in agriculture, and harassment of the inland slave trade. At the end of this period each member might renew his contract or exercise the option of returning to England.

Clarendon thought this 'a very estimable plan', and asked the Doctor to draw up the instructions for the expedition's staff; these he flatteringly published almost verbatim.

On 8 February 1858, after quibbling over terms of reference, Livingstone received a formal appointment as 'Consul in the District of Quilimane on the Eastern Coast of Africa',* which carried a salary of £500 a year. Livingstone enjoyed his new official status; from now on he was rarely seen without his gold-banded consular cap.† At the same time official letters bearing the Queen's name, and signed 'your affectionate friend, Clarendon', were written for later presentation to Sekeletu, Cazembe, Shinte and other potentates. These enjoined them to co-operate with Livingstone's expedition on the Zambezi since 'this is, as all men know, God's pathway into Central Africa', and prompted them

* A commission in the Livingstone Museum, Zambia assigns the appointment to 'the independent tribes in Eastern Africa'. This perhaps was superseded.

† No uniform was provided for consular staff and the famous cap was Livingstone's creation. He only rarely wore a cloth to shade the neck, although he is often so portrayed.

too that, since the English had 'derived all our greatness from the divine Religion we received from Heaven', it would be as well if the Chiefs also studied it in the hope of similar benefits.[10]

Clarendon again became belatedly concerned about the Portuguese Government's reaction to news of Livingstone's expedition. For in the long term the replacement of the slave trade by legitimate commerce could only be implemented by establishing the apparatus of civil government in the interior. Inevitably this would become a threat to the Portuguese sovereignty in Mozambique, and deny their hope of linking it to Angola. Livingstone hoped to dispel such fears by a personal approach to King Pedro, but an outbreak of yellow fever in Lisbon prevented his visit. It would in any case have been fruitless for the Portuguese attitude to the Zambezi Expedition had become extremely sensitive.

Portuguese settlers had been established in Mozambique since the early sixteenth century. The colonists then gradually pushed up the Zambezi as far as Zumbo. When Livingstone came down the river in 1856, metropolitan Portugal's power had been curbed, while Mozambique's prosperity was badly affected. The colonial authorities were continually harassed by rebellions and the intrusions of warrior tribes. Not long before Livingstone's arrival, Tete itself had been sacked.

The Lisbon government was no doubt sincere in attempts to suppress the slave trade in Mozambique, but many of its officials connived at and even participated in the slavers' activities. Mozambique in short was far from being a model colony and the Portuguese did not relish the prospect of a man of Livingstone's calibre exposing its iniquities. They feared that he might 'change his status of explorer to that of conqueror', or inspire another spasm of humanitarianism in Britain which would end up by depriving Portugal of her colony. Their anxiety was justified by Livingstone's later aspirations, but King Pedro could scarcely exclude from his dominions a British expedition whose intentions were demonstratively humanitarian. When Livingstone asked for co-operation in making the river 'a free pathway for all nations', Lisbon shrewdly called his bluff by refusing a request to include Sena and Tete in his consulship saying that both ports were closed to foreign trade. Livingstone was relieved to learn, however, that the Portuguese recognised that their territory did not extend far 'beyond Zumbo', since the Batoka plateau, his intended *point d'appui*, lay well upstream from this limit.

The Portuguese government only acted decisively after the Zambezi Expedition sailed from England. Then on 5 May 1858 Lisbon informed Whitehall it was considering closing the Zambezi to foreign shipping, and a month later decreed the building of a custom house at the mouth of the Zambezi and restricted navigation of the river to ships flying the Portuguese flag. Livingstone's hopes of enlisting British commerce in his crusade to civilise Central Africa were thus ruined, for no merchant could expect profit from ventures thus crippled by heavy custom dues. Before the much-vaunted Zambezi Expedition was fairly started, the linchpin had been removed.

Livingstone's final weeks in England were passed in such a flurry of activity that he complained he had 'scarcely time to think in this whirl'. There was staff to be selected and equipment purchased for despatch to Birkenhead, the port of embarkation. As his wife was accompanying him, arrangements had to be made for maintenance of his children and these were only concluded with the appointment of trustees, on 9 December 1857, to administer the fund he had set aside for their needs. He had hoped to get away by 14 February, which would allow them to pass through the Zambezi delta during the healthy season. But business was difficult to finalise in a London crowded for the wedding of the Princess Royal, which was responsible for exasperating delays. However, Livingstone was summoned to Buckingham Palace on 13 February for an audience with Queen Victoria. Her Majesty was very gracious and assured the Doctor that her thoughts would follow him through Africa. But Prince Albert, still concerned for his cousin's interests, had recently declined to be patron to the U.M.C.A. and his manner was so hostile that Livingstone 'felt gagged before the Queen', and considered that this 'arch enemy' should be termed 'the greedy' rather than 'the good'.

That same evening Dr and Mrs Livingstone, with their staff, joined three hundred and fifty celebrities to be entertained at a farewell festival in the Freemasons' Tavern where the Grenadier Guard's Band competed with the Duke of Argyll's piper in playing 'suitable and chiefly Scottish airs'. They were feeling the strain now; only the day before the Livingstones had hurried down to Brighton for John Smith Moffat's wedding, and there, still smarting from Tidman's 'animus', he made a covenant to pay his brother-in-law a salary of £150 a year which allowed him not only to marry, but to work as a free-lance missionary with the Matabele mission rather than be bound to the mandarins of the L.M.S.

'The Wonder of His Age'

The expedition staff was formally enrolled on 22 February. Afterwards Livingstone had a final interview with Clarendon and travelled up to Scotland with his wife for a tearful parting from his children and mother. After attending to business with his solicitor, Braithwaite, at Kendal, he and Mary arrived at Birkenhead on 6 March 1858 to join the steamer *Pearl*. At last the great adventure of the Zambezi Expedition could begin.

11

'Missionary Travels'

Some time after learning of Livingstone's journey from Linyanti to Luanda, that percipient publisher, John Murray III, met Sir Roderick Murchison and discussed the possibility of Livingstone writing a book about his African travels for publication under his imprint. Murchison duly wrote to the Doctor informing him that 'Mr John Murray, the great publisher, is most anxious to induce you to put together all your data and make a good book'. This letter missed Livingstone, but three days before Christmas 1856, Murray called on him in London and renewed the suggestion. Livingstone accepted the proposal in principle[1] and Murray followed it up with a written offer of a generous two-thirds of the profits. Four days later, concerned because other publishers had approached Livingstone, Murray wrote again confirming the terms and adding the promise of two thousand guineas as a first instalment of royalties on publication.

The idea of writing a book had been in Livingstone's mind for some time. On 10 September 1852 he informed his brother Charles that he was considering 'a work in imitation of White's *Natural History of Selborne*' and went on to explain: 'I admire the wonderful works of God, and the wisdom he had displayed in the animal kingdom; and as I have already some facts not known in works of natural history, I think a work written after the manner of White, with neither tawdry sentimental reflections nor idolatrous spouting about Nature, but with a manly acknowledgement of the Divine wisdom and special operations in all the developments of instincts and adaptation[2] might find a publisher.'

Eight months later Livingstone returned to the subject: 'My thoughts run on a book of travels, but when I reflect on what is necessary for such an undertaking, I give up in despair.' A little later he wrote to his wife from Linyanti to tell her that in England he hoped to deal with his 'arm arrangements' (presumably a reference to having the false joint in his humerus ankylosed) and perhaps publish a book; 'but this', he added, 'must be a profound secret'.[3]

Any doubts about embarking on a literary project disappeared when Murchison, at the R.G.S. welcome-home meeting, publicly renewed his advice to write a travelogue.[4] The very next day, at the L.M.S. meeting, Livingstone announced his 'intention of doing that instead of making those public appearances which are urged upon me'—a sarcastic reference to the Society's intention of making him a 'public beggar'. So Livingstone gladly accepted Murray's offer, hoping that the book would solve his financial difficulties, free him from the L.M.S., 'satisfy public curiosity', and provide an excuse to shut himself away from the attention of his admirers.

'I begin tomorrow to write my book', he told Murchison briskly on 21 January 1857; then in lodgings at 57 Sloane Street, London, and subsequently in the more deliberate isolation of the house overlooking Hadley Green, he produced a manuscript of 300,000 words in a remarkably short time, although distracted (but delighted) by the antics of his children. The burden of composition weighed heavily upon him: 'Ugh!' he told a friend, 'writing a book is worse than travelling through rough swamps', and he sighed at his inability to match the flowing phrases he admired in *The Edinburgh Review*. Yet this long record of remarkable personal enterprise, which concentrated particularly on the trans-African journey, was in Murray's hands within six months, and the book was published before the end of the year.

The timing was fortunate. Books on exploration were in great demand at the time, and this product of the most literate and intelligent of the British explorers ranked high on the list of such works. Profiting from Livingstone's fame, *Missionary Travels* was tailor-made to be a bestseller. Yet many of Livingstone's biographers have tended to ignore the book's importance, doing no more than draw attention to its admittedly faulty construction before dropping the subject as though an embarrassment. But *Missionary Travels* merits far more sympathetic attention, not least because it played an important part in shaping contemporary European attitudes to Africa, and remains a living book which is still read today.

Livingstone's exciting story covered an immense range of subjects, and it was admirably told. A natural instinct for the choice and handling of words allowed him to make them sparkle in the lyrical passages describing the beauties of Africa, and then rasp with magnificent indignation over the injustices inflicted on its people. His accounts of the land and its fauna are so vivid that the reader catches the very smell of Africa as he turns the pages, while the naively simple structure of the book suggests that each one of these readers has been especially taken into the author's confidence.

But *Missionary Travels* was also a feasibility project which, after studying the problems of heathen Africa and the enormous potential of its natural resources, provided a practical scheme to tackle those problems and develop these resources, by means of a civilising mission to the continent.

Essentially the book is a revised version of Livingstone's private journals, a replay of the jumbled thoughts and multifarious activities he had recorded. Some passages were repeated nearly verbatim from the Journal; others show signs of hurried editing. But the author simply did not have sufficient time to sand-paper every phrase, and this provides *Missionary Travels* with its peculiar flavour of spontaneity, artlessness and candour—an impression of almost total recall. Admittedly dull passages do occur in the text, but even these serve to suggest the tedium of nineteenth-century travel in Africa.

Two quirks of style, due rather to haste and carelessness during transcription than to artifice, give the book an unusual sense of immediacy. One is the constant copying of the date from the Journal into the text. The other is the repeated change of tense from the past into the present, examples of which are very numerous. In consequence, when Livingstone is on the move, the reader finds himself travelling with him; he feels himself to be part of the expedition.

Livingstone occasionally interrupted the narrative by expounding on some facet of personal philosophy or his views on mission policy. Yet he notably omits the pious reflections that appear in his journals, and which abounded in contemporary missionary writing. Indeed it was the publisher's reader who gently suggested that Livingstone might like to add something to the manuscript about his own conversion and faith, since otherwise 'many religious people would set the book down as a merely intellectual affair, and [think] that I was not a religious missionary at all'. Rather grudgingly the author complied by inserting the last paragraph on page 4, adding in a covering letter that 'I will not refer to the religious feelings again nor to the evangelistic labours to which these impelled me'.

135

There were other facts which Livingstone glossed over when transcribing his journals. In *Missionary Travels* he writes little about the implication of corrupt Portuguese officials in the slave trade, or of the difficulties in African travel, or of ill-usage by hostile tribesmen. These omissions were motivated by a wish to avoid mentioning anything which might discourage future European advance in the continent. For, like a sundial registering only the sunny hours, Livingstone was so influenced by his mandate to redeem a continent that he tended to embellish those things he deemed creditable to Central Africa and ignored those detrimental.

The winning candour with which the public endowed the author of *Missionary Travels* was therefore unjustified. Livingstone cannot be acquitted of leaving a false impression that the newly-discovered African interior was served by a noble navigable river, and whose untapped resources needed only the injection of British initiative and capital to become another Eldorado. Events were to prove that both premises were false.

Yet a fertile imagination is sometimes more productive than barren fact, and it is easy to forgive Livingstone's discreet shifts of emphasis on Central Africa. The book's merit lay less in the accuracy of facts or the viability of plans, than on its success as a propaganda vehicle, its contribution of original scientific knowledge, and its interpretation of the African character. This fostered European interest in the sub-continent, and focused world attention not only on the existing slave trade but also, for example, on the role of insects in disease. Of even more consequence, the book revealed that Livingstone had not only explored Africa, but had extended his exploration to the African mind. For the first time Africans stepped out of a printed page as distinct personalities. It was no accident that in the first edition of the influential *Races of Men* published in 1850, its author, Robert Knox, asserted that Negroes were shaped differently, walked, thought and acted differently from white men, but in the second edition ten years later he presented them as members of a race of great energy whose attainments could equal those of Europeans.

Livingstone in his book stresses the fact that chance hindrances repeatedly bore fruit. He recalls that Boer hostility drove him to further discoveries; that the migration of Setswana-speaking Makololo opened the way into the interior for him and for Moffat's translation of the Bible; that from Linyanti he had been led first westwards rather than to the east where he would have been embroiled in war, and that his decision to take the Makololo back home from Luanda spared him from drowning in the *Forerunner*. Only towards the close does he indicate his awareness of being the designated instrument of God, and he ends on a note of rare nobility: 'I humbly hope that it [the unseen hand] will still guide me to do good in my day and generation in Africa'. It leaves in the reader's mind the impression that *Missionary Travels* in the first instalment of an adventure story, whose sequel must be eagerly awaited.

Use of the journals permitted rapid progress in writing. Nine chapters were completed within ten weeks.[5] During May 1857 Murray learned 'I am now in Angola', and on 6 July he was 'going down the Zambesi'. Later in the month Livingstone despatched the final chapters to the publisher.

Livingstone now became greatly concerned with the accuracy of the book's illustrations. A proposed picture of 'the lion encounter', he told Murray, 'is absolutely abominable. I entreat you by all that's good to suppress it. Everyone who knows what a lion is, will die laughing at it. . . . It's like a dray horse over me.' Murray had the picture altered. Livingstone similarly begged the publisher to have his artist carry the metal bangles right up Shinte's legs. The harassed author grumbled too about his own likeness in the book, writing 'My friends all call out against the portrait by Philips, and Vardon says it will do for anyone between Captain Cook and Guy Fawkes.'

Livingstone wrote the entire manuscript by hand with some limited assistance from his brother Charles. Attempts at dictating the text to a Mr Logsdon failed since he felt 'quite unable to dictate continuously or give a connected narrative without seeing the preceding part of the sentence', and poor Mr Logsdon was dismissed with 7/6 for his pains. Murray sent the manuscript to his reader, Mr Binney, who then greatly vexed the author with suggestions for improving the text. Livingstone flatly refused to accept advice to alter the sound of animal noise in the Chobe swamps from 'splash, guggle, jupp'. He was nettled when Binney thought the phrase 'horses imported from ships' was incomprehensible, yet grudgingly acceded to a prudish insistence that the word 'urine' be omitted from the description of the Bushman method of curing animal skins in the waterless desert. He positively declined, however, to find a substitute word for 'circumcision' in the account of the *boguera* ritual. As is usual, the author had many second thoughts after despatching the manuscript, and wrote anxiously to Murray asking him to make the insertion on page 170 'But it may be a sort of Ant-Lion (*Myrmuolao*) as they often walk backwards.' Murray made the alteration after improving the phraseology.

Livingstone's deepest grievance against Binney concerned his efforts to 'emasculate' the narrative. Frequently he protested at the effect this had on his style, and his final broadside was pure Livingstone: 'My dear fellow', he told Murray, 'Every iota of his labours must go. I think you will not find me cantankerous or difficult to deal with in any other matter.'

Livingstone also shared other authors' trials at the leisurely progress made by a famous cartographer who had been engaged to draw the map in the book: 'That ruffian Arrowsmith', he groaned, 'is putting all the blame for his delays on me,' and he sounded almost pleased when the 'ruffian's' difficulties induced 'an attack of partial paralysis' in the unhappy man.[6]

The book appeared on 10 November 1857 and was splendidly received. The first edition was sold out at once, and Livingstone was gratified to receive his cheque for two thousand guineas. By 1859 his royalties amounted to twelve thousand pounds and they continued for years afterwards. Of interest to the bibliophile are the eight variants of the book's first edition. An extra page describing the author's courtship of Mary Moffat has been tipped into some copies. In others the lithographs are tinted, while the illustration opposite page 66 appears in several different forms, Livingstone's figure being absent from one of them.[7]

Before publication, Queen Victoria graciously accepted a copy of *Missionary Travels*, and Murchison gave it 'a glowing character'. This was a good start and the reviews which followed were ecstatic. Charles Dickens gravely accounted the author to be 'as honest and courageous a man as ever lived', while a flamboyant journalist thought of him as 'an Aladdin wandering through his new palace, with its infinite series of chambers, each a treasury. He is a Marco Polo, recounting the marvels of Nigritian Carthy.' Livingstone was delighted, and his anxiety to increase sales drove him on Christmas day to inform Murray (in words which would seem familiar to generations of publishers) that 'yesterday on going through Manchester a friend of mine wishing to have my autograph in a copy of the book sent round the town & searching for it in vain. . . . I think it well to mention this and also that the new ones have not yet reached Glasgow.' He need not have worried: the book was paid the ultimate tribute of piracy.

Hardly noticed in the tempest of applause which greeted *Missionary Travels* were the laments of pious critics that the work was not more evangelistic in spirit, and the disparagement of cynics who enquired why the Portuguese, who had been established for three hundred years in Mozambique, had yet accomplished so little in exploiting this terrestrial paradise if the Zambezi was navigable. Indeed it does seem extraordinary that shrewd statesmen, hard-headed businessmen and missionaries alike accepted Livingstone's utopian account of Central Africa without question. Admittedly (and predictably) the armchair geographer Desborough Cooley found some faults and gleefully pointed out that the author had made an error in the relative positions of Linyanti and the Kafue,[8] while another unkind colleague referred to the book as Dr Livingstone's first attempt at fiction writing. Only later did real disillusionment with *Missionary Travels* set in; it even set Robert Moffat pronouncing his son-in-law's book 'a pack of lies', while James Stewart, who was to be second only to Livingstone in his service to Central Africa, came to believe that the author used 'accursed lies' when he described the Zambezi valley in such glowing terms.

But all this lay in the future. What was important in 1857 was that the publication of this book, which was significant at so many levels of interest and understanding, greatly increased the impact of Livingstone's addresses to the public, and made it see in Central Africa a field for profitable atonement of sins committed against the continent during the slave trade era.

12

Return to the Zambezi

Nothing in the whole course of African exploration compares in drama with Livingstone's Zambezi Expedition. This central episode of his career was born in an air so full of promise that it might have been the dawn of the seventh day; it ended in a wintry midnight of despair. The disappointments and tragedies which occurred during its course were very fully reported. During these six years Livingstone wrote many official despatches, a journal and carried on copious correspondence, and also compiled a log of events which has not yet been published. There was a formidable documentation of the expedition too by its other participants, for in this extravaganza of frustration and recrimination, Livingstone was surrounded by a large cast of supporting actors. Their journals fluently reveal the ebb and flow of his moods, from black misanthropy to sanguine exaltation, both modified by surges of teleological thinking.

Livingstone had not originally planned to re-enter Africa with white companions, but he had become captive of his own hyperbole. The very success of his crusade in Britain resulted in his acquiring official status, complex equipment and a European staff. With a leader like Livingstone, who was suspicious and sensitive to criticism, the venture into pestilential country was inevitably disturbed by contention. But all seemed to go well at first. Livingstone even believed that his associates had been selected under divine scrutiny, noting that 'the arrangements which have ended in giving me suitable Christian comrades may be taken as evidence of a gracious smile on my enterprise now. I feel very thankful indeed that there is no cross-grained specimen among them.'[1] But by the end of the enterprise he remarked that 'nothing but insanity would lead me again to become a servant of servants or a leader of . . . Europeans'.

But apart from the effect of his own irascibility, the expedition was doomed from the start. It was based on three false premises: that the

Zambezi was navigable, the Portuguese co-operative, and the framework of African culture so brittle that there would be no difficulty in effecting a social revolution among the tribesmen.

Livingstone gave little thought to the difficulties that might lie ahead when the shallow draught screw steamer *Pearl* slipped her moorings at precisely 12.50 p.m. on 10 March 1858 and headed down the Mersey through sleet and rain.

On board were Livingstone's six assistants. He had selected the members of his staff somewhat casually as though they were of scant importance to his plans. Certainly he had no intention of accepting a contender for the command of the expedition from amongst them; when Samuel Baker, a possible rival, made an offer of his services, it was ignored. Moreover Livingstone had insisted on the Government investing him 'with magisterial power as a consul', and before sailing required his assistants to sign an agreement that 'we . . . hereby bind ourselves to consider Dr Livingstone as leader of that expedition and to obey all reasonable directions we may receive from him'.

At first the staff regarded the Doctor with awed respect, but soon felt wounded by his marble aloofness, unaware that it was contrived to mask the vulnerable man within. A communication problem arose for Livingstone never took them into his confidence, and they became resentful of his high-handed leadership. But contract, propinquity and mutual dependence linked them together; like a chain gang they were jerked along through an alien environment by a man sometimes unbalanced by manic-depressive disorder and always obsessed by his manifest destiny. One by one they came to detest Livingstone.

Cocooned as he was in certainty that he was working under the rubric of divine support, Livingstone regarded his companions as mere instruments to be used in God's design. He was unconcerned for their interests, and lacked insight into their problems. He viewed their illnesses as malingering, disagreement as insubordination, and failure as culpable negligence. Never once did Livingstone think of them as a band of brothers. Instead he was morbidly suspicious of his colleagues' intentions, supposing them to 'have the belief that the depression of their chief is their own exaltation. It often happens that his failure is the subordinate officers' success. There is besides the temptation to steal a march on him by appropriating a discovery, and even in cases of the grossest misconduct, the latter may count on the sympathy of the newspaper class who consider themselves as the chosen companions of the oppressed, and the terror of tyrants.'[2]

His companions formed an unusual sextet. The navigator and second-in-command was Commander Norman Bedingfeld whom Livingstone had met in Luanda. Bedingfeld was a touchy naval officer and, as Livingstone knew, a trouble maker who had twice been court martialled for 'quarrelsome conduct'. Bedingfeld imagined himself to be the expedition's real commander and the Doctor a mere figurehead, so that his admission to the company was like planting a time bomb in it.

Dr John Kirk, doctor and botanist, was twenty-six. He was a thin rather delicate man who combined common sense with reliability, but eventually left the expedition nourishing a deep grudge against its leader.

George Rae came from Blantyre and this perhaps explains Livingstone's unusual solicitude for him. Rae's talents as a brilliant engineer were respected; he himself was not. He was a habitual gossip; a rather illiterate colleague once declared that Rae 'is a Thing and no better than a crawling two faced mischief making man'.[3]

Richard Thornton was only twenty when he was recommended by Murchison as the geologist. The Doctor found him difficult to handle and discharged him for 'inveterate laziness'.

Thomas Baines lasted only a few weeks longer than Thornton: during 1859 he was discharged in disgrace. Engaged as an artist and store-keeper, Baines's work in the first sphere was exemplary, but he found difficulty in keeping track of the stores scattered, unlocked, along the Zambezi, and his unavoidable neglect was construed by the Doctor as dishonesty.

The sixth assistant—the Doctor's brother, the Reverend Charles Livingstone, was the most important member of the staff so far as a study of Livingstone is concerned. Charles was a tall, thin man whose early years had been passed in the same humble circumstances as David's. He emigrated to America where he combined study at Oberlin University with manual labour. Eventually he emerged as an ordained minister. In 1851 having been refused a post by the L.M.S., Charles received a call to the Congregational Church at Plympton and a year later married. He was subsequently translated to Lakeville, but his health gave way and in 1857 he travelled to England, alone.[4]

The nature of Charles's illness was concealed by the family, but it is clear from his correspondence that he had suffered a nervous breakdown.[5] During the coming expedition both Kirk and Stewart referred darkly to his 'complaint'[6] and in 1864 he is known to have relapsed into a condition that 'renewed his mental difficulties'.[7]

In England Charles found his brother David a national hero, and he applied to join his Zambezi Expedition. Livingstone accepted him, hoping a new environment would 'prevent a complete breakdown of [his] health',[8] and provide him with the opportunity of taking advantage of the commercial potential of Zambezia.

Livingstone kept these reasons for Charles's enrolment to himself, and instead indicated he was variously engaged as a general assistant, photographer, scientist engaged in meteorological and magnetic observations, as agent for the development of African trade (since residence in America had presumably made him an expert on cotton cultivation) and as the expedition's 'Moral Agent to lay a Christian foundation for anything that may follow'.

It was a bewildering number of assignments, and Charles has always been assumed to have failed lamentably in them all. But the results of his photography, now almost entirely lost, appear to have been reasonable and there is good evidence that his scientific work was satisfactory.[9]

Unfortunately Charles's 'mental difficulties' made him hard to live with; they antagonised his colleagues and led James Stewart to describe him as the expedition's 'evil genius', while even the saintly Bishop Mackenzie 'who tried to like everyone was obliged to confess that he failed in that case'.

Charles's conduct was typical of manic depressive disorder. Because of a cyclothymic temperament he suffered periodically from a sense of insufficiency, bouts of gloom, accessions of despair and extravagant grief, as when he broke a photograph of his wife or feared her letters were going astray. But these phases of depression alternated with shrill rages, accusations of persecution and witchcraft, and outbreaks of physical violence, leading to assaults even on his brother.

These symptoms of Charles's disintegrated personality are important for the light they throw upon David Livingstone's character. For the condition of manic depressive disorder is genetically determined and strongly familial, although its manifestations may be mild when the dominant gene is of 'diminished penetrance'. People who do not exhibit the florid symptoms of the disorder may yet show strong emotional arousal, and in those with disciplined minds the malady often spurs them on to great achievement.

Charles's symptoms were repeated in a much less overt form by his brother David: Livingstone's inherited cyclothymic personality made him similarly liable to alternating periods of elation and despair, but through discipline, passionate conviction and dedication he could usually control their grosser manifestations, although they were frequently revealed in the privacy of his journal. The appreciation that Livingstone was mildly deranged by manic depressive disorder is so important to the proper understanding of his ambivalent behaviour that the malady has been more fully described in the Introduction.

Graphologists claim to analyse a man's character from his handwriting. It may be significant that one distinguished graphologist, after studying David Livingstone's script, believed that it demonstrated 'interior disharmony. . . . His stability and balance turned on conviction rather than on perception.'[10]

Charles did not complete the personnel of the expedition. Livingstone found that his wife refused to be abandoned again to the old dreary round of boarding houses. So he reluctantly agreed to her coming out to Africa again hoping that the *Pearl* would carry the expedition quickly through the unhealthy country of the lower Zambezi, and that Mary's influence might smooth the edges of his own acerbity when dealing with the staff. Accordingly the passenger list included the names of Mrs Mary Livingstone and little Oswell whom his father had nick-named 'Zouga'.

* * * * *

The *Pearl*'s first few days at sea were rough, and her passengers were subdued by sea-sickness. But by 14 March 1858 they were all so far recovered that the Doctor was able to establish a routine on board; each morning the staff was to be elevated and fatigued alternately by morning prayers and Setswana lessons. Four days later, their attention straying to the play of colours on Tenerife, they assembled to hear the Foreign Office's instructions for the expedition. By now the social strata on board had been established: Kirk, Bedingfeld and Charles Livingstone were the officers who gave orders: Baines, Rae and Thornton were the N.C.Os. who took them. At Freetown twelve Kroomen—skilled African sailors—were engaged to work the steam launch. Soon afterwards Livingstone distributed his personal orders, laboriously written out for each member of the expedition except the favoured Charles. Covering several sheets of foolscap, they explained Livingstone's objects, bade his companions regard themselves as the cultural representatives of the Christian West, exhorted them to influence the natives by exemplary conduct, and ended with a stern warning to avoid constipation at all costs, since this together with lack of exercise brought on malaria.

Unlike the others, Mrs Livingstone's sickness had not improved and now her husband drew the inevitable conclusion that she was 'affected with the nine months complaint'. After pondering the matter he decided to drop her and Oswell off at Cape Town so that she might go to Kuruman for her confinement. Mary was heart-broken and refused to be comforted by an assurance that she could rejoin the expedition during 1860. Livingstone outwardly accepted the separation as 'rather a sore trial to us both',[11] but to Young he confessed, perhaps hypocritically, that the separation was 'like tearing the heart out of one'.

Leaving the Cape on 1 May 1858 the staff was instructed to take two grains of quinine each day in a glass of sherry. Livingstone's institution of malaria prophylaxis was a significant medical breakthrough since it permitted Europe to open up Central Africa with comparative safety. He demonstrated that while the members of the expedition adhered to a strict prophylactic regime (which not all of them did) they escaped severe fever; when they relaxed the precaution towards the end of 1858 for some years (believing the highlands to be healthy) malaria became a problem and they suffered accordingly.

On 14 May the *Pearl* stood into what was confidently believed to be one of the Zambezi's mouths and the launch (named the *Ma-Robert* after Mrs Livingstone) was unloaded and quickly assembled. Unfortunately very little was known about the river's delta (Livingstone having omitted to see it two years earlier) and it took eight days to discover they had ascended the Luawe River which does not join the Zambezi.

So the search for the true mouth was extended eastwards and after deciding against taking the ship over the dangerous Luabo bar, they came on 4 June to the narrow Kongone mouth.

Reconnaissance revealed that the Kongone channel led to the main river but it was clear that the *Pearl* could never get through its shifting shoals, and on 16 June 1858, the first and only council during the expedition was therefore assembled and the decision reached to send her back to other duties. 'So now', sighed Kirk, 'we are on our own resources,' and all hope of a quick and easy passage to Tete had vanished. For the next nine days the *Ma-Robert* and the naval escort's boats ferried the expedition's stores to Nyika (or Expedition) Island, where the prefabricated house, destined originally for the middle Zambezi, was erected as a base depot. It was a curious contraption of wooden walls, a thatched verandah and corrugated iron roof. From here the party took the launch up river in relays during July and the first half of August, to dump provisions at Shupanga, Sena and Tete. Now a great deal depended on the *Ma-Robert* and she proved a grievous disappointment. Her faults were numerous and infuriating: the engine developed so little power that her crew had the mortification of being over-hauled by fully laden canoes; the specified load threatened to sink her so provisions had to be towed behind; her engines wheezed so abominably that Livingstone dubbed her 'The Asthmatic' and expostulated that her engine was only 'fit to grind coffee in a shop-window'; it took four hours to raise steam in 'our ricketty £1,200 grunt' and mountains of wood to move her at even walking pace (although she went better on locally obtained coal, which with some satisfaction the Doctor announced was the first to be taken from this part of Africa); worst of all 'this nondescript half-canoe and whole abortion of a vessel' leaked like a colander.

Livingstone relieved his feelings by reviling the *Ma-Robert*'s builders —Sir Macgregor Laird and his brother. He charged them with planting an inferior article on him, ostensibly 'for the good of the cause', but really 'to effect a second job out of this expedition', and he found it difficult to rid his mind of this 'couple of sinners cultivating philanthropy for the sake of the "main chance" '. He even accused Laird of deceiving him during the *Ma-Robert*'s trials by furtively using coal for fuel instead of wood.*

Even more disappointing than the 'Asthmatic's' performance was 'God's Highway'. When Livingstone passed down the Zambezi during 1856 it was in flood; now the river was so low that only with the greatest difficulty could they get even the tiny launch up river. It grounded on shoals and sandbanks with maddening frequency.

Still worse for the party's morale was Livingstone's undignified quarrel with his second-in-command. Commander Bedingfeld believed himself to be indispensible as the launch's navigator and behaved, according to the Doctor, as though he were 'the sole head and I [a] mere nominal leader'. As always, Livingstone's suspicions about a colleague's intentions were

---

* But Livingstone eventually believed that the *Ma-Robert*'s poor performance was yet another providence which directed him to his true destination—the Shire Highlands.

most sharply expressed during one of the hypomanic phases of his disorder, and a year later we find Livingstone accusing the wretched Bedingfeld of joining the expedition 'to exalt himself, and [he] began to scheme his own promotion by my fall'. But before their clash, Livingstone was notably depressed; fearing criticism from his staff he was absurdly secretive about his plans and declined to confide them even to his second-in-command. This riled Bedingfeld; angry words were spoken, until after 'row number four' Bedingfeld handed in his written resignation.

Shaken by the effect this might have in the Admiralty and 'to avoid being publicly criticised for working on Sundays', Livingstone attempted to appease Bedingfeld by begging him 'to do your duty in a manly way, for writing long letters to each other is more like boarding school girls in a pet than like men engaged in a great work'.

Although finding this excessively tactless, 'Cr. B.' did withdraw his resignation, but Livingstone found him 'constantly carping [and] complaining' (it is the first occasion that we shall note the Doctor's alliteration when ruffled), and the next 'row' was not long delayed. When the *Pearl* left the expedition, Bedingfeld objected to the *Ma-Robert* escorting her over the bar. By now Livingstone had decided that Bedingfeld's tantrums were due to constipation and answered with some helpful advice: 'there is often a peculiar condition of the bowels which makes the individual imagine all manner of things in others. Now I earnestly and most respectfully recommend you to try a little aperient medicine occasionally and you will find it much more soothing than writing official letters.' On 28 June Bedingfeld replied that 'your letter . . . is the most insulting I have ever received', and asked to be relieved of his duties at the first opportunity.

After anxious consultation with his staff, Livingstone accepted the resignation. Next day the Doctor displayed his versatility by navigating the launch up river, leaving Bedingfeld pressing Kirk, Rae and Baines to testify in writing that he had been prepared to remain on duty until a replacement arrived. The good-natured Baines was foolish enough to comply, thereby notching up a black mark in the Doctor's mind.

It was typical of Livingstone that he never forgave Bedingfeld for his behaviour, but not until the next year, when hypomanic, did he find the words which adequately translated his feelings: 'I never before met with such a bare-faced dirty hypocrite as he. (He suffered from a venereal irritable bladder).'

When he arrived in England Bedingfeld demanded an enquiry into his dismissal. It found against him, but four years later he was promoted to Captain, and retired a Vice-Admiral.

*　　*　　*　　*　　*

On 9 August 1858 the expedition set off up river again with the *Ma-Robert* towing a loaded pinnace and canoe. From Shupanga Livingstone continued with Charles, Rae and Baines. The Zambezi here was very low and the Doctor was disgusted 'to see his pet river go and dry up to a two foot stream'. Near Sena Livingstone rather casually took note of the Shire River joining the Zambezi, and learnt that its course was unknown to the Portuguese because of the hostility of the local tribesmen. It was not until 8 September that the launch reached Tete, with Baines bringing up the pinnace behind and making coloured charts of the river which have the delicacy of Chinese paintings.[12] At Tete the Makololo, left behind two and a half years earlier, welcomed Livingstone with 'transports of joy'. Thirty of them had died during his absence, including six murdered by Bonga, a half-caste rebel, who wanted parts of their bodies for 'medicine'.

After stowing the stores in a house lent by Tito, Livingstone's host of 1856, the *Ma-Robert* dropped down river again to keep a rendezvous with H.M.S. *Lynx*. On the way they stopped to wood at Shiramba, near Lupata Gorge. While the men were felling an ebony tree, Livingstone measured a gigantic baobab nearby. It was hollow, and, going within, Livingstone found 'bark inside as well as out'. Almost exactly a hundred years later Mr Quentin Keynes found Livingstone's monogram carved on the inner bark, and a half-caste living nearby assured him that his father, Senhor Ferrao, had watched the Doctor carve it. At the coast Livingstone heard that the *Lynx* had lost six sailors when her cutter, carrying provisions for him, capsized crossing the bar. In contrast to the extravagant distress displayed after a similar accident in 1856, the Doctor brushed this news aside as of little consequence; it was an indication of the way he had come to regard those assisting him as expendable instruments in achieving God's plan for Africa. The Navy subsequently lost more lives when provisioning the expedition, which led to many bitter recriminations.

Coming up river again, Livingstone was preoccupied with the Kebrabasa Rapids. He had gambled heavily on their being passable by the launch, whose sections he knew were too heavy to be carried, and was concerned now lest they were more formidable than he had reported. There had even been some wild talk of blasting a way through them and 'opening wide the gates which have barred the interior for ages'.

After only five days at Tete, Livingstone went on in the *Ma-Robert* with Kirk and Rae. Next day, 9 November, they entered the Kebrabasa gorge and struggled up stream for four miles before landing on the right bank.

The Zambezi above and below the gorge is a gentle river, but at Kebrabasa its waters for over thirty miles are compressed into a winding channel only fifty yards across. On each side, walls of shining rock, polished as though with boot black, rise up precipitously into a succession of mountains, sheer and unscaleable. The shadowed river bed, writhing like a monstrous serpent, is filled with immense boulders, grotesque in shape and larger than houses. Where they are heaped together the water probes its way between them or leaps over the rocks in roaring waterfalls.

It was clear at once to Kirk that the gorge 'was an impediment to the further progress of our launch'. Livingstone stared disbelievingly at the scene, silent and appalled. It was the worst moment of his life. The Zambezi after all could not be 'God's pathway into the interior'. He turned back to Tete deeply depressed.

All that he had promised the public depended on the navigability of the Zambezi. Now it seemed that God had deserted him. He poured out his anguish in the Journal: 'Things look dark for our enterprise. This Kebrabasa is what I never expected. No hint of its nature ever reached my ears. . . . What we shall do if this is to be the end of the navigation I cannot now divine, but here I am, and I am trusting him who never made ashamed those who do so. I look back on all that has happened to me. The honours heaped on me were not of my seeking. They came unbidden. I could not even answer the letters I got from the great and noble, and I never expected the fame which followed me. It was thy hand that gave it all, O thou blessed and Holy One, and it was given for thy dear son's sake.'

After the first shock had worn off Livingstone made a more thorough survey, with his entire staff, a Portuguese guide and some Makololo to act as carriers. Leaving Tete on 24 November 1858, they disembarked on the northern bank of the river and pushed on up the gorge on foot, with Livingstone in his anxiety setting a tremendous pace over the broken ground.

The other members of the party were quite unable to keep up, and even the Makololo said that Livingstone was insane. Disgusted by their demoralisation, Livingstone went on with Kirk to the top of the gorge. There at Morambua cataract they found water falling twenty feet in thirty yards. It was the final blow. They grimly made their way back to the launch and were at Tete again on 6 December 1858. Livingstone remained there oppressed by the thought of having fallen from grace and distressed too by the realisation that now it would be impossible to keep a rendezvous with his wife. His great spirit was daunted, and he noted that 'I have been troubled with unusual langour several times. . . . Find it difficult to write my despatches'. Yet, apt as always to distort unwelcome facts to fit into what he conceived to be the holy design, he preferred to mislead the British Government and his friends. On 17 December 1858 Livingstone told the Foreign Secretary that, in the opinion of *all* his staff, 'a steamer of light draught of water, capable of going twelve or fourteen knots an hour, would pass up the rapids without difficulty when the river is in full flood', and he asked him to replace the *Ma-Robert* with a more powerful vessel. (The Foreign Office did in fact arrange to send out the *Pioneer* to serve the expedition—but she was never tested against the cataracts.) Livingstone similarly informed Maclear that 'I have not the smallest doubt but a steamer of good power could pass up easily in flood', while the Admiralty was assured that a powerful vessel could pass even the top cataract and that the existence of the rapids was almost an advantage since the Portuguese instead would have to go by land, an expensive process which would make them more likely to co-operate with the expedition.

During the next phase of hypomania this extraordinary man even succeeded in deluding himself that Baines, who had gone up again to the cataracts during the rainy season with Charles, had reported 'favourably on the possibility of passing'.[13] This typical affective reaction was untrue, but to some extent he rationalised it in his book *Narrative of an Expedition to the Zambesi and its Tributaries*,* when he managed to give the impression that he had accompanied this third reconnaissance of the gorge.

The period of depression reached its climax towards the end of 1858 and presently gave way to a hypomanic mood. During it Livingstone became bitterly critical of the disgraceful way his staff's endurance had

* Hereafter called *Narrative*.

failed during the first testing march. He saw his companions as encumbrances and himself far better off without them. His mind began to dwell especially on the futility of employing a geologist and a painter who had proved so feeble. As his thoughts were directed to their shortcomings, the idea of their dismissal grew into a petulant resolve and finally into an obsession, and six months later both Baines and Thornton were expelled.

These dismissals, indicative of an inability to master random impulses, remain the worst blots on Livingstone's reputation. Although anticipating events, they can be conveniently considered here.

For some time neither Thornton or Baines had got on with the overbearing 'Moral Agent' who greatly resented their not having 'shown him quite as much respect as he liked'. Charles was also aware that the Portuguese in Tete were far more friendly to them than to himself. This he resented and complained to his brother that Thornton neglected his duties and malingered, while Baines not only painted portraits of his Portuguese friends with Government material, but pampered them with titbits from the stores.

During the February of 1859 we find Livingstone noting that Thornton 'has been inefficient of late' and 'evidently declined to geologise and has done next to nothing last three months. Gorges himself with the best of everything he can lay hold of without asking.' Four months later, Livingstone in a fury handed the young man an official letter of dismissal.

After Thornton left, Livingstone felt constrained to excuse his action. To the Foreign Office he wrote in his queer alliterative way that 'The case of Mr Thornton . . . was one of complete collapse consequent on change of climate'; to Murchison Livingstone complained that Thornton had met his remonstrances with 'sneers about Scotchmen'; in his journal he was scathing about this youth who was a 'disgrace to the Expedition and the English name', and dismissed his symptoms as being due to 'hysteria, the fits of laughing and crying, rising in the throat and flatus, resembling exactly that met with in females'.

Livingstone's persecution of Baines was even more relentless. He began to distrust the storeman after learning of his testimonial to Bedingfeld. Concerned that its wording might reflect on his own actions, the Doctor could not rest until he had seen what Baines had written. On 19 September 1858 while at Sena he therefore addressed a somewhat artful letter to 'My dear Baines', which ended with an inconsequential 'By the way,

Bedingfeld referred in an official letter to a certificate signed by you. I think it desirable to give Her Majesty's Secretary of State the exact words to which you signed your name.'

Baines did not reply, so on 3 November 1858 after the expedition's personnel were reunited at Tete, Livingstone tackled him on the subject.

Baines at the time was delirious with fever, but Livingstone managed to extract from him an admission that he had written something like 'We certify our belief that Captain Bedingfeld is willing to retain command of the *Ma-Robert* till a suitable successor be appointed.'

There the matter was temporarily dropped, until Charles took a hand in the affair, and taxed Baines with handing over expedition property to the Portuguese. He was rewarded with some form of confession from the delirious man (although Baines said later that this was 'little more than a repetition of words he had himself used in accusing me'), together with a rambling request to be placed in confinement. Then Rae added to Livingstone's growing fury by telling him that Baines had stolen a piece of serge from him.

On 23 June 1859 Livingstone duly noted that 'Baines had been heady for three weeks and made away with Expedition goods to a large amount while so affected. Asked them to put him in confinement.' He then called on him for an explanation. The wretched man admitted that some goods had gone astray when he 'did not know what he was about', but offered to pay for the missing articles, and according to Livingstone, asked to stay with the expedition without salary. Somewhat mollified Livingstone was content to admonish Baines 'not to paint any Portuguese likenesses' in future.

But only a few days later Livingstone flared up again, writing 'While Baines made so free with the goods of the Expedition, he took very good care of his own and was both sharp and mean. Gave soap to everyone that asked for it; made away with the wine of the Mess, treating the Portuguese with it, yet held back from paying more than his share; wished to make Rae pay half his washing, Baines having 90 pieces and Rae only four. Has a piece of serge in his possession belonging to Rae, gave away some dozens of bottles to Generoso etc. . . .'

The Doctor then breathlessly despatched a letter threatening Baines with dismissal, and renewing his charges of 'skylarking' in Tete and 'painting Portuguese portraits' without permission. Ten days later in a frenzy of rage he discharged Baines.

Baines hoped to be allowed to defend himself on the various charges of inefficiency, dishonesty, wilfully damaging a whaler, and 'skylarking', and he had a good case. It was virtually impossible to supervise the expedition's scattered stores. The whaler had indeed capsized at her moorings during a squall, and Baines had been too weakened by malaria to salvage the craft for some time although it was now 'not a whit' worse. He had certainly painted portraits for his Portuguese friends, but the Doctor himself had asked him to do this on at least one occasion, as Livingstone's Journal entry for 22 November proves. The presents to his friends were for services rendered and of trifling value. Finally there were absolutely no grounds for supporting Livingstone's suggestion that Baines's skylarking was part of a sinister plot to ingratiate himself with the Portuguese at the expense of his colleagues.

But at the time Livingstone was away, broadcasting news of Baines's wickedness to his friends. 'He took to stealing and debauchery',[14] he told them, and had even engaged in orgies with his Portuguese friends. Then Livingstone had Kirk search Baines's baggage for incriminating material. Kirk found nothing of importance except a possible deficit of sugar, but, as instructed, brought Baines down to the coast where Livingstone was waiting to lay fresh charges of his victim owing him money and drawing cash at Tete after his salary had been stopped. He treated him like a pariah: 'I do not allow Baines to come to our table', the Doctor noted on 23 November, 'but send him a good share of all we eat ourselves. He lives in a whaler with a sail as an awning over him.'

There remained only one final hypocritical scene of accusation and disavowal before the sordid affair ended. Livingstone summoned Baines to his hut and subjected him to a torrent of questions. According to Kirk, Baines showed 'no presence of mind in making replies'. He either maintained a stubborn silence or gave explanations that were confused and ineffective. He laughed hysterically when questioned about the piece of serge claimed by Rae, and 'sneeringly denied that any loss had occurred'.

Baines's version of the scene at his grilling is probably more accurate. He says that he challenged Livingstone to produce proof of his charges, and assured him that his 'so called confession [was] made in a moment of delirium'.[15] He then offered to make his own way to Tete where his innocence could be proved, or alternatively stand trial at the nearest

British port. Changing his tactics, Baines next enquired 'how could I carry away four barrels of sugar, etc., when the house was frequented by seventy Makololo and numerous natives of the village'.[16] Livingstone does not appear to have answered this awkward question.

Baines was then sent off by cruiser in disgrace looking 'like a man of 60',[17] his 'sole wardrobe' consisting of two shirts and two pairs of trousers in a small canvas bag.[18] At Cape Town, Baines recruited public support and obtained Rae's retraction of his earlier accusations. Then on 6 February 1861 he published Livingstone's letter of dismissal and his own defence in the *South African Advertiser and Mail*. This was embarrassing to Livingstone, but he refused to withdraw his charges or admit any error of judgement. Instead the Doctor pursued Baines with accusations which became more sweeping and absurd as time went on. Early in 1860 he informed Maclear that 'We found a large parcel of hollow brass ornaments which he [Baines] had stolen from my private property in his box.'[19] In 1862 Livingstone's log speaks of Baines 'associating with convicts; spent weeks together painting their degraded faces',[20] and he reminded Murchison that 'after losing the best part of two years' provisions, I allowed a thief whom I twice caught in the act of stealing to go unpunished'. When writing the *Narrative* of the Zambezi Expedition, Livingstone confided to Murray that 'Baines could not draw human faces without charicaturing them',[21] and, like a non-person, never mentioned him in the text by name. As late as 1870 he was still denouncing the artist with all his old malevolence, demanding from Baines's mother (whom he referred to as 'the old hag') some articles which were improperly in her son's possession. In November 1871 he remembered more misdemeanours and rambled on that 'Baines turned all our stores off to his own advantage as he thought—then forged issues of 12 months' cabin fare from 8 persons to 3 persons in 3 months and one of the persons was himself. He offered to pay me—confessed his theft *twice to me*.'[22] That same year Livingstone shocked Stanley with a repetition of his bitter charges against Baines, and he carried them with him to his grave. Yet the Doctor always thought of himself as the injured party and sighed that 'Baines, Bedingfeld and Thornton have been causes of great grief to me'.[23] It was typical of him that he did not consider the grief he had caused the three men. Indeed the whole unhappy episode reveals the rigidly condemnatory attitude to which the combination of cyclothymia with a providential doctrine can lead a man. If Baines never quite succeeded in effacing the stigma on his name, he did at least manage to prick Livingstone on one of his tenderest spots when he announced that the Doctor had in fact made no new discoveries in Central Africa, since 'the Portuguese had been all over that ground two hundred years ago'.

13

Nyasa

After the shocking discovery that Kebrabasa closed the Zambezi to navigation, Livingstone brooded at Tete through the last days of 1858. There slowly it came to him that it was unwarranted, even unseemly, to doubt the workings of divine purpose in placing these cataracts across his course. After all the manifold and signal mercies shown to him, Kebrabasa must surely be another providence, furnished by the Almighty, to guide him to his appointed path. Perhaps the Shire fitted into the holy design, for it was closed to the Portuguese by their fears. It might have been 'reserved' for him as the intended entry into Africa for Christianity; it could even lead to highlands more fertile and salubrious than the Batoka Plateau, and to a people whose needs exceeded all others.

Impulsively Livingstone decided to examine the Shire. Some months later when his survey pointed to this river enjoying all the hoped for advantages, and sure again of God's favour, he contritely wrote, 'It is presumptuous not to trust in him implicitly and yet this heart is fearfully guilty of distrust. I am ashamed to think of it.'

For once on the Shire it was clear that all so mysteriously wrong with the Zambezi came right in this new river. They cruised up-stream comfortably, untroubled by shoals, admiring the wide and fertile valley that ended to the east in the scarp of the Shire Highlands.

The Manganja tribesmen* living in the valley must have been bewildered as they watched them with mingled alarm, hostility and fascination. Day and night crowds of warriors, fingers taut on drawn bows, watched the little steamer pass by. Livingstone's purpose on the trip was only reconnaissance and the establishment of friendly contact with the natives. He would occasionally go ashore, shouting to an invisible audience that he was one of the English and therefore their friend. Long

---

* A people of Cewa stock, who on the lake shore were known as the Nyanja, and in the Shire Valley as Maravi and Manganja.

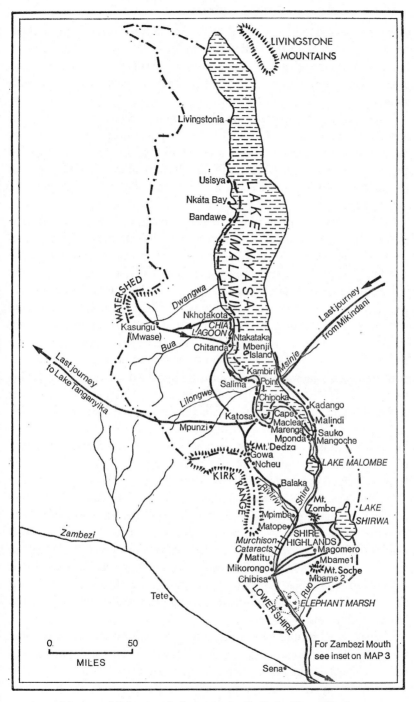

Map 4. Livingstone's Journeys in the Lake Nyasa Region

afterwards an old chief recounted that as the 'burning canoe' approached, he hid his warriors in the reeds ready to fire off a shower of arrows. But he relaxed when the Doctor stepped ashore, swept off his cap and smiled at him. 'How', concluded the chief, 'could I give the sign to kill a man who smiled?'

Livingstone was delighted by the brimming river, by the splendid scenery which he believed himself to be the first European to see, and at the opportunity which was opened before him of bringing the Gospel to an immense populace. 'When will this fertile valley resound with the church-going bell?', he asked in his diary, echoing the lyrical prose of earlier days.

On 6 January, after passing the Ruo mouth, the launch followed a channel through a vast evil-smelling swamp where hundreds of elephants were moving like grey galleons across the boggy waste. They named it the 'Elephant Marsh'. Beyond they passed a red cliff on which stood the village of a powerful chief named Chibisa, and now the site of Chikwawa. Ten miles further, they heard the sound of falling water ahead and came to the first of the cataracts which block the Shire for more than thirty miles. Their presence did not greatly dismay Livingstone, for he learned that a well-trodden path passed round them, and he was confident that this could easily be widened into a road. He named the cataracts after his friend Murchison, while a nearby eminence, Chiperone, was tactfully named Mount Clarendon. From Africans he learned that two lakes lay only a few days' march away to the north. Then, after painting a large V.R. and the date in red on a prominent rock at the foot of the lower cataract, and vainly waiting a few days to obtain a 'fix' from the stars, the launch steamed quickly down to the Zambezi.

Back at Tete Livingstone settled down with renewed zest to his correspondence which happily compared the virtues of the Shire to those of the Zambezi as an ingress to the heathen heart of Africa. Nascent colonial ambitions had been aroused by the sight of the lovely highlands beyond the cataracts, and now on 5 February 1859 he informed Murchison that 'I think 20 or 30 good Christian Scotch families with their minister and elders would produce an impression in 10 years that would rejoice the hearts of all lovers of our race'.

Livingstone's attitude to white settlement in Africa requires some study. He neither doubted the validity of western civilisation, nor lapsed into sentiment about the romantic savage. Although without any sense

Nyasa

of colour prejudice he was a robust patriot, genuinely believing the British (whom he always referred to as 'the English') to be the 'salt of the earth' and 'a superior race'. This stemmed in part from a conviction that Britain had perfected the most democratic form of government and had therefore a duty to export that system to less fortunate countries. 'It is on the Anglo-American race that the hopes of the world for liberty and progress rest,' he wrote at the end of *Missionary Travels*, and now he was sure that vigorous exploitation of the comparatively empty but fertile territories he had discovered could be best accomplished by dotting them with white settlements. This would improve African standards and create employment for the British poor.

During 1857 Murchison had encouraged Livingstone's proposals for the commercial development of the Zambezi valley and had suggested to the Foreign Office that Portugal 'might readily part with her Colony of Quilimane and Tete &c . . . which in our hands might be rendered a paradise of wealth'. A little later, when organising the Zambezi Expedition, Livingstone revealed the true scale of his colonial aspirations in a private letter to a confidant, Professor Sedgwick, writing 'That you may have a clear idea of my objects I may state that they have something more in them than meets the eye. They are not merely exploratory, for I go with the intention of benefiting both the African and my own countrymen.' He then went on to explain that 'All this [expedition's] ostensible machinery has for its ostensible object the development of African trade and the promotion of civilisation, [but] I hope it may result in an English colony in the healthy highlands of Central Africa. (I have told it only to the Duke of Argyll)*. . . .' The parenthesis was incorrect. Before sailing Livingstone informed another friend 'sometimes my mind ventures nevertheless to indulge in the idea of an English colony yet springing up in some districts which my feet have trod and that would be a glorious thing for the progress of Africa'.[1]

This was the crux of his thinking. European settlement in Africa would benefit the Africans and provide creative employment for the humble people from whom he sprang. 'It is the mission of England', he wrote, 'to colonize and to plant her Christianity with her sons on the broad earth which the Lord has given to the children of men.'

* But the Duke may have been partly responsible for these settlement aspirations, since he had exclaimed to Livingstone 'what a glorious thing it would be for the civilization of Africa if a colony could be planted in the interior'.

159

Nyasa

During 1859, after recognising the strategic importance of the Shire River and the fertility of the highlands beyond, the subject of colonisation was fostered in his mind. On 13 May Livingstone informed Palmerston, 'I think colonization by our own countrymen would complete what your Lordship began by suppressing the slave trade'. On 5 July he reported to Miss Coutts that 'I am becoming more & more convinced that a small English colony in the Highlands of Africa is indispensible to working out her civilization and producing a sensible effect on American slavery'.[2] By August the accent was placed on the benefits for the British poor and he told Murchison, 'I am becoming every day more convinced that we must have an English colony in the cotton-producing districts of Africa. . . . Everything possible is done for the blackguard poor at home but nothing for the honest poor. This would meet the case. . . .' That October in his Journal Livingstone wrote 'Colonization from a country such as ours ought to be one of hope, and not despair. It ought not to be looked upon as the last and worst shift that a family can come to, but the performance of an imperative duty to our blood, our country, our religion and to human kind.' Then he goes on to reflect that 'It is a monstrous evil that all our healthy, handy, blooming daughters of England have not a fair chance, at least, to become the centres of domestic affections . . . national colonization is almost the only remedy. English women are in general the most beautiful in the world, and yet our national emigration has often, by selecting the female emigrants from work houses, sent forth the ugliest huzzies in creation to be the mothers, the model mothers, of new empires. Here, as in other cases, state necessities have led to the ill-formed and un-informed being preferred to the well-formed and well-inclined honest poor, as if the worst, as well as better, qualities of mankind did not often run in the blood.' Livingstone went further and asked Young 'to try and get some good families to settle in the Highlands', and officially requested permission from Whitehall to 'take possession of new discoveries such as Lake Nyasa in the name of Her Majesty'. Although rebuffed, some two years later he wrote again to Murchison wondering whether 'Lord Palmerston ever entertained the idea of buying out the Portuguese in East Africa. It would be cheaper than keeping the six men-of-war on that coast and might be wise on the score of political economy.'

He had returned to the conviction that moral example rather than individual conversion would most benefit the 'trodden down' heathens, while colonisation, he said, would bring the Africans into contact with Christian settlers, whose communal influence would lead them to a better economic life and higher ethical principles. Yet Livingstone never seems to have appreciated that such settlements would ultimately require the establishment of some kind of civil or even theocratic apparatus of government.

It mattered not; for his suggestions were coolly received in London. On one plea Palmerston minuted, 'I am very unwilling to embark on new schemes of British possessions. Dr L. . . . must not be allowed to tempt us to form colonies only to be reached by forcing steamers [up] cataracts', while Washington at the Admiralty deplored Livingstone's action in raising such 'a wild subject which should not receive the sanction of H.M.G.'.

But it must be emphasised that Livingstone's anxiety to establish white artisan enclaves was not inspired by 'Colonialism'. This was made clear during the later perilous voyage to India when he noted: 'The idea of a colony in Africa, as the term colony is usually understood, cannot be entertained. English races cannot compete in manual labour of any kind with the natives, but they can take a leading part in managing the land, improving the quality, in creating the quantity and extending the varieties of the productions of the soil; and by taking a lead too in trade, and in all public matters the Englishman would be an unmixed advantage to every one below and around him, for he would fill a place which is now practically vacant.' In particular he believed that English settlement would be the best method of eliminating the slave trade, since he looked for 'a bodily transplantation of all our peculiarities as a Christian people and for a specific object, bending all our energies to the destruction of the trade in bodies of men'.[3]

As it was, Livingstone never once raised the flag during his travels: although he correctly diagnosed the causes of Africa's ills he did not apply to them the therapy of imperialism. He preferred the establishment of European enclaves in salubrious areas with no domination other than moral over the hinterland. These nuclei were to feed a stream of civilising impulses into the surrounding country. His aggressiveness was cultural rather than political; the only time he recommended bloc annexation was when he wished to deny the Shire Highlands to the Portuguese and the slave trade.

Thus Livingstone was the precursor of Imperialism rather than its progenitor. The stimulus that led to the 'Scramble for Africa' came from

Brussels, Paris and Berlin after his death. Yet when this extension of European power was initiated, Great Britain found it useful to resurrect Livingstone's idealism as justification, indeed as an obligation, for participating in the 'Scramble'. Thus, even from the grave, Livingstone modified his country's approach to Africa, for Britain reflected his humanitarian ideal when, instead of making a series of cynical takeovers designed to exploit the wealth of the annexed territories, she adopted the principle of the dual mandate, which embraced the duty of raising her new subjects to such a level that they would ultimately achieve self-government.

And in one especial area, Livingstonian sentiment rather than an expansionist policy later directed Whitehall's tactics: when Britain proclaimed a Protectorate over the Nyasa country it was a belated response to Livingstone's wishes. For his countrymen could never bring themselves to abandon the Lake of Stars with which they so closely associated him, nor the descendants of the faithful Makololo who had settled on a bluff overlooking the Shire River.

Back at Tete on 2 February 1859, Livingstone at once turned to making preparations for the proper exploration of the Shire Highlands. He loaded the launch with fifteen Makololo and proceeded easily up the Shire to the cataracts with Charles and Kirk.

He now went out of his way to gain the friendship of Chief Chibisa, and found this easy as both men had a little Portuguese. As always, he treated the chief with marked respect, for in Africa he accepted the local power structure as a valid form of political authority.

Livingstone felt confident enough now to leave the launch, and toiled with his party past the cataracts on foot. At the end of a week they emerged into the great Shire Plateau which extends northwards for fifty miles to the mountain mass of Zomba. This was cool, healthy, well watered country, some of the most beautiful in the continent, a happy blend of Europe and Africa, a land far more suitable for European settlement than the Batoka Plateau. Everywhere they saw signs of cotton cultivation, and six years later the Doctor was to strain the credulity of the readers of his *Narrative* with a bland assurance that the quality of the cotton grown here was 'considered at Manchester to be nearly equal to the best New Orleans'. But in the midst of all this beauty, the travellers became aware of a shadow creeping across the highlands; clans of warlike

Yao (whom Livingstone called Ajawa) had invaded the Manganja country, initiating a generation of massacre and counter-massacre. The Yao were already established around Zomba, and, incited by Portuguese slavers, were harrying neighbouring villages and carrying off captives to sell into slavery.

On 18 April the party came to a lake named Shirwa or Tamandua, far larger, Livingstone assured his companions, than Ngami, for in those days Shirwa stretched from the spurs of Zomba mountain almost to the Mlanje massif. Local Africans told them that beyond Shirwa and separated from it by only a narrow strip of land lay a much larger lake. It went under various names; 'We patronise Nyinyese'—the lake of Stars— Livingstone told Oswell* and informed Miss Coutts it must be Lake Maravi that 'runs up well to the equator'.[4] Satisfied with what had been achieved and determined 'rather to gain the confidence of the people by degrees than to explore', the Doctor led his party back to the boat, passing close to the site of modern Blantyre. At the Shire mouth they turned down the Zambezi hoping to keep a rendezvous with a man-o'- war at the bar and take on fresh provision. As they went Livingstone was busy extolling the splendid prospects for the Shire Highlands to friends and Whitehall. One passage emphasised his difference from contemporary explorers, for he wrote that though his descriptions of Lake Shirwa 'will probably attract attention ... the discovery is not the chief object in view, though that lies in the way. The great object is the promotion of the welfare of men.'

No warship lay at the coast but they were startled to see a custom house being built at the Zambezi mouth, a sure sign of Portuguese determina- tion to close the river to foreign shipping. Kirk could not blame the Portuguese, pointing out that 'they are fools to let us in at all and it is what we would never have done to foreigners in Australia or the like'. But they all recognised that it signalled the ultimate failure of the expedition. They were back at Tete on 23 June 1859.

On 15 August Livingstone again turned into the Shire and began the third ascent which would bring him to his lake of stars. He anchored the *Ma-Robert* at Dakanamoio Island which, due to the changing course of the river, is today part of the mainland. During this part of the journey Livingstone's thoughts were much concerned with the activities of rival explorers. He had learned at the coast of the splendid discovery of Lake

* Though in fact he finally gave the lake the name of Nyassa meaning 'large water'.

Tanganyika by Burton and Speke, and feared lest they turned south to reach Nyasa, which he regarded as his special preserve.*

This anxiety coincided with hypomania and frayed the Doctor's temper. Nothing seemed to please him and none among his companions was spared his criticism, not even brother Charles who had left behind the essential chemicals for photographic work. The African crew were in frequent trouble: on 18 July Livingstone beat an insubordinate Makololo with a cook's ladle and nine days later thrashed a troublesome stoker, having shaken Kirk with the advice that he should 'break their heads' if the crew was troublesome. One day Livingstone's wrath was turned on Kirk. It was no more than a petty incident but throws light on the fitful peevish workings of Livingstone's mind. Kirk had gone ashore to collect botanical specimens and was late returning to the launch. After waiting for twenty minutes Livingstone decided to teach him a lesson for 'sporting', and steamed up river, leaving Kirk to stumble along the bank until his punishment was considered adequate. Two days later a more serious incident occurred: the *Ma-Robert* tangled up with the two canoes she was towing and a Makololo drowned, but Livingstone found a way— so typical of his tendency to pick on an unrepresented person for any mishap—of blaming it on Macgregor Laird.

On 28 August Livingstone struck into the hills with Charles, Kirk and Rae. They were vexed by the guide's apparently deliberate attempts to mislead them and only later realised he thought their objective of 'Nyanja Mokulu' was the Elephant Marsh. On 7 September, when under Mount Zomba, they became seriously ill after drinking 'mulligatawny soup of amazing strength'. Livingstone believed that the trouble lay in the cook's heavy hand with condiments, but Kirk was probably justified in suspecting an attempt to poison the entire party.

They were still feeling the effects of the mulligatawny on 14 September when they saw a sheet of water ahead, but it was the small Lake Malombe. Kirk was disappointed that day for another reason: the end of their two-year contract was approaching and now Rae upset him with news of the Doctor's 'stingy' edict that their pay would cease with embarkation in Africa and not, as he had believed, on their return to England.

On 16 September, after trudging past Malombe, they saw the wide

* The subject of Snr Candido's claim to the discovery of Nyasa has been considered in the author's *Livingstone's Lake*. Mr V. L. Bosazza has kindly drawn my attention to an extremely accurate map of Lake Malawi dated 1800, another indication that it was well known then to the Portuguese.

9. Livingstone's sketch of a fish in Lake Nyasa

10. Livingstone's sketch of dead slaves probably made on 29 June 1866 when his journal entry reads: 'I saw another person bound to a tree and dead—a sad sight to see'.

waters of Lake Nyasa shining in the distance. They reached the lake next day two miles east of the Shire outlet, and stared out over the ravishing view which belongs to Italy rather than to Africa. In the evening, as the sun dipped behind the great rampart of Dedza Mountain and the golden surface of the water was shot through with lilac, they came to the Shire mouth and the village of Sauko, a friendly chief. Here the four men spread their blankets under the pendant roots of an enormous banyan tree. It had been a day of triumph, one of major discovery, but Livingstone was strangely unimpressed. He had neglected his Journal for three weeks, signalling a depressive phase, and merely jotted down 'Reached Lake Nyassa from which the Shire emerges'.

A large Swahili caravan was encamped nearby and that evening some of the slavers visited the white men. They offered three little girls for sale and then two men secured in gorees.* Livingstone bought some malachite from the 'awful blackguard looking lot', and sent it to Maclear, suggesting that some of it be used in making brooches for the ladies at the observatory, and asked particularly that 'my friend Miss Drew may have a bit'.

The slavers' visit was significant, for with it a keypiece of Livingstone's thinking dropped into place: he appreciated that chance (or 'Providence') had let him to precisely the most vulnerable spot on the slave route from the interior to the east coast. Nearly all the slavers' roads converged here on the Shire River, which the 'great slave path—a path of suffering'[5] crossed by ferry. That night he could think of nothing else but that the Shire was 'the jugular vein' of the slave trade, and that a steamer placed on the upper river and lake would 'cut off slaving at its source'. Once again he distinguished a Heavenly purpose in his having 'been led on from one step to another (my wife thinks from an unsettled roving disposition) . . . and now see the prospect in front spreading out grandly'. The more materialistic Charles decided instead to 'turn trader for the sake of the boom which opening up this region will confer on Africa'.[6]

Livingstone was being less than candid when he singled out Charles as turning 'trader'. As early as June 1857 he had decided that both he and his brother Charles should make some profit for themselves out of the coming Zambezi Expedition by exploiting the cotton, coal, sugar and buaze in Zambesia. So the two men advanced £100 to buy goods for resale

---

* These slave-taming sticks were made from a young barked tree with forked ends for fastening round the captive's neck.

in Africa and asked James Young and Braithwaite to join them in the venture. Livingstone's decision to ask the Government to provide a steamer for use on Lake Nyasa was motivated not only by the attempt to destroy the slave trade but also by its commercial use. Livingstone further considered allowing Kirk to go home at the end of his contract, but Rae was allowed to become a junior partner in the undertaking; the business proposition may also have influenced Livingstone in sacking Baines and Thornton. As it was the project was allowed to lapse after the abandonment of the Shire Highlands by the U.M.C.A. missionaries who settled there during 1861.[7]

They left the lake next day because, as Livingstone informed Oswell, 'We had left Macgregor Laird's precious punt in sinking condition and had to hasten back.'[8] The march was directed at first on Zomba. Livingstone and Kirk climbed to its summit near the present Ku Chawe Inn and were delighted by the beautiful scenery of the plateau. Then they marched southwards, just to the east of the present Blantyre road until they regained their old route running past the site of Limbe to Mbame's village at Soche near Blantyre. They reached the *Ma-Robert* after an absence of forty days during which they had covered well over two hundred and fifty miles on foot. They had seen a good deal of cotton growing, but not enough to justify Livingstone's announcement that here lay 'the finest cotton field in the world' with 'reasonable prospects of great commercial benefits to our own country'.

One is constantly surprised by the amount of time that was squandered during the course of the Zambezi Expedition, and now almost nothing was accomplished during the following seven months. The *Ma-Robert* during this time seemed to steam aimlessly up and down the Zambezi.

To begin with they rested near Chibisa. Charles, according to Kirk, was 'horribly disagreeable company', while Livingstone was losing a great deal of blood from a combination of dysentery and haemorrhoids. News that the *Lynx* was shortly expected spurred him to copious correspondence, and in five days he got off thirty-seven letters to friends as well as a long despatch to Lord Malmesbury, the new Foreign Secretary. When steaming downstream, he was cheered to receive a package of mail, including a letter from his wife which informed him that a daughter had been born at Kuruman nearly a year before, on 16 November 1858.

The *Ma-Robert* reached Kongone on 10 November 1859, but not until 3 December was contact made with *Lynx*. The end of the expedition's two-year term was now approaching. Livingstone was in a fever of anxiety to learn whether an extension had been officially sanctioned, and the reaction of the Foreign Office to his request for a more powerful steamer and the dismissal of three of his staff. So it was a cruel disappointment when the precious mail was lost in the surf. Unwilling to embark on any new exploration without Whitehall's sanction,[9] Livingstone resolved to send Rae home to supervise the construction of a steamer for Lake Nyasa, while he himself fulfilled his pledge to the Makololo by leading them home after their long detention at Tete. Kirk and Charles who, without enthusiasm, had decided to extend their service, were to go with him. Rae, instead of leaving in *Lynx* with Baines, had wished to remain a little longer with the expedition, possibly because, as Kirk suggests, he entertained fond hopes of seducing the wife of one of the Portuguese planters at Sena. At Shupanga they found the Governor of Quelimane building a second custom house, which set Livingstone writing, 'He is a bigamist, having during his residence in England married an English woman and left her. She has been made blind by his syphilis and is in want. She was supplanted by a Portuguese lady by whom he has grown up daughters. . . . This case shews one of the benefits English girls derive from foreign marriages.'

They were at Tete on 2 February 1860 only to learn that, due to a bad harvest, the march to Sesheke must be delayed. Thornton turned up in Tete at this time having spent six months exploring the Luangwa valley, and Livingstone's Journal shows that the Doctor salved a guilty conscience by offering him a passage home, though Thornton turned it down.

Livingstone was never a man to sit doing nothing, and he did not relish the prospect of hanging about in Tete. Quite impulsively he decided to go to the coast again and send off Rae. (The records do not reveal whether the engineer had been satisfied by his dalliance at Sena.) No ship appeared so they went up-river again to drop Rae off at Mazaro, from where he made his way to Quelimane. He was 'on duty still' and continued to draw his pay. Disregarding Livingstone's instructions to take passage via the Cape, Rae went home by Aden and was rewarded by being ship-wrecked in the Red Sea. Meanwhile at Shupanga Livingstone was agreeably surprised to find one letter had been recovered from the mail lost from *Lynx*. It was from Bishop Gray of Cape Town and told him that four British Universities had combined to send out a mission to the Zambezi.

Back at Tete the party was coldly received by the Portuguese, for as

Livingstone writes in his Journal 'we are more obnoxious than ever in consequence of a false translation made in Tette of some parts of my book by Generoso, in which he puts in names of certain inhabitants and makes use of insulting epithets respecting them'. From this time Livingstone detested the Portuguese. They had dared to lay claim to his own discoveries, had 'an inkling of our drift' towards establishing a colony in Shire country, and were proposing to close the Zambezi. Instead of realising that the Portuguese regarded him as a political adventurer, he preferred to attribute their animosity to his 'standing protests against vice and uncleaness'. He condemned them now as an 'utterly effete nation, stamina all consumed by the venereal', and approached the boundaries of dementia as he raved about 'the filthy diseased' settlers who 'cultivated skin diseases and drunkeness more than horseflesh and are asses themselves', and his belief 'that there is not one Portuguese in the country without the venereal disease, either hereditary or acquired'. One can almost sense his feeling of relief when he found the right phrase and denounced his erstwhile friends as members of 'an utterly effete worn-out used up syphilitic race'.

Three weeks at Tete were devoted to preparing for the journey to Sekeletu's, and Livingstone's attempts to assure his flagging companions that their walk would take only six months, which, as usual, when travelling on foot, proved astonishingly accurate. But his brother refused to be comforted; 'Mr. C.L. is sore against going up to Sekeletu', wrote Kirk, 'He is for risking nothing in the way of health for the men, although they did bring the Doctor down.' His distress culminated in a hysterical quarrel with his brother on the eve of their departure. The Portuguese so unbent as to lend two donkeys for the march, though with the proviso that they were not to be used by the detested Charles. It was dampening to discover that the Makololo heroes of 1856 were unenthusiastic at the prospect of returning home; most of them preferred to remain at Tete. In the end sixty agreed to leave, but of these thirty slipped back during the march. A motley crowd of carriers had been recruited with difficulty from the Portuguese slave-owners to carry up the presents for Sekeletu, and the long march to Makolololand began at 2 p.m. on 16 May 1860.

14

The Long March

During the 1,200-mile march in the second half of 1860, Livingstone was again the alert inquisitive man of earlier years, and his account of the journey, which occupies nearly a third of *Narrative*, is one of the best travel stories ever told. He was delighted to have regained control of events and relieved to be independent of the wretched *Ma-Robert*. In *Narrative* the reader shares again his interest in the marvels of nature, while his difficulties with Charles and the desertion of the Makololo are blandly ignored.

Livingstone's straggling column would march about six hours each day; then while the Africans made camp the white men went out shooting for the pot. They travelled along the northern bank of the Zambezi, making detours to avoid the mountains round Kebrabasa and the hilly country where the great wall of the Kariba dam now tames the river. They rested a short time at Zumbo which Livingstone described as 'the most charming picturesque site in the country', although he was critical of its people who, since the priests' departure, had acquired 'not a single art, save that of distilling spirit by means of a gun-barrel'. He noted too that the Batonga on the Batoka Plateau, who today show a high incidence of lung cancer, were 'the most inveterate smokers in the world'.

Presently they reached villages owing allegiance to Sekeletu, and the progress became 'a triumphal procession'. From the Victoria Falls the party travelled by canoes to an uninhibited welcome at Sesheke (now Mwandi village and occupied by a United Church of Zambia mission).

Sekeletu was ill and had moved from Linyanti to a village across the river near the site of modern Schuckmannsburg. His condition puzzled Livingstone and Kirk who believed it to be either pemphigus, herpes or leprosy.[1] In fact it seems that Sekeletu was suffering from a variety of pemphigus named *Forgo Selvagem* or 'Brazilian Wildfire', a contagious disease prevalent in Brazil and also seen in tropical riverine Africa.

Before the institution of modern therapy, those affected died within five years.

So far treatment for Sekeletu's disease had included the execution of several Makololo chiefs for bewitching him, and the liberal application of cow-dung poultices to open sores on the limbs and face. After the customary consultation with the local 'doctor'—a 'witch of Endor type woman'[2] —Livingstone treated the sores with zinc sulphate and silver nitrate dressings. But after he left, Sekeletu became blind, a recognised complication, and died during 1864.

Although gratified by his presents (especially an accordion) Sekeletu chided Livingstone 'for not bringing Mrs L. to be a shield against Moselekatse'. For years the Makololo had hoped the Livingstones would settle among them; their presence would protect them from Mzilikazi, and perhaps allow the tribe to move to the healthy Batoka Plateau. Now Sekeletu even offered a part of his domain for an English colony as an inducement.

Livingstone sadly declined. Years earlier he had abandoned the Bakwena for a more pressing duty, and now the Shire Highlands had been revealed to him as his 'proper sphere' in Africa. 'I hope to return to Makololo in time', he assured John Moffat a shade uneasily, 'but having been led . . . to open a field I never contemplated exploring, and there found a field which, if diligently cultivated, will bear powerfully on slavery and the slave-trade, I think it duty to render whatever aid lies in my power.' But this second desertion troubled him. Because of their misplaced loyalty the Makololo had denied themselves contact with traders from the south and west, and the opportunity of arming their warriors with muskets. This proved disastrous, for within a few years a Barotse rebellion wiped out the tribe. Even more distressing for Livingstone were the details he learned of the catastrophe which had overtaken the Makololo mission, and the shocked realisation that his own behaviour might be accounted an even blacker betrayal.

Much harsh criticism has been levelled at Livingstone for his lack of concern for the members of the Makololo mission and its tragic failure must be considered in some detail.

It will be recalled that in the first flush of his triumphant return to Britain, Livingstone had recommended, even pressed, the L.M.S. to establish missions among the Matabele and Makololo. Thereafter he had withdrawn from the Society and his advice was hardly sought as the

Makololo mission slowly took shape under the veteran Henry Helmore
and young Roger Price.

Tidman's prickly dignity allowed him to make only one casual approach
regarding the mission's entry into Makolololand. In reply the Doctor
merely suggested that its route should either follow his old tracks through
Botswana or proceed through Matabele territory whence his launch might
assist in the Zambezi crossing. Livingstone afterwards pointed out that,
given more opportunity, he would have also advised Helmore to take a
horse to search for waterpoints in the Kalahari but 'Helmore did not
write me even'. Then in a spasm of irritation Livingstone added a vicious
aside—'a precious mull they made of it'.

Livingstone was shrewd enough to understand Tidman's reason for
ignoring him. 'I have a strong impression', he wrote later, 'that having
come under their ban, an attempt was made by means of poor Helmore to
shew that they could do everything without my aid—not a word did he
write to me and it is a question if the red tape bound Dr Tidman to
silence.'[3] He further informed his mother-in-law, again with slight
refraction of the truth, that 'Tidman never wrote a word about the
mission, and even Helmore gave me not one syllable about his movement
... Dr Tidman told a friend of mine that he could not write me [due to]
red tape'. Livingstone also stated that, after starting his journey from
Kuruman, Helmore sent no messages about his progress which might have
made him alter his own movements (at the time directed to the exploration
of Lake Nyasa), although 'had we known that their arrival at Linyanti
took place only a few months before ours we should have strained a point
to aid them with every means in our power'.[4]

The mission party, consisting of Mr and Mrs Helmore, Mr and Mrs
Price (Mrs Price was pregnant and gave birth in the desert) and four
Helmore children, arrived safely at Kuruman. From there Moffat un-
accountably allowed the party to trek on through the Kalahari at the worst
season of the year. But they were sustained through the next terrible
months by the thought of being met on the Chobe by the experienced Dr
Livingstone. When, after many tribulations, their wagons jolted into
Linyanti on 14 February 1860, Livingstone was thousands of miles away,
waiting for *Lynx* at the coast. Helmore's first question at Linyanti was
'Where is the ngaka?', for, as Price wrote, 'We all expected to find that
Dr Livingstone had either been there or was there then, and we were
greatly disappointed on finding that nothing had been heard of him'.[5]

171

Worse, Sekeletu was unfriendly. He felt offended because the missionaries had brought him no muskets, and feared that these new arrivals might make off with some of his subjects like Livingstone. He sealed the missionaries' fate by refusing them permission to move onto the highlands until after Livingstone's long-anticipated arrival. So the two men busied themselves with building huts and preaching to the people.

Then malaria struck the party. The first death occurred on 2 March 1860; by the end of April only Mr and Mrs Price and two of the Helmore children remained alive. Price, by this time convinced that Sekeletu had poisoned their food, was determined to escape, but only after payment of iniquitous ransom did Sekeletu finally agree to his leaving Linyanti with a single wagon. Ironically Livingstone was at that time approaching Zumbo. Price was then made to pay extortionate toll to cross the Chobe. Beyond, in the Mababe Depression, Mrs Price died. He buried her, but later was horrified to learn that the Makololo exhumed her corpse, and took the face back to Linyanti to be used as 'Medicine'.[6] Price then pressed on with the children and miraculously reached Kuruman alive.

Sekeletu assured Livingstone on his arrival that the Makololo had liked Helmore but found Price arrogant and bad tempered; he insisted that the missionaries died of fever,[*] and indignantly denied any suggestion that he had murdered them. Had he done so, he added, he would never have allowed four members of the mission to escape. Livingstone accepted Sekeletu's version of the affair. Charles, however, was sure that 'the oily tongued vagabond' Sekeletu 'treated Helmore very badly',[7] and Kirk agreed with him, doubting the chief's explanation that a revolver he habitually brandished had been traded with Price for ivory.[8]

Towards the end of August Livingstone saddled the old horse he had left in Sekeletu's care during 1855 and rode to Linyanti for medicines and personal papers remaining in his wagon there. All his property was intact, even the magic lantern. Livingstone visited the missionaries' graves nearby (whose sites are now lost), and piled up animal horns and bones over them for want of stones.[9] To his surprise Price had left no message for him.

Livingstone's immediate reaction to the tragedy was a characteristic tangle of grief, criticism, concern lest some of the responsibility be laid on him, and contrition that he had failed to arrive in time to treat the stricken

---

[*] The Helmores almost certainly died from Blackwater fever, a complication of malaria (see the author's *Rulers of Rhodesia*, John Murray, 1968).

missionaries with quinine in place of the 'little Dover's pulv homeopathy' which was available to them.

His mind dwelt for weeks on the events leading up to the calamity: 'I cannot imagine what kept Helmore so long on the way', he told Bishop Gray at Cape Town and asked 'Did they use any remedy? Was it fever? What symptoms did they observe?'. To another friend he explained, 'I regret this extremely, as at the very time they were perishing we . . . were curing the disease'.

Although Livingstone was troubled by his failure to help the Makololo missionaries, he felt that the chief blame lay with the Directors who had not sought his advice, and who had despatched into malarial country a group of Europeans without a doctor or even the most elementary knowledge of the treatment of fever, although he himself had pointed out the merits of quinine therapy in *Missionary Travels*. He reported the fate of the Helmore party to Tidman in language cruelly devoid of feeling, although careful to explain that 'having been unexpectedly detained in the lower parts of this river . . . I was too late to render the aid which I had fondly hoped to afford'.

As for Price, he had committed the unforgiveable sin of criticising Livingstone's favourite tribe, and the Doctor did not hide his opinion that he was responsible for the disaster by provoking Makololo hostility. In his log-book the Doctor noted that although the tribesmen all liked Helmore, they had no use for Roger Price.[10] He contemptuously told John Moffat that Price 'evidently lost his head—no great thing of a head at the best, I fear'. He so doubted Price's account of his ordeal as to assure Mrs Moffat that 'no traces of the terrific suffering remained on your new son-in-law'.* Livingstone even explained to Agnes that 'Poor Price spoiled a great deal at the Makololo by sheer want of tact, then got frightened & came away declaring he was poisoned and Betsy married him out of pity I suppose', while a friend was surprised to learn that 'Mrs L.'s new brother-in-law is a donkey'.[11] When he came to write *Narrative* Livingstone compressed his account of the tragedy into two pages, and repudiated the murder charge against Sekeletu's Makololo by explaining that 'the spear, and not poison, is their weapon'. Moreover he contrived to avoid mentioning Price by name in the book, referring to him as 'the missionary associate of Helmore'. Such scorn was unjustified: for the remainder of his long life Price laboured nobly among the Tswana

* Elizabeth Moffat married Roger Price on 23 October 1861.

people and is still remembered among them as 'the great Lion of Bechuanaland'.

Livingstone was stunned when Tidman made it clear that he preferred to accept Price's account of the tragedy rather than his own, especially as Livingstone's was 'derived from the testimony of Natives', and he was even more distressed by the whispering campaign conducted by the Directors against him. 'Their agent, Mr Farebrother', he told John Moffat, 'goes about the country telling at public meetings that I am morally responsible for the loss of the missionaries at Linyanti', and he repeated the charge to Mrs Moffat: 'Mr Farebrother, agent of the Society, goes about lecturing and bringing all the blame of failure on my shoulders'. The memory, or perhaps an uneasy conscience, rankled. As late as 1871, Livingstone in his greatest extremity reminded Kirk that 'another Secretary of the same Society indulged in a tirade in a London church against me as "morally guilty of the death of Mr Helmore"'.

His involvement with the unhappy mission ended on a characteristically tactless note. Late in 1861 Livingstone enquired of Tidman whether the L.M.S. intended to renew attempts to evangelise the Makololo. If so, he went on, 'I may possibly be able to render some assistance—My friend Helmore unfortunately neglected to give me any information, and it is to avoid the pain I suffered in consequence of being left in the dark till aid was unavailing that I now beg leave to trouble you'. Tidman's reply is not extant.[12]

* * * * *

'This has been an unfortunate Expedition for quarrels', wrote Dr Kirk when he returned from Sekeletu's. Indeed the violent feuding between the two Livingstone brothers was the most extraordinary event of the long march.

It is not mentioned in the carefully laundered *Narrative*, but Livingstone's bewildered dismay at Charles's accusations was recorded in his journals, and Kirk too put down as much as he could remember of the unseemly conduct of the two ordained brothers.

The trouble began on 13 May 1860 at Tete. The cause was trivial. Livingstone reproached his brother for tearing a pillow. Charles in return sharply criticised his brother's leadership of the expedition. A fierce altercation followed with, according to Kirk, 'Mr C.L. using most improper expressions to a superior officer, Dr L. saying that he [Charles] had been a failure from the beginning and that the only mistake made was in bringing him out'. Afterwards the Doctor poured out his indignation in the journal: 'My brother informs me that the members of the expedition did not get orders what to do, and were always at a loss of how to act. . . . All were willing and anxious to help if only I would have told them. He never told me this before.' He defended himself by recalling his policy of abstaining 'from multiplying orders', but he was clearly worried by Charles's tantrum, writing 'as he seems to let out in a moment of irritation a long pent up ill-feeling, I am at a loss how to treat him'. He concluded with a highly critical assessment of his brother in his several capacities.

The two men were reconciled during the early part of the march, but on 11 July there was another dispute during which Charles shouted out a stream of hysterical abuse about his having been employed in 'the service of the Devil, and that when he came out, he thought he came out with a Christian gentleman'. In the evening Dr Livingstone, with bemused incredulity, again scratched down his brother's accusations: 'Manners of a cotton spinner, of the Boers; didn't know how to treat men. An old filthy pillow that I got the benefit of it; that I cursed him, that I set the Devil into him, etc., and asked if it was not his work to take time for me, and repeated again and again that I had cursed him. What part of Botany is Sunday cursing. Seemed intent on a row. Would be but a short time in the Expedition; regretted that he was on this journey. Would rejoice when he could leave it.' The entry ended with a bewildered 'So far my brother Charles'.

A week later, having remembered another of his brother's grievances, Livingstone jotted down in his diary: '(*I have to do all the hunting and carry the game too—C.L.*) (*They eat the meat fast enough but it is impossible to get them to go for it*).'

'At Zumbo', according to Kirk, 'the two made up the quarrel and went on lovingly until Sesheke* when they had another round but this was nothing. It began about grub'. On this occasion, Rae learned that Charles 'behaved disgracefully' and the Doctor retaliated by telling him that he 'rued the day the expedition had received him as a member'. This led up to what Kirk termed 'the grand row' at Sinamane's on the way back to Tete. Sekeletu had provided the Europeans with a Makololo escort, and Charles suddenly decided to 'change from joking to kicking with iron-nailed heavy boots the chief man. Only the high personal regard for Dr

* Kirk by error wrote Sechele.

Livingstone averted bloodshed in this case. The spear was poised',
continued Kirk, 'and needed only a stroke of the arm to send it to the
heart.' Then Charles became manic: 'He returned the kindness', says
Rae, 'by *striking* Dr. L. and tearing the coat off his back'.[13] Kirk confirms
this and rather incoherently reported his amazement at watching Charles
'tearing with nails so as to draw blood and tear clothes, his brother saying
he was serving the Devil, indulge in epithets such as "the cursing Consul
of Quillimane" repeated over and over again.'

The quarrel at Sinamane's may have been the most fiery between the
two men, but it was almost the last. There was a minor scene when they
got back to Tete, but four days later Kirk was relieved to find that the
brothers had 'smoothed' over their troubles, and six weeks afterwards
commented that Charles lately 'has not taken any of those rum fits of
anger'. Looking back at it afterwards Dr Kirk decided that 'His conduct
up country was like that of a madman ... I cannot come to any other
conclusion but that he was not right at the time'. Charles had given a
classic exhibition of the symptoms of a man suffering from manic
depressive psychosis.

So far as Livingstone was concerned, he later treated his brother
generously. Charles was allowed to remain with the expedition and to
co-operate in writing *Narrative*, but Kirk was probably right when he
surmised that he was only kept on out of charity.

* * * * *

On the way back from Sesheke, with sixteen new Makololo porters,*
Livingstone made a more determined effort to measure the Victoria Falls.
Leaning over the projecting ledge on Garden Island, he lowered a
weighted line, marked by a white rag, which snagged at 350 feet, still an
estimated 50 feet above the water. This exercise enchanted the local
Africans: twenty years later a visitor learned that the Ngaka pulled up a
white fluttering bird and some pearls from the river. Using his instruments
Livingstone also estimated the length of the Falls and, recalling the date
'by way of assisting the memory', told Russell it was about 1860 yards.

The party also explored the rain forest on the southern bank and here
the Doctor made an 'awful attempt' to paint the tremendous spectacle
from its best vantage point. One copy was sent to Murchison, and another
may be seen in Livingstone's notebook. For once Livingstone regretted

* Nine were destined to become chiefs in the Shire country.

having got rid of Baines, for he wished he had been present to paint the scene. Baines did so brilliantly two years later.

Leaving the Victoria Falls on 27 September they made a four-hour detour to see a stronghold of the Batoka on the south bank, and then went on to see the Moemba Falls. This gave 'smoke', the Doctor wrote, 'and sounds much' but was 'nothing after those of Victoria'. Even today these falls have been seen by only a few Europeans. The party crossed the Kalomo on 2 October and went on to examine a fine coal field near Manyerere (Kamawendere) on the south bank,* which was presumably an outlying section of the great Wankie field. A few days later they reached Sinamane's village. They had been trying to buy canoes ever since leaving Moemba Falls, and at last acquired sufficient for the party.

On 15 October Livingstone made a curiously characteristic note that 'people who brought presents of meal asked politely if they might smoke near us—this from naked people is better than is met with in Railway carriages'.[14] On the 17th they were off the Bume River, which is now a resort on Lake Kariba. Next day they entered the Kariba Gorge and 'slept ... below a remarkable detached rock'. On the 22nd they went ashore to shoot for the pot at Nchokomela, and a little later nearly lost their canoes in the Mupata Gorge (which Livingstone called Karivua). Passing through Zumbo they visited the *Zimbao* or court of Sekua Nagela near Pinkwe Hill. The following Sunday was spent at Chicova, and next day, 12 November 1860, they entered Kebrabasa Gorge.

Livingstone was still obsessed with demonstrating the navigability of Kebrabasa, if only by canoes, and made a 'mad attempt' to shoot these formidable rapids, quite content to risk twenty men's lives to prove his point. One of the canoes capsized and Kirk lost most of his property. Forced ashore, they tramped on to Tete, their morale lower than ever before. 'I have no desire', wrote Kirk, 'to be any longer on' the expedition. But mail was waiting for them in the village and it contained much good news.

---

* It has been asserted that Livingstone set foot on Rhodesian soil only at the Victoria Falls. But he certainly came to the south bank at Manyerere, and also stopped at villages within Rhodesia which are now submerged in Lake Kariba.

15

The U.M.C.A.

The gloom of the weary men was transformed by the news at Tete. It included a despatch from the new Foreign Secretary, Lord John Russell, which agreed to extend the expedition's duration, commended Livingstone's discovery of Lake Nyasa, announced the replacement of the *Ma-Robert* by a more powerful steamer (already on its way out), approved the exploration of the Rovuma, and confirmed the imminent arrival of a band of Anglican missionaries.

This was so encouraging that Livingstone shrugged off its admonition to moderate his criticism of the Portuguese, a refusal to provide a steamer for Lake Nyasa (which meant he would have to finance the project himself), and an abrupt dismissal of his colonial aspirations.

Behind the despatch lay a good deal of debate in London. Some influential officials advised the recall of the expedition because Livingstone's explorations were alarming the Portuguese, while paradoxically it was they who were reaping the only benefit from them. Russell, sensing that public opinion would disapprove the abandonment of the enterprise at this stage, turned to Washington for advice.

Washington's attitude to the expedition became equivocal. He was disturbed by Livingstone's deviations from its original objectives, and was uncompromising in his opposition to providing a third steamer. At the same time he was anxious to help in suppressing the slave trade, and deplored the Portuguese closure of the Zambezi, even suggesting letting 'the Zulus loose upon them'. So somewhat grudgingly he agreed to Lord John Russell's proposal to extend the expedition's term.

The new ship, *Pioneer*, was now approaching Kongone with a band of priests, representing the advance party of the U.M.C.A., on board her escorts. This was the fruit of Livingstone's famous appeal at Cambridge, and he felt confident that from now on the fortunes of the expedition were bound to improve. He had already decided that the newcomers would work in the Shire Highlands where their very presence and the title of a bishop's see would stake out a claim to British protection. There, he hoped, they would become the nucleus for a larger white settlement. Livingstone would have preferred an undenominational mission but he recognised the influence of the Anglican church, and even if odiously Puseyite, felt that 'anything is better than heathenism'.

He happily went down-river to meet the missionaries, until, as though aware of its coming supercession, the *Ma-Robert* sank near Chemba. Her passengers escaped with most of their possessions and saw the year out at Sena where Charles had one of his 'rum fits' again, and 'another pass of words with Dr L'. They reached Kongone on 4 January 1861, and waited there for almost four weeks for *Pioneer* to arrive.

She came in on 31 January followed by two cruisers with the missionaries on board. 'I hail their arrival', wrote Livingstone, 'with very great satisfaction.'

Their leader, Charles Frederick Mackenzie, a man in his thirties, had accepted the title of 'Bishop . . . to the tribes dwelling in the neighbourhood of Lake Nyassa and the River Shire'. He was the epitome of 'muscular Christianity', athletic yet a *Munthu Wokoma Ntima*—a man of sweet heart. Brought up by two spinster sisters he had matured gracefully. He 'seemed raised above the earth', one of the sisters recalled when he left for the Zambezi, and 'nearer Heaven than ever',[1] while a U.M.C.A. priest agreed that Mackenzie was a man 'to rob you of your heart'. Mackenzie and his priests are important for the light they throw on Livingstone's character. The bishop's relations with him reveal the cycloid rhythm of Livingstone's moods; Scudamore, a lumbering, diffident and lovably absent-minded man, brought out that streak of tenderness in Livingstone which he felt for the truly humble; Rowley's disapproving pen uncovered Livingstone's sensitivity to criticism; Procter's patent weakness after succeeding Mackenzie as head of the mission, exposed his contempt for human failure; Waller's moral strength, on the other hand, disclosed the depths of friendship which Livingstone fostered in kindred spirits.

The priests represented all shades of Anglican opinion, which at that time was divided into High, Low, and Broad sections. The High Church (exemplified by the celebrated Dr Pusey) approached Catholicism in its doctrine and ritualism, while it was fashionable for its priests to drone through their services with pedantic unction. The Low Church was fervently evangelical. Both looked down on the Broad Church, because of its tolerance and easy-going ways. The novelist Willa Gibbs once parodied their attitudes as being either 'low-and-lazy, broad-and-hazy, or high-and-crazy'.

The most senior of the clergy, Lovell Procter, who had become engaged during the voyage but had left his fiancée in Natal, was definitely Broad Church. Livingstone summed him up as 'very orderly and sedate and in love', and believed he would 'make an excellent parish priest' which is exactly what Procter became after being gently wafted from one English living to another by the random workings of Anglican patronage.

We are indebted to Procter for providing us with a description of Livingstone at this time. He found him 'most unassuming & courteous in manners, talks little & only to the purpose, combining good sense with a vigorous mind &, so to speak, calm enthusiasm. He looks strong & inured to the climate; he has that tough wiry frame which is just the one we should imagine calculated to undergo all he has done. I was delighted with him. He is sensible, decided & clear, & while sanguine enough, properly calculating and cautious. . . . In manners he is simple & un-affected and unassuming, with great cordiality & frankness, a little shy but quite self-controlled. He speaks little but to the purpose, clear and unhesitating. In person he is above middle height, strongly set & wiry; he is exactly like the portrait in his book, but without the look of pain & severity there given. He speaks with a Scotch accent & from long intercourse with the natives his English is a little broken'.

'Parson Rowley', the second clergyman, had been successively of the Baptist and Quaker persuasions[2] and now with his adoption of the Anglican denomination was by far the most narrow and devout of all the new missionaries. David Livingstone (whose own pen must be counted among the most unwearied in history) was incensed by this 'sad, blether-ing fellow' for neglecting his mission duties and 'perpetually writing'. The results included a record of his service in book form, a highly coloured account of mission life in *Macmillans*, and a well-publicised criticism of Livingstone for *The Times* which greatly influenced British public opinion.

Scudamore can be fitted into the Broad Church category. After his death 'dear Scude' was remembered for being 'so mild, gentle, sweet tempered & artless. . . . If anything like selfishness could be attributed

11. The author with Alan and Ian Henderson in 1972 at the site of
Livingstone's first crossing of the Chobe

12. The author at the remains of Livingstone's house at Mabotsa with
     the present chief of the village

to him, it must be in the pleasure he felt in the constant exercise of unselfishness'.

Horace Waller, the egocentric lay-superintendent of the mission, later to be ordained, was perhaps the most interesting of what the Doctor snidely termed 'the Parso tribe'. Waller was Low Church and a stern advocate of the rights of the oppressed, being incapable of restraining his noble indignation when these were transgressed. Erratic to begin with, Waller emerged at the end of the ordeal on the Zambezi as a man better focused and far more purposeful than before. Livingstone did not find it easy to make friends, but his friendship with Waller, though slow to develop, became one of the most rewarding in his life. Indeed one of the minor regrets of Livingstone's later years was that Waller had not married his daughter Agnes.[3] Waller was one of the pall-bearers at Livingstone's funeral, but he performed a far greater service when he edited his last journals.

Rounding off the party were two white artisans and three African converts from the Cape whom Livingstone, with unconscious humour, pronounced to be 'noted blackguards'.

*　*　*　*　*

Now that Whitehall's despatch had given approval, Livingstone could think of nothing else but undertaking an exploration of the Rovuma, which he learned had a good harbour, and 'belongs to nobody'.[4] This 'no doubt', he said, 'will be the path to the lake.'[5] From now on, the theory of an easy connection between the Rovuma and Nyasa was like an unseen star which would eventually come to light, simply because he believed God had placed it there. Mackenzie, having already reluctantly agreed to plant his mission in the Shire Highlands, was anxious to establish himself there without delay. Livingstone, however, persuaded him to inspect the Rovuma first. But the river turned out disappointing; it was falling and *Pioneer* was frequently aground. So, fearful of being stranded until the next rains, Livingstone turned back on 16 March 1861, when only thirty-one miles up river.

It was now he learned that Mackenzie, in a moment of incredible folly, had despatched instructions for his sisters to join him in the highlands.*

* The bishop's misconception of the hazards in Africa a century ago were so grotesque that he also arranged for an English gun-smith with a wife and six small children to join the mission. Fortunately the U.M.C.A. balked at the expense, and after litigation compensated the gun-smith with £40.

This prompted Livingstone to send for Mary. After the birth of her daughter, Anna Mary, at Kuruman, Mrs Livingstone had returned to Britain to be with the other children. There she was plunged into 'religious gloom . . . which found vent in terrible expressions'. She was short of money, desperately discontented with her lot, and upset by learning that a 'Doctor of Divinity' had suggested she had been abandoned 'because her husband cannot live with her'. As early as February 1861 Livingstone had told his daughter Agnes, 'I suspect Mama must come to me'; soon afterwards he received a letter from Mary telling him that after complaining to the wealthy Miss Coutts about the long separation, she had replied in words which, when passed on to Livingstone, 'ran into me like a big dose of smelling salts—and I promised forthwith to send for my *worse* half as soon as I can get up a house for her'.[6] After Mackenzie's decision he felt he could strain his wife's impatience no longer, and on 20 March Livingstone told her to 'embrace the first opportunity to come out'. Mary accordingly arranged to travel part of the way with Rae when he brought out the new lake steamer.

Back at the coast Livingstone's 'rousers' helped Mackenzie through his first attack of fever, although he tactlessly announced that 'the cure is worse than the disease'. Then friction developed between Livingstone and Lieutenant May, Master of *Pioneer*, which had all the makings of a second Bedingfeld incident. Fortunately good sense prevailed and May withdrew to England, but the episode quickened Whitehall's anxieties about Livingstone's character, and set Washington musing 'he does not easily brook a rival near the throne'.

Livingstone jauntily accepted the additional responsibilities of navigating *Pioneer*, and steamed off to Johanna to load up with U.M.C.A. stores and fifty apprehensive passengers of all races for the voyage back to Kongone, which was reached safely on 1 May 1861.

Livingstone so far had been full of praises for *Pioneer*. She was a copy of the Queen's yacht *Elfin*, and a 'product of the Admiralty' rather than of a false philanthropist. But as she steamed into the Zambezi it was evident that she drew far more water than specified. For some time Livingstone concealed his chagrin but eventually confessed she was 'too deep for exploration'.

As they bumped their way slowly up the Shire, the fledgling evangelists of the U.M.C.A. learned what it felt like to be a member of one of Livingstone's expeditions. They had accepted his airy assurance that the passage to Chibisa would take a mere twenty days and Mackenzie even anticipated being there 'before Trinity Sunday'. In fact ten miserable weeks went by before they reached their destination.

The new missionaries were dismayed by the everlasting axing of trees and cutting them up, and the backbreaking work of hauling the ship off successive sandbanks from a small boat rowed ahead. It was worst in the Elephant Marsh, where Mackenzie sighed 'well here we are, not having made more than 6 or 7 miles in the last three weeks'. But Waller was filled with admiration for Livingstone. 'Never shall I forget the untiring patience of the Doctor at this time,' he wrote, 'always cheerful, never tired with the hundred and one questions put to him by those who were bored with the monotonous laying out of anchors and "guess" warps, walking round capstans and lowering boats.'

But, like a reward for all the hot exertions of the day, the *Pioneer*'s company enjoyed the grace of each African sunset as they relaxed together: 'We have fine evenings on the quarter deck', wrote Kirk, 'smoking and talking, after being at work all day, often wet too. We must amuse ourselves so we have grog before going to bed.' During these starlit evenings Livingstone was amazed by the speculative 'puerilities' with which the clergymen sustained their doctrinal arguments. Each in turn would toss a novel idea into the air or challenge their companions' orthodoxy with enormous gusto. Rowley was particularly polemical: it was 'rare fun after Rowley got a little gin into his head', Charles remembered, 'the bishop had frequently to check him by punching his side'.[7]

As time dragged on, the clergymen lapsed into the disenchantment that affected everybody who followed in Livingstone's tracks. Whispers of criticism were heard about his eulogistic descriptions of the Shire. When they looked for his 'vast' wealth of cotton, 'only one small bundle was brought' for sale and it cost more than it would fetch in Manchester. Crocodiles there were in plenty, but no sign of the vaunted game. Rowley tells us of one artisan who, after learning the art of tanning 'in the expectation that hides were everywhere, the only hides he could find to tan were those of our little boys' who were later assembled in the mission school.

Animosity in *Pioneer* was by no means one-sided. The old hands watched the growing discomfiture of the 'parso tribe' with disparaging scorn, and regaled themselves with stories that the priests ate more than their fair share of rations. Procter in particular proved 'a great eater and very fond of jam and jelly. . . . He was found one night by the officer of the watch licking the jam pots.' They were greatly diverted too by the discovery that the store of dates was dwindling, and Kirk unkindly 'set a rat trap in the date box', although he was persuaded to wrap a cloth round its teeth. It went off, reported Charles, who evidently shared his brother's taste for alliteration, 'but did not hold. . . . Had it held we should have seen a picture of a pilfering parson with his paw in the box'.[8]

But Mackenzie was a benign influence; his readiness to put his hand to any task reminded Livingstone of 'my good father-in-law'. He got on famously with Livingstone who had only one reservation about the bishop: he was 'lacking in decision of character' and thus 'easily moulded by others'.

Their relations strained but still intact, the crowded company finally reached Chibisa on 7 July 1861. A week later they set off for the highlands, though only after the usual delay caused by a prolonged argument among the porters concerning the distribution of their loads. This so infuriated Mackenzie that he was seen prodding the carriers along with his crozier (which they believed to be a new model musket) and hauling one of them to his feet by its crook. Charles Livingstone recorded the scene and the culprit's indignant complaints that 'the Bishop shoved him, struck him with his big stick, and the moment he sat down to rest a few seconds, hauled him up and poked him on with his long crook-headed stick'.[9]

Climbing up to the escarpment with light hearts the party soon reached the lovely rounded Shire uplands, which Mackenzie thought 'as fine as Natal', while Charles enthusiastically described 'the clear sunshine, with the valleys full of masses of white vapour which is slowly curling up the mountain's side'. Theirs was one of the stirring marches in Christian history. In the van tramped Livingstone, wearing his heavy blue serge suit, and peaked consular cap with the faded gold lace round the crown; beside him marched Mackenzie crozier in one hand, 'elevated and well in view', and a loaded double-barrelled gun in the other, while a tin of oil hung around his neck and a bag of seeds on his back. He was well aware of the incongruity 'of the contrast between my weapon and my staff, the one like Jacob, the other like Abraham who armed his trained servants to rescue Lot'.

The march could scarcely have been undertaken at a less auspicious time. By now the slave traders had tightened their grip on the highlands and the whole country was alive with demented refugees fleeing from Yao warriors who were the 'hunting dogs' of the Portuguese and Arab slavers. Indeed the march was the highwater mark in the fortunes of the Zambezi Expedition. As Livingstone sadly noted in *Narrative*, the venture 'in spite of several adverse circumstances, was up to this point eminently successful . . . we had opened a cotton-field which . . . was 400 miles in length. We had gained the confidence of the people wherever we had gone; and supposing the Mission of the Universities to be only moderately successful . . . a perfectly new era had commenced in a region much larger than the cotton-fields of the Southern States of America.' But, he goes on, they 'came into contact with the Portuguese slave trade', and to this he ascribed all the misfortunes that followed.

The second morning brought the party to Mbame's village a few miles south of Mpemba Hill. There the white men rested in huts while new porters were engaged. Mackenzie and Procter had lagged behind chanting doxologies together until they joined Scudamore who was bathing in a nearby stream. They were not with Livingstone when he learnt that a slave coffle was approaching. It was hustled along by the whips of half a dozen black drivers who were 'shouting and trumpeting as if they had been performing a capital game before Her Majesty at Balmoral'. Again in a hypomanic phase, Livingstone decided to intervene. Calling on his companions to load their rifles, he ran out to meet the coffle. Unnerved by the sight, the slavers 'darted off like mad' but not before their leader was recognised as one of Tito Sicard's domestics, sure evidence that the local Portuguese were exploiting the expedition's discoveries by extending their slaving operations. He was 'a rather goodlooking, dapper little fellow', Livingstone wrote when he sent Murray one of Kirk's photographs of the coffle to be copied into *Narrative*.[10]

The eighty-four men, women and children thus abandoned were promptly freed. The bishop's baggage included a saw, and with it the gorees were quartered and then used symbolically as fuel to cook a meal for the captives. Amid much hand-clapping and ululation, calico was next handed out to the liberated slaves who promptly attached themselves to Mackenzie as a ready-made congregation.

The released Africans gave a horrifying account of their ordeal. Two women had been shot for attempting escape, while another, unable to carry both her load and baby, had seen the child's brains dashed out on a stone.

Livingstone had never before physically interfered with the activities of the slave traders and he knew it would provoke the Portuguese. But at the time he was more concerned with Mackenzie's reaction. The bishop had already resolved to use fire-arms in self-defence, but had not reached a decision about employing them aggressively. Distressed by Livingstone's pugnacity, he presently sought guidance in the collect for the first Sunday after Epiphany, which reads 'Grant that the people may both perceive and know what things they ought to do and also may have grace and power faithfully to fulfil the same. . . .' Thus encouraged, he sturdily informed the Bishop of Oxford that 'Livingstone is right to go with loaded gun and free the poor slaves; and . . . we are right, though clergymen and preachers of the Gospel, to go with him, and by our presence, and the sight of our guns, and their use if necessary (which may God avert), to strengthen his hands in procuring the liberation of these people'. In his diary the bishop wrote, 'surely all will join in blessing God that we have such a fellow countryman' as Livingstone.

During the next two days sixty-four more captives were released at gun point. Then, on 23 July 1861, a more serious clash occurred with the slavers probably on the slopes of Ntonya Hill.

Livingstone that morning was in trouble: a haemorrhoid had prolapsed. Kirk was away harrying another slave coffle, so Waller was persuaded to use the lancet. He did this fearfully, 'so extensive was the enlargement', but the patient's stoicism again set him eulogising, 'our captain, guide and staunch friend throughout, the God-fearing lion-hearted leader . . . a man of men he is'.

Livingstone then led the party towards a Yao village. Presently they knelt down with the bishop to pray, like medieval crusaders, that their purpose might be fulfilled. But above Mackenzie's voice they heard wails and exultant shouts; looking up they saw a long slave coffle approaching the village, while Yao women ran out to greet the slavers 'as did the Israelitish women of old, to welcome back the victors'.

Livingstone walked towards them, calling for a parley, but the Yao rushed forward firing arrows and an occasional bullet. The whitemen were taken by surprise. 'So little did we intend to fight', the Doctor wrote afterwards, 'that I was unarmed and had to borrow a revolver in case it came to close quarters, and after a few rounds our ammunition was expended—but they made off.' According to Kirk six Yao were shot and most of the bewildered captives ran away, leaving only two children to swell Mackenzie's congregation. Then Livingstone fired the village and carried off a large quantity of booty. It was unusual behaviour for a missionary.

Moving on, the party came to Magomero, where, in the shadow of a curious square-shaped mountain, they discovered an easily defended tongue of land projecting into a river. Livingstone accepted this secure position as another 'sign'. 'We seem to be invited', he noted, 'to stand in the gap and arrest a flood of slavery', and he persuaded Mackenzie to set up his station there. Its site can now be identified by the two crosses standing near the Nasawa Young Pioneers Training Base.

As huts were being marked out, the captives were sent off under Charles's supervision to make gardens for themselves. Later Livingstone gleefully reported that the women promptly 'took off all their clothes and danced around him instead of commencing to hoe. He left them and came up much ashamed and declaring that he could do nothing with them'.[11]

A week later, before leaving Magomero to make a proper exploration of Lake Nyasa, Livingstone advised Mackenzie against becoming further involved in tribal fighting. 'You will be oppressed with requests for aid', he told him, 'but don't go.' Magomero, he insisted, must be a refuge for the oppressed and only defended if directly attacked.

Once on his own Mackenzie 'inaugurated a regular system of work for all' and conducted daily services (which were assumed by his flock to be concerned with brewing war medicine). He also resumed his correspondence with supporters at home, reporting the promising (though unfortunately bloody) start to the mission and requesting two hundred blankets to prevent immoral practices among his African dependants in the cold weather. And he tried to ignore the atrocities going on around Magomero.

But on 9 August a deputation of Manganja chiefs, supported by a tail of tribesmen, begged him for armed assistance against the Yao, and for the next two days the missionaries prayerfully examined their consciences together. One can sympathise with their dilemma. Could they, as men of peace, condone the atrocities on tribesmen whom they regarded as their flock, or should they defend their people?

The debate continued until Mackenzie learned fuller details 'of barbarities perpetrated'; then 'his blood', in Kirk's memorable phrase, 'rose and theories vanished' and the missionaries agreed to fight the Yao provided the Manganja chiefs gave a pledge never to engage in slaving themselves.

This condition was quickly accepted by the chief and next day Mackenzie gaily wrote that he had 'consented at last to head an army' against the slavers. He declared a holy war, and even considered sending home for military assistance in the coming campaign.

Such militancy differed from Livingstone's fighting in self-defence. The missionaries had deliberately set themselves up against the Yao as rulers of the highlands and they became the aggressors.

Mackenzie had been brought up on stories from the classics, and remembering the three Punic wars, he jestingly called the fighting which followed 'the Second Ajawa war'. With a ragged army of eight Britishers and a thousand badly armed Manganja, he boldly attacked Yao settlements on the slopes of Zomba. He was seen to drop 'a chief with a red cap on his head',[12] and Waller surprised himself by shooting a slaver through the forehead at sixty yards range.[13] At least seven Yao were killed and three villages burned. Mackenzie 'seemed rather proud of the affair' but Rowley 'could only find relief in tears'. There was another flare up of fighting in October when the missionaries again inflicted casualties among the Yao and burned more villages.

Unfortunately Mackenzie had rushed intemperately to the conclusion that the Yao were wholly evil and the Manganja innocent, persecuted people. He only realised there was little to chose between the two tribes after watching Manganja warriors seizing Yao children for sale into slavery, and discovering that the majority of the Magomero community was Yao.

It was the ethics of his own militant policy which most perturbed the bishop. He asked himself whether his office carried the right to kill the people of his own diocese. He had good reason. Although a clash between the slavers and white men in Central Africa was bound to occur, should fighting be initiated by clergymen?

Certainly when the news reached Britain, High Church opinion was overwhelmingly critical of Mackenzie's actions, holding it to be no part of a missionary's duty to shed human blood, however great the provocation. At a meeting attended by three hundred mission supporters, Dr Pusey described Mackenzie's conduct as 'a frightful thing' and explained that 'the Gospel has always been planted, not by doing, but by suffering'. But for the most part the expedition members supported Mackenzie's aggression: Charles, on hearing of Pusey's outburst, pointed out rather ponderously, 'all very well Mr P., if you were in Africa and saw a host of murderous savages aiming their heavily loaded muskets and poisoned arrows at you, more light might enter your mind . . . and if it didn't great daylight would enter your body through arrow and bullet holes'.[14]

Livingstone's feelings on the matter were typically ambivalent. Two years earlier he told a quaker friend, 'I love peace as much as any mortal man. In fact I go quite beyond you, for I love it so much I would fight for it', but now he was inclined to reject Mackenzie's militant policy. He was worried about its effect on his own public image, noting anxiously to Murchsion that 'what you will say to gentlemen killing those whom they were sent out to convert, I can easily guess', and informing Whitehall that 'a missionary ought in all lawful things to identify himself with the interests of his people, but it is doubtful whether this should extend to fighting for them'.

His opinion, however, slowly changed and a year later Livingstone was writing cautiously, 'to my mind the case was one of necessity—of dire necessity, and no one clergyman or layman would engage in it willingly any more than he would choose to perform the office of the common hangman'. But it was only after meditating beside Mackenzie's grave that Livingstone summed up his, and perhaps our own, feelings in a way that few other people would have managed so well: 'At first I thought him wrong in fighting', he wrote, 'but don't think so now. He defended his 140 orphan children when there was no human arm besides to invoke.' It was the sort of epitaph his 'good bishop' would have cherished.

16

The 'Hetty Ellen'

Mackenzie's troubles still lay in the future when Livingstone launched a four-oar gig fitted with a sail on the upper Shire at Matope and went on to Lake Nyasa with Kirk, Charles and one sailor as companions.

One would have imagined that the pioneering voyage which followed would have been one of the most splendid experiences in Livingstone's life, yet he looked back on it with aversion. It coincided with one of his 'downs', the weather was appallingly hot and the lake tempestuous, he was miserably sea-sick and two robberies reduced the men to their underclothes and near starvation due to the loss of their calico currency. To add to their troubles, fighting on the eastern shore prevented them from investigating Livingstone's theory that the lake was drained by the Rovuma.

Sailing up the lake's western coast, Livingstone was appalled at the suffering caused by the slave trade. Near the great slave emporium of Nkhotakota, this 'devilish trade in human flesh' had turned the lakeshore into an abomination. At one place they burned more than a thousand gorees which had been piled up for future use and Livingstone sighed 'O, when will Christ's holy gospel enter into this dark region'. He later learned that each year nineteen thousand Africans were exported from the area and many more died during raids or the horrific marches to the coast. It seemed more essential than ever to place a steamer on the lake and strangle 'this trade of hell'.

Farther north, conditions were even worse for the lakeshore was being devastated too by the Angoni (Mazitu), another off-shoot of the Zulus, who left the beaches strewn with corpses; 'as an Englishman loves to kill game', Kirk reported, 'so they [the Angoni] kill men for sport'.

A group of Makololo accompanied the gig on foot along the winding shoreline and their dilatory progress slowed down exploration, but still a great deal of survey work was accomplished. The lakeshore was accurately mapped (its southern end being whimsically likened to the shape of Italy's 'boot'), and a conspicuous promontory, later the site of the first mission in Malawi, was named after Maclear. But the Europeans found the lake Africans unattractive and were irritated by their blatant curiosity: 'sheer over-modesty ruined me', Livingstone told a friend, 'I had before slipped away a quarter of a mile to dress for church, but seeing a crowd of women watching me through the reeds I did not change my old "unmentionables" ', and these were all he had left when the party was robbed a little later.

Livingstone was forever enquiring about the lake's length but every answer was different. Information about the Rovuma was equally bewildering, although the general consensus that its source lay fifty miles from Lake Nyasa, was reasonably accurate.

Livingstone's depression at the time is reflected in his Journal entries which are terse and uninteresting. Even the beauty of the scene beyond Bandawe failed to lift his spirits, for this 'abode of lawlessness and bloodshed' reeked of slaughter and the lakeshore was 'literally strewed [with] human bones and putrid bodies'.

He never reached or even saw the end of the lake. At Nkata Bay he joined the land party in the hills, lost touch with the boat for four days and was in mortal peril from Angoni war-parties. 'What on earth made you run away?' he shouted at Kirk when the two parties were reunited, and when Kirk tried to explain, Livingstone ruffled him still further by breaking in with 'Nothing like taking the first word and laying the blame on someone'.

By then their provisions were almost exhausted and with a sickening sense of frustration, the boat was put about. 'This is the first time I ever returned without accomplishing all I set out to do', Livingstone wrote with pardonable bending of the truth. He had, however, seen the great wall of mountains, later to be named after him. They appeared to close in on the lake, and led Livingstone to believe Lake Nyasa to be a hundred miles short of its real length.

They came slowly down the west coast delayed by adverse winds and mocked by pugnacious Africans who thought them fleeing from the Angoni. Below Kambiri Point the Makololo decided to strike off on their own. The Doctor attributed this to his refusal to sail round each bay to protect them, but African tradition asserts that the Makololo were sulking because he had forbidden them to hunt elephants on the Sabbath. When the boat finally pulled from the lake into the upper Shire on 26 October, it seemed fitting that the miserable expedition ended to the sound of distant gun-fire, saluting another triumphant Arab man-hunt.

At the top of the cataracts the gig was hung up on a tree for future use. Then the party tottered down to *Pioneer*, with Charles's beard now quite white, and according to Hardisty, its unschooled engineer, like men who were 'nothing but sking and bone'.[1]

Livingstone refused to employ the mutinous Makololo in *Pioneer* again, so these sixteen men proceeded to write a saga of their own. Like medieval freebooters carving out a principality, they settled in Chibisa's old village, attacked Yao slaving parties and after retaining the best looking girls, sent the captives to Magomero. Very soon each man enjoyed the favours of six wives, while their muskets and prowess in battle attracted a following of eighty Manganja warriors. They became a power in the land, but called themselves the children of 'Doto Livisto', and delighted in airing their English vocabulary—which consisted of 'look here', 'thank you' and 'good morning, Sir'. They were generally a nuisance to the Magomero missionaries although a support in time of trouble. Years later the renegades became a factor in the 'Scramble for Africa' since Britain would not allow these men, who had been touched by the Livingstone Legend, to fall under Portuguese control. Their descendants remain the chiefs and headmen today of villages on both sides of the Shire.

The rains began early that year and Livingstone was anxious to get away quickly on the rising river. Had he done so, the coming tragedies would have been avoided. Unfortunately he was obliged to wait until three sailors convalescing at Magomero rejoined the ship. During the delay a new recruit for the mission, the Reverend H. de W. Burrup, arrived at Chibisa, followed by a Dr Dickinson and an artisan named Clark. They confirmed that a cruiser, with Mrs Livingstone, Mrs Burrup and Miss Ann Mackenzie* on board, was expected at the Zambezi mouth early in January. Next day Bishop Mackenzie arrived at the Cataracts from Magomero in response to a testy letter from Livingstone which informed him that, because of the shallow Elephant Marsh, *Pioneer* would be unable to bring his sister further up river than the Ruo mouth. In the same letter, Livingstone turned down a request from Procter to go down river and provide an escort for the ladies with a curt intimation that *Pioneer* was

---

* Mackenzie's second sister had surprised everyone by getting married to the Archdeacon of Pietermaritzburg, and did not come out to the Zambezi.

'not a passenger ship'. To Mackenzie Livingstone also made it clear that he disapproved his proposal of 'leaving his most important post at this critical time to bring up his sisters', and in a curious generalisation later explained 'He seems to lean on them. Most high church people lean on wives or sisters . . . I would as soon lean on a policeman.' Eventually a compromise was reached: Mackenzie and Burrup were to rendezvous with *Pioneer* at the Ruo mouth on New Year's Day and conduct the ladies to Magomero. *Pioneer* left the Cataracts on 15 November 1861, with Charles hatching up a plan to leave the expedition at the coast,[2] while Livingstone still in his ungracious and dejected mood was recording morbid suspicions about his staff.

His hope for a quick trip down-river and a punctual rendezvous with the cruiser was frustrated by being grounded for 'five weary weeks' in the Elephant Marsh. Malaria was rife, quinine prophylaxis not being reinstated until 17 December,[3] after the expedition had suffered its first casualty when the ship's carpenter died. There was no sign of Mackenzie at the Ruo which was eventually reached on 7 January. Livingstone pressed on down river now desperately worried about his wife, who was presumably waiting in the delta, and concerned too as to whether Rae had succeeded in bringing out the ship for the lake. On 23 January, *Pioneer* reached the coast at Luabo Mouth (which could provide better firewood than Kongone). There they waited impatiently until, on 31 January, HMS *Gorgon* was sighted towing a 'dirty little brig', the *Hetty Ellen*. *Gorgon* was flying flags to announce 'I have a steamship in the brig'. Livingstone signalled back 'Welcome news'. 'Wife aboard' continued *Gorgon*. 'Accept my best thanks' replied Livingstone. It all seemed remarkably civilised.

That afternoon Captain Wilson brought *Gorgon* in on false bearings since he had taken the Luabo for Kongone. Then, while he made a perilous crossing of the bar in a rowing boat with Rae, the mission ladies* on board led the now uninhibited naval officers in the singing of rounds.

*   *   *   *   *

A new cast of actors now temporarily joined the Zambezi Expedition. It included five ladies. One of them, Mrs Livingstone, was gaily aware of this incongruity, predicting that the 'regular cargo of ladies [would]

---

* Miss Ann Mackenzie, accompanied by a house-keeper Jessie Lennox, her maid Sarah, and young Mrs Burrup.

take Livingstone by storm', and she looked forward to 'his look of surprise when he sees what a lot'. She did so next morning when *Pioneer* steamed over the bar towards *Gorgon* and the ludicrously named *Hetty Ellen*. Ignoring the cruiser Livingstone made straight for the brig, climbed aboard, embraced his wife and went with her below to pore over photographs of their children.

A seaman in *Gorgon* vividly remembered the impression Livingstone made that day. 'There was something powerful about him', he said, 'that drew men to him, white and black alike. . . . His eyes were wonderful —keen and with a twinkle of humour about them. And his thin face was deeply tanned. When he spoke to me, or shook hands with me, there came into his eyes an expression that I have seldom seen so marked in any other eyes. His soul shone through them. They showed you what was in the man . . . and withal he was as gentle as a child.'

Next morning *Pioneer* towed *Hetty Ellen* and two paddle-boats across the bar. The missionary party, with a horrifying amount of luggage, had been packed into the boats together with a handful of officers who carried orders to do what they could for Livingstone, and fifty armed ratings intended to show the flag at Magomero and protect the mission. Forty sections of Rae's new boat *Lady Nyassa* were also stored in *Hetty Ellen*. Livingstone had paid £6,000 for her, and Rae added £200 as a speculation in case she was used, as he hoped, for trading. Rae had supervised the *Lady Nyassa*'s construction and brought her out to Africa himself in *Hetty Ellen*.

In a low state, Livingstone was all indecision and irresolution as the mission stores and the sections of *Lady Nyassa* were laboriously transferred to *Pioneer*. 'Everything', groaned Charles, 'is in confusion', a Naval officer had never seen 'such constant vacillations, blunders, delays and want of common thought', while another newcomer, James Stewart, was sharply critical of Livingstone's 'woeful want of arrangement'. To make matters worse the ladies were half-distracted by the commotion, and Rae reported that he had found *Pioneer*'s engines in a deplorable state.

But Mary was in excellent form, delighted to have rejoined her husband, and prattling pleasantly to everyone. When Livingstone wrote to tell John Moffat he would send her to the highlands if she got fever, she added 'do not believe him' in the margin and drew a profile sketch of her head with a derisive thumb touching the nose.

She had good reason to feel relieved for she was now free from the embarrassing attention of one of the new missionaries, the Reverend James Stewart, which had caused grave scandal during the voyage.

Stewart, a strict Non-conformist, had come out to Africa to examine the prospects for a Free Kirk Industrial Mission in the Shire highlands, and Livingstone welcomed him as another potential nucleus for a white colony. He was a tall, good-looking, bearded man of thirty-one, and almost maudlin in his admiration for Livingstone; after poring over *Missionary Travels* Stewart had labouriously and precisely defined his hero's status as a botanist, geologist, zoologist, doctor, explorer, missionary and statesman.

Stewart sailed out to Africa with Mrs Livingstone, and she welcomed the attention he lavished on her, and which he hoped would ingratiate him with her husband. They enjoyed long conversations in her cabin far into the night, and explored Cape Town together. But Rae's arrival at the Cape in the *Hetty Ellen* soured their relationship. Rae, who had met Stewart briefly in Scotland, made no attempt to hide his opinion that the newcomer was not a missionary but a bogus trader and libertine. Eventually the two men quarrelled openly, and on 27 October the distraught Stewart noted in his journal that 'some appalling charges seemed to be about to be brought against me. I went to bed at one, stunned and confounded.'

Stewart travelled with Mrs Livingstone to Durban, where they joined the U.M.C.A. contingent—the four ladies, and Miss Mackenzie's chaplain—who alternatively winced and gloated over Rae's stories about Stewart's behaviour. Then the whole party went on to the Zambezi mouth in the *Hetty Ellen*. There was no sign there of Livingstone and the brig steamed north for news. At Mozambique Captain Wilson of HMS *Gorgon* met them and acted with decision. He towed the *Hetty Ellen* back to Luabo and there the *Pioneer* was duly sighted.

The old hands of the Zambezi Expedition, influenced by Rae, treated both Stewart and Mrs Livingstone with reserve. Livingstone, however, fortunately pronounced Rae's 'appalling charges' to be mere 'tittle tattle'. But the gossip had mortified Mrs Livingstone, and in Kirk's opinion it predisposed to her final illness.

Yet as they came to know Stewart better, his companions on the Zambezi decided that his only transgression had been indiscretion. They conceded that his nocturnal visits to Mary's room were to bring comfort to her when she was depressed, laudanum when hysterical, and censure when intemperate. But the slander continued to worry Stewart and years later he brought up the subject in a letter to Livingstone in which he begged him to have not 'the shadow of doubt in his mind' about the innocence of the relationship, protesting that 'to Mrs Livingstone I always acted with the same ease and freedom as if she had been my mother'.[4] This was unnecessary; Livingstone had always accepted Stewart's innocence. He leaned on him when Mrs Livingstone died, and afterwards offered Stewart £150 a year to be associated with himself as an independent missionary. Indeed the only concession he made to the scandal appeared in *Narrative* where Livingstone implied that Stewart did not join the expedition until the April of 1862.

Eventually Stewart forgave Rae for initiating the slander against him and blamed the unpleasantness of 'that old hag', Miss Mackenzie, who delighted in squeezing the last drop of drama out of every situation. For she continued to revel in the gossip: when leaving the coast she was still broadcasting her exciting suspicions, Stewart noted gloomily, and 'relieves the tedium of the delay at the bar and will further relieve it on the voyage down by industriously repeating all the scandal. . . . That she did not originate it is no palliation . . . she industriously propagating what she knows at most to be mere gossip'.[5]

Within a year Stewart abandoned his adulation of Livingstone and became his most carping critic. The fabric of his admiration was not rent by a single disagreeable episode; rather it slowly frayed. Several factors were involved: Stewart's pride had been injured by his cold reception in Africa, which he ascribed at first to Rae's hostility and the 'Puseyite prejudice' of 'a set of snarling arrogant Episcopalian curs', but soon his resentment focused on Dr Livingstone, like a child whose illusion of a father's infallibility has been shattered. As he travelled through country discovered by the Doctor, Stewart found it vastly different from that so glowingly described in *Missionary Travels*. He convinced himself that he had been lured into a wild-goose chase by Livingstone's 'accursed lies', and when he finally left the expedition wrote in his diary, 'I part with Dr L, and have no wish whatever to see him again'. In a final theatrical gesture Stewart flung his erstwhile treasured copy of Livingstone's book into the Zambezi with a muttered 'so perish all that is false in myself and others'. On reaching Scotland he continued to criticise the Doctor with blistering ferocity. Yet, after Mackenzie's martyrdom, antipathy towards the 'Episcopalian curs' turned into sympathy and admiration. The aversion for Livingstone mellowed more slowly. It happened that Stewart accidentally retained one of the Doctor's letters lent to him by Mary; when he read it again in 1864 he found it contained a long passage referring to Livingstone's difficult struggle through the Sansureh swamps during 1853, whose description in *Missionary Travels* Stewart had condemned as grossly exaggerated. Obliged now to accept its truth, Stewart wrote to Livingstone admitting that he had misjudged him. The Doctor's reply was magnanimous and the breach began to heal. Next year Livingstone 'spoke very kindly of Stewart' to a parson in Bombay, and hoped 'that he may yet join him in Central Africa'. Finally at the Doctor's funeral in Westminster Abbey, Stewart went through some form of spiritual resurgence, and it brought him back to Lake Nyasa to establish the great mission station which he himself named Livingstonia.

17

Tragedy

Perhaps the most significant decision taken during the Zambezi Expedition was that made on the evening of 31 January 1862 after Rae boarded the *Pioneer*. He then positively refused to accept Livingstone's instructions to assemble the *Lady Nyassa* at the Zambezi mouth, where *Gorgon*'s crew could be called upon for assistance. Beset by irresolution the Doctor finally agreed to load the sections in the *Pioneer* for reassembly at the Ruo mouth.

Already Livingstone's timetable was upset. His wait at the cataracts for the convalescent seamen prevented his taking advantage of the full river in November; the subsequent failure of the rains resulted in the *Pioneer* grounding for weeks in the Elephant Marsh, and this led to her missing *Hetty Ellen* on her first call at the coast. Now Rae's decision meant the abandonment of all hope of getting *Lady Nyassa* to the Murchison Cataracts before the river fell again, and this condemned the Europeans to spend an unhealthy season on the lower Zambezi.

No less than ninety passengers and crew were packed on board and, when *Pioneer* finally moved unsteadily up the river, she was listing badly with one paddle frequently out of the water. Already Stewart was entertaining doubts about Livingstone. Conversation in the evening was, he decided, 'of the lightest kind, often riddles or finding a word formed the amusement', and when continued on Sunday, it set Stewart muttering that the talk was 'little befitting the day: Greece, Queen &c'[1] A naval officer, similarly disturbed by the lack of Sabbath observance, feared that Livingstone's 'fame as an explorer has eclipsed that of a missionary'.

Miss Mackenzie was concerned about her brother, who by now must have been waiting six weeks or more at the Ruo mouth. Livingstone, however, reassured her that there had been no sign of him when he passed the rendezvous on 7 January, so presumably Mackenzie knew of *Pioneer*'s delay in the Elephant Marsh. Unfortunately *Pioneer*'s progress up river was now slowed down by sandbanks, changing currents and defective performance of her engines, which Rae blamed on the inadequate maintenance provided by Hardisty, the ship's engineer. Realising that she would never reach the bishop's rendezvous before the river fell again, Captain Wilson on 17 February 1862 abruptly announced his intention of taking the mission ladies on in *Gorgon*'s gig. So, late that afternoon, poor agitated Miss Mackenzie tottered into the boat clutching Mrs Burrup's arm, while Wilson, Dr Ramsay of *Gorgon*, and eleven bluejackets followed. Kirk acted as escort in a well-manned whaler.

Only after twelve hellish days did they reach Malo Island opposite the Ruo mouth,* where the headman assured them he had not seen the bishop. They anchored that night in mid-stream, never dreaming that they lay only a hundred yards from Mackenzie's freshly-dug grave. Then they rowed on to Chibisa which was reached on the evening of 4 March, with most of the sailors now prostrated with fever, while Miss Mackenzie had become so ill that they feared she would die. Here they finally learned the dreadful news that the bishop had succumbed to malaria five weeks earlier, while Burrup had been carried up to Magomero to die.

It turned out that after leaving Livingstone at the cataracts in mid-November, Mackenzie sent off two priests to prospect a cross-country route to the Ruo mouth. They were detained by a hostile chief and the bishop wasted time by leading a punitive expedition against his village. Accompanied by Burrup, he only reached the appointed rendezvous, arranged with Livingstone, on 11 January 1862, several days after *Pioneer* had passed by, and there he settled down with Burrup on Malo Island to await its return.

They were in a terrible predicament. The local headman was unfriendly, the two men suspected they had been deserted by Livingstone, and were tormented by a growing anxiety for their womenfolk. Worst of all they had lost their precious supply of quinine when their canoe overturned.

Inevitably they went down with fever and soon were too weak to leave their hut. We know little of the way Mackenzie and Burrup spent the next three weeks except that they passed some time by learning quotations from the 'Epistle to the Romans' in the original Greek, and we can be certain that Bishop Mackenzie drew comfort from those beautiful and challenging words of St. Paul which begin 'whosoever shall call upon the name of the Lord shall be saved'. Presently Mackenzie fell prostrate

* The river during the last century has altered its course and the island has been submerged.

whenever he tried to stand up, and became wrapped in a hallucination of living at Magomero with his sisters. As his condition deteriorated he sometimes roused himself to tell the Makololo, who had accompanied the two men, that Jesus was sending for him. Then, after bleeding heavily from the nose and mouth, Mackenzie sank into coma, and on the last day of January 1862 the first bishop of the Universities' Mission to Central Africa died. 'God be thanked he was the man he was', wrote Waller movingly when he heard the news, 'death had no horrors for him and even the pangs felt at its approach by all beings whom mortality claims, seem to have passed unheeded by him.'² It was another magnificent epitaph.

Burrup somehow found the strength to carry the body across to the mainland that evening and watched as the Makololo dug a grave under an acacia tree. He did not notice that his friend was buried with the head to the west. Too dark for him to read the prayer book, Burrup murmured what his fevered mind remembered of the burial service. Then he returned to Magomero where two weeks later he died. When the station was subsequently abandoned, local tribesmen exhumed the corpse and cut off the head to be used as fetish. But Mackenzie's grave remained inviolate and was a place of pilgrimage, until quite recently when the bishop's body was reinterred at Blantyre in Malawi.

Only towards the middle of March did Wilson get his mourning ladies back to Shupanga, where *Pioneer* was now moored. Livingstone silently watched Miss Mackenzie and Mrs Burrup being carried aboard, and then went down to his dimly lit cabin, grieving over a friend and for the effect his death would have on his own crusade. He was heard murmuring 'this will hurt us all'. (He was right: Murchison and many others withdrew their support from the U.M.C.A. on the presumption that no mission could be sustained in the presence of the slave trade.) Then he collected himself and his journal entry that day reads, 'I shall not swerve a hair-breadth from my work while life is spared'.

Next day, 15 March 1862, Livingstone set off down-stream with the bereaved ladies, and, favoured by a strong current, reached Kongone the day after. Unfortunately only a few hours earlier *Gorgon* had been blown out to sea by a gale and did not return until 2 April. It was a trying time for everyone. Kirk felt furious at Mrs Livingstone's attentions to Stewart, and wrote angrily in his diary that 'Dr L. does not see how he has been thoroughly humbugged by this fellow. If only he knew the use he made

Tragedy

of his wife, he would change his tune.' Wilson was in a ferment to get away having heard, wrongly, that war had broken out with America. When her birthday and wedding anniversary came round Mrs Burrup 'cried hysterically, or walked about all night never closing her eyes'.[3] Miss Mackenzie was almost equally distraught, but was somewhat comforted when Livingstone read the service on Sunday since 'even with his very bad pronounciation, he cannot spoil the liturgy'.[4] Livingstone was equally ungracious when he noted that 'Miss Mackenzie bears up very well: people who have a competence hold out wonderfully'. Then he added a shocking sentence about the bishop's death, so typical of his lack of control, that 'this sad loss will have one good effect: better men will be sent out and no one hereafter come for a lark or to make a good thing of playing the missionary for a few years and then reaping laurels'. What made things worse was his repetition of this heartless remark before Miss Mackenzie.

By now Livingstone had turned against the U.M.C.A. missionaries. They had become an embarrassment to him since their militancy in the highlands. He was riled by his wife's account of their hostility to Stewart and upset by Rowley's recent article which condemned his over-optimistic report of the Zambezi. Finally he suspected that the panicky accounts of near-famine conditions reaching him from Magomero were grossly exaggerated.

Gorgon at last sailed away, with Miss Mackenzie so far recovered as to be brimming over with gossip about Stewart and Mary, and carrying Dr Meller of *Pioneer* too who had obtained reluctant permission to re-cuperate from malaria at the Cape. Livingstone was left to load his ship with more sections of the *Lady Nyassa*, and steam back to Shupanga. A greater grief awaited him there.

His wife looked sallow and unhealthy, according to Kirk who thought that her previous indiscretions in eating and drinking had undermined her health, and he was convinced too that the gossip about herself and Stewart was preying on her mind. Probably she had not taken quinine, for at Mariano on 21 April 1862, Mrs Livingstone went down with fever, a consequence of the long wait in the delta for *Gorgon*. Five days later, failing to respond to treatment, they moved her into the old and spacious Shupanga house. It was a single storey, whitewashed building with a tiled roof, lying before a semicircle of high bush, and facing across a sloping lawn onto the Zambezi and the majestic mountain mass of Morumbala.

Tragedy

The house which still stands today was, in 1862, unfurnished, and the men improvised a bed from three tea cases and a mattress. Treatment continued to be unavailing, and early on Sunday 27 April Livingstone saw that his wife was falling into coma; he sent for Kirk at 3 a.m. and the two men remained at her side until she died at 7 that evening. An hour before the end James Stewart was surprised and gratified to be summoned to the house, to commend the dying woman to God. After their prayers ended, Livingstone leaned over his wife's inert body, calling 'My dearie, my dearie. You are going to leave me. Are you resting in Jesus?'. He wrote later that Mary 'looked thoughtfully up. I think it meant yes'. Then the breathing ceased. The ensuing silence was broken by a question from Stewart. 'Yes', Livingstone answered, Mary's face had indeed assumed 'the very features and expression of her father'. That night Kirk and Stewart laid out the body, while Rae hammered a coffin together, and the others dug a deep grave beneath the baobab, close to where an officer in Owen's expedition of 1821* had been buried forty years earlier.

Stewart ended his account of Mary's death with a heartless 'It was altogether a day to remember, this long bright hot and clear Sabbath at Shupanga'. A little later he buried a packet of Livingstone's letters which Mary had lent him. He did so furtively and without being seen, at night in the woodland behind the house.[5] One he inadvertently retained.

At 1 p.m. next day Livingstone, supported by Charles, followed the coffin to the freshly prepared grave. Behind them walked three men who would serve as his own pall-bearers—Waller, Kirk and Young. Charles was struck during the service by the number of birds resting in the branches of the baobab, 'and some pretty canaries . . . singing sweetly in the adjoining trees'.[6] Livingstone declined a Portuguese offer to fire a salute over the grave.

Mary's death came as a staggering blow. Livingstone's written words reveal grief, incredulity, and a hard, gruff man's love for his wife. The sincerity of his letters belies the shocking impression made by the cold and factual account of Mary's death which appeared in *Narrative*. To Moffat he wrote 'I loved her when you gave her over to my charge and the longer I lived with her, the better I liked her'. Lady Murchison learnt that 'It will ease my achnig [sic] heart to tell you about my dear departed Mary Moffat, the faithful companion of eighteen years', and he ended 'I feel as

* Captain W. F. Owen led an expedition which surveyed the West and East African coasts between 1821 and 1826.

if I had lost all heart now'. He informed Mrs Fitch of the death of 'My beloved partner whom I loved and treasured so much for eighteen years', and went on 'she was a good wife, a good mother and a good but often fearful and dejected Christian. . . . Our love did not die with the honeymoon, though that was spent in hard work in the Bechuana country, and the last three short months after an unexpected separation of four years were as pleasant as any I had spent in her society . . . one is strong only until he is tried. I have a sore heart'. With this letter Livingstone enclosed some of Mary's hair 'cut off when in our last attempt to rouse her from the comatosed state we applied a blister to her head. It is all tangled, having been uncombed for some days'.[7]

He assured his friends that he was so depressed as to be willing to die. But there was no intention of questioning the workings of divine Providence: 'I feel greatly distressed at times and weep bitter tears', he wrote, and then added 'Though I hope it does not imply rebellion against God'. Nevertheless a note of bitterness crept into his correspondence as he realised that Mary's death could be blamed on Hardisty's neglect of *Pioneer*'s engines, which had prevented their leaving the fever-ridden delta on schedule.

Yet even through the grief, Livingstone's indomitable spirit presently emerged. 'I shall do my duty still but it is with a darkened horizon I set about it', he told Murchison, and his heart leaped as he saw the *Lady Nyassa* taking shape by the river's edge, looking 'strong and beautiful'. He did not allow misery to turn him from his dedication to 'duty', and within a day or so of Mary's funeral, employing an almost Nietzschean 'will to power', was hard at work, preparing the little ship for launching.

But after that April evening in 1862, he was often haunted, when depressed, by his own death. On 16 May 1862 he 'expressed a willingness to go'; that September he jotted down 'Am I to be a martyr in my own cause. . . . Am I to experience that this cause is to be founded on my sacrifice & cemented by my suffering . . . since the death of my Mary I often feel that I have not long to live but I will do my duty for all that'. Next month he confided to Maclear, 'I have been thinking a good deal since the departure of my loved one about the region whither she has gone', but he sounded more hopeful now and added, 'There will be work there as well as here'. Writing in his journal on 19 May he speculated on his own allotted resting place in dreamy words that became famous: 'I have often wished that it might be in some far-off still deep forest, where

I might sleep sweetly till the resurrection morn, when the trump of God will make all start up into the glorious and active second existence'.

And as the first anniversary of Mary's death came round he wrote in his log book: 'I feel often that I have not long to live and say "My dear children I leave you. Be manly Christians and never do a mean thing. Be honest to man and to the Almighty One".'[8]

18

River of Death

With the deaths of Mackenzie and Mrs Livingstone the Zambezi Expedition entered its final phase. Already the outlook was grim: *Pioneer* lay stranded at Shupanga, *Lady Nyassa* was not yet assembled, Portuguese hostility was increasing, while the Governor of Tete would presently announce that 'slave hunting was not contrary to Portuguese law'. Famine and war were devastating the Shire valley, the U.M.C.A. had proved a 'drag' on Livingstone, and the expedition's extended term was approaching its end.

The difference between success and flat failure depended on whether Livingstone could get *Lady Nyassa* onto the lake before Whitehall recalled the expedition, and by now the morale of its men at Shupanga had collapsed. Things were even worse at Magomero where the missionaries were reaping the whirlwind of the 'Bishop's War'. Dysentery swept through the station and carried off fifty Africans, while the crops failed so badly that three boys liberated by Mackenzie sold themselves into slavery for the sake of a meal. Thieving had become common; one day the altar cloth in the new chapel was stolen—but this mattered little since the priests could no longer celebrate the Eucharist as the Communion wine was finished.

Of greater concern was the gathering strength of the Yao, and by the end of February the missionaries knew they would either have to fight again or withdraw from Magomero. After prayerful discussions Procter decided to evacuate the station, and with a horde of followers he made his way towards the Shire with 'greater precipitancy than we ever intended'. It seemed somehow appropriate that somewhere along the line of retreat Mackenzie's crozier was broken. On 6 May the column stumbled into Mikorongo, close to the Makololo stronghold at Chibisa, and there they settled down, alternately comforted and distressed by the piratical Makololo.

Meanwhile work on *Lady Nyassa* was continuing at Shupanga and she was triumphantly launched on 23 June 1862. But the river was still too low to move her to Chibisa, and rather than waste time Livingstone decided to make another exploration of the Rovuma, although hindsight suggests it would have been wiser to go up-river in a light boat and begin the road past the cataracts. But success on the Rovuma might encourage the expedition, while, for Livingstone, it would diminish 'the pain which daily visits to the grave kept up' and allow him to forget the problems facing the U.M.C.A.

The second unsuccessful attempt on the Rovuma is valuable for providing three fresh vignettes of Livingstone. The first was drawn by Kirk: Livingstone, then 'more than usually unsociable,' was 'uncomfortable at sea and looks so. When the weather gets foul or anything begins to go wrong, it is well to give him a wide berth, most especially when he sings to himself. But the kind of air is some indication. If it is "The Happy Land", then look out for squalls and stand clear. If "Scots wha hae", then there is some grand vision of discovery before his mind. . . . But on all occasions humming of airs is a bad omen'. The second vignette comes from Captain Gardner of *Orestes* who reported 'During the last few days I had seen a great deal of Dr Livingstone and got to like him very much. He is modest, gentle and quiet and utterly fearless and thus inspires confidence among the native tribes.'* The third was an African chief's description of Livingstone as 'a short man with a bushy moustache, and a keen piercing eye, whose words were always gentle, and whose manners were always kind, whom as a leader it was a privilege to follow, and who knew the way to the hearts of all men'.

Kirk would not have agreed with so flattering a portrayal at the time, for there is a point when steadfastness of will thickens into senseless obduracy, and when mild hypomania becomes psychotic. So while Livingstone tried to force a rowing boat up the Rovuma, Kirk's journal shrilled with denunciations of his leader. On 13 September he wrote: 'His determination seems to amount to infatuation', on 18 September: 'The infatuation which blinds him, I cannot comprehend . . . It seems madness and to follow a man running such risks for the empty glory of geographical discovery is more than I would consent to . . . I can come to no other conclusion than that Dr L. is out of his mind.' And finally on 25 September: 'Dr L. is a most unsafe leader.'

* Gardner like so many of Livingstone's associates was later to turn against him.

River of Death

One other event on the Rovuma must be reported. On 19 September, as the expedition dragged their boats over a succession of shoals, tribesmen armed with muskets and bows crowded to the river bank and forbade them to go farther. Livingstone eventually obtained permission to pass with a gift of thirty yards of cloth. Yet soon the Africans began 'jumping about and pointing out their backsides at us as a sign of contempt', and then opened fire on the boats. 'There was not an instant to lose', wrote Kirk excitedly, 'I took aim and down with the fellow with the gun and [seeing a second African] ordered my coxswain to drop him, which he did instantly. Both fell stone dead.'

Such an event would not enhance Livingstone's reputation and he was careful not to refer to it in his letters, or even his diary. In *Narrative* he glossed over the incident by reporting that 'All our assailants bolted . . . save two, one of whom was about to discharge a musket and the other an arrow, when arrested by the fire of the second boat'. Few other men would have thought of using the euphemism 'arrested' for 'killed'. Yet strangely four years later, when he came back to the Rovuma for the third time, Livingstone was so wrapped up in the doctrine of providentialism that, reminded of the incident, he mused 'It may have been for the best that the English are thus known as people who can hit hard when unjustly attacked'.

* * * * *

Livingstone was desperately depressed on the way back to the Zambezi. At Quelimane he looked like a cat with his tail between his legs and at Kongone admitted feeling down-hearted.[1] He spent the Christmas of 1862 miserably at Shupanga, surrounded by Mary's memories, horrified by reports of famine in the Shire valley, and furious with Rae who, knowing they must come out again at the cataracts, had again refused to fit engines into *Lady Nyassa*. This meant that when they set off up river, she would be towed by *Pioneer*. Rae had replied to Livingstone's remonstrances with 'language before the men calculated to disturb order and subordination', but his co-operation was vital and Livingstone had given way, though not without noting in his confidential log that 'Rae has behaved with great duplicity, accusing Baines of having stolen his goods, then giving him a certificate that he had no reason to believe he had stolen any *public property*. I shall use him but be wary of trusting to him in the least degree'.[2] Hardisty was therefore correct in thinking he' his only puting up

207

with him until he can do without him, then he will spurn him like a dog'.[3]

Kirk by now was almost equally unco-operative, following a nasty scene at the Shire mouth when he asked permission to climb Morumbala. Livingstone initially agreed, then changed his mind. Nevertheless on Sunday 18 January, the day of rest, certain that no work would be expected, Kirk went off to climb the mountain. As he scrambled up he saw that Livingstone had sent the crew out wooding and was getting up steam preparatory to moving up river. There was nothing he could do but return. Livingstone received him with biting sarcasm. Next day Kirk wrote furiously in his diary, 'Dr Livingstone's word of honour will not have much value in my mind again . . . I have been *grossly misused*, Dr L. breaking away from his word. . . . His subsequent conduct in changing plans which completely tied us to the vessel, must have been simply some low sort of revenge.' His irritation with 'the hypocrite' was revived a little later when he wrote, 'Dr L. told me that there were to be no more Sunday excursions, a nice piece of cant piety from him, seeing that he had the natives wooding during the very time of Divine service'.

On 25 January 1863, with the two boats lashed together, they entered the Elephant Marsh, that headquarters of broken hopes and disillusionment. They spent the best part of a month there, for even in February the river was falling, and Kirk at last reached the obvious conclusion that a sailing yacht would have been far more useful in these shallow waters than any number of expensive steamers.

The last remnant of team-spirit among the expedition's members vanished in the marsh. Just how far discipline had relaxed is revealed by Rae's behaviour. He refused to mess in *Pioneer* and Livingstone, after 'feeling much perplexed as to what course to take', again gave in. 'Rae's turning rusty', noted Kirk, 'is the most serious thing for the Doctor', and he thought the chances of getting *Lady Nyassa* onto the lake were now 'infinitesimally small'.[4]

Livingstone's disjointed entries in a note-book bear witness to his gloom in the marsh. On 1 February 1863 he sighed, 'How to live a real Christian life amidst all the worry & cares of our condition'. The following day there is a brief entry, 'came to first sharp bend & failed'; next day: 'tried and failed'; on the 5th: 'failed'; on the 14th: 'Patience patience river rising a little'; 16 February: 'dragging vessel'; and so the entries continue in grievous frustration.

River of Death

He was appalled by the misery of the surviving Africans in this once thriving valley. Crops had failed and they were constantly harried by slavers. The stench of famine and death lay everywhere. The river banks were a frieze of horror, strewn with corpses, and only occasionally did they see a few emaciated figures staring vacantly at the ships, helpless in the face of disaster. From one survivor Charles learned that a single trader had carried off 450 women to the slave market, after killing all their menfolk.[5]

Rowley described the Shire as 'literally a river of death'. Too weak to dig graves the villagers threw their dead into the river. The crocodiles were so gorged with human food that they disregarded the bloated corpses floating down with the current in ghastly procession. Each morning the *Pioneer*'s paddles had to be cleared of their grisly catch of bodies. Charles calculated that a corpse passed him every three hours, while Rowley once saw a body of a little boy floating by with a tiny arm thrown up. He rescued the child and baptised him Moses before he died. 'He could not sink,' Rowley explained afterwards, 'his stomach was so inflated.'

Livingstone was tortured by the thought that this collage of suffering had resulted from his having opened a way into the Shire for a slave trade which was now protected by Portuguese law. All his efforts to improve the Africans' lot had done them nothing but harm; every new path he had pioneered had served to bring in Satan's forces. He did not doubt that the blame lay with the local Portuguese, and the old hope of the Rovuma route to the lake flitted into his mind again as he thought of obtaining a small motor boat with only a ten-inch draught. Although the project came to nothing, Livingstone was to use the Rovuma route when he re-entered Central Africa during his last journey.

On 16 March 1863, when *Pioneer* lay immobilised in the Elephant Marsh, an urgent request for help came from the missionaries at Mikorongo. Livingstone and Kirk hurried up by canoe and found that Scudamore had died some time before from cellulitis affecting the larynx, while Dickinson was recently dead from blackwater and Clarke racked by epileptic fits. This was the Doctor's first visit to the new station and he was highly critical of the missionaries' conduct. Already, when in a hypomanic mood, he had criticised the brethren for not learning Chinyanja, and for drinking too much, while on hearing that Waller had brought ten muskets for defence, he sneered 'I suspect that the missionaries don't believe with the venerable Dr Pusey that "their duty is to suffer not to do" '. Later, when the mood returned, he further denounced the priests for 'idling their time away catching butterflies',[6] and actually assured Mrs Moffat that the three Europeans who died at Magomero 'did so from sheer idleness'.

Leaving Kirk to attend to Clarke, Livingstone wearily returned to *Pioneer* on 19 March. He was fifty that day and rather pathetically noted 'this my wife said last year is my birthday'. Next week he finally got the boats up to Mikorongo, and on 10 April reached the cataracts. Livingstone immediately selected a camp site at Matitu where the Mwambezi stream runs into the Shire, and, suddenly optimistic again, laid out a vegetable garden to supply labourers working on the projected road. In it he 'sowed English peas, beans, lettuces and Kuruman parsnips, water melons. . . . Nasturtium seed, spinach and cabbage, and put up a box for bees'. He then turned to the task of road construction, surprised and delighted that Thornton had rejoined the expedition.

After his dismissal in 1859, Thornton had prospected for a legendary silver mine, explored the Luangwa valley and came back to recuperate at Tete on 2 February 1860, by coincidence at the same time as Livingstone returned there from the discovery of Lake Nyasa. He then declined the formal offer of a free passage home and went on to Zanzibar where he joined an expedition to Kilimanjaro. While thus employed, Livingstone learned that Whitehall recommended his reinstatement.

The Doctor already regretted Thornton's dismissal. He badly needed some demonstrable results from the expedition to lay before the Cabinet, and Thornton's geological findings would provide something more tangible than his own accounts of failure and Kirk's sketchy botanical records. Moreover Thornton's return would silence the mounting criticism at home about Livingstone's maladroit handling of his staff. Accordingly, while at Shupanga on his way to meet Bishop Mackenzie, Livingstone addressed a letter to Thornton, offering to recommend his re-engagement to the Government. But its wording lacked generosity; he gave no indication of acting on official advice or of willingness to withdraw his charges of laziness; instead the letter suggested that the offer was made from charity. Anxiety to get hold of Thornton's scientific material even led Livingstone to assure him that 'my recommendation would come with all the greater force if accompanied with a proper report of your geological researches for the use of H.M. Government'.

Thornton turned down the offer on the grounds that he had been discharged without proper enquiry, but next year he made his way back to the Zambezi and met Livingstone at Shupanga on 14 July 1862, when the re-engagement offer was renewed. Thornton now accepted, but on his own terms: he obliged Livingstone to withdraw his previous charges and allow him to work where he pleased without the necessity of submitting reports through him.

Thereafter, while Livingstone reconnoitred the Rovuma, Thornton 'geologized' until he followed *Pioneer* up the Shire in a small boat. He briefly went on board in the Elephant Marsh, but on 13 February, to Livingstone's disgust, pushed on to Mikorongo. There he volunteered to go with Rowley to Tete for food. He was so 'haggard and done up' on his return as to be unable to resist the next attack of malaria. He died on 21 April. His grave can still be seen beside the Mwambezi.

Although Livingstone later demonstrated his lack of charity by accounting Thornton a 'fool' for undertaking so hazardous a journey for the 'lazies', he was in a pliant mood at the time of Thornton's death and said he 'felt the blow extremely'. This change of mood is revealed in another incident. Two weeks earlier Livingstone had repelled Waller's criticism of thieving by the Chibisa Makololo, retorting angrily that they had probably learned it from the missionaries. But feeling ashamed of his bad temper, on the day Thornton died, he wrote Waller a charming apology for 'saying something to you which I ought not to have said, but I was too much of an ass to confess it. I ought not to have said that the Makololo began to capture sheep and goats under episcopal sanction. . . .' The *amende honorable* quite won Waller's heart and to the end of his life he was Livingstone's man. Thornton's death completed the demoralisation of Livingstone's companions. On 26 April 1863 Charles plucked up courage and asked permission to go home. Kirk did the same next day. Livingstone accepted both resignations, though ungraciously (yet privately wrote he felt 'lightened' by them). To Kirk he insisted 'in a very disagreeable manner' that he travelled home by the Cape rather than Aden which Kirk preferred. Next day Kirk was further distressed to find Livingstone's 'manner is still very distant', and ascribed it not to a cyclic temperament, but to his being 'savage at being jammed up here, the more so as it is his own doing', and then Kirk touched angrily on his leader's inability to 'get on with many whites under him. He cannot make them happy.'

But before the two men could leave the cataracts, Livingstone developed severe dysentery. Kirk attended him devotedly, noting with surprise the patient's unexpected craving for native beer and tinned sardines. Only on 17 May was Livingstone able to attend to business, but he was weak and 'quite disheartened'. Procter thought him 'more pulled down & older all of a sudden'.

Kirk departed on 19 May 1863 with Charles, and on 7 October landed at Southampton, his smouldering dislike of Livingstone rekindled by the last churlish behaviour and a misapprehension that Livingstone had reported unfavourably on his service. To James Stewart, Kirk's pen dripped gall as he wrote that Dr Livingstone 'is about as ungrateful and [slippery a] mortal* as I ever came in contact with, and although he would be grievously offended to think that anyone doubted his honesty, I am sorry to say that I do . . . I don't think he would exactly say what he knew was untrue, but for all practical purposes the result is the same, and in him I believe all kindly feelings to be absolutely extinct.' Kirk's bitterness was unabated a year later when he announced, surely unfairly, that Livingstone 'would give all for a C.B. or, better, a K.C.B.'.

Such venom was unjustified. Livingstone in fact soon passed into a mood of energy and optimism, and he behaved generously to Kirk after his departure. While he dropped down river to the coast, the Doctor was writing to him, 'I am sure I wish you every success in your future life. You were always a right hand to me and I never trusted you in vain. God bless and prosper you'. Letters reflecting Livingstone's concern continued to follow Kirk: 'I feel naturally very anxious about you and the rest', he wrote on 8 August 1863, and assured him after returning from the Shire Highlands: 'I was very anxious about you all and often thought of you during our tramp'. It was during this 'tramp' that the Doctor paid his second-in-command the highest compliment in his power, for, as he explained in *Narrative*, 'our wish to commemorate the name of Dr Kirk induced us . . . to call the whole chain of mountains from the west of the Cataracts up to the north end of the Lake, "Kirk's Range" '. After his own return to England Livingstone announced that Kirk 'never once failed to do his duty like a man', and used his influence to obtain for him the post which led to Kirk's distinguished career in Zanzibar.

Dr Livingstone was beset by requests to quit during that last week of April 1863. Dr Meller of *Pioneer* next asked to leave, explaining that his

---

* Kirk's usually clear writing is blurred here, perhaps by his inner fury; the passage appears to read 'slippery tury and mortal'.[7]

three years' contract was about to expire, but Livingstone balked at the thought of losing a second medical man, and coldly explained that Meller's sick leave during 1862 could not be counted as contract service. In fact he did not allow Meller to leave for another three months. As we have come to expect, Livingstone's denunciations of Meller, when hypomanic, reflected his contempt for anyone who failed him: he blurted out that he 'got into a mortal funk on poor Thornton's death and went about telling each of the men in turn that unless invalided at once he, (M), would not be responsible for his life'.

All through May the cataracts road was pushed slowly forward through difficult wooded country intersected by deep gullies. There now only remained with the expedition Rae, Gunner E. D. Young, four white sailors from *Pioneer*, some Johanna labourers working on the road and a handful of the Makololo. Livingstone felt relief in having fewer mouths to feed and no one to criticise him, and provisions could be eked out until further supplies reached Matitu.

19

Recall

One of the cherished facets of the Livingstone legend insists that he was on the point of carrying *Lady Nyassa* to the lake when, on 3 July 1863, he received a despatch from the British Government recalling the expedition, and that only this prevented its final success. Nothing could be farther from the truth. By then Livingstone had already conceded defeat and ordered the dismantling of *Lady Nyassa* to cease, and was in fact relieved by the recall since it meant that Whitehall would bear some of the onus for failure.

As early as 17 April 1863 he had noted that 'if the government looks on this as I do we may expect to be withdrawn'. Next week he told Waller, 'I should not wonder in the least to be recalled', and at the end of the month drafted a despatch for Russell stating that the desolation in the Shire valley made retirement advisable and suggesting that 'it will be better to screw the steamer together again and sell her in India'.[1] By 1 May he had tidied up this draft, so that the relevant part read: 'looking at the fearful desolation that has followed in our footsteps, should the same system be likely to prevail, will it not be better to screw her together again, navigate her over to India and hand her over to the authorities.'[2]

There is also evidence that Livingstone actually welcomed the despatch. He told Waller, 'I had come to the conclusion that no good could be done by the expedition while the [Portuguese] were allowed to follow in our footsteps and spoil all by their slave forays'. Two days later he informed Kirk, 'our recall has not been unlooked for by me', and even told Moffat that 'our recall came as a relief from suspense'.[3]

For by mid-June 1863 provisions were becoming scarce at the cataracts. Livingstone, believing he might find food on the lakeshore, accordingly set off to retrieve the gig and search round the lake. He discovered the gig burnt out, however, and returned to *Pioneer* for one of her boats, only to find that Bishop Tozer, Mackenzie's successor, had arrived at Mikorongo, and with him carried the anticipated instructions of recall.

Posterity has set up Tozer as one of the villains of the Livingstone saga. He is displayed as a mean-spirited cleric who brought down the final curtain on all the hopes and aspirations borne to Africa by the Zambezi Expedition. Certainly Tozer was very different from Mackenzie. An ugly pocked face was topped by flaming red hair. Instead of a crozier, he carried an umbrella, and jauntily affected a sailor's blue jacket and holland trousers. The general effect of Tozer was depressing. He quite lacked his predecessor's radiant spirit; his actions were governed by logic rather than emotion.

Bishop Tozer was an untravelled man of thirty-three when suddenly translated from a rural rectory at Burgh-cum-Winthorpe to Central Africa. He landed at Kongone from H.M.S. *Orestes* on 8 May 1863 and there received 'very unsatisfactory reports' about the U.M.C.A.. On the way up-river he paused to inspect Morumbala (where he found Livingstone's glowing description 'extravagant'),[4] and reached Mikorongo on 26 June.

Tozer saw his duty clearly. He had been sent out to advise on the unhappy state of the mission, like an eminent specialist called in to give his opinion about a seriously sick patient. He had already made up his mind about the diagnosis: all the mission's troubles, he believed, stemmed from Livingstone's 'war-like advices' and Mackenzie's militant policy. As for treatment, this too had been chosen. It was to be surgical. To Captain Gardner, Tozer confided his intention of withdrawing the mission to a safer place—which meant near the coast.[5]

The surviving missionaries at Mikorongo greeted his views with anguish. Rather than retirement down the Zambezi they advocated advance, preferably to Mbame's kraal on the site of modern Blantyre. Tozer rejected this advice. As for Livingstone's stand against the slavers, Tozer was decidedly on the side of the Portuguese. He denounced the forcible liberation of slaves as 'highway robbery', since they were the property of the man-hunters at Tete, and when taking a service at the mission, tactlessly coupled a prayer for Queen Victoria with one for the King of Portugal.

As Tozer waited for Livingstone's return from the highlands, he re-examined his problem with clinical detachment. He had opened the despatch he was carrying, and learnt of the expedition's recall, which

215

would further prejudice the mission's viability through loss of contact with the outside world thus far provided by the Royal Navy. Secondly he appreciated that although four of the mission staff were already lying in their graves, there was little to show for their sacrifice. Not a single convert had been made nor any cotton bought, famine reigned where crops had flourished, the country previously considered ripe for evangelisation was now ravaged by inter-tribal war, and such vast amounts of money and goods had been squandered by the mission that its supporters at home were growing uneasy. The Universities at Durham and Dublin had already dissociated themselves from the venture after learning of Mackenzie's campaign, and the only solution now, Tozer felt, lay in withdrawing the mission to a more accessible site—like Morumbala.

On 4 July he went up to meet Livingstone in *Pioneer*. The short interview was polite but strained. Livingstone thought Tozer 'a good and courteous man', but counselled against retreating to Morumbala. He argued that this would abandon the Shire Africans to the slavers, and that Morumbala lacked people to teach, while the mission would fall under Portuguese control and become subject to 'their acknowledged immorality'.[6] Finally, and less convincingly, Livingstone said that a mission there would intrude on a future Portuguese missionary field and lead to what he quaintly called 'eggregious schismatics'.

Later, Livingstone admitted he could not collect all his thoughts together at the interview and had vaguely agreed that a move to Morumbala might be termed prudent.[7] This slip convinced Tozer that he had won him over to his plan. It was only when Livingstone considered the consequences of the move more clearly, and learned that Tozer intended to take a mere handful of 'teachable' boys to Morumbala, that he perceived the scheme to be cowardly, heartless and dishonourable.

Horace Waller was equally incensed by the bishop's policy, and determined to get the women and children out of the slavers' clutches. When opposed by Tozer he resigned from the U.M.C.A., and on his own responsibility shepherded these helpless waifs and strays down to the coast and eventually to the Cape where their descendants still live. Livingstone supported Waller's stand, and added a few youths to the party.

Apart from this gesture, Livingstone could do no more than fulminate about Tozer's 'dastardly retreat', first to Morumbala and subsequently to Zanzibar, during a prolonged excitable period, even telling him he would make him regret it 'till his dying day'. He was scathing about Tozer in *Narrative*, writing that he had 'acted as St Augustine would have done, had he located himself on one of the Channel Islands, when sent to christianize the natives of Central England'. But when he revised the proofs, being depressed, Livingstone had second thoughts: he told Murray 'I am at a loss what to say about Tozer [though] it wont do to say he is a good pious donkey'. Yet he eventually allowed the insulting passage to stand. Tozer's name was added to those who had ruined the divine plan for Africa. As late as 1872 we find Livingstone ranting that because of Tozer's retreat his diocese was occupied by the 'Lord of all Evil', while Christian priests from the safety of a 'mere chaplaincy of the Zanzibar Consulate' spent their time peering in awe through telescopes at the heathen mainland from which they had been ejected.

In all honesty one ought to take Tozer's side in this dispute. But somehow our sympathies always lie with Livingstone. Tozer took a logical and brave decision when he withdrew the missionaries successively to Morumbala and Zanzibar, and he was vindicated by their subsequent advance to Lakes Tanganyika and Nyasa. But the world prefers ideals and lost causes to logic, and Bishop Tozer paid grievously for his dialectical resolve. His cautious policy may have saved lives and money but it made no appeal to the evangelistic fervour of Great Britain, or to the mission's financial supporters. And Livingstone's venomous criticism marked him as a missionary who had cravenly refused to put his faith to the test. Tozer's health eventually broke down; he resigned from the see of Zanzibar in 1873, and, after briefly filling bishoprics in Jamaica and Honduras, was invalided to England, helpless and miserable. For years he battled against increasing paralysis and loss of speech. Death came to him in 1899 as a merciful release. No less than Mackenzie must he be accounted a martyr to the Christian cause in Africa.

* * * * *

Tozer's lack of tact was demonstrated when handling the official despatch he carried: from Mikorongo he forwarded it to the cataracts by an artisan who hailed the ship with 'no more pay for you "Pioneer" chaps. I brings the letter as says it'. Livingstone was more affected by the method in which his instructions were delivered than by their contents. For this open despatch had been freely discussed at Cape Town and among the U.M.C.A. missionaries before it reached him, so one sympathises with his indignant protest to Earl Russell* for the 'very unmerited humiliation' to which he and his companions had been exposed.

The despatch in any case was brusquely worded. After paying brief tribute to Livingstone's difficulties it stated that 'Her Majesty's Government cannot however conceal from themselves that the results to which they had looked from the expedition under your superintendence have not been realised'; it continued with a reference to the expedition's 'heavy charge' and added that staff salaries would cease on arrival in England or on 31 December 1863, whichever was earlier. It next directed Livingstone to hand over *Pioneer* to the Navy as quickly as possible; then, as though an afterthought, provided him with a little latitude, 'if you should, however, think that advantage would result from your postponing the final withdrawal'.

Waller felt Whitehall's decision far more strongly than Livingstone. He was haunted by the thought of Christian influence in the Shire valley being replaced by the devil's, and summed up his feelings in words of protest which ring through the years: 'why don't the very rocks groan on those beautiful hills—the lamp is flickering and soon enough it will be dark enough, aye, even for the Portuguese slave-trade! Oh, how I dread all this. . . .'

The British Cabinet has earned itself obloquy for withdrawing the expedition, but in fact there was little option. Just as in 1857 the Government reacted to public opinion by launching the venture, so in 1863 it responded to general demands for its recall. For Livingstone had fallen from his pedestal. His ecstatic account of Central Africa was disproved, while the divinely revealed 'God's Highway' had turned out to be impassable. His behaviour, too, had made a host of enemies among the relatives and friends of Bedingfeld, Baines, Thornton, Kirk and Stewart. Ten clerics publically castigated him for having liberated slaves at gun point after Rowley accused Livingstone of hunting 'for slaving parties in every direction',[8] and of instigating Mackenzie's war. The Royal Navy expressed concern at its losses when provisioning a fruitless project on the Zambezi, while Washington finally withdrew his wavering support from what he described as 'desultory operations'. Criticism was particularly trenchant at the Cape, whence one of Baines's friends wrote home that 'everyone in this country now looks on Dr Livingstone with distrust'.[9]

* Lord John became Earl Russell in 1861.

Things were even worse on the diplomatic front, for Whitehall was gravely embarrassed by Lisbon's denunciations of Livingstone's conduct. Even his erstwhile friends in Mozambique referred to him as 'a rascal, scoundrel and hypocrite',[10] and, according to Stewart, 'spit when his name is mentioned'.

The general disenchantment with Livingstone found final expression in a savage attack launched in *The Times* on 20 January 1863. It included a passage reading: 'We were promised cotton, sugar and indigo . . . and, of course, we got none. We were promised trade; and there is no trade, although we have a Consul at £500 a year. We were promised converts to the Gospel, and not one has been made . . .' and so it went on column after column. This made a tremendous impact. The feeling grew that Livingstone, after imposing himself upon the public, had somehow defrauded it. And only two weeks later Russell trimmed his sails to the shifting gusts of general opinion, and composed the despatch recalling the expedition.

*   *   *   *   *

After receiving the official notice of recall, any other man but Livingstone might have rested comfortably at the cataracts until the river rose sufficiently to allow him to take his two ships to the sea. But its arrival coincided with a euphoric phase, and the very next day Livingstone decided to occupy the time by resuming his search for food on Lake Nyasa; more particularly he hoped to discover whether a river flowed into its northern extremity, and to establish the slavers' routes and the number of their victims. Feeling 'about half a horse-power stronger' at the prospect of exploration, he set off up the escarpment.

'I suspect Dr. L. has gone to the Lake again, seeing that his only chance is to return with something new in his hand', mused Kirk in England when he heard the news. But how little he understood his man: the new journey was impelled still by the old clear motive of alleviating Africa's misery.

Livingstone took with him twenty Makololo and Shupanga men, together with porters to carry a small boat. They launched it on the upper Shire, but five of the Shupanga hands 'wishing to show how much cleverer they were' promptly jumped into the boat, which overturned. Livingstone watched it swept over the upper cataract with remarkable restraint. 'It was evidently so well meant', he wrote, 'and the fellows looked so crestfallen, the case was like that of a little child trying to bring a vessel to Papa and dropping it, [so] I could not be angry.' He continued his journey on foot. With him on this rapid march he took the ailing steward of *Pioneer*, Thomas Ward, supposing that his anaemia would benefit from the exercise —and strangely enough this rude therapy turned out to be effective. One must, however, sympathise with the poor man, who 'strove manfully to keep up but when we halted he was often to be seen spread out like a dead frog and at last fell behind confessing that his legs were bad'.[11]

For two months Livingstone was once again the man of 1854. He begins his account of the journey in *Narrative* with 'It was with light hearts [that] we turned our faces north', and from the following chapters we gain the impression, not of a frustrated explorer, but of a squire examining his ancestral domain. They marched beside the Shire from Matope and then up the Rivirivi valley, and through Balaka, Ncheu and Gowa. Livingstone continued past the present Mua mission to reach the lake shore close to Ntakataka, where he was well received by chief Katosa. He next followed the route of the modern railway line to Salima, and beyond to Chitanda. Livingstone, happy to be alone among Africans, was continually euphoric in his observations. The natives seemed far less ugly than before, their harsh music no longer irritated him, and he thought the valley of the Livulezi 'formed as beautiful a landscape as could be seen on the Thames'.

After paying some patronising attention to the local fishing industry at Chia, Livingstone came a little wearily on 10 September 1863 to the busy slave emporium of Nkhotakota which had greatly prospered since his previous visit. Here he had hoped 'to have lived and help to stop this wretched traffic'. On the edge of the town he seated himself 'under a magnificent wild fig-tree', which still stands today in the U.M.C.A. compound,* and waited confidently for hospitality from the slavers living there; and, after hustling away his old acquaintance ben Habib, with a slave train, Jumbe's lieutenants did treat him courteously.

Nkhotakota is surely the most sinister of towns. This place, made by the slave trade, remains utterly evil. The memory of old peril still lurks in the dark labyrinthine passages between its huts. The wails of driven slaves even now linger in the town's stale air and every evening return to screaming life as flights of bats dart by against the darkening sky, like regiments

---

* Though its Livingstone association is disputed by other trees named for Marenga and Jumbe, the dynastic title of the district's ruler.

of anguished spirits. A tortuous track runs past the sprawling huts to the old dhow harbour on the lake. This *Via dolorosa* of Malawi is dark and gloomy, being overhung by great kapok and mango trees, planted last century by Arab man-hunters, and saturated now with the foul fetor and matter of bats. It is part of the old slave trail that ran from Cazembe to the sea. At night this haunted way lies apprehensive and deserted, but by day is thronged by wandering people: women bargain noisily over fish rotting in the sun; the men, holding hands like casual lovers, stroll by chattering ceaselessly together, examining wares displayed by hawkers, strumming marimbas or listening to transistors perched uncomfortably on bony shoulders. As they pass they stir up a black dust which was powdered long ago by the dragging feet of countless slaves, and it rises like a cloud of monstrous memories which are past European knowing or experience.

Yet what is most alive in this malevolent town remains its association with Livingstone. His remembered presence has imparted an unexpected lustre to it; and there it is very easy for an imaginative eye to recreate his sturdy figure trudging up the gentle slope with the ship's steward in 1863.

A few days' march west along the slave trail brought Livingstone through Kasungu to the watershed overlooking the swamps in which he was destined to die. He heard there of a Lake Bemba or Bangweulu lying ten days' march to the west, from which a great river, the Luapula, flowed northwards to another Lake, Mweru. For two days Livingstone hesitated, longing to go forward, well aware that he stood on the brink of brilliant discoveries which would have indeed given him 'something new in his hand'. But he remembered too his obligation to take *Pioneer* down river with the rains and feared that 'Lord Russell meant to take away my salary' if he delayed.

So on 29 September he turned back, deviating from his old route when east of Kasungu hill. At Molamba he came again to Lake Nyasa, 'had a delicious bath', and beyond revisited chief Katosa to present him with a marine officer's coat. Then the party returned through Ncheu and down the Lisungwe valley to *Pioneer*. The gruelling march left the Doctor with sun-stroke, tinnitus, and deafness, but he announced proudly he 'never did so much and that in the hot season'.

Feeling 'much chagrin' at not having marched westwards from the watershed, Livingstone waited two months for the river to rise. Only on 19 January 1864 could he take the two steamers downstream. With their passing all hope drained from the country where he had expected to found a British settlement.* He stopped briefly to pick up remnants of Mackenzie's flock, and there was time for another stop to visit Mary's grave, where he gathered a handful of leaves from the great baobab for Agnes. 'I am sorry to leave her dust in this land of slaves', he wrote, 'but she was free & will rise at the sound of the trump of God.'[12] On 12 February *Pioneer* reached the coast; there the Doctor grimly handed her over to a Naval officer, and took up his quarters in *Lady Nyassa*.

*   *   *   *   *

Livingstone's immediate concern was to dispose of *Lady Nyassa*, and he persuaded the captain of a cruiser to tow her to Mozambique. But the only prospective purchasers were Portuguese who would use the ship as a slaver so Livingstone went on to Zanzibar. Again no suitable buyer appeared and almost casually he decided to take the little ship to Bombay for sale. He left Zanzibar on the last day of April 1864.

Nothing during his lifetime approaches the cold-blooded audacity which made Livingstone cross the Indian Ocean in so frail a vessel. She was never intended for a voyage of over two thousand miles on the high seas and could carry coal for only eight days steaming, far less than the most optimistic estimate for reaching Bombay. So Livingstone would have to rely largely on sail, and if delayed until the monsoon broke in early June, *Lady Nyassa* could scarcely hope to survive its wild seas.

The crew was a scratch one, consisting of three European seamen (two of whom were sick for most of the voyage and the third mutinous), seven Shupanga men and the two boys rescued from the mission, Chuma and Wikatani. Rae was supposed to have looked after the engines, but changed his mind and announced his intention of working instead with a sugar planter on Johanna. Livingstone said goodbye to this last member of his staff with unconcealed scorn, telling Maclear that he 'left us out of sheer terror'. There was no time to replace him.

The voyage to Bombay occupied forty-five days, but it is dismissed very briefly in *Narrative*. Livingstone's journals, however, reveal that during this time he was a prey to constant anxiety. For days on end the little ship lay becalmed; then she would be lashed by tumultuous storms. On 26 May even Livingstone lost heart, and turned away to seek shelter in

---

* It drew heart again when E. D. Young brought another group of missionaries back to the ake a decade later.

Aden, but almost at once a favourable wind blew up and he changed back on course. On 12 June 1864 his courage was rewarded—and his ability as a navigator demonstrated—when the Indian coast was sighted. Next day *Lady Nyassa* crept into Bombay's bustling harbour. As he recalled, 'the vessel was so small, that no one noticed our arrival'.

He spent only a short time in India, for most of its as guest of Sir Bartle Frere, Governor of Bombay, who became a close friend. Livingstone's hopes for Africa revived during the stay when a group of merchants offered to finance the establishment of a British settlement on the Somali coast, and all thoughts of selling the *Lady Nyassa* were abandoned. But the promised settlement never materialised and later the vessel was disposed of for a mere £2,300, and even this was soon lost when the bank, in which it was deposited, failed.

In Bombay Livingstone paid off the ship's crew, found temporary shelter for the mission boys, borrowed money for his passage and embarked for home on 24 June 1864. At Suez he examined the canal then under construction and reached London on 23 July. The Zambezi Expedition had become a part of African history.

The great design was an admitted failure, and an anticlimax to all Livingstone had previously accomplished and predicted. Russell rightly accounted it 'a melancholy story—the expedition leaves the slave trade stronger and more prevalent'. Yet there were tangible results to show for Livingstone's years of trial. The Shire river, Lake Nyassa and the Rovuma had been explored, while British attention was drawn to the slavers' ravages and the strategic value of the Shire valley. And the tide of Christian advance had only temporarily receded. Within the next few decades all that Livingstone had hoped for was consummated; the shores of Lake Malawi would be dotted with mission settlements, a steamer plied her waters, licit commerce flourished, the slavers were expelled and the lake people lived under British protection. For good or evil Livingstone's demonstration of a political vacuum was a factor in initiating the 'Scramble for Africa'. The Zambezi Expedition may have been a grievous disappointment, but it moulded the future of a sub-continent.

20

Newstead

Livingstone's welcome in England during 1864 lacked the rapture of 1856. People remembered that last homecoming as the morning star of a day which had never dawned; now they accepted the Zambezi Expedition as a costly failure. Livingstone was a giant with a limp, and anyway there were several rival hero-explorers now in Britain. The exploits of Burton, Speke, Grant and Baker in their search for the Nile sources had produced far more brilliant results than anything accomplished by the expedition to the Zambezi.

Few banquets were given for Livingstone in 1864, requests to lecture were rare, no invitation came from the palace, and even the Geographical Society's welcome was tepid. Lord Russell was particularly cold, having learned that the Doctor had broken Portuguese law when he smuggled his waifs past the Zambezi custom house. Kirk also greeted his return without warmth; it seemed only Murchison's friendship had survived.

Indeed, immediately after Livingstone's arrival in London, Murchison carried him off to a reception at Lord Palmerston's. Following the Prime Minister's cue, polite society opened its doors to Livingstone, and an anxiety to expose the iniquities of the Portuguese slave trade 'in the proper quarter' made him dally in London for a week. On 25 July, in a hastily purchased dress suit, Livingstone dined at Lord Dunmore's before going on to a reception at the Duchess of Wellington's to meet half the country's peerage. Next day was divided between his publisher and frigid officials at the Foreign Office. On 29 July Livingstone called on Gladstone who was 'very affable', and went on to 'a very agreeable party' at the Palmerstons. He did not, however, find time to call on Dr Tidman, although the two men exchanged curt notes, and later on Livingstone found it inconvenient to accept an invitation to speak at one of the L.M.S. meetings in Exeter Hall.[1]

He escaped at last to Scotland on 31 July 1864, but his happiness at the prospect of joining the children was marred by an increasing concern for his eldest son, Robert.

Born early in 1846, Robert was a spirited child whose conduct soon worried his parents. 'He is excessively obstinate at times', Livingstone wrote of the four year-old boy, 'it often causes us sorrow.' Perhaps because he was psychologically marked by inherited genes, Robert exhibited furious tantrums, and felt so deep a repugnance for any form of mental exertion that his father prophesied his only hope of employment lay in 'cab driving or the hurdy gurdy'.

Mrs Livingstone on her own could not control the boy; but her departure for the Zambezi in 1861 made things worse by removing the last remaining domestic prop, and his behaviour became still more unruly. His mother had confided him to the care of a board of trustees and the elderly maiden aunts at Hamilton. These two prim spinsters were so shocked by their nephew's conduct that they never afterwards mentioned him by name.[2] The trustees too lacked imagination; they overruled Robert's desire to join the Navy, which might have instilled some discipline, and his peccadilloes continued. When Rae rejoined the expedition he let it be known that Robert was 'a wild blackguard'.

After his wife's death Livingstone decided that his eldest son had 'a deal of the vagabond nature of his father' and must join him in Africa. He sent him the passage money, but Robert promptly squandered it.[3] 'I don't think Robert is to be trusted', Livingstone sighed,[4] but 'Paraffin' Young* still did, for the boy wheedled the fare out of him.[5] He was quite destitute when he landed at the Cape, but succeeded in working his way to Durban.

But Robert came no further; after Kirk quit the expedition Livingstone's letters followed him down river, imploring him to make contact with his son, and assist him in obtaining an onward passage, a charge which Kirk failed to fulfil. The Doctor's concern was all the more disquieting since he had learned of his being criticised as an irresponsible parent, and that a 'cousin accused me of being deficient in my duty to my children while engaged here in this expedition'. Thereafter Livingstone heard little of Robert until the July of 1864, when he received a pencilled note from him announcing he had enlisted in the American Federal Army.

---

* Sir James Young, chemist and originator of the paraffin industry, had known Livingstone at the Andersonian and remained a life-long friend.

225

It appeared that after reaching Natal, Robert made his way to Isipingo where he knew Robert Moffat junior had gone to live. Unfortunately Uncle Robert had just died but his aunt helped him with a little money. Then, having missed a chance of accompanying Tozer to the Zambezi, Robert made his way back to Cape Town where he lodged uncomfortably in the Sailors' Home. There, according to the intolerant Kirk, he was 'doing no good and they will be glad to see him shipped off somewhere else'[6]—which was exactly what happened. Robert worked his passage in a brig to Boston and found war raging between the States. He was promptly drugged, kidnapped, and forcibly enlisted under an assumed name in the 3rd New Hampshire Regiment of the American Army. So the note to his father was headed 'Rupert Vincent, N.H. Vols., 10th Army Corps, Virginia', and told him that he was in a hospital near Petersburg, suffering from exposure and battle fatigue.

We have a photograph of Robert Livingstone taken just before this time. Troubled eyes and a dour mouth, inherited from his father, give him a disgruntled expression, but there is also gentleness about the face. That trait came out in the assurance he gave in the letter that 'I have never hurt anyone knowingly in battle, have always fired high, and in that furious madness which accompanies a bayonet charge and which seems to possess every soldier, I controlled my passion and took the man who surrendered prisoner'. Robert went on to say that 'My craving for travelling is not yet satisfied', and then penitently added that 'I have changed my name, for I am convinced that to bear your name here would lead to further dishonour to it'. The sad letter ended with

'God is punishing me for what I have done,
  I remain,
    your quondam son, Robert.'

Livingstone's fears for Robert were now immeasurably increased, and expressed in mordant words. He wrote that his son 'will in all probability be hewn down like so many others',[7] and feared that his 'bad boy . . . will be made manure of for those bloody fields'. He felt relieved in October to learn that Robert had been captured and hospitalised first at Petersburg, then at Salisbury. The Doctor pulled what strings he could, and devoutly hoped that his son would be released, and even join him on the third journey to Africa which he was planning. 'If only I had Robert (if alive) home to go with me', he told Maclear, 'I should do pretty well.' But Kirk snorted that though 'I had always thought he [Livingstone] had tried the effect of relatives on Expeditions enough, it seems he is game for another.'

By June 1865 Livingstone began to fear the worst and observed gloomily that 'Robert we shall never hear of again in this world I fear; but the Lord is merciful, and just, and right in all His ways. He would hear the cry for mercy in the hospital at Salisbury.' Three years later he was still without definite news of Robert's fate, and only in 1871 did he learn for certain from Stanley of his death.

Robert had in fact been wounded and captured during an engagement at Laurel Hill in Virginia on 7 October 1864. He died in hospital at Salisbury, North Carolina, in the following December. They buried him in a mass grave. After hearing these details Livingstone requested Stanley to arrange for his son's body to be removed to the cemetery at Gettysburg.[8] But Robert Livingstone still rests at Salisbury, in a grave whose surroundings have been made into a beautiful remembrance garden. His sorrowing father could only find solace from the thought that his son had died in the worthy cause of emancipating the American slaves.

*   *   *   *   *

Livingstone rejoined his children on 3 August at Hamilton. Agnes, now sixteen, delighted him by being 'quite grown up and very good', and he decided she must house-keep for him in London, even making enquiries for a small cottage. Anna Mary was a charming little girl of five, whose tongue seemed 'the real perpetual motion', though she was rather frightened of her father whom she had never seen before. Oswell was delicate, and Thomas too, suffering from haematuria—bleeding from the bladder—probably the result of bilharzia, though Livingstone blamed it on the 'abominably drained school in Scotland'.

Livingstone went presently to consult the eminent surgeon, James Syme, in Edinburgh about his piles. Syme advised surgery; but the bleeding had stopped, Livingstone felt embarrassed at the thought of the undignified operation and deluded himself that 'this complaint had been my safety valve', and he declined the operation. It was a grievous decision since his death in 1873 can be attributed to haemorrage from piles which had been irritated by chronic dysentery.

On 17 August Livingstone paid a three-day visit to the Duke of Argyll's seat, Inveraray. He was delighted by the warmth of the Highland tenants' welcome, and by the fishing too when he took eleven salmon one morning. On leaving, Livingstone pronounced this 'the most charming visit I ever paid'. He refused Lord Kinnaird's invitation to Perth which the Queen was visiting since he did not 'like to appear running after royalty', but did take advantage of the offer of a free steamer trip to visit the Livingstone ancestral home, on the island of Ulva. Memories of his family still lingered there, the weather was fine and invigorating, and he was intrigued to see the poor remains of the bothy where his grandfather lived. The cottage in which the Doctor stayed on the island is still pointed out to its rare visitors.

He went back to Hamilton before the end of the month to prepare the speech which he had been persuaded to deliver to the British Association in Bath. On the way he perturbed James Stewart by calling on him in Glasgow to pick his brains for the coming book, and left him worrying whether he had been justified in traducing Livingstone's character.

Dreading the ordeal of 'public spouting' again, Livingstone installed himself at 13, The Circus, in Bath. The town was agog, for the two most controversial of the Victorian explorers, Speke and Burton, were to address the Association next day on the Nile sources. They were violently antagonistic on the subject of this geographical enigma; Speke (rightly) judged Lake Victoria to be the true source, while Burton insisted it was the Lusize River flowing out of Lake Tanganyika. Livingstone disliked both men, but the issue revived his interest in the Nile.

Unfortunately the Nile debate never took place for Speke went out shooting beforehand, and when the audience assembled, lay dead with a gaping wound in his chest. His gun had gone off as he climbed a wall, but many people suspected he had preferred suicide to meeting Burton in public debate.

Four days later Livingstone delivered his own address to a gathering of 2,300 people. To his embarrassment, he was supported on the platform by the controversial Bishop Colenso, whose heretical views, it was assumed, he shared. But his speech was well received: after proclaiming the accomplishments of the Zambezi Expedition (which Dr Meller condemned as 'a series of lies')[9] he launched himself into a scathing criticism of the Portuguese administration in Mozambique, which was repeated in *Narrative*.

From Bath Livingstone journeyed to Newstead with Agnes on 26 September 1864, to stay with William Webb, an old friend of Mabotsa days. The next seven months turned out to be among the happiest in his life.

Newstead Priory, usually spoken of as an Abbey, was founded in 1171 and handed over at the Dissolution to Sir John Byron who converted the buildings for domestic use, retaining the ruined church and handsome cloister. Lord Byron, the poet, inherited the estate in 1798, and a subsequent owner built a new wing which included the Sussex Tower. After being briefly considered as a residence for Edward, Prince of Wales (his father finally decided instead on Sandringham), the Abbey was bought by Webb on his return from Africa. Now Livingstone was lodged in a comfortable suite in the Sussex tower. His room, which was used as an air-warden's post during the last war, can still be seen.

Webb's feeling for interior decoration was bizarre: he cluttered the Abbey and even the cloisters with hunting trophies (some of the lion skins are still in place), so that Agnes sometimes thought the whole house was inhabited by stuffed animals. But Livingstone greatly enjoyed the comforts of this country home. As his cares dropped away, he romped with his host's children and amused them by inventing ridiculous names for his enemies. He ate hugely, topping off breakfast with scones, jam and clotted cream, and he grew positively stout.

Out of doors Livingstone interested himself in Webb's experiments in fish-spawning, and felt 'a foot taller' when he shot five rabbits. He amazed the Webbs by the breadth of his religious views: when Agnes was confirmed into the Anglican church, the Doctor took communion with her and afterwards accepted the Sacrament every Sunday in Newstead's little chapel.

Livingstone welcomed many friends to the Abbey. Charles arrived one day with his wife. His mental difficulties had recurred, but he seemed to be improved by working with Livingstone on his new book. Livingstone in return credited Charles with joint authorship of *Narrative* and used his waning influence to secure him a consulship at Fernando Po where he somewhat reluctantly went. Dr Kirk too spent some days at Newstead and the unhappy breach with Livingstone was temporarily healed. One of the Prime Minister's confidants, a Mr Abraham Hayward Q.C., also came down at the end of January, carrying an enquiry from Lord Palmerston as to whether 'there was something he could do' for Livingstone. Probably a decoration or a pension was in Palmerston's mind, but the unworldly missionary merely suggested that the Cabinet used its influence at Lisbon to open the Zambezi and Shire to foreign navigation; later Livingstone reproached himself for not having asked instead for a settlement in favour of his children.

Just before Christmas Murchison was at Newstead with his wife, (who amazed the company by demonstrating fourteen varieties of patience) and showed interest in Livingstone's suggestion that great benefits would flow from another attempt to find a path beyond Portuguese influence to Nyasa country, and a broad hint that he (Livingstone) might assume the task as a salaried official. So when Murchison declared he would do what he could with the Government, Livingstone began to plan his final expedition. For though he was happy to be with Agnes his heart was still in Africa and the familiar struggle between family obligations and his 'duty' was agitating his mind again when he told Murray, 'I ought to have been off ere now; though I have every comfort that I can desire here, I often take a sore longing to be in Africa. My family is my only chain'.[10] He was concerned too by news about his favourite tribe: 'My heart is very sore for the Makololo,' he wrote on 23 March 1865, 'a letter last night tells me [of] a complete smash up such as we expected has taken place. In fact there is now no Makololo tribe. Sekeletu died & they got to fighting among themselves. Then the black tribes rose, killed his successor and dispersed the remainder who fled leaving all their wives & children.'[11]

The necessity to work on the new book required a lengthy stay at Newstead. On returning to England, Livingstone had intended to do no more than publish a 'trumpet blast' in pamphlet form, denouncing Portuguese iniquities in Africa. But gradually the scope of the project enlarged; it became a tirade against the slave trade and a justification of the Zambezi Expedition, which pointed to its achievements and vindicated Livingstone's leadership. The manuscript was written in a sunny room of the Sussex Tower on a large black carved table. News of the project leaked out, and Meller scoffed that Charles had joined his brother 'to concoct their precious book, and a curious composition of untruth it will be'.[12] He was not entirely wrong: *Narrative* was essentially a propaganda vehicle and a *tour de force* in the art of covering up. No mention was made of quarrels during the expedition, and only scanty reference to the setbacks which plagued its course. In fact the book is more remarkable for what it leaves out than for what it reveals.

Livingstone had use of his brother's diaries when writing *Narrative*, but

Newstead

the fiction of Charles's indispensable co-operation necessitated writing the book in the third person, and the irritating use of the royal 'we' gives it a flat objective style which contrasts sharply with *Missionary Travels*, and indeed with *Narrative*'s own vigorous preface written later in the first person. The author's attempts at humour seem laborious, and since it was not written as a day to day account, *Narrative* lacks its predecessor's ease of flow, while the chronology is sometimes difficult to follow. Livingstone drew on the help of Rae, Waller and Stewart when writing the book, though Kirk declined to contribute a section based on his own botanical notes.[13] Ironically, apart from a note of praise for Kirk, Livingstone paid no tribute to them, while Baines and Bedingfeld were not even mentioned by name. Nor did he give credit to all Baines's drawings, which were worked up as illustrations, after ascertaining from Whitehall that they were public property.[14] Instead they were accompanied by a sycophantic acknowledgement to Lord Russell.

The book was written in haste, with Agnes and members of the Webb family recruited to turn out fair copies. As though Livingstone wished to ignore unhappy memories, few unpleasant episodes were mentioned, but occasionally a note of bitterness crept into the text when setbacks, which would have previously been accepted as the inscrutable workings of Providence, were blamed on evil men who were hampering the Lord's design. Towards the end of writing the manuscript, the afternoon walks at Newstead were abandoned, and Livingstone worked far into the night with a new-fangled gas lamp lighting the table in the tower, until he tumbled into the huge four-poster bed, reputedly Lord Byron's, which is still preserved in the house. One senses that the author's interest at the end was flagging, and the book seems finished off in a hurry.

By 30 January, Livingstone told Murray that only the account of the last march to Lake Nyasa and the voyage to Bombay remained to be completed,[15] but three weeks later he had made such disappointing progress that he decided the dangerous crossing of the Indian Ocean need only be a 'short' passage—no more than a 'note'—which in fact it was. Sometimes he took especial care with his prose, and 'spent four mortal days in rewriting the Victoria Falls'.[15] Contrarily his reference to the vital setback to his plans at Kebrabasa was brief and casual.

'O for Finis', he sighed on 7 February 1865, 'catch me at another book', but it was not until 15 April that the last word was written. Even then he had a good deal of revision to do, and a week later was still 'working like

231

a galley slave' on the draft. Publication, originally expected for the summer, was delayed until the completion of Arrowsmith's map, and the book did not appear until after Livingstone left England. It never enjoyed the tremendous success of *Missionary Travels*, but a creditable 10,000 copies were sold in five editions.

This record of the Zambezi Expedition may be disappointing, but it had several redeeming features: the accounts of the long march to Linyanti and the last journey to Nyasa include good passages of descriptive writing. Thus on page 517 we read that when leaving the lakeshore 'In looking forward we seem to be ascending the long slope of a range of mountains; but the nearer view consisted of a succession of beautiful tree-covered rounded hills; the narrow footpaths were perpetually leading up steep inclines and down descents to running rills, whose sides were fringed with fine, large evergreen trees; the deciduous trees having parted with their leaves, were now enjoying the rest of winter, though only twelve degrees from the equator. The people in the villages into which we entered were generally employed in making very neat fish and other baskets of split bamboos, or in beating the bark of trees into cloth . . . the castor-oil plant is extensively grown also and oil is extracted from the seeds for the purpose of lubricating the body and more especially the hair, which is worn very long. From the careful way in which many train out their hair into different-shaped masses, it has less of a wavy curl than the wool of a long-fleeced sheep—the oil seems to keep it straight.'

He took particular pains over the illustration of his wife's grave, made from one of Kirk's photographs, fearful least it be inexact in any detail. Thus he asked that the thickness of the baobab tree be increased so as to conform with its real girth.[17] This concern contrasted sharply with the cold indifference of the passage describing Mary's death. He was delighted to discover that Baines's picture opposite page 28 of the book, by chance, exposed the falsity of a Portuguese assertion that a navigable river, the Mutu channel, permanently connected the Zambezi to the Cuacua River and thus to Quelimane, for the illustration demonstrated that the channel lay well above the water level of the Zambezi except during the flood season.[18]

The illustration opposite page 356 must be especially considered too: this depiction of a coffle of slaves proved to be as notable a piece of propaganda as Clarkson's use eighty years earlier of the famous diagram showing how 450 slaves were packed into an appallingly small space for the passage from Africa to America in his *History of the Abolition of the African Slave-trade*. It did much to revitalise British abhorrence of the trade still surviving in East Africa, and played a part in leading to its suppression.

Finally we should note that right at the end of *Narrative*, Livingstone's imperial aspirations for the British and their Anglo-Saxon cousins across the Atlantic found expression again when he advocated the replacement of the ruling Portuguese in Mozambique by English colonists, and the annexation of Cuba by the United States.

On 25 April 1865 Livingstone bade an affectionate farewell to the hospitable Webbs and travelled up to town with Agnes, where he was shocked next day to learn of President Lincoln's assassination. In London he tore himself away from *Tom Brown's Schooldays* to speak to a Royal Academy banquet held in the Crystal Palace, and afterwards gave some highly-strung evidence to a Commons committee examining conditions in Africa, during which he indignantly denied that the teaching of Christianity adversely affected the natives. On 19 June a telegram informed him of his mother's death. Within three years Livingstone had lost his wife, eldest son and mother. He hastened up to Hamilton for the funeral, then shyly attended the prize-giving at Oswell's school before travelling south. He would never again see his native Scotland. His last recorded words there were 'Fear God, and work hard'.

Livingstone was now greatly concerned with providing for Agnes. Father Lemue, who long before had officiated at his wedding, put him in touch with a niece, Madame Hocédé, who had been governess to the Queen's children till her indiscreet chatter about the Prince Consort's mortal illness led to her dismissal. Madame now ran a 'superior' school in Paris for Protestant English girls. After long negotiations Livingstone agreed to entrust his daughter to her care, though his friends warned him repeatedly that the Paris of the Second Empire was in fact the Second Babylon. Unknown to the trustees, he asked Murray to superintend the quarterly payment of school fees to Madame Hocédé, while Mrs Murray agreed to choose her clothes when Agnes came out of mourning. Madame was to be sent £120 annually together with a small sum set aside for laundry. Ten to twenty francs an hour were to be allotted to Agnes's French teacher whereas her German tutor had to be satisfied with a meagre five francs.[19]

Livingstone fretted too over the ubiquitous Thomas Baines who had arrived in England, with demands that his wrongful dismissal be publically admitted. Livingstone, however, kept quiet about Baines's 'orgies' at Tete and slipped away to Paris with Agnes a week earlier than expected. When Lady Murchison called, she was surprised to find him gone.* 'Someone had twitted him with being more fond of enjoying the comforts of civilisation than with enduring the hardships of the wilderness', Baines informed his mother, displaying gross ignorance of Livingstone's real character, while she in turn jeered that 'he ran away when a friendly meeting was oppened [*sic*] to him in England'.[20] So when Dr Livingstone embarked at Folkestone on 13 August 1865, there were no cheering crowds to see him off but only Kirk and the faithful Waller.

He spent a few days settling Agnes in with Madame Hocédé, and left his daughter sadly confused by telling her that the dome of Les Invalides was Notre Dame.†[21] Then he went on by train to Marseilles (much worried by the French habit of smoking in carriages) to embark for Bombay, where he had left *Lady Nyassa*. Anxious letters sped back to Paris by every post. In one he bade his daughter to 'avoid all nasty French novels. They are very injurious, and effect a lasting injury on the mind and heart.' From Bombay she presently learned that he was ready to set out again for Africa.

---

* A letter in John Murray's possession, dated 7 August 1865, suggests that 'a medical emergency' at Newstead called Livingstone unexpectedly from London.

† Agnes, in turn, confounded her family by announcing her engagement to Madame's brother,[22] but soon broke it off and returned to Scotland.

21

The Last Journey

By 1864 most of Africa's geographical puzzles had been solved, for in a remarkably short time Burton, Speke, Grant, Baker and Livingstone had revealed the continent's chain of inland seas. But a few tantalising problems remained: did the lakes communicate, was Speke right in claiming that Lake Victoria Nyanza was the source of the Nile, where lay the Congo's source, and what was the configuration of the central African watershed? It was inevitable that one day Livingstone would go back to Africa to seek the answers, and when Murchison suggested that he did so under the auspices of the R.G.S. he gratefully agreed, only insisting that he combined some missionary work with exploration.

Murchison persuaded the R.G.S. to subscribe £500 for the new venture, but it was accompanied by tactless instructions 'from two blockheads' on the committee to chart his route carefully and allow the Society's secretary sight of his notes before their publication. Livingstone was so disgusted by the tone of the letter that he threatened to 'remain in Africa altogether'.

Russell displayed even worse manners when pressed to support the expedition. Having learned from Meller 'the truth about everything' on the Zambezi,[1] he offered only £500 towards Livingstone's expenses and declined a salary, although previously he had 'promised [it] distinctly . . . before Sir Roderick'. As for a consular appointment, Russell refused to do more than give Livingstone an honorary, 'milk and water' commission to the tribes between Mozambique and Abyssinia, but at least it provided him with some sort of official status. To make the pill more bitter, Whitehall's official instructions were drawn up by a clerk named Murray who displayed the 'most exuberant impertinence' by warning the Doctor against causing the Government any more embarrassment. This 'effrontery', wrote Livingstone, 'gnaws at my heart on every touch of illness or dispondency' and made him promise 'to live after they [the

F.O. officials] are dead and rotten'. All Murchison's efforts to modify Whitehall's 'stringent letter' unhappily failed since Russell was suffering from gout and Clarendon was away with measles.[2] James Young, however, was more generous than the Government, subscribing £1,000 towards the venture, while Livingstone himself raised a further £800 by lecturing in India.

Livingstone had made his plans while finishing *Narrative* and indeed publicised them in its preface. He intended to enter the interior by the Rovuma, examine the unseen head of Lake Nyasa and then study the hydrography of the watershed. Here he anticipated finding the sources of both the Nile and Congo, feats which would suitably crown his career. But the most cogent reason for embarking on this last journey was not the 'éclat' of discovery; it was compelled by the old high motive of alleviating human misery. The 'settling' of the watershed, as he explained, was 'a purely geographical question [and] had no interest for me. I want to do good by opening up a path north of the Portuguese.'[3]

Yet he undeniably savoured fame, and knew full well that the discovery of the Nile source, the greatest trophy of Victorian exploration, would make him a national hero again, allow him to outshine the detested Burton, and gain the admiration of his new friends—the politicians and noblemen who had taken the place of the 'old squad' at Ongar and his scientific contacts.

The Nile, the world's longest and most famous river, was known to receive only one sizable tributary, the Blue Nile, during its long course through the desert; but its origin was a mystery, though there were theories in plenty. About 460 B.C. Herodotus had learned that the river flowed from one of two fathomless fountains, and the Zambezi issued from the other, while two snow capped mountains stood nearby, deep in the African interior. During the 1st century A.D. Greek traders brought back reports of such mountains near a group of lakes which seemed to confirm Herodotus's hearsay evidence, and when Ptolemy compiled his famous *Geography*, he depicted the Nile rising from two huge lakes whose feeder streams lay at about latitude 10° South.

Ptolemy's concept was slavishly copied by cartographers during the following centuries, until James Bruce found the source of the Blue Nile in Abyssinia during 1770; but still the question of the main stream's origin remained unsolved.

It had attained something of the interest awakened today by space exploration, and several British expeditions were launched into the African interior to solve the problem. In 1858 Burton and Speke identified Lake Tanganyika, and then Speke went on alone to find Lake Victoria Nyanza which he at once claimed to be the true Nile source. He confirmed this inspired guess in 1860 when he followed the lake's outlet until it could be identified as the historical Nile. At about the same time Samuel Baker announced the discovery of Lake Albert Nyanza (now Lake Mobutu Sese Seko) and claimed it as a second source. The altitudes of these lakes are relevant to Livingstone's own search for a higher Nile source: roughly, Tanganyika lies at 2,500 feet, Victoria at 3,700 feet and Albert at 2,000 feet.

The question of the true source now depended on identifying the farthest issue of the headwaters of these lakes. Burton believed it lay at the head of one of Tanganyika's feeders; Livingstone agreed that it lay south of Lakes Tanganyika and Albert, and, since so much else of Ptolemy's map had been confirmed, considered it would be found on the Central African watershed at about 10° South.

He had himself crossed that watershed during the trans-African journey, and in 1857 stated in Edinburgh that the Nile and Zambezi sources lay close together in this region. Again, in 1863, Livingstone had climbed another part of the watershed and learned of lakes lying to the west which drained into the northward flowing Luapula River. This he predicted would turn out to be the Nile, and believed it would be comparatively easy to follow it downstream to the identifiable Nile, and upstream to what must be the river's true source.

*   *   *   *   *

Livingstone's last journey was planned on a far less elaborate scale than the Zambezi Expedition. He took no Europeans with him, although he would have liked Kirk to come, but Kirk declined on the grounds that the appointment carried no salary, he was shortly to be married, and had his own career to consider. Livingstone accepted this and obtained the post of Agency Surgeon at Zanzibar for him, from which he was subsequently promoted to Consul. Livingstone's hopes of Robert accompanying him too were disappointed; he thought of one of Tozer's men whom he liked, but eventually decided he 'would rather go alone than with anyone untried'.

Despite his earlier protestations, there was little missionary work done on this expedition, and it differed in other ways from the previous

237

ventures: its objectives were never precisely defined and throughout the next seven years we are quite often uncertain of Livingstone's intentions; indeed his movements seemed less often dictated by resolve than by contingency. Several further factors added to the comparative obscurity of this last rambling journey: many of the letters written by Livingstone went astray; his journals were edited with such tact by Waller that he omitted all passages which might reflect on Livingstone's reputation, particularly those of vituperative criticism of his enemies; and most of the area he explored chanced to fall outside the later British sphere of interest, so far less was learned from local Africans by Livingstone's compatriots.

Livingstone was unconcerned now with European settlement or planting missions. Instead he trudged through Central Africa believing that God, in His chosen time and for good purpose, would direct his steps to a required destination. Initiative was so far surrendered to providence that Livingstone would wait for weeks at a time for some 'token' to reveal his proper course, and whereas his earlier travels stand out on the map in crisp and flowing lines, those of the final journey twist about like a child's random pencil tracings. The rhythm of his mood-changes, moreover, had altered with such added emphasis on enervating depression, that after reading his old friend's journals, Oswell gasped 'how quiet and gentle he has grown'.

Though tormented by malnutrition, sickness and infirmity, Livingstone during the last years is not a man to be pitied. He was, in Stanley's words 'a contented soul', labouring as he most wished to do, living where he preferred to be above all other places.

During this time many Africans became familiar with the haggard, bearded, benign aging man,* who was often hungry and sick, yet for some incomprehensible reason wandered from one village to another, halting only to rest and ask innumerable questions or speak of a mysterious redeemer who was his master. He became a recognised part of the African scene, and a curiously permanent one too, for her people still speak of him. No doubt because he seemed a little crazy, they treated him with the kindness and respect they paid their own elders, who would soon join the ancestral spirits.

---

* Livingstone was just fifty-three when he began the last journey and had turned sixty when he died.

* * * * *

The Last Journey

Livingstone first went to Bombay to recruit staff and sell *Lady Nyassa*, having decided against sailing her to Africa against the monsoon. Hospitably received again by Frere, he lived up to his host's gubernatorial style. A fellow guest found Livingstone 'much stouter, better and healthier looking than he was last year', but remarked with faint disapproval that 'he was dressed very unlike a minister—more like a post-captain or admiral. He wore a blue dress coat, trimmed with lace, and bearing a Government gilt button. In his hand he carried a cocked hat.' Livingstone caused a stir too in church by wearing 'a blue surtout, with Government gilt buttons, and shepherd-tartan trousers'. He again met the local merchants who agreed to establish a trading station in Africa outside the Portuguese zone, but the project was later quietly dropped.

On Frere's advice Livingstone recruited twelve sepoys and a Havildar from the Marine Battalion at Bombay, to protect his caravan. These men, he airily assured John Murray, were 'good well-drilled Indians who have roughed it in the Persian Gulph'.[4] From the Church Missionary station at Nasik, where rescued African slaves were educated, he enrolled nine 'Nassick boys' as porters. He also re-engaged two Yao youths, originally rescued from the slave coffle at Mbame's, Chuma and Wikatani. Both knew a little English and had sailed in *Lady Nyassa* to Bombay. Chuma was a man of great potential who received much praise as one of Livingstone's 'faithfuls'; he was sharp-witted but his irresponsibility infuriated his master, who was particularly distressed when he 'ran off with a concubine',[5] and deserted 'in his hour of utmost need'.[6] Finally he took on the Shupanga men—Susi and Amoda—who had likewise served in *Pioneer* and *Lady Nyassa*. Both remained faithful, though Susi absconded temporarily during 1868 and, according to Livingstone, was 'a habitual thief'.[7]

In Bombay and, later, in Zanzibar, Livingstone stocked up with bales of calico and beads for currency, with clothing, medicines, a tent, cooking utensils and a few luxuries like coffee and sugar. For relaxation he bought an accordion, and he carried two Bibles (one of which was small enough to go into his pocket for 'emergency reading'), the one volume edition of Smith's *Dictionary of the Bible* (the gift of Lady Franklin),[8] and (surprisingly) Forbes's *Duty and Powers of Justices of the Peace in Scotland*,[9] sure evidence that he intended returning to Britain and was not already swayed by any martyr complex. All these goods were broken down into seventy and fifty pound loads, suitable for porters.

Livingstone also took baggage animals—camels and Indian buffaloes—
to Africa, hoping that 'a beast of burden that defies the insect pest . . .
will be a boon' to the continent.[10] In the event most of the beasts died
after eating poisonous plants in Zanzibar, while the survivors quickly
succumbed on the mainland to the sepoys' bad treatment. Finally he
bought a mongrel poodle, named Chitane, which 'had more spunk
than a hundred country dogs [and] took charge of the whole line of
march'.

For some time Frere had intended to placate the Sultan of Zanzibar
with the gift of the steamship *Thule*, and he considerately commissioned
Livingstone to make the presentation. This saved him passage money and
was 'a great lift to me in the eyes of the Arabs'. Livingstone's depression
in Bombay thawed as he prepared to leave for Africa, and on 4 January
1866 he jotted down an invocation of the pleasures ahead in his notebook:
'When one travels with the specific object in view of ameliorating the
benighted natives of Africa every act becomes enobled. While exchanging
the customary civilities—Receiving a night's shelter, purchasing food for
the party—asking for information—or giving answers to the Africans'
polite enquiries as to the objects of the travellers—we begin to spread
information respecting that people by whose agency their land will yet
be free from the cursed slave trade. The mere animal pleasure in travelling
is very great; the elasticity of muscle imparted by brisk exercise. Fresh
& healthy blood circulates through the brain—the eye is clear, the step
firm and the day's exertion has been enough to make repose thoroughly
enjoyable. The influence of remote chances of danger either from men or
wild beasts. Our sympathies are drawn out to our hardy humble companions by a community of interests and perils, and made us all friends.
[One word indecipherable] the mind meanwhile is made more self
reliant—confident in resources with greater presence of mind—The body
& limbs become well knit—the muscles lose all their fat and are as hard
as a board—the countenance bronzed, no dyspepsia. The sweat of one's
brow is no longer a curse when one works for God. It is converted into a
blessing. It is a tonic to the system—the charm of repose can only be
known after severe exertion.'*

Next day the *Thule* began the voyage to Zanzibar. The ship rolled

* This was the original wording. Livingstone later tidied the passage and rewrote it into the
Journal under the date of 26 March 1866. Waller used this well-known second version under
the later date when he edited Livingstone's *Last Journals*, thus giving the impression that it
was written soon after landing in Africa.

abominably. The sepoys and many of the crew were prostrated by seasickness which the Doctor escaped, thanks to placing a bag of powdered ice on his spine. At one critical moment, the ever-versatile man took over from the skipper to save the ship from foundering.[11] *Thule* dropped anchor at Zanzibar on 28 January 1866.

Zanzibar was the great entepôt of the East African coast, and boasted the world's largest slave market. It had no sanitary system; ordure was simply piled on the beach, and Livingstone thought it should be 'called Stinkibar rather than Zanzibar'.

Four thousand Arabs lorded it over the island's 200,000 Africans, most of them slaves. In addition there were several thousand Swahili* 'middlemen', some seventy Europeans, and an influential colony of Hindu merchants locally known as banyans, through whose hands were channelled the goods which bought ivory and slaves on the mainland. Some of the Europeans on the island were also involved in the slave trade; one, named Fraser, ran his large clove plantation with slave labour; he would sadden Livingstone's last months.

Livingstone was received in style by a brass band rendering 'God save the Queen' when he paid his formal call on Sultan Majid. Majid promised him a firman—a sort of passport requiring assistance from his subjects on the mainland—and dismissed him to the strains of 'The British Grenadiers'. Livingstone had 'difficulty in preserving his official gravity' and told Agnes 'Wee Willie Winkie' would have been more appropriate, in one of his few references to his small stature.

The Zanzibar Arabs regularly took large caravans of Swahili and armed slaves into the interior. Having chosen a target area, they raided for months at a time to capture slaves. They marched these unfortunates down to the coast, the adults carrying tusks, losing terrifying numbers on the way. It was estimated that for every five Africans captured, only one reached the coast alive. Whole areas of Africa were being depopulated by the slavers; the Continent was literally bleeding to death in 1866, and the misery of her people continued to haunt Livingstone until his death. 'The sights I have seen', he once wrote, 'are so nauseous that I always strive to drive them from memory.'

In Zanzibar the surviving captives were fattened up for sale in the slave market. Livingstone visited it one day, and told Agnes the slavers 'go about . . . with a woman or child held by the hand calling out "seven

* Africans, usually with Arab blood, who had assumed Arab ways.

dollars, seven dollars" '. Other captives sat in dejected lines. An Arab would come to them, size up a girl, open her mouth, make more intimate examinations, and finally throw a stick twenty yards, to watch, like a horse dealer, "her paces."'[12] Some of the human chattels were intended for domestic slavery in Zanzibar, which was relatively lenient. But the majority were packed into dhows for ghastly voyages, made longer by the necessity of avoiding naval patrols, to the Middle East, India and even China.

The carriage of slaves to Zanzibar was still legal in 1866, but the Sultan had been induced to outlaw external trade beyond. Yet he was powerless to enforce this prohibition, and the Royal Navy patrols, based on Zanzibar and the Comoro Islands, intercepted only a fraction of the dhows. Englishmen who came in contact with the slavers detested their cruelty; one sailor summed up his feelings as 'if the devil don't catch these fellows, we might as well have no devil at all'. Livingstone's attitude to the Arabs was to become ambiguous; he was amazed that these men had lost the zeal for proselytisation which had carried Islam to so much of the world, for the slavers were concerned with profit rather than conversion.

He was surprised too that, despite their sufferings, the Africans held the Arabs in respect. They regarded their system as no more than an extension of their own domestic slavery which was sanctioned by tribal custom. Far from rejecting Islam, the Africans envied those of their fellows who were allowed to embrace it. There was much in Islam to attract them: unlike Christianity it was untainted by racial bias; it accepted their own chattel concept of women and plurality of wives; conversion required no more than the repetition of a few easily-learned words; the prospect of a Mohammedan paradise after death, where each of the faithful was attended by four luscious virgins, was far more attractive than the Christian Heaven; and Islam put muskets into its converts' hands, with all the opportunities and prestige that went with them in nineteenth-century Africa.

By the time of his arrival at Zanzibar, Livingstone had further formulated his plans. He intended to disembark his expedition at the Rovuma mouth, and follow its course to what he believed was the northern end of Lake Nyasa. From there he would march northwards to Lake Tanganyika and continue up its eastern coast to Ujiji. This he would make his base for further explorations westward. A squalid fishing village today, Ujiji in 1866 was important as the terminus of the great caravan route to the

The Last Journey

interior, which ran inland for seven hundred miles from Bagamoyo on the coast opposite Zanzibar. It passed through several other Arab colonies, of which Unyanyembe was the most important. Ujiji, moreover, had become the jumping-off point for the unknown country of Manyema, which was reported to be a treasure house of easily-won ivory and slaves.

In Zanzibar, on the British Consul's recommendation, Livingstone contracted with the firm of Ladha Damji to send up regular supplies to Ujiji. The firm was represented by a fat banyan, named Koorji, a man with small intelligent eyes and a permanent crop of carbuncles. Koorji was confident there would be no difficulty in despatching caravans inland in accordance with Livingstone's instructions, and he assured him that his agent at Ujiji, Thani bin Suelim, could be depended to guard his stores until the expedition's arrival.

For several reasons, Livingstone decided against reaching Ujiji by the established road. He still believed the Rovuma would provide a route to Nyasa; he wished to explore the lake's northern end and decide whether it drained into Tanganyika; he had no wish to identify himself with the slavers by following their road, especially as it meant treading in Burton's footsteps; and he had promised the Bombay merchants to find a site for a trading station, which both parties envisaged as lying near the head-waters of the Rovuma.

Livingstone was confident that the British Consul would personally ensure that Koorji honoured his contract and engaged suitable pagazi to carry his goods up-country, while Kirk's arrival on the island would be an additional guarantee that provisions reached him safely. Indeed Livingstone regarded himself as part of a triple alliance to suppress the slave trade: he was its forward agent, Kirk would man the vital middle station, while Waller secured the main base among the humanitarian circles at home.

Livingstone was detained longer than expected in Zanzibar, awaiting H.M.S. *Penguin* to ferry his expedition to the mainland. She arrived eventually early in March 1866, carrying ten pagazi recruited in Johanna, whose leader, Musa, had served briefly in *Pioneer*. On 19 March *Penguin* sailed for the mainland with the expedition crowded on board, towing the strange menagerie of baggage animals in a dhow. Shifting sand had blocked the Rovuma mouth, so *Penguin* went on Mikindani beach to disembark the expedition. When she steamed away, Livingstone was to see only one more white man during the remaining seven years of his life.

243

22

Tanganyika

After spending a few days at Mikindani, engaging porters and making camel saddles, the march inland began on 6 April 1866. The people were friendly, and remembered Livingstone from previous visits. Eleven years afterwards an old man presented a passing missionary with a coat given to him by Livingstone, 'whose manners', he said, 'were always kind'. It is among the treasured relics in the Blantyre museum.

Unfortunately Livingstone had to rely on a philandering guide who zigzagged to successive villages pursuing his lustful aspirations, and discipline was bad from the start; the caravan straggled so badly that once it was spread out over nearly a hundred miles, and only closed up on hearing rumours of marauding Angoni. This threat presently made Livingstone veer south-west from his intended course. But still villages were deserted in the wake of slavers, food was scarce, and everywhere he saw ghastly signs of the Arabs' passing. Corpses were found bound to trees; groups of men lay still clamped in gorees, moribund from hunger. In his notebook Livingstone drew several ghoulish sketches which vibrate with the shock and horror of these scenes.

Hardly less shattering was the trouble with the baggage animals. The sepoys goaded the camels ferociously, and within a month already two were dead. By then Livingstone seemed to have lost control of the column; he was incapable of making a firm decision; instead of commands, he cajoled, temporised, entered into arguments, and usually submitted to his followers' demands, however outrageous they might be.

'I have to be silent', he wrote of their treatment of the animals, yet it was the hired porters' behaviour which first blighted his hopes of a quick march to Nyasa, when they insisted on turning back. From then on he had to rely on engaging local pagazi to carry the stores in short stages from one village to another. Most of the Nasik boys turned out to be lazy ruffians who took to 'murder, slave-stealing and robbery', crimes that Waller was

3 A coffle of slaves

careful to avoid mentioning when editing the journal. They deliberately 'lost' their loads, and once joined the Indians in bribing a guide to direct the column to the coast so that they might quit the expedition. In the end the sepoys became the worst affliction: they dawdled along the path, averaging less than four miles a day, and repulsed Livingstone by their foul habits. On 20 May he determined to send them back—and then relented. They repaid him by flailing the last camel to death and afterwards ate the buffalo calf, which led Livingstone to complain mildly of his experiments being 'vitiated'. Finally he lost his temper and gave two offending sepoys a few cuts with a cane. They responded with accusations to the 'Nassickers' about their leader's 'strange practices' and he feared their complete subversion of these boys. Finally, on 15 July, the sepoys were dismissed. The Havildar remained a little longer before he deserted.

Well over three months were spent in covering the three hundred and fifty miles to the town of Chief Mataka, who (it was an ominous reflection on the slavers' influence) wore Arab dress. His territory reminded Livingstone of the Shire Highlands, and seemed a suitable site for the Bombay merchants' station, but we hear no more of the project, and another of his attempts to colonise the African wilds withered away.

Marching on through country devastated by the Arabs, Livingstone reached Lake Nyasa on 8 August 1866, close to where the Msinje stream enters it. He had at last established communication of a sort between the lake and Rovuma, and indeed this route was used when the U.M.C.A. returned to the interior. Livingstone was delighted to see *his* lake again because 'to come to Nyassa was like visiting an old home I never expected to see. The roar of the waves and dash in the breakers or rather rollers was quite exhilerating.' He remained a few days on the lake shore, writing letters, making vain attempts to contact some Arabs to arrange for his party to be ferried to the western shore, and saddened by their dhows sailing where he had hoped *Lady Nyassa* would patrol. Then he moved tentatively north to circumvent the lake but decided to pass round its familiar southern end when threatened by Angoni, and perhaps too because he realised he had underestimated its length. On 9 September he was at Kadango, and four days later reached Malindi on the lake's heel opposite today's Palm Beach Hotel; there in his Journal he bemoaned the U.M.C.A.'s failure to establish themselves on the lake, unaware he was writing where that mission would soon establish a flourishing station.

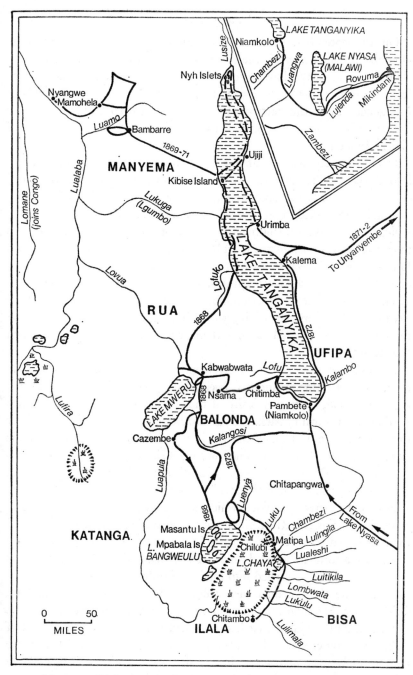

Map 5. Livingstone's Last Journey. The inset shows the journey from Mikindani to Lake Tanganyika, 1866–7

On 13 September, while camped near the Shire outlet, Livingstone gloomily brooded over all the river had meant to him in the past, and sighed 'now . . . slave dhows prosper'. Instead of crossing the river by the ferry, he made a detour to visit the Yao chief Mukate in the foothills of Mangoche. Then the party moved down the escarpment, passed over Malombe by canoe, and continued across Cape Maclear to the town of Chief Mponda.

Here they were near Wikatani's home, whence his father had sold him into slavery. Wikatani now claimed to have met a brother (the word covers so wide a relationship among Africans that a charge of lying would be unfair), and asked to be released. Unable to keep him against his will—which would have substantiated Arab reports that his porters were no more than slaves—Livingstone let him go sadly. A more serious desertion followed soon afterwards. At Marenga's the Johanna men heard rumours of Angoni raids in the Kasungu district. Livingstone promised he would avoid this area, but on 26 September the carriers walked away when he gave the order to march. Livingstone admitted later that he felt inclined to shoot their leader, Musa, but then decided he was well rid of such 'inveterate thieves'.

By now the party was 'inconveniently small'; there remained only Susi, Chuma, Amoda and six Nasik lads. But Livingstone was in a euphoric mood, writing lyrically of the country's beauty and there was no thought of turning back. He was further encouraged a few days later to receive a warm welcome from an old friend, Katosa, resplendent in his naval coat. From him he obtained porters. Climbing up the steep escarpment towards Dedza, Livingstone passed unknowingly by the Bushman rock paintings on Mpunzi Hill, which would have given him a clue to the nature of the cave dwellings which so intrigued his last years. They crossed the Lilongwe River fifteen miles above Malawi's new capital, and then zigzagged across country to avoid Angoni warriors. On 12 November Livingstone forded the headwaters of the Bua and ten days afterwards tramped over the watershed into modern Zambia.

Meanwhile the Johanna men were heading for the coast, and on 6 December 1866 reported to Consul Seward in Zanzibar that Livingstone was dead. Musa related that his party had crossed the northern end of Lake Nyasa by canoe, and that the Johanna men then fell behind on the march. They were startled to hear a flurry of fighting ahead, and, on going on after dusk, found the bodies of Livingstone, his servants and the Nasik boys strewn along the path. Livingstone, Musa said, had been nearly decapitated and stripped, so they could bring no relics back.

Musa's account was intended to provide him with a cover story for his desertion and an opportunity to claim back pay. Questioning failed to shake him, and Seward reported sadly that 'this brave and good man [Livingstone] had crossed the threshold of the unexplored'. On 7 March 1867 all England learned of the tragedy.

But Waller and 'Gunner' Young, an Able Seaman who had grown to admire Livingstone while serving in *Pioneer*, both knew Musa for a liar and refused to accept the story. Murchison, suspicious too, gratefully accepted an offer from Young to lead a small expedition to Africa to verify the report.

Set beside the fumbled improvisations of Livingstone's last journey, Gunner Young's expedition to Lake Nyasa is a model of efficiency and despatch. He sailed for the Cape on 11 June 1867 with three white companions and the sections of a steel boat christened *The Search* which was modelled on the *Lady Nyassa*. They quickly assembled the boat at the mouth of the Zambezi and moved up river with Young carefully tending the graves of Mary Livingstone, Scudamore, Mackenzie, Dickinson and Thornton. He had no difficulty in recruiting two hundred and fifty porters at Chibisa and carried the boat's sections past the cataracts, thus demonstrating the practicability of Livingstone's earlier scheme. Early in September he launched *The Search* on the upper Shire, and at the lake's south-east corner came across evidence of the Doctor having passed that way. Clearly Livingstone had circumvented the foot of the lake and Musa's account was false. Young next sought information on the western shore, where Marenga identified Livingstone's photograph, described his appearance exactly and told Young that the Johanna men, after following the white man through his village, returned declaring that their time was up and they had left the Doctor's service. Young was back in England by 21 January 1868, his task brilliantly completed.

But already news had come from Zanzibar that Livingstone had been 'sighted' after the alleged date of his murder, and in April 1868 Agnes received a letter from her father.[1] A few days later Murchison electrified a meeting at the R.G.S. with the 'glorious tidings' of Livingstone's safety. The build-up of anxiety for him had quickened everybody's interest; now he seemed invulnerable. When the curtain descended on him again, his friends discounted rumours of his death, and did not wake up to his final desperate predicament until too late.

Musa was handed over for punishment to the Sultan of Johanna who kept him manacled in chains for eight months before sending him back to Zanzibar for final judgement. Kirk, however, feeling that Musa's punishment had been severe enough, arranged for him to be freed. Much later, during 1870, Livingstone learned of Young's relief expedition, and in his loneliness found comfort in the thought that the Government and friends had combined to send out a search party to find him.

* * * * *

Meanwhile Livingstone and his reduced band, having crossed over the watershed between Nyasa and the Luangwa River on 22 November 1866, unknowingly followed the route Lacerda pioneered (over sixty years before) towards the town of Cazembe, paramount chief of the Balonda.

The country was very beautiful but only coarse millet was available as food and this caused a relapse of Livingstone's old enemy, dysentery. 'Too ill to march', he noted ominously on 6 December. Then, on Christmas Day, his four milch-goats strayed. Their milk had rendered his millet porridge more palatable, and he noted gloomily that 'the loss affected me more than I could have imagined'. He was so thin now that he took his belt in three holes, and told his son Thomas that he constantly dreamt of roast beef.

The last day of 1866 was spent on the rim of the Luangwa valley, where he finished the journal for the year on a despondent note: 'it has not been so fruitful or useful as I intended. Will try to do better in 1867, and be better—more gentle and loving'. When the march was resumed, one of the porters slipped on a steep slope and damaged the chronometers he was carrying; for the next few months, Livingstone's latitudes in consequence were some twenty miles out.

On 15 January they came to the wide Chimbwe River, close to the road now linking Dar-es-Salaam with Lusaka. His people were so preoccupied when wading across that the Doctor's poodle was forgotten and left to drown. Livingstone was hardly consoled by his companions calling the river 'Chitane's Water', an honorable name that was retained on the map for many years. Five days later a far more serious loss occurred: his medicine chest was stolen by two deserting porters. It made Livingstone 'feel as if sentence of death ... had, as in my poor friend Mackenzie's case, been passed upon me', and in his Journal he lamented that the loss 'gnaws at the heart terribly'. Yet the consequences were less serious than he feared. By now Livingstone was becoming immunised to malaria by repeated attacks; apart from one severe bout at Lake Tanganyika, his subsequent attacks were comparatively mild. This was particularly evident during the four months he spent with Stanley, who was frequently prostrated by malaria, while he escaped.

Livingstone now had to decide whether to return to Zanzibar and replace the drugs, or continue the march to Ujiji: he decided on the latter course since he was now nearer Ujiji where he anticipated finding stores, and in any case felt confident of Divine protection. As he told Murchison, he intended to fend off fever with 'native remedies and trust in the watchful care of a Higher Power'. He even conceived that the loss might be yet another 'providence', writing 'this [loss] may turn out for the best by taking away a source of suspicion among more superstitious, charm-dreading people farther north'. He also found excuses for the two errant porters. From now on Livingstone, in pursuance of his New Year prayer, periodically became a man of almost saintly indulgence: when an Arab deliberately misled him about the nature of the country ahead, and thus lost him five months' travelling time, he merely sighed, 'I regret this deception, but it is not to be wondered at'; at Lake Bangweulu he 'resolved to bear with meekness' the refusal by hired canoe men to honour their contract; when two of the 'faithfuls' deserted he admitted, 'I do not blame them very severely in my own mind for absconding: they were tired of tramping, and so verily am I'; and he gladly accepted the return of the contrite prodigals a little later, noting 'I have faults myself'.

On 28 January 1867 Livingstone's small party arrived at the Chambezi River which should have provided the key to the hydrography of Central Africa. Unfortunately the Doctor failed to interpret its significance. Inaccurate Portuguese reports, and the similarity of their names, led him to conclude that this southward flowing river represented the headwaters of the Zambezi. Only at the end of the year did he learn from Chief Cazembe that it fell into Lake Bangweulu, and was continued north-wards as the Luapula and Lualaba rivers, and might therefore be the upper Nile.

Three days' march from the Chambezi brought Livingstone to the court of an important Bemba chief named Chitapangwa, who refused him permission to move on for three harassing weeks. The chief was suspicious about Livingstone's reasons for coming to his country, and, in what seems a remarkably modern gesture, 'when told it was for a public benefit, he pulled down the underlid of the right eye' to demonstrate his incredulity. Livingstone found the waiting 'hard', but added typically that 'all may be for the best; it has always turned out so'.

Fortunately this was a 'land of plenty',[2] and here too Livingstone met a party of Swahili travelling eastward. He prevailed upon them to wait while he feverishly completed a despatch for Whitehall and letters to his friends. One asked the Consul at Zanzibar to send an additional caravan of stores and medicine to Ujiji. Unfortunately when Churchill, Seward's successor, received the letter nearly a year later, he reasoned that by then the Doctor would have long since left Ujiji, and ignored the request. A letter to Agnes told her he was so emaciated that his bones were 'nearly bursting through the skin'.[3]

The party moved on at last past the site of modern Kasama, with Livingstone busy ticking off names of successive villages like a tourist itinerary. After a steep descent on 1 April, he was rewarded by sight of Lake Tanganyika, locally known as Liemba.

Next day they reached the lake at Pambete, near modern Niamkolo, with Livingstone 'excessively weak', but confident that 'the Highest will lead me'. The lake's 'surpassing loveliness' deeply impressed him, and he tested Clarendon's classical knowledge with the assurance that 'it is as perfect a natural paradise as Xenophon could have desired'.*

Here Livingstone suffered his last severe attack of malaria, and in the dangerous cerebral form, exhibiting 'fits of total insensibility with the entire loss of power over the muscles of the back'.[4] Fearful that local Africans might harass the sick man, his companions spirited him away to an uninhabited island, where Livingstone in his delirium concluded they intended to imprison him—and felt very ashamed on his recovery.

He was soon able to resume the march, moving northwards up the western lakeshore as far as the Lofu River. He was in a disinterested frame of mind, and only three short journal entries appear during the next six weeks. Then, after hearing of fighting ahead, Livingstone turned back, as he would never have done earlier. Unfortunately this was before reaching Tanganyika's effluent, the Lukuga River, which would have

* Lord Clarendon returned to the Foreign Office from 1865 to 1868.

solved some of his geographical problems. Livingstone instead determined to examine the two lakes lying to the west, and made for Chitimba's village where he knew he could obtain information from Arabs gathered there. They were at war with a powerful chief named Nsama, and after seeing Majid's firman, insisted on taking him into their stockade until peace was concluded.

So for the next three months the Doctor rested in the Arab camp until the fighting ceased, feeling oddly attracted to the 'gentlemen subjects of the Sultan' whom he compared favourably to the brutal man-hunters of Kilwa. Even their raiding, he noticed, was conducted leniently, and he actually drafted a despatch for Clarendon commending their 'mode of trading in ivory and slaves', and depicting it as its most 'attractive' form. Perhaps it was because he felt meek, though he easily 'glided into a growl', that he became, temporarily, so indulgent to the slavers.

Thus began Livingstone's close association with the Arabs. During the years ahead, as he often gratefully acknowledged, they repeatedly succoured him, or escorted him through dangerous country. The association undoubtedly placed Livingstone in an ambiguous position, and lost him influence among the Africans. Moreover the slavers' marching-rate was provokingly slow, as they stopped repeatedly to trade, and this greatly impeded his progress.

Thirteen years earlier, Livingstone had refused to travel with Silva Porto because he was a slaver. But now the moods of passivity occurred more frequently, and his sense of divine mission had strengthened. So he saw nothing paradoxical in accepting assistance from these indubitably wicked men whom God had placed in a position where they might help in consummating the Holy Design. His mandate overrode all personal scruples. The only real paradox lay in the fact that, whereas before the slavers had followed in Livingstone's pioneering tracks, now he followed theirs.

When peace returned Livingstone travelled slowly westwards towards the two lakes, in company with the notorious Tippu Tip. But for most of October the caravan lay stalled, and when at last they seemed ready to start, Livingstone groaned in the journal that authority was 'found in the Koran for staying one more day here. This is very trying. . . . Nothing can be more tedious than the Arab way of travelling.'

We obtain more evidence of Livingstone's new tolerance for the 'gentlemen' slavers when the march was resumed from a lyrical passage in the

Journal describing the passage of a slave coffle: 'The long line of slaves and carriers, brought up by their Arab employers, adds life to the scene; they are in three bodies and number 450 in all. Each party has a guide with a flag, and when that is planted all the company stops till it is lifted, and a drum beaten, and a kudu's horn sounded. One party is headed by about a dozen leaders, dressed with fantastic head-gear of feathers and beads, red cloth on the bodies, and skins cut into strips and twisted: they take their places in line, the drum beats, the horns sound harshly, and all fall in. These sounds seem to awaken a sort of *esprit de corps* in those who have once been slaves. My attendants now jumped up, and would scarcely allow me time to dress when they heard the sounds of their childhood, and all day they were among the foremost.' The female slaves, he adds, 'held up bravely'.

As Livingstone approached Lake Mweru, the inaccuracy of his chronometers was storing up trouble for the future. They possessed extremely delicate 'escapements' which were liable to damage by sudden jolts. This had occurred earlier in the year, and more recently during an earthquake.*5 Now their readings made him place his longitudes fifty miles out and in the opposite direction to the previous error, so that when he drew his maps, he included seventy miles of space that did not exist. It subsequently resulted in his distorting the shape of Lake Bangweulu so that its long axis lay east and west instead of north and south.

Going ahead of the slave train which halted at the important depot of Kabwabwata, Livingstone reached Lake Mweru on 8 November 1867. It was a major discovery, yet he dismissed it in the journal without enthusiasm or animation. But when he resumed a more exhilarated mood, Livingstone described its real beauty in such glowing terms that it set Stanley writing of Mweru being surrounded 'on all sides by high mountains clothed to their tips with the richest vegetation in the tropics', while the lake's waters gushed out 'through a deep rent in the bosom of the mountains . . . with the thunder of a cataract', before they expanded into the 'calm and broad Lualaba'.

* When one chronometer was eventually returned to the Foreign Office, it was reissued as a less accurate 'deck watch'.

23

The Last Great Discovery

Even before reaching Lake Mweru Livingstone had decided against moving directly to Ujiji. For Cazembe's town lay tantalisingly close, and he determined to accompany a small party of Arabs who were visiting it. So he set off south after making a closer examination of Lake Mweru, and commenting sagely on the unlikely association there of endemic goitre and filaria infestation which blew up a man's scrotum like a balloon.

On 18 November 1867 they came to the Chungu River a few miles from Cazembe's court, where the Brazilian explorer, Lacerda, had died. Three days later Livingstone marched down a broad approach avenue, passed 'a cannon dressed in gaudy cloths', and 'burst through' a shouting crowd demanding tribute into the Londa capital. He was greeted by a salute of musketry, fired by the adherents of a white-bearded Swahili trader named Mohamad bin Saleh who had been confined to the town for the last ten years because of some half-forgotten offence. There was a second Arab at Cazembe's, Mohamad bin Gharib (or Bogharib) who proved a generous and upright man, and whose only offence in Livingstone's eyes was his making 'ostentatious prayers à la Bedingfeld'.

On 24 November 1867 Livingstone was formally presented to Cazembe, who wore a crown of yellow feathers while his legs were enveloped in a vast pleated skirt like a reversed crinoline. Cazembe ruled a territory that is now divided between Zaire and Zambia. He was notorious for his cruelty; many of his subjects were short of a hand or ear; behind him stood the official mutilator holding a scimitar and gigantic pair of scissors.

But to Livingstone he was courteous and informative, speaking of gold and copper mines in Katanga, and confirming Livingstone's growing belief that the Lualaba might prove to be the lower Nile.

Livingstone spent a month at Cazembe's, mildly interested in its African life, and attracted to the queen, in whose face he detected a flattering resemblance to Mrs Webb. He met an old man who remembered

Lacerda, and was intrigued by a dwarf who amused the court like a Tudor jester. He also used time to finish a despatch for Whitehall and many letters, although only a few of them reached their destination; but one got through to Kirk, now established at Zanzibar,* which repeated the instructions to provision him at Ujiji. And—it was an unfortunate kindness—he persuaded Cazembe to liberate his captive, Mohamad bin Saleh. We shall see how the kindness was repaid.

By now Livingstone was desperately homesick. No letter from his family had reached him since leaving Zanzibar, and he sighed, 'I am so tired of exploring, without a word from home'. So when he learned of Mohamad's intention of leaving at once for Ujiji, Livingstone accompanied the caravan. Only gradually did he realise that Mohamad's sole desire was to get away quickly from Cazembe's and, when once safely distant, to begin trading again. Worse, Mohamad turned some of Livingstone's attendants against their master by 'selling the favours of his concubines to them, thus reducing them to a kind of bondage'. Mohamad's delaying tactics meant that Livingstone was not to reach Ujiji until 14 March 1869.

The intervening fourteen months were probably the most wretched of his career, and only redeemed by the sudden spurt of energy which led to the discovery of Lake Bangweulu. The journal for this period is a confused report of weeks spent splashing through wet mud during an incontinently wet season, of attacks by Africans on the Arabs, and of desperate illnesses from which he nearly died.

For two whole months the caravan was 'detained by a superabundance of water' near Kabwabwata, an Arab stronghold, though, on 16 March, Livingstone was able to visit the Lovua branch of the Lualaba flowing strongly northwards from Lake Mweru. But any suggestion of his visiting Lake Bangweulu was met by the Arabs with assurances that this was tantamount to suicide. Then, quite suddenly on 12 April, Livingstone decided to put it to the test and break away. Next day he assembled his remaining attendants—and three of them mutinied, Susi and Chuma being among them; in his new hypomanic mood Livingstone scuffled with Susi, and even fired his revolver at him, but fortunately missed. Then Livingstone moved off with his five loyal men. Amoda deserted next day. Only Abraham, Simon, Gardner and Mabruki were left with the Doctor.

* Churchill went on leave in July 1869, and Kirk became acting Consul. Churchill returned briefly to office towards the end of 1870.

The Last Great Discovery

It is possible to sympathise with the deserters; they longed to reach the safety and comfort of Ujiji, and now their demented master had turned his back on it. Livingstone refused to feel down-hearted; he felt confident that the Lualaba was indeed the Nile and on the way south even drafted a despatch for the Foreign Office in which he wrote: 'I may safely assert' that the Nile sources lay far south of Lake Victoria, and more or less where Ptolemy had placed them. Delusion could go no further.

During the enviable time of well-directed energy on the march to Bangweulu, Livingstone was again the radiantly optimistic, enterprising, energetic man of the periods of his great achievement, hasty in his judgements and prepared to take unjustified risks. He marched south along a course marked roughly today by the Kawambwa–Mansa road, and came to the shores of Bangweulu on 18 July 1868. Next morning he crossed to Masantu Island.

But Masantu lacked any eminence from which he could gain a general view of Bangweulu, or even decide where the lake proper ended and the surrounding swamps (so reminiscent, he thought, of the Nile's inundations) began. He went on to Mpabala Island by canoe, from where he could see Chilubi standing out of the water. Livingstone took it for an island; in fact it is a promontory on the mainland. His men refused to go farther, and so denied him the chance of recognising Bangweulu's eastern shore, or of appreciating its proper shape.

As it was, he thought the swamps to the east were part of the lake, and since he had to account for seventy extra miles of space, envisaged Bangweulu as being four times its real size, with its long axis running east-west. When he came back to the area towards the end of his life, he was, as a result, utterly lost.

He began the journey back to rejoin the Arabs on 30 July, and on reaching them sketched a map which correctly showed the Chambezi being continued through Bangweulu and Mweru by the Luapula and Lovua branch of the Lualaba. Then he learned that an Arab party was going to visit Manyema, lying west of Tanganyika. This presented too good an opportunity of inspecting the lower Lualaba to be missed; the march to Ujiji was again postponed, for, as he rejoiced, the way was 'opening out' before him.

But war with Cazembe put an end to the project and the caravan resumed the march to Ujiji on 23 September. It numbered five hundred fighting men but dared not pass Kabwabwata, and there on 20 November

257

1868 fought off a heavy attack by Bemba tribesmen. By now utterly dependent on the Arabs, Livingstone had to wait until they decided to move north again on 2 December. Then on New Year's Day 1869, he went down with pneumonia. Undoubtedly his life was saved by Bogharib, who personally administered medicines and nourishing food, and had the invalid carried on in a litter. Livingstone was convalescent again by the time they reached Lake Tanganyika at the Lofuko river mouth on 14 February.

Syde ben Habib owned canoes here, and after some haggling lent one to Livingstone. He embarked on 26 February and was paddled slowly northwards, forced by violent storms to hug the coastline. Unknowingly he passed the Lukuga River and missed another opportunity of examining the lake's outlet. On 11 March they were at Kibise Island, from which they crossed the lake. Three days later Livingstone saw the white houses of Ujiji shining in the sunlight, and his spirits lifted, for here at last he felt certain of finding letters and provisions.

He was sorely disappointed; there was no news from his family, no medicines, no nutritious food, and no newspapers. Only a fraction of the provisions sent up from the coast had reached Ujiji; almost everything had been stolen or left behind at Unyanyembe. Livingstone received only a little coffee, sugar and tea, together with a few bales of calico of such poor quality as to be useless for bartering. The blow was staggering.

We must turn for a moment to consider the attempts made to send supplies to Ujiji. Koorji despatched those originally ordered by Livingstone soon after he left Zanzibar. A few months later Seward sent up additional packages. His successor, Churchill, unfortunately ignored Livingstone's instructions of 2 February 1867, but when the two letters written towards the end of that year reached Zanzibar safely, Churchill consulted Kirk and sent another caravan up-country.

So in theory adequate stores should have been waiting at Ujiji. In fact each caravan was systematically pilfered. This was hardly surprising; Livingstone himself had been unable to prevent theft of his stores during 1866, and the half-castes leading the caravans from Zanzibar were all dishonest. The original provisions sent by Koorji were in the charge of a Swahili named Musa who was particularly unreliable. He took two years to cover the seven hundred miles to Ujiji, partly because he was delayed by fighting between the Unyanyembe Arabs and a formidable tribal warrior named Mirambo, and also because he dawdled. Not being sure that Livingstone was still alive, he saw no point in hastening to succour a dead man—and felt no compunction in robbing one.

Livingstone angrily dismissed Musa, and during the next few weeks felt slightly less aggrieved when a few of the missing packages arrived up from Unyanyembe. One contained fifty-two back numbers of *Punch* which he devoured greedily.

Livingstone was content to rest for four months at Ujiji. By 14 March he was feeling better, but for the next ten weeks he was in one of his 'downs'. He felt apathetic, and the daily journal entries are either short or entirely omitted, while nothing at all was entered between 27 April and 16 May. The Arabs at Ujiji were outwardly friendly, but with good cause they treated him with reserve for in his correspondence he condemned them as 'the vilest of the vile'. And they had no compunction in intercepting the forty odd letters he wrote, only two of which reached their destinations. One was addressed to the Sultan and asked him to use his influence in sending up more provisions by reliable freemen and with an armed escort. The second letter was for Kirk and contained the plea that 'I earnestly hope you will do what you can to help me with the goods and men'.

Livingstone must have considered going down to Zanzibar himself to obtain the medicines and porters he needed so badly, but he rejected the idea because he was sure his personal requests to Majid and Kirk would be honoured. He preferred to regain his strength for the geographical work ahead, and to formulate his ideas about the Nile and the hydrography of the African heartland.

He believed that plants in the Lake were drifting to the north, which supported Burton's theory that Tanganyika drained into Lake Albert, and so formed part of the Nile system. But then there was the Lualaba. This, Livingstone concluded, must be another arm of the Nile, or—the thought was oppressive—the upper Congo. Only a little more effort now seemed required to set the pieces of the puzzle in their proper places. If the Lualaba and Tanganyika's effluent river proved to be the two arms of the Nile mentioned by Ptolemy, then there was the additional exciting prospect of finding the remains of the ancient city of Meroe at their confluence where his *Geography* had placed it. Short expeditions to the head of Tanganyika and into Manyema would supply the answers. 'Slowly and surely', wrote Livingstone after his spirits returned, '[I] saw the problems of the fountains of the Nile developing before my eyes.'

The first obvious step was to explore the head of Tanganyika and follow any emergent river to Lake Albert. But he had no calico to hire a canoe, the Arabs refused him currency and there were reports of fighting on the northern lakeshore. Such apparent 'providences' could not be ignored, and Livingstone decided instead to go into Manyema and follow the Lualaba to Lake Albert and on to where he could identify the historical Nile. His adoption of this radically different and much more hazardous plan can only be understood against the background of Livingstone's teleological thinking. Optimistically (he had entered an 'up' that June) he anticipated that his task could be completed within five months, before the 'new squad' of porters arrived from Zanzibar in response to his last letter. In fact Livingstone spent the next two years in Manyema.

* * * * *

According to Henry Morton Stanley, Manyema a century ago was the most remarkable and romantic region in Africa. It was unknown to the rest of the world when Burton saw it across the waters of Tanganyika during 1856, but in 1869 Manyema was becoming embraced by the expanding Arab gun-frontier as traders entered the fabled elephant eldorado in their hunt for ivory and slaves.

Today Manyema is part of Zaire. It strikes the modern visitor still as a savagely beautiful tropical paradise. Nature there seems at its most exuberant. Everything is green. Forests of towering trees rise from verdant glades and rounded hills. Clear streams run through the valleys. The air is scented and heavy. Its light-skinned people, especially the women, are among the most handsome in Africa, and Livingstone repeatedly recorded his admiration for these 'remarkably pretty creatures'.

But 'savage', not 'beautiful' or 'pretty', is the operative word when describing Manyema. The immensely tall grass, growing so profusely, is as sharp as a flourish of swords; the hills, so attractive from a distance, are overgrown with thorns and virtually unclimbable; the forests lie still as death and weirdly menacing; the heat is intolerable; malaria abounds; and the rains during the wet season turn each stream into a raging brown torrent. Travel in Manyema is an exercise in exhaustion, and its people, though good-looking, were, as Livingstone was now to discover when he crossed Lake Tanganyika on 12 July 1869, also unruly, insolently inquisitive, and addicted to cannibalism.

24

Manyema

Because he was with Arabs, Livingstone took almost four months to reach Bambarre, only a hundred miles from Tanganyika, but never seen by a white man before. It was now only ten days' march—four forced marches—to the Lualaba.

Livingstone was greatly impressed by the new country of Manyema for which he saw a great future, telling Thomas, 'the day for Africa is yet to come'. Another rambling letter to Agnes reminisced over past events—Helmore's illness, Tozer's iniquities and Speke's folly in claiming Lake Victoria as the Nile source when so small a quantity of water drained from it. But again he ended with a noble sentiment: 'I am glad that a kind Providence enabled me to do much that will reflect honour on my children'.

On 1 November 1869, in company with a small caravan, Livingstone pressed on westwards as far as the wide Luamo River, only twenty-five miles from the Lualaba. But the local tribes had suffered terribly at the slavers' hands, and 'all were our enemies'. They refused to provide canoes, and the caravan turned back to Bambarre.

By now the town was filled with Arabs, for the ivory rush had begun. Among them was Bogharib, and Livingstone decided to accompany him in another attempt to reach the Lualaba, this time making a wide sweep north to avoid the hostile villages.

The second attempt began on Boxing Day, but the Wamanyema were as hostile as ever, his dysentery relapsed, and the caravan was forced into 'winter quarters' for five long months. Livingstone again fell into depression; he made no attempt to go on alone, and his journal entries are scrappy and more than usually concerned with his own symptoms.

Only in June 1870 did his spirits revive, and, although the Nasik boys had mutinied at the prospect, Livingstone pushed west again with only Susi, Chuma and Gardner. But early next month he was overtaken by a new affliction which enforced his return to Bambarre: 'for the first time in my life', Livingstone noted, 'my feet failed me'. He had fallen victim to one of Africa's scourges—Tropical Ulcers.

Until recently these 'irritable-eating ulcers' were prevalent in the tropics, and became a major problem during African campaigns in the last two wars. They are caused by infective organisms entering an abrasion, generally on the exposed lower limbs, of those people whose natural resistance has been impaired by malaria, dysentery, hookworm infestation, or general malnutrition. Hideous, rapidly enlarging ulcers then appear, measuring up to a hand's breadth in size; their margins are raised and undermined; the sloughing tissue at the base is bathed in grey-green pus, and discharges a bloody ichor. If untreated the ulcers may eat away muscles, tendons, nerves and even blood vessels. Livingstone gives a detailed first-hand description of the condition and rightly suspected that it was spread by contagion, for he noted its appearance in epidemic form in an adjoining Arab camp, where it 'carried off' thirty slaves.

Fearful of missing the expected 'new squad' of pagazi, Livingstone 'limped back to Bambarre' on 22 July 1870 and there he remained until 16 February 1871.

These seven months were the most revealing of his life, for during them he escaped from the reality of loneliness and discouragement into the realms of imagination and visionary transcendentalism.

For the first three months he was confined to his hut, fearful that his physical condition might prevent his finishing his task, and he thought seriously of retiring 'while life lasts'. But, after accepting advice from Arab neighbours, he treated his ulcers directly with powdered malachite. Even today copper sulphate compresses are used in the treatment of Tropical Ulcers, and Livingstone's lesions quickly healed. On 10 October 1870 he was able to leave his hut.

During these waiting months he had been tormented by pain, and 'in agony for news from home', but in late August, his mood lightened again; although physically still crippled, his mind began to explore a whole new realm of consciousness in which he confused imagination with reality, but it set every object in the hut dancing and flaming with kaleidoscopic life.

Livingstone had always gained much pleasure from the Scriptures, and now he noted that he 'read the whole Bible through four times whilst I was in Manyuema'. His immaculate personal Bible can be seen today at

Blantyre, but the smaller copy, presumably used by his attendants at his regular services, is much thumbed, especially at Psalms 23, 40–43, 45, 90, 95–112. Grimy fingers have turned often to Proverbs and the Pentateuch too, but the Book of Job, so relevant to his circumstances, was apparently rarely consulted.

His newly aroused activity led to the resumption of his correspondence, though he never knew if it would reach its destination. Writing materials were short, but he improvised ink from the juice of a plant named *Zugifaré* by the Arabs, whose reddish colour led to the suggestion that he used his blood for writing. Any scraps of paper that came to hand were pressed into service, even old cheque-book stubs and minutes of R.G.S. meetings which fortunately had wide margins. A letter of this time to Agnes includes another of those noble phrases: 'I hope to present to my young countrymen an example of manly perseverance.'

In addition he made lengthy notes on all manner of subjects. There is a report on his personal philosophy and a detailed account of 'The winds of Africa'. A scientific memorandum on malaria notes it 'is one of the great barriers to the advances of Christian nations into the interior of the continent', while a particularly interesting paper asserts that the similarity of the shells and fish of Lake Nyasa to those of Galilee 'lead me to the inference that a chain of lakes once extended from Palestine to South Africa', indicating his geographical comprehension of the Great Rift Valley which runs from Galilee to the Zambezi.

There were less taxing diversions. Livingstone spent a good deal of time observing the behaviour of a new pet, locally called a 'soko'. It has usually been assumed to have been a chimpanzee, but Livingstone himself described it as a gorilla, and his description suggests it was a sub-species, the mountain gorilla, since it nested, killed leopards, and attacked men, biting off their fingers.

He also turned his attention to the mysterious African addiction to 'safura' or earth-eating, finding it prevalent among slaves, and possibly a manifestation of their insecurity. This condition, geophagy, still exists in primitive communities.

Another medical communication concerned the disorder of Broken Heart. It was common among new captives who 'ascribed their only pain to the heart, and placed the hand correctly on the spot, though many think that the organ stands high up under the breast bone'; he concluded that 'it seems to be really broken-hearts of which they die'. While modern medicine agrees that intense grief can induce a heart attack, the malady described by Livingstone was a lingering one, which neither then nor today is properly understood.

Stranger notions wandered through his mind at Bambarre. He was vastly intrigued by Arab accounts of cave-dwellings in Rua, to the west of Mweru. 'Always something new from Africa', he noted, misquoting the proverb, and described lines of houses excavated on a mountain-side, capable of holding ten thousand people, and decorated with paintings of animals made by dark men with slanting eyes. Probably he was describing Kiwakisi Caves in Zaire, which consist of numerous connected vaults decorated with Bushmen paintings.

Such were some of the more pedestrian among the flights of thought that swept through Livingstone's mind as he lay in Manyema in a rough hut.

But there were also exalted ones—ones that were typical of the cyclothymic personality. Elevated by the joy now possessing him, Livingstone conceived that he had been appointed to a new and vitally important task—confirmation of the Sacred Scriptures of his faith. 'Surely my work is with the Lord, and my judgement with my God', he wrote when looking back on this sojourn at Bambarre.

On 18 August 1870, two Arab visitors told him that in Katanga lay four fountains, from each of which a great river flowed, and, as Livingstone noted excitedly, 'a mound rises between them, the most remarkable in Africa . . . [which] would serve exactly the description of the Garden of Eden in Genesis'. He had thought often about the hillock described by Herodotus which gave life to the Nile; as early as 1855 he learned that the Zambezi emerged from a hill named Kaombo, and two years later told an Edinburgh audience that the Nile source lay nearby. Now the Arabs' description appeared first-hand confirmation of Herodotus's account.

His mind became infatuated by the Nile, and a delusional mind-image acquired a reality more insistent than his surroundings. Livingstone had with him a copy of a map compiled by Speke to illustrate his explorations. To this he now added Mweru with the Lualaba issuing from it. Then on the back he made a sketch of the 'remarkable' mound which he annotated as 'a hill without stones', about a mile across. Around it he placed the four 'coy fountains' of the classics.

As fantasy soared, he conceived that there were three, or even four,

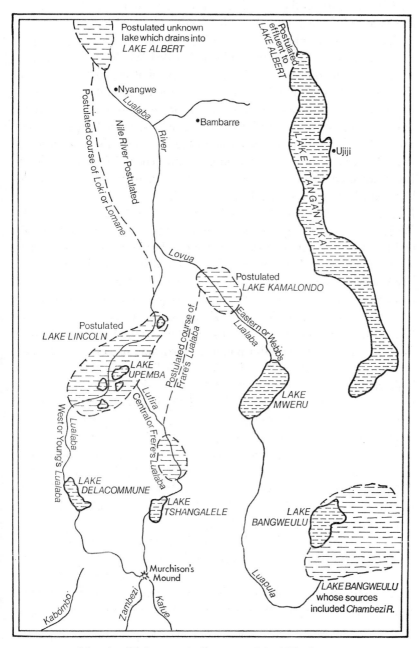

Map 6. Livingstone's Concept of the Nile Sources

Manyema

separate lines of northern drainage from this watershed. He even gave names to them which honoured his friends.

His concept comprised the familiar Bangweulu–Luapula–Mweru–Lualaba sequence to the east, and was labelled Webb's lacustrine river; it was made to broaden out in the country of Rua into a lake named Kamalondo. Kamalondo does not exist but the breadth of this part of the Lovua and the imprecise African words for bodies of water excuses the error. On the west a second Lualaba, which he named after 'Paraffin' Young, flowed northwards from one of the four fountains until it joined Webb's Lualaba below Kamalondo. On the course of Young's River, Livingstone enlarged Lake Upemba and its surrounding swamps into a lake called after President Lincoln,* which continued as the known Lomani (or Loki) River to Webb's Lualaba. Finally Livingstone called the Lufira River (rising from an adjoining fountain) the central Lualaba or Frere's River, and visualised it flowing either into Young's or Webb's River. Thus he made the rivers of Young and Frere originate from the 'remarkable' mound, which he placed on the watershed just north of modern Solwezi. Nearby on the south Livingstone postulated two more fountains giving rise to the Zambezi and Kafue. In fact the Lunga and Kafue sources lie close to this point while the Kabompo rises a little to the west. Livingstone indicated a possible fourth line of northerly drainage through Lake Tanganyika which he still believed fed Albert Nyanza. This riverine theory fitted many of the facts. Where he went tragically wrong was to assume that his three Lualabas joined to form the Nile. In fact they represent the headwaters of the Congo. Later, Livingstone would reach the lower Lualaba and calculate its altitude at about 2,000 feet, an awkward figure since it approximated to that of Lake Albert, and this lay well 'downstream' to the north. But he got over the difficulty with three different suggestions: that Baker's calculation was wrong; that the Lualaba by-passed Lake Albert; and by inventing another lake which extended the Lualaba to Lake Albert.

It was a complex thesis, and perhaps Livingstone was embarrassed by the number of sources he had postulated. For he had placed them at a pair of fountains near the mound, in the heads of the Chambezi or Bangweulu's feeder streams if these were longer, and in the rivers filling Lake Tanganyika. The remainder of his life was spent trying to

* 'A monument', Stanley later explained with pardonable optimism, 'more durable than brass, iron or stone.'

266

demonstrate these separate sources and proving that the Lualaba was the historical Nile.

But he was ever haunted by a nagging concern that the Lualaba might turn out to be the Congo. He tried to dismiss this disturbing thought by ascribing the Congo's origins to the Kasai, Quango and Lubilash, and by falling back, sub-consciously, on his teleological doctrine, for the Lualaba had surely been 'reserved' for him for some good purpose; it would provide him with new fame, not for personal satisfaction but only to increase his prestige and so advance the completion of the Holy design. 'The Nile sources are valuable to me', he told his elder brother John, 'only as a means of enabling me to open my mouth with power among men.'

Before we leave Livingstone's fallacious thinking on the Nile, we must note that his other friends were not forgotten when he named the coming discoveries in wishful anticipation. One fountain was to be called after Palmerston and others after Oswell, Frere and Young, while the hillock itself was styled 'Murchison's Mound'. These names were never to appear on maps, and although the heights he had glimpsed at the head of Nyasa are still known as the Livingstone mountains, Stanley's suggestion that the mighty Lualaba be called the Livingstone River was rejected by Leopold II.

Livingstone always gave the impression that he remembered Herodotus's account of the Nile from his boyhood; in fact Smith's *Dictionary of the Bible* recounted the story, and we can imagine the eagerness with which the Doctor pored over its pages and then turned to the Old Testament for additional information. The dictionary also described the rise of Moses to power in Egypt, adding that he 'advanced to Saba, the capital of Ethiopia, and gave it the name of Meroe, from his adopted mother Merrhis, whom he buried there. Tharbes, the daughter of the king of Ethiopia, fell in love with him, and he returned in triumph to Egypt with her as his wife.' Livingstone's deluded mind quickly kindled to the notion that he would find the ruins of Meroe as he descended the Lualaba-Nile.

Indeed he became engrossed with the opportunity this would give him of confirming the truth of the Pentateuch, now challenged by Darwin and Colenso, although logic and his geological knowledge of the earth's antiquity must have told him this was flying in the face of reason. And, for him in his present mood, it was only a small step to imagine that at

Bambarre he had been led to the land of the Old Testament in order to demonstrate a unity with the sacred past. With facile optimism he recalled Arab descriptions of a handsome white race living in Manyema—who must surely be the descendants of the lost tribes of Israel. The ivory doors and pillars which the slavers said they had seen in Manyema could only represent the work of men whose traditional memory retained an image of Solomon's ivory palace. The Arabs lent more credence to these fantasies by speaking about their own cherished tradition of Moses travelling through this part of Africa. Livingstone had already pondered over this legend. As early as 24 February 1868 he had gravely noted that some Arabs 'believe Kilimanjaro mountain has mummies as in Egypt and that Moses visited it of old', and eight months later he referred to their tradition of Moses living at Meroe.

So now at Bambarre the following entries appear in the journal: 'One of my waking dreams is that the legendary tales about Moses coming up into Inner Ethiopia . . . may have a substratum of fact. . . . I dream of discovering some monumental relics of Meroe,* and if anything confirmatory of sacred history does remain, I pray that I be guided thereunto. If the sacred chronology would thereby be confirmed, I would not grudge the toil and hardships, hunger and pain, I have endured—the irritable ulcers would only be discipline.' The content of his waking trance was transmitted in a lighter mood to W. C. Oswell: 'I am dreaming of finding the lost city of Meroe at the confluence of the two head branches. The reality reveals that I have lost nearly all my teeth—that is what the sources have done to me.' He repeated his aspiration to Braithwaite, but the subsequent sentence reads differently: 'If I should find something to confirm the precious old documents [as] the scriptures of truth, I would feel my toil rewarded'.

Entries about the coming quest crowd into the journal. On 25 October 1870, after explaining that his presentiment of death had now 'weakened', he breathlessly remarks that 'an eager desire to discover any evidence of the great Moses having visited these parts bound me, spellbound me, I may say, for if I could bring to light anything to confirm the sacred oracles, I should not grudge one whit all the labour expended'; and eight days later, 'I have also an excessive wish to find anything that may exist proving the visit of the great Moses and the ancient kingdom of Tirhaka'.

---

* The ruins of Meroe in fact lay far away to the north beyond Khartoum, and had been examined by Bruce in 1772.

And so, believing himself to be on the very threshold of glorious discoveries, Livingstone laid his plans for the next step when the porters sent up by Kirk arrived at Bambarre. The clear course would be to descend Webb's Lualaba until he reached the recognisable Nile (privately he expected this would be at Petherick's branch flowing through the Bahr el Ghazal), even though the Wamanyema were now fighting the Arabs and travel would be dangerous. So the earlier he went the better.

At last on 27 January 1871 solid news reached Bambarre of the approach of a caravan, and on 4 February ten of the long-expected porters arrived. The Doctor's impatience and anticipation exploded into joy and gratitude to Kirk for having despatched them.

The joy and gratitude were sadly premature.

For it is difficult for us to commend Kirk's attempts to succour Livingstone; they seem little concerned with his welfare. Admittedly Kirk faced formidable difficulties in getting a caravan up-country. After receiving Livingstone's letter, written four months earlier, on 2 October 1869, he turned for help to Koorji, who eventually enrolled fifteen shiftless Mohammedan slaves as porters. Kirk blamed his difficulty in getting suitable men on an approaching cholera epidemic, but Stanley later succeeded in engaging 192 free men for his own expedition.

Kirk's choice of a Mohammedan Swahili tailor named Shereef as leader is still less excusable. Even a short investigation would have shown him to be a worthless man who was more concerned with trading on his own account up-country than with carrying vital provisions to a white man marooned in the interior.

Shereef's caravan with £500 worth of stores left Zanzibar at the end of October 1869, and faithfully repeated the dismal story of the earlier expeditions. Shereef stopped continually to sell off his own stock *and* the goods consigned to Livingstone. The pagazi would not hurry, and only on 10 December 1870 did they reach Ujiji, having taken fourteen months for a three-month journey.

Shereef declined to go farther since he had divined in the Koran that Livingstone was dead, and settled down comfortably in Ujiji, living on the sale of the remaining goods. But he did send on seven pagazi to Manyema.* Unaccountably joined by three other men, they arrived at

* For the record their names were Farahani, Feruz, Amur, Bilale, Ambarre, Ramadan and Chakusa.

Bambarre on 4 February 1871. With them they carried a letter from Kirk, a supply of quinine and a mere £4 worth of provisions.

Livingstone quickly discovered that these 'banian slaves' were useless, and he referred to their conduct as a 'mauvais sujet', one of the few occasions he used a French phrase. They positively asserted that Kirk had instructed them to bring him down to Zanzibar.

They demanded—and got—an advance of pay,* and then went on strike for double wages, to which Livingstone again had to agree. Then they refused to go on from Bambarre unless accompanied by sixty guns, and when Livingstone remonstrated, they told him they took orders from their banyan masters. They only agreed to march when threatened with a pistol, and the party finally quit Bambarre on 16 February 1871 with Susi, Gardner and Chuma leading the ten villainous pagazi.

It was a relief to be on the move again, and Livingstone, on 9 March, was delighted to learn that the Lualaba went 'rolling majestically *to the north*,† and again makes even easting'. But soon the wretched porters mutinied and Livingstone doubted 'whether the Divine favour and will is on my side'. On 29 March, however, they came to the town of Nyangwe on the bank of the Lualaba, and his fears were again allayed by learning that the river overflowed its banks each year 'as the Nile does further down', and although its water was darker than at Cairo, the current ran 'about two miles an hour away *to the north*'.†

It was disturbing, however, to find the altitude of Nyangwe was hardly more than Lake Albert,‡ but when he followed the Lualaba downstream to about 4 degrees it broadened out, and this lent substance to his theory of a great 'unknown lake' extending to Lake Albert. He could go no farther; the pagazi insisted on turning back because of fighting ahead. Livingstone had reached his furthest west. He returned to Nyangwe (as he would never have done in a more resolute mood); four months later he escaped from the town, baffled and at the nadir of his fortunes.

No canoes were available to him for hire at Nyangwe, and he had no money to buy one. In any case the Arabs did not relish his moving

* Bogharib and other Arabs appear to have advanced money for their wages.
† My italics.
‡Livingstone told Stanley that he found the altitude to be over 2,300 feet. When Stanley himself visited Nyangwe in 1876 he calculated it to be only 1,454 feet which conclusively disproved it being the Nile. It is odd that Livingstone's measurement was so far out; perhaps it was another example of wishful calculation.

beyond their control, and, although kindly, refused to help him cross or go down the river. Twenty years earlier Livingstone would not have accepted the rebuff; now he submitted patiently, trusting it was intended for some good. This he presently recognised when an Arab canoe was lost down-river at an unsuspected cataract. 'I was prevented going down to the narrows', the Doctor wrote on hearing this news, 'we don't always know the dangers we are guided past'.*

The 'dreary waiting' continued. Some of his letters at this time stress his admiration for the Manyema women, and may have accounted for a rumour in Zanzibar that he had settled down with an African princess. Another solace was his fascination with the great open-air market at Nyangwe, held three times a week. There, for long afterwards, he was remembered kindly as Douad; when Stanley came here five years later, he was hospitably received as Livingstone's friend and one greyhaired African told him that Douad had saved him 'from being robbed many a time by the Arabs, and he was so gentle and patient and told us such pleasant stories about the wonderful land of the white people. Hm', The aged white was a good man, indeed.'

Livingstone's trusting patience seemed rewarded on 18 June 1871 when the amiable Dugumbe arrived in Nyangwe at the head of five hundred fighting men, intending to settle down and exploit the Lualaba's western bank. He helped Livingstone materially, and (for a price) tentatively offered to help him explore Lake Lincoln and visit the four 'coy fountains' although he would not hear of his crossing the Lualaba. But he would not commit himself to a definite start. 'I am distressed and perplexed . . . all seems against me', Livingstone wrote in his journal on 14 July 1871. Once more his faith was wavering. Next day the whole situation was altered by a monstrous atrocity.

*   *   *   *   *

The massacre Livingstone witnessed at Nyangwe on 15 July 1871 haunted him for the rest of his life. There is an unbelieving flavour to his description of the scene; the pages in the journal seem to explode with loathing and outrage.

That morning Livingstone went as usual to the market and wandered among the women who had come to display their wares of fish, salt, oil,

---

* Livingstone never revealed how he reconciled the existence of this cataract with the calm waters of his 'unknown lake'.

goats, pigs, produce and vegetables. He listened to the customary haggling at the booths, then, vaguely disturbed because he had seen several villages burning on the far side of the river, he sauntered back towards his house. Suddenly a group of Arabs infuriated by the price asked for a single fowl began shooting into the defenceless crowd, and were joined in the killing by a group of armed slaves, who 'seemed turned into demons'. It was an exhibition of the slavers' deliberate policy of terrorising the Wamanyema.

Nyangwe became a scene of indescribable confusion as the Wamanyema tried to escape by canoe or on foot. Livingstone watched helplessly as their canoes foundered and the fugitives were taken by crocodiles. About four hundred people, mostly women and children, perished that morning. For Livingstone it was a ghastly culmination of all the horrors he associated with the slave trade.

'My first impulse', Livingstone writes, 'was to pistol the murderers', but he was restrained by Dugumbe, who himself took steps to save some of the fugitives. Livingstone then hustled the survivors into his house, after bravely hoisting his consular Union Jack. Next day fourteen cowed and trembling headmen from the burnt villages of the far bank came over to ask him to make peace and to protect them; but ironically now, when the Wamanyema were at last prepared to assist him, and Dugumbe was positively placatory, Livingstone could not bear to stay a moment longer with the Arabs. His plan of accompanying Dugumbe to Katanga was abandoned: 'I cannot remain among bloody companions', he explained, 'and would flee away.' Although poised, as he believed, on the brink of success, he saw no alternative but to escape like Christian from the accursed city, and return to Ujiji. 'I was near a fourth lake in this central line', he told Maclear, 'and only eighty miles from Lake Lincoln on our west, in fact almost in sight of the geographical end of my mission when I was forced to return.' All his efforts seemed to have ended in failure; he would never know that his cause was vitally helped by the massacre at Nyangwe. For his account so horrified Britain as to cause the despatch of Frere's mission of enquiry to Zanzibar, and so led to the suppression of the African slave trade.

The three months' journey back to Ujiji was a continuous nightmare and somehow during it Livingstone lost thirteen days from his calendar reckoning. He was in agony from piles, and troubled too by his only remaining footwear—a pair of painfully tight patent-leather French shoes. In appalling heat, discouraged and fatigued beyond telling, he stumbled back with his treacherous porters through hostile country. The party was stoned, then ambushed, and Livingstone escaped death by inches when a spear grazed his back. Afterwards they ran the gauntlet through the forest for five mortal hours. At Bambarre he rested for ten days, 'reduced to a skeleton'. Then he struggled on to Lake Tanganyika, his spirits maintained only by the thought of the stores he would surely find sent up by Kirk. He crossed to the town on 23 October 1871.

That evening the blow fell: he found Susi and Chuma weeping bitterly. 'All our things are sold', they told him, 'Shereef has sold everything for ivory.' It was an even more shattering disappointment than the one he suffered here in 1869.

Fortunately he had left a small quantity of calico in the care of a friendly Arab in Ujiji. This, together with the sale of his watch, gun and instruments, would allow him to pay his way for another month. Then, as he told his brother John, he would make his way northwards down the Lualaba, alone if necessary, in the hope of falling in with Samuel Baker.*
For he was beginning to have doubts about Kirk's loyalty: his choice of Shereef and the banyan 'slaves' to succour him seemed at best inefficiency and at worst an utter lack of concern. If the thought entered his mind of returning to Zanzibar, it was banished. He would never again seek the aid of Her Britannic Majesty's Consul, whom he had thought to be his friend.

Indeed Livingstone seemed to have reached the end of the road; within a few weeks he would literally be a pauper, and could scarcely expect to live much longer. His own words exactly describe his condition. 'I felt as though I were the man who went down from Jerusalem to Jerico but no priest, Levite, or a good Samaritan would come my way.' But miraculously the good Samaritan was at hand.

---

* Whom he had learned was leading an expedition up the Nile.

25

Livingstone and Stanley

No episode in the history of exploration has so caught the public imagination as Livingstone's meeting with Henry Morton Stanley at Ujiji on 10 November 1871.* Events had conspired to make it sensational as well as picturesque, for by the end of 1871 the British people had suddenly become deeply concerned for Livingstone's safety. An earlier uneasiness had abated when he was reported alive in 1868. Thereafter, occasional messages came from Zanzibar to say he had been 'sighted' by some Arab; fitful enquiries were made from time to time; and there were some wild theories about his whereabouts: Murchison thought his friend would presently appear on the West coast of Africa; Cooley guessed Livingstone was imprisoned at Cazembe's court; Baker, about to lead an Egyptian Army into the Sudan, believed he would meet him on the Nile. But Livingstone's reputation for invulnerability carried the day, and no one did anything concrete about his disappearance.

. . . except for Mr James Gordon Bennett, the enterprising owner of the *New York Herald*, who sent his star reporter, Henry Morton Stanley, to Aden to seek news of Livingstone. Stanley could learn nothing and presently moved on thankfully to cover Spain's civil war.

Then in October 1869 Kirk telegraphed from Zanzibar that Livingstone had recently been seen in Ujiji. Although he doubted the accuracy of this report, Bennett, during a dramatic interview in Paris soon afterwards, instructed Stanley to make another attempt to 'find' Livingstone. First, however, he was to complete other journalistic assignments which would take at least a year. It has never been explained why Bennett imposed this delay, Stanley may even have invented it, but it was a most fortunate decision.

Stanley's departure from Paris towards the end of 1869 passed

* This date is not necessarily correct. Both men were out in their reckonings, but accepted 10 November after adjusting their calendars on the 1st day of Ramadan, the 14th.

unnoticed, but while he pursued Bennett's itinerary through Egypt, Palestine, Turkey and Russia, public anxiety mounted. In May 1870 the British Government reacted by voting £1000 for supplies to be sent up to Livingstone; then on learning that Ujiji was cut off by Mirambo's warriors, it called on the R.G.S. to help organise a relief expedition. This was commanded by a Lieutenant Dawson and included young Oswell Livingstone. It sailed for Zanzibar by the newly-opened Suez Canal on 7 February 1872, and reached the island six weeks later—but by then it was already well behind Stanley. Dawson sent two members of the expedition across to Bagamoyo to prepare for the inland march. They began recruiting pagazi on 27 April 1872, but next day Stanley's advance guard reached the coast with news that Livingstone was safe. Against all odds, instead of his compatriots, an American journalist had 'found' him.

The news broke in England on 2 May 1872 and was subsequently amplified by the publication of two despatches from Stanley while Bennett basked happily in the glow of the greatest 'scoop' in history.

The despatches recounted how Stanley approached Ujiji on the morning of 10 November 1871. The Stars and Stripes were borne before him; his men were sounding kudu horns, beating drums and firing off salutes. The noise brought Livingstone from his house. He wore the consular cap, a red woollen jersey, grey tweed trousers and the tight shoes. Crowds of Africans, too, poured into the streets to welcome the caravan as Livingstone waited under a large mango tree close to the lakeshore.* Here he was joined by a group of Arabs. Then the hubbub diminished and the crowd parted to allow Stanley's approach on horseback. He was wearing smart white flannels, a well-chalked sola topi with a newly folded puggaree, and shining Wellington boots. He spurred his horse forward and then dismounted, walked forward, doffed his helmet, bowed and said 'Dr Livingstone, I presume'.

The greeting was made all the more ridiculous by Livingstone's dignified reply of 'Yes, that is my name'. Stanley's four words would become an over-worked music hall gag, and even now, people meeting anywhere in the world find it amusing to say 'Mr X, I presume'. The unfortunate remark haunted Stanley for the remainder of his life.

But Henry Morton Stanley was very far from being a fool. After

---

* A monument was raised at the meeting-place. The lake then temporarily receded, so that until recently the monument stood some way from the water.

Livingstone, he was to become Africa's greatest explorer. He was born John Rowlands at Denbigh of unmarried parents during 1841, the year of Livingstone's arrival in Africa. Brought up amid crushing poverty he was placed in a workhouse at St. Asaph when only six. There, after absorbing the elements of a general education, according to his own account he escaped from the insitution and its sadistic master. Though grudgingly lodged by relations he was never accepted as a member of the family, and in 1858 we find him writing contritely for help to an uncle: 'It is a hard case on me', he said, since he could find no work and had 'nowhere to go'. He signed himself 'your humble nephew, John Rowlands'.

Spurned by his relations, the outcast worked his passage as a cabin boy to New Orleans where he jumped ship and took a job as a junior clerk. There too he met a wealthy merchant named Henry Hope Stanley who, being childless, adopted several children including John Rowlands. He quickly regretted this latest acquisition to his family; the boy was so troublesome that his foster father soon sent him away to work on an Arkansas plantation, which he quickly left, however, to find work with a local trader. Here Rowlands acquired skill with firearms and when the Civil war broke out he enlisted in the Confederate army.

By now he had taken his adopted father's name of Henry Stanley (and later exchanged the middle name of Hope for Morton after experimenting with Morelake, Moreland and Morley). He was wounded and captured at the Battle of Shiloh, and imprisoned at Camp Douglas near Chicago.

Conditions there not being to his liking, Stanley cheerfully changed sides and enlisted in the Illinois Light Artillery, but was quickly discharged as medically unfit. He then made his way back to north Wales, but his mother rebuffed him so, he says, he returned to the States and worked first as a deckhand on a merchantman, then as a clerk in Brooklyn and finally signed on in the Federal Navy. After being present at the bombardment of Fort Fisher, Stanley deserted together with a youngster named Lewis Noe. Afterwards he freelanced for *The Missouri Democrat*—and discovered a rare ability to string words together.

This seemed likely to come in useful during his next adventure, when Stanley, Noe and a third man went off to seek copy in Asia Minor. But there they were captured by brigands and beaten up, while Noe was raped. After being rescued by the American Minister in Constantinople, we find Stanley masquerading as a United States naval officer in Denbigh where he treated the inmates of St. Asaph's workhouse* to tea and cakes, and an entirely fictitious account of his career. He then returned to America.

There, at the age of twenty-six, he obtained an assignment to report on General Hancock's campaign against Red Indians until, in 1867, he persuaded the *New York Herald* to send him out to cover Lord Napier's invasion of Abyssinia. Thanks to surreptitious bribery Stanley scooped the world with a report on the fall of Magdala and the Emperor Theodore's suicide, and in June 1868 he could exult, 'I am now a permanent employee of the *Herald*'.

In this capacity he sought news of Livingstone at Aden, and then covered the war in Spain until summoned to Paris by the *Herald*'s proprietor, who gave him his new Livingstone assignment. He finally reached Zanzibar on 6 January 1871 and at once began preparations for the hazardous march into the interior.

He was abundantly fitted for the task. Stanley was a tough and thrusting man who was determined to gain fame; he spoke often of acquiring 'kudos' for himself, and he did not mind whom he hurt in the process. Moreover, he had become a brilliant reporter; Stanley knew exactly how to draw every iota of drama from a story, and intended to win as much 'kudos' as possible from the Livingstone assignment.

Queen Victoria later summed Stanley up as 'a determined, ugly little man with a strong American twang', but when he was excited, his voice resumed the sing-song rhythm of his Welsh forebears. His face was round and red; drooping lips were set off by a wispy moustache and beard. He had high cheek bones and penetrating grey eyes, which Mrs Webb of Newstead said were 'like small pools of grey fire, but the least provocation turned them into grey lightning'.

Unfortunately Stanley never got over the stigma of his illegitimacy. He was fiercely, absurdly touchy, and throughout his life, in conversations, correspondence and several profitable exercises in autobiography, he constantly tangled truth with mendacity. In Zanzibar he presented himself as an American, and took such dislike for Kirk that he decided to hide his real reason for coming to the island. But Stanley got on well with the American Consul, and with Fraser too, whose connections with the slave trade had brought him unpleasantness from Kirk. Indeed it was

---

* The workhouse still stands, now grandly renamed 'H.M. Stanley Hospital'.

Fraser who suggested to Stanley that the British Consul was not over-concerned with supplying Livingstone with the provisions he needed so desperately.

For his part Kirk distrusted the disingenuous Yankee who insisted he was mounting an expensive expedition merely to explore the insignificant Rufiji River. Other things about Stanley seemed suspicious too, so Kirk was evasive in his replies to ponderously vague enquiries about Livingstone's possible whereabouts. According to Stanley, Kirk also represented Livingstone to him as a splenetic mean-spirited misanthrope, who would probably march off in the opposite direction if he heard someone was looking for him. It seemed to confirm Fraser's suggestion that Kirk was Livingstone's adversary rather than his friend.

Unhappily Stanley soon discovered fresh evidence of Kirk's negligence when he crossed over to Bagamoyo on 4 February 1871. The caravan despatched three months earlier by Kirk and Churchill, in response of the British Government's grant of £1000, lay stalled at the coast.

Kirk had not bothered to supervise the pagazis' departure or even enquire about their progress until on or about 18 February, when he crossed to the mainland to hasten it on its way. Even then he decided to combine the trip with some hunting.

According to Kirk's despatches, he quickly got the caravan moving inland and followed it for two days before going shooting. Stanley's account differed. He insisted that Kirk allowed a week to go by before he visited the quarters of the pagazi, only to discover that the caravan had just left. Nor, said Stanley, did Kirk follow it inland. Livingstone unreservedly accepted Stanley's account, while Stanley afterwards missed no opportunity of accusing Livingstone's 'quondam companion' of negligence of his old friend. However when Stanley wrote his breezy best-seller *How I found Livingstone*, his censure there of Kirk raised such a storm of protest that in subsequent editions he deleted the unkindest remarks. But the damage was done, and although Sir Reginald Coupland had sprung to Kirk's defence,* inevitably his reputation suffered, and today Kirk is remembered as the man who 'lost' Livingstone, while Stanley remains the intrepid explorer who 'found him'.

* * * * *

Stanley did himself very well for his expedition into the interior. He

* In *Livingstone's Last Journey*, Collins, 1945.

Livingstone and Stanley

spent £4,000 on six tons of equipment, which included a bearskin, Persian carpet, enamel bath, silver goblets and two bottles of expensive champagne to celebrate the anticipated meeting. At Bagamoyo he enrolled 192 men whom he sent up the Ujiji road in five contingents: the first group left on 18 February, while he himself, mounted on a magnificent bay horse, led the last party out of town on 21 March. Subsequently Stanley was presented with an intelligent little slave boy named Kalulu, who became his 'butler', and later accompanied him to England and America where he proved an enormous success on Stanley's lecture platforms.

Stanley was a harsh leader. He quickly reduced two seedy white companions to wrecks. One tried to shoot him after being knocked down for some misdemeanour. In the end they separately begged to be left behind on the line of march, and both perished miserably in the wilds. Thereafter Stanley transmitted orders through his factotum, Bombay. Bombay had served with Speke, who had knocked out his front teeth. His new master proved equally irascible, and twice whipped him soundly. For Stanley was a firm believer in the persuasive powers of a whip; he used it once on the hysterical wife of one of his porters and noted the incident with relish in *How I found Livingstone*. This too was tactfully omitted in subsequent editions.

If power can be defined as the ability to force other men to act according to one's wishes, then Stanley was a man of power. Men of his type would civilise Africa during the next decades, but they also mortally offended her people by an arrogant assumption of racial superiority. They behaved quite unlike the Doctor. The tragedy of Africa is that men like Stanley seemed to mark the continent more indelibly than Livingstone. Certainly Stanley drove his porters rather than led them; and whereas Livingstone is remembered as a man walking across Africa with a Bible in his hand, posterity sees Stanley striding across the continent brandishing a scourge. The impression is in part justified: 'This selfish and wooden-headed world', Stanley once observed, 'requires mastering as well as loving charity'. He differed in another way from Livingstone: deep down Stanley disliked Africa and its people. 'I do not think I was made for an African explorer', he admitted, 'for I detest the land most heartily.'

Yet whatever may be said about his methods, there can be no doubt about their efficacy. His cumbrous caravan reached Unyanyembe in eighty-four days, and he would have got there even earlier had he not stopped to conduct autopsies on baggage animals in the hope of disproving Kirk's warning against taking them into tsetse country.

Unyanyembe, a town of a thousand houses, was the capital of Majid's mainland ivory-and-slaving domain, and its Arab compound, called Tabora, has given the modern town its name. Stanley found most of the provisions brought up for Livingstone lying in the town, and being 'rapidly made away with'. He also came across a packet of mail addressed to Livingstone. Kirk had given it to a man named Kaif Hallech, or 'How do you do' in Arabic. When 'How do you do' refused to carry the mail to Ujiji, Stanley unhesitatingly put him in chains and dragged him on with the caravan.

But even Stanley was delayed by the Arabs' war with Mirambo, and he only got away from Unyanyembe on 20 September 1871. After skirting Mirambo's territory he finally entered Ujiji on 10 November.

With the luck of a born journalist, he had arrived at exactly the right moment. Livingstone was not lost in the geographical sense (for he knew exactly where he was), but he was destitute and in despair. Indeed there seemed something pre-ordained about Stanley's movements; Fate (or, as Livingstone would have said, God) appeared to have controlled them. For the two men met as though they had marched to an agreed rendezvous. Even Stanley was impressed by Livingstone's predictive doctrine: 'Had I gone direct from Paris . . . I might have lost him', he wrote later, 'had I been enabled to have gone direct to Ujiji from Unyanyembe I might have lost him . . . I began to recognise the hand of an overruling and kindly Providence.'

After the meeting under the mango tree, Livingstone motioned Stanley to the verandah of his house. A rather strained conversation followed until Stanley remembered the bottles of champagne, and gave the toast 'Dr Livingstone, to your very good health, Sir'. Thereafter the two men began to talk more easily.

The Arabs presently withdrew and the crowd drifted away, leaving them chatting far into the night. There were many adventures and world events to discuss (the Doctor was particularly surprised to hear of the Second Empire's ruin); and all through the long conversation, Livingstone patiently refrained from reading the letters Stanley had brought him, or even from enquiring the reason for his presence in Ujiji. 'It was not my business' he explained later in an example of mid-Victorian reticence which deserves to be as well remembered as Stanley's greeting. Only late at night did the Doctor open his letters; from one he learned that the Government had voted £1,000 for his relief and intended to pay him a salary. For his part Stanley rejoiced that he had squeezed so much information out of Livingstone and could soon hurry back to civilisation with his story.

Yet he remained with Livingstone for four months, and assumed the unwonted role of a disciple. Although so unlike in character, the two men did possess certain traits in common. Both were deeply religious and both were stubborn and brave, prodigious in energy, and intolerant of other men's weaknesses, whether physical or moral. Neither bore criticism well nor tolerated ridicule. And they each possessed that peculiar quality of toughness combined with curiosity which makes a dedicated explorer. Even their differences curiously complemented each other's. So these two self-willed men, cast into such unusual intimacy, were able to discuss a host of subjects without friction; one of the few on which they differed was as to the relative merits of Gladstone and Disraeli, Livingstone predictably preferring the liberal statesman.

Yet sometimes Stanley's personality must have grated on the older man. He was cynical, brash and without much social conscience. He never told Livingstone of his real origin; only after becoming famous did Stanley allow that he was really John Rowlands and came from Denbigh.*
Livingstone occasionally felt called upon to reprove his friend's harshness to African servants, but he never uttered a critical word to others about him—except when he admitted to Agnes that Stanley's 'temper was bad'. Rather he was filled with gratitude for his 'Good Samaritan'. 'You have given me new life', he assured him repeatedly, and told his friends that Stanley 'acted as a son to me'. A father–son relationship, which Stanley, the outcast, subconsciously craved was thus quickly and firmly established. Now Stanley had not only found for himself a father, but to him he had brought life. Never was a psychological defect so perfectly corrected.

Livingstone had good cause for gratitude. His predicament that first week in November was terrible, and almost certainly without Stanley's aid he would have died before the year was out. Now he was sustained by

* He eventually resumed his British nationality, became an M.P. and was honoured with the Grand Cross of the Bath.

companionship, medicine, and nourishing food. His newly-sharpened appetite amazed Stanley; Livingstone put on weight, and even the bleeding stopped for a time.

The two men talked interminably together and drank prodigious quantities of tea. One evening Stanley recorded the Doctor taking nineteen cups while he himself had eleven. Sometimes Stanley sat with notebook in hand taking down Livingstone's reports of his pilgrimage for transmission (not without errors) to the readers of the *Herald*. He also persuaded Livingstone to write two long letters to Bennett for publication. They are curious documents, whose style owed so much to Stanley's journalese that it was seriously suggested they were forgeries.

Stanley, using 'very strong arguments', several times advised Livingstone to return with him to civilisation, to recruit his strength (and obtain dentures) before resuming his work in Africa. He even dangled before him the prospect of the honours—perhaps a knighthood—awaiting him at home. But the appeal merely drew a sharp: 'Yes but impossible: Must not, cannot, will not', for Livingstone was certain that his friends would want him to complete his work first.

He had other reasons for refusing Stanley's advice: retirement would mean employment in 'an unhealthy consulate to which no public sympathy would ever be drawn'; he did not wish to see Kirk again; he would no more hang on to Stanley's 'tail' than to Moffat's years before; and in any case Livingstone believed he was on the verge of making the greatest geographical discovery of the age, which would endow him with such prestige that he could stamp out the last vestige of the slave trade.

About a week after his arrival, Stanley gave up the idea of a quick return to Europe, and instead suggested that they explore the northern end of Tanganyika together, and discover whether an effluent river really did join it to Albert Nyanza. So for four weeks the two men, travelling in separate canoes hired by Stanley—one flying the Union Jack, the other the Stars and Stripes—were paddled comfortably round the lake shore. They quickly settled the geographical question by finding that the Lusize—the supposed effluent—flowed into the lake. Here Livingstone, whimsically, named a tiny archipelago 'New York Herald Islets', a name which they bore for many years. Several times during this 'picnic', Livingstone restrained the trigger-happy American from engaging hostile tribesmen. One comic incident occurred, when Susi, after joining Bombay in a drinking bout, squeezed into his master's bed;

amazing to relate, Livingstone sleepily made room, believing him to be Stanley.

Now that Tanganyika could be excluded, Livingstone turned all the more eagerly to proving that the Lualaba was part of the Nile system. For this he would require reliable pagazi, and Stanley promised to send up a suitable team when he returned to the coast. It was further agreed that Livingstone accompany Stanley as far as Unyanyembe to recover what remained of his stores, and subsequently to shepherd the new porters past Mirambo's army. So after celebrating Christmas together, the two men sadly made preparations for Stanley's return.

Stanley's feelings ran deep. We would have expected this tough careerist to be at least mildly contemptuous of his companion's meekness and piety. Instead he regarded Livingstone as a truly saintly figure, and looked back on the months they spent together as the supreme experience of an eventful life. Instead of Kirk's misanthrope, Stanley had found the immaculate man. 'A happier companion, a truer friend', he wrote, 'I could not wish for.' It was Livingstone's gentleness rather than his moral grandeur which most touched Stanley. From this 'Christian gentleman', he said, he learned 'the doctrine of forbearance', a claim which few people who studied Stanley's later career would have endorsed. After leaving, Stanley, without any sense of sentimentality, informed Livingstone that with 'very few amongst men have I found I so much got to love as yourself. In the qualities which go to make the man & the gentleman, I find you possess more than any other that I remember.' And he described their time together as having been spent 'in an Elysian field'.

Our knowledge of Livingstone has been vastly enriched by the several eulogistic descriptions Stanley wrote and they are all the more precious to us because they are the last we possess. But they also formed the basis of the hagiography which has ever since mantled Livingstone's figure. The adulation was genuine; Stanley assured Agnes that 'the very name of Livingstone has a charm in it for me. I loved him as a son'. And twenty years later he told her that her father's 'memory is always with me'.

No doubt sometimes Stanley was baffled by the depths of his friend's character, but his word-portrait of Livingstone remains a sort of testament. One passage reads: 'Of the inner man much more may be said than of the outer. As he reveals himself, bit by bit, to the stranger, a great many favourable points present themselves, any of which taken singly might well dispose you towards him. . . .' Showing penetrating insight,

Stanley also tells us that Livingstone 'lived all his life almost, we may say, within himself—in a world of thought which *revolved inwardly*,* seldom awaking out of it except to attend to the immediate practical necessities of himself and his expedition. The immediate necessities disposed of, he must have relapsed into his own inner world, into which he must have conjured memories of his home, relations, friends, acquaintances, familiar readings, ideas and associations, so that wherever he might be, or by whatsoever he was surrounded, his own world had attractions far superior to that which the external world by which he was surrounded had.'

Stanley is interesting too when examining Livingstone's faith: he wrote of 'a man deeply imbued with real religious instincts. . . . His religion . . . is of the true, practical kind, never losing a chance to manifest itself in a quiet practical way—never demonstrative or loud. It is always at work, if not in deed, by shining example. . . . In him religion exhibits its loveliest features. It governs his conduct towards his servants, towards the bigoted Mussulmans—even all who come in contact with him. Without religion Livingstone, with his ardent temperament, his enthusiastic nature, his high spirit and courage, might have been an uncompanionable man and a hard master.' It was a brilliant personality analysis but incomplete; later on Stanley wished that he had said more about his subject's 'humour and sly fun', and the 'endless fund of high spirits, which now and then broke out in peals of hearty laughter'.

Stanley could detect only a single flaw in Livingstone's character—his continuing resentment towards Baines, Bedingfeld and Tozer, and it drove him to confess 'I felt the faintest fear that his strong nature was opposed to forgiveness, and that he was not so perfect as at first blush of friendship I thought him'. Stanley even declared it 'a weakness to dwell on these bitter memories'. But after delivering this homily his 'autobiography' returns to adulation: 'I have met few so quickly responsive to gaiety and the lighter moods, none who was more sociable, genial, tolerant and humerous' as this 'contented soul'.

Yet if he criticised Livingstone's bitterness towards his old companions, Stanley paradoxically encouraged his growing antipathy for Kirk. The story of that unhappy quarrel, so fiercely debated, so obstinately denied, must be briefly considered, for it 'marred', as Waller once gravely noted, 'the last moments of the Doctor's life'.

* My italics.

Stanley was not exactly untruthful when he described Kirk's neglect of Livingstone, but he subtly stressed those points which reflected against the Consul. Thus he repeated Kirk's description of Livingstone as a 'misanthrope', and condemned his apathy in getting the last caravan away from Bagamoyo, suggesting that he preferred instead to go hunting. By the time Stanley had finished, Livingstone was convinced that all his troubles stemmed from Kirk's contemptuous indifference.

As with previous 'betrayals', suspicion led to harsh decisions. When Stanley returned to the coast, he carried with him three letters for Kirk from Livingstone. The first was an official complaint about Kirk's conduct; it began with a formal 'Sir', referred to his 'private trip' to shoot on the mainland, and commented bitterly, 'I may wait twenty years and your slaves feast and fail'. Another letter affronted Kirk by insisting that he handed the £500 remaining from the Government grant to Stanley. Livingstone also pointedly gave Stanley a cheque for this sum in case the Consul had dishonestly 'made away' with it.[1] He further commissioned Stanley, not Kirk, to select the new porters for him at the coast, and on a scrawled scrap of paper gave him discretion to turn back any 'slave' pagazi already despatched by Kirk whom he met on his way down-country. As a final insult Livingstone handed several letters, an official despatch and his Journal (from 28 June 1886 to 20 February 1872) to Stanley, explaining that he feared Kirk might keep them to prevent exposure of his misconduct. Stanley was instructed to give the Journal to John Murray for safe keeping, rather than to any member of the Livingstone family.* The pocket books, we must note, remained with the Doctor until his death.

At Zanzibar, Kirk felt 'crushed' by the 'very uncourteous tone of these official letters' and 'their ungenerous personal insinuations', and feared that they might jeopardise his career. Although he replied in temperate terms to express the 'greatest grief and indignation' at Shereef's conduct, afterwards, according to Livingstone, he 'publicly declared . . . that he declined to do anything for me because he should only get insulted',[2] and even spoke of him as that 'damned old scoundrel'. Kirk certainly denounced Livingstone in furious terms to the Foreign Office and added that Stanley had persuaded the Doctor to pay a visit to America, which, he commented spitefully, 'I am now glad to think is not likely to be for three years'.

---

* In fact Stanley handed the Journal over to Agnes.

Other letters written by Livingstone at this time bear witness to his distrust of Kirk. Agnes learned that 'I may go to my grave or elsewhere before he will stir a hand or foot for me', and that 'Dr Kirk has failed me miserably',[3] so badly in fact that he would 'beg the government to send no more money unless a consul is sent who will think more of aiding a brother officer supposed to be a personal friend'. Finally he accused Kirk of envying his fame and of picking 'holes in my character', writing that Kirk 'carps & nibbles at my character and tells fibs, as for instance that I dont write my geographical positions but put down a dot which I alone understand and otherwise blethers'. Later he suggested to Agnes that Kirk was trying to get him back to England so that he might 'finish up the sources' of the Nile himself.

These suggestions could only have come to Livingstone from Stanley; what most infuriated him was the hint that Kirk was hoping that he, not Livingstone, would discover the 'coy fountains' of the Nile. To Waller, Livingstone noted sourly that the Consul's behaviour had made him 'a gape and not a disciple of David Livingstone';* Braithwaite learned that Kirk 'has been a sore disappointment. I got him the situation and he is too lazy and indifferent to serve David Livingstone'; and the Doctor told his brother in Canada, that the Consul's 'killing simplicity' had cost him his two years of wasted effort, £1000, and two thousand miles of useless tramping. Kirk, he went on, had even sent a paper to the Geographical Society for publication which suggested that he, Dr Livingstone, ought to retire and leave younger men to complete his explorations.[4]

We do not know how all these letters were answered, but those to Agnes prompted her to sum up her feelings, and perhaps our own: 'I am not at all satisfied about Dr Kirk, and I think there is a good deal to be explained. Papa blames him in my last letter . . . I do not think he wilfully neglected Papa, but I do not think he exerted himself as he should have done.'[5]

On his return to Europe, Stanley added fuel to the flames by slandering Kirk in public. He even announced that 'He had a mission from Livingstone to describe [Kirk] as a "traitor" ', and never publicly withdrew this charge. The dangerous statement was published by English papers, together with an assertion that Livingstone had sneered 'I don't think he [Kirk] will be Consul any longer after this'. Public reaction to

---

* It is interesting to note how Livingstone refers to himself in the third person as this reflects the exalted concept of self seen often in the hypomanic phase of cyclothymia.

these charges made the Government despatch Sir Bartle Frere to Zanzibar to examine Stanley's allegations. Fortunately for Kirk, Frere's report allowed him to continue the career which brought him such great distinction.

*   *   *   *   *

On 27 December 1871 Livingstone and Stanley left Ujiji to begin the journey to Unyanyembe. They passed down Lake Tanganyika by canoe to Urimba and began their march on 7 January 1872. The two men made steady progress despite Stanley's repeated fever and Livingstone's distress from piles which prevented him riding a donkey provided by his companion. Stanley was much impressed by the way Livingstone 'tramped' the 250 miles 'like a man of iron', and near Unyanyembe carved the Doctor's initials on a tree, which is now lost. They entered the town on 18 February in the Stanley manner with flags flying and the escort firing a salute. As he pushed open the splendidly carved door of the tembe* where he had lodged before, Stanley grandiloquently announced 'Doctor, we are at last home'.

It was hardly home but the house seemed comfortable enough as they passed the next month together. Livingstone's regard for Kirk was not improved by his receiving only a single packet from Zanzibar during this time, whereas Stanley had several from the American Consul. Livingstone now completed the letters begun at Ujiji, confident for the first time since 1866 that they would reach their destinations. Most went to Britain, six were for Bombay and there were the two controversial ones addressed to Bennett.

They angrily inspected Livingstone's remaining stores at Unyanyembe and found nearly all had fallen a prey to white ants. Stanley's provisions too had suffered, but there remained enough for him to provide the Doctor with sufficient for four years. This last manifestation of generosity deeply touched Livingstone.

By 13 March 1872 Stanley's preparations were complete. That night, he tells us, Livingstone poured out his gratitude to him, while he wept unashamedly at the prospect of abandoning his surrogate father. In the morning Stanley toyed with breakfast, hardly able to speak. Then Livingstone accompanied him out of town. Within half a mile they came

---

* Arab house built round a courtyard; its door is preserved in the Africana Museum Johannesburg.

to a large tree and stopped in its shade. An emotional parting followed whose memory remained so evocative that Stanley once told Agnes 'I almost fancy it is palpable'. Then he strode off to enduring fame while Livingstone turned back to re-enter the shadows. Scarcely a year of life was left to him.

26

Unyanyembe

While Livingstone waited at Unyanyembe, Stanley made a forced march to the coast, which was reached on 7 May 1872. He was particularly fond of recounting one incident during the march: when the porter carrying Livingstone's journals slipped while fording a river, Stanley pointed his revolver at him, shouting 'Drop that box and I'll shoot you'. The threat was effective, and the precious papers were brought over safely.

Stanley was surprised to find elements of the English Search and Relief Expedition at Bagamoyo, including young Oswell Livingstone. Now, with Stanley's news, its whole object was frustrated, and successive resignations removed the senior officers until only Oswell was left. Stanley met Oswell again in Zanzibar and persuaded him nevertheless to lead the pagazi he intended to recruit up to his father at Unyanyembe; but two days later Oswell changed his mind after an interview with Kirk. Livingstone subsequently accused Kirk of urging Oswell 'to show the white feather', and, worse, of criticising him in words 'not usually conveyed to a son against his father'.

Oswell excused his decision on the grounds of delicate health, inexperience, and the inconvenience of interrupting his medical studies; but still one wishes he had joined his father, and lightened the burden of loneliness in the months ahead. Livingstone was contemptuous of Oswell's behaviour, especially after receiving a letter from him which explained his real reason for coming out to Africa.

Oswell told Livingstone that he believed the Government intended awarding his father a considerable grant of money and a pension; now, he wanted to take him back to England so that he and the family might benefit from it, and perhaps persuade him to write another best-seller before he died. Oswell's letter also reprimanded Livingstone for neglecting his family.

After reading this explanation, Livingstone wrote in his diary:

Unyanyembe

'Received a letter from Oswell dated Bagamoyo 14 May which awakened thankfulness,* anxiety and deep sorrow'. He told Agnes that Oswell had reproached him about his lack of concern for his children, and added that by returning home, Oswell had failed to 'gain a little credit that may enable him to hold up his head among men and not be merely Dr Livingstone's son'. He was more forthright to John, telling him that Oswell's letter was 'the most snobbish and impertinent I ever received or read', while its writer was as 'poor a specimen of a son as Africa has ever produced'. Livingstone suspected that his two spinster sisters at Hamilton had incited Oswell's attempt at extortion, and grumbled that although he had 'devoted all my money to these neer do weels . . . they forget the hand that fed, clothed, and lodged them & say I forgot them'.

Charles Livingstone was equally indignant when he learned of his nephew's pusillanimity, and wrote to his own son: 'what a thundering Ass your cousin O. has made of himself. He had one of those golden opportunities, so exceeding rare and which never return . . . and can now only snap and snarl at Stanley'.[1] But later on Livingstone himself was able to recognise yet another providence in his son's timidity: 'to die alone', he wrote in a notebook, 'will give me an influence which I pray may be turned for good in the abolition of this nasty slave trade'.[2] For lonely martyrdom would increase his hold over men's minds.

* * * * *

Stanley, with his usual efficiency, recruited fifty-six pagazi for Livingstone at the coast. They included twenty men from Stanley's own caravan, and a number from the S & R Expedition, including six Nasik boys—Matthew Wellington, Jacob Wainwright and his brother John, Benjamin and Richard Rutton, and Carus Farrar.† A competent African named Manwa Sera led the column, while Susi and a man named Chowpereh acted as N.C.O.s during the following months; a lad called Majwara became the Doctor's personal servant.

Stanley was preparing to leave for Europe when the caravan was ready to start inland, and he asked Kirk to see it off. An ugly scene followed, when Kirk, in Stanley's words, protested: 'I must decline. I will do

---

* A possible reason for Livingstone's thankfulness is discussed in the following chapter.

† Matthew Wellington survived until 1935. In old age when taken to watch a film of Livingstone's life, he started forward crying 'Master, Master'. Wainwright had been on Speke's expedition and wore a commemorative medal inscribed 'Discovery of the Nile sources', which understandably irritated Livingstone.

nothing privately for Dr Livingstone; officially I will. I shall not expose myself to needless insult again.' Stanley's account seems factual, for Kirk reported to Whitehall that the request was 'positively and at once declined, and I informed him that I could not after what Dr Livingstone had done and said, act in any but an official capacity'. Oswell also refused to see the caravan off, and the duty fell to the dragoman at the American Consulate.

Stanley embarked the same day, 29 May, looking forward to a hero's welcome in England. During the voyage he worked at breakneck speed to turn his notes into book form. The result was a verbose and sensationally worded volume. Perhaps because of its bad taste and vitriolic criticism of Kirk, John Murray showed no anxiety to publish the book, but under another imprint it proved a sensational success. Possibly the illustrations made a contribution to its popularity—particularly the picture of a naked girl being prepared as the main course for a cannibal feast.

*   *   *   *   *

Stanley landed at Marseilles during the early hours of 23 July 1872, got off a short despatch to London, and roused two sleeping journalists to give them his news. Their report in the *Daily Telegraph* two days later caused a furore because of the severe criticism of Kirk. Then, while Stanley was fêted in Paris (at one banquet he was so carried away after being served 'Poulard trufflée à la Stanley', that in his speech he referred to his 'mission from Livingstone to describe [Kirk] as a traitor'), England digested the news. Admiration for Stanley's feat and relief for Livingstone's safety was combined with chagrin that an American should have succeeded where a British expedition had so signally failed. And since the despatch was so censorious of Kirk, the public felt deeply perturbed that such a man was employed in H.M. Consular Service.

Earlier rumours of Stanley's sucess had been derided. Murchison's successor at the R.G.S. had suggested that instead of Stanley having relieved Livingstone, Livingstone had probably rescued Stanley from a dangerous situation, while newspapers even implied that the American's story was a hoax, and his 'Livingstone papers' forged.

But there could be no doubt now about the *coup*. Ingratiating relations met Stanley at Dover, and England proceeded to make proper amends for her previous cavalier behaviour. The Geographical Society was particularly fulsome in its congratulations; everyone wanted to see

Stanley's model at Madame Tussauds and his portraits in safari clothes
with Kalulu; the Queen commissioned a portrait of him and presented
him with a jewelled snuff box; and *Punch* excelled itself with verses
which began

'Charge, Bennett, charge. On, Stanley on.'

But Stanley soon turned the public against him. His attacks on Kirk
misfired because of the British predilection for the underdog, and his
appearances in scientific circles fell flat since he loyally upheld
Livingstone's unlikely theory that the Lualaba was the Nile. He made an
especially bad impression when he addressed three thousand people,
including the exiled Emperor Napoleon III, at a British Association
meeting: there he took his audience briskly through his African
adventures, moved on to the character of the man he rescued, and ended
with a blistering disparagement of Kirk. That same evening Stanley was
the Guest of Honour at a convivial dinner given by the Brighton and
Sussex Medical Association. This time he indulged in pantomime when
recounting his exploits and drew such guffaws from the tipsy doctors that
after dropping a sovereign on the table, he strutted from the room, and
refused to answer chastened requests to return.

As soon as possible Stanley called on Agnes and handed over several
letters from her father together with the manuscript journal, which she
prudently lodged with the Union Bank of Glasgow.[3] He went on to an
uncomfortable interview with Horace Waller.* Connected now to Kirk
by marriage, Waller felt concerned about the effect of Stanley's criticism
on this member of the 'triple alliance'. He thought that 'low fellow'
Stanley's hostility was 'Satan's work', and felt delighted to catch him out
in a 'barefaced lie'—although the unabashed American merely shifted
his cigar from one side of his mouth to the other. 'We must be careful
of Stanley, I can see', Waller wrote conspiratorially to the secretary of
the R.G.S.

Stanley next visited Newstead, where he slept in the bed associated
with Byron and Livingstone. Mrs Webb thought him 'a perfect Ishmaelite
with his hand against every man, and feeling every man's hand raised
against him'. Then he crossed the Atlantic, leaving Britain fearful that

---

* Waller was later to edit these journals for publication in book form, from which
Livingstone steps out as a man of superb dignity and pathos. But, regrettably, Waller omitted
a good deal of manuscript material which he believed might damage his hero's image. One of
the most important tasks now facing Livingstone scholars is the republication of these papers
in their original form.

Unyanyembe

Livingstone might still need help. Two expeditions were therefore quickly organised to make contact with him. Both were too late.

*   *   *   *   *

A heavy weight of loneliness descended on David Livingstone after Stanley left him. He must now wait, as patiently as possible, for the new pagazi from the coast, and he calculated they would arrive during the middle of July. In fact they did not appear for another month, and Livingstone only quit Unyanyembe on 25 August 1872.

The tembe where he had lodged was the finest in the town, built round a courtyard in which grew twelve pomegranate trees. There, occasionally, Livingstone would turn from his correspondence and devotional exercises to inspect the provisions left behind by Stanley, or to receive turbanned, white-robed Arab friends who squatted on the Persian carpets spread across the floor, and recounted local news.

During the five months of waiting, Livingstone was more fidgety than during the longer detention at Bambarre, especially after the expected date of the porters' arrival passed. Typical Journal entries are: 3 July; 'wearisome waiting, this . . .', 5 July, 'Weary, weary!'; 7 July, 'waiting wearily here . . .'; 30 July, 'Weary waiting this, and the best time for travelling passes over unused'; 4 August, 'wearisome waiting . . . but [typically] this delay may be all for the best'. Co-operation with omnipotence undoubtedly helped morale.

Unaware of the aura and acclaim which was gathering about his name, he was cut off from the world except for an occasional message from Stanley as he hastened down the road, but one day, from Agnes, he received four shirts, one of which would serve him as a shroud.

Although he still brooded over finding the fabulous fountains, the mystic intensity of the previous year had waned, and increasingly he feared that the Lualaba might not be the Nile. 'I am even now not at all "cocksure" that I have not been following down what may after all be the Congo', he wrote on 24 June, and added, with a flash of his old humour, 'who would risk being put into a cannibal pot and converted into black man for it?'.

Returning to his ideas for the establishment of missions in Central Africa, he considered the possibility of bringing in Christian Africans from the west coast, but, one day, reverting to his aversion for settled missionaries, he made a ringing call for help to his own people: 'Come on, brethren, to the real heathen. You have no idea how brave you are till you try. Leaving the coast tribes, and devoting yourselves heartily to the savages, as they are called, you will find, with some drawbacks and wickedness, a very great deal to admire and love.'

At Unyanyembe Livingstone developed his contempt for Kirk and fell into a kind of frenzy as he discovered new and discreditable reasons for the Consul's conduct. He was certain that Kirk was jealous of his fame and even hoped to supersede him as Britain's foremost explorer. The lonely man remembered his naivety four years earlier when he confided to this false friend that 'you cannot imagine how I should like to get a run with you again in the wilds',[4] and he jotted down that Kirk's reports to the Foreign Office about his efforts to supply him 'were only half truths', while a presumptuous account of Lake Bangweulu was 'a sally of audacious ignorance as if the mantle of *Inner Africa laid open* had been picked up by him'.[5] Livingstone wrote too that he had discovered the reason for Kirk's neglect: Kirk had been bribed by Ladha Damji (the banyan in Zanzibar) to allow his firm to handle Livingstone's provisions, and when Kirk realised its inefficiency, he could scarcely complain or interfere, lest his dishonesty be exposed.[6]

After realising his own folly (the first we hear of it) in refusing a consulate on the African coast offered by the Bombay Government, Livingstone wrote a little incoherently in a notebook, 'I was so short-sighted for my own interests and now I see that Dr Kirk had no sort of compunction in trying to supercede me by Banian treachery. The eagerness with which he recommended that I should retire & leave the rest to other travellers—strong urgings to S & R Expedition to resign & go home—and the culpable negligence of placing all my supplies in Banian hands & there leaving them tell a tale—If Dr Kirk had ever got the offer of the Nile he would not have had the additional strain put on his moral nature which the prospect of superceding me after he had acquired his two perquisites—a salary & position to fall back upon for which he at first declined. His public recommendation to me to retire & leave the rest to others is ominous. The other plan to which Government looked, points to a private affair of himself and his advice to the S & R Expedition to dwindle and then the strong urging to go home may not be less than his extreme greed or low villainy, but I trust in the mercy of the Most High to finish my work.'[7]

This tirade was written during a manic mood, and it is interesting to note that only a little earlier we hear another voice of Livingstone, a meek and uncritical one, when in one of his 'down' phases. He informed the Foreign Office 'I regret very much . . . that Dr Kirk viewed my formal complaint against banyans as a covert attack upon himself. If I had foreseen this, I should certainly have borne my losses in silence. I had never any difference with him, though we were together for years, and I had no intention to give offence now.' This message set Waller excitably telegraphing the Geographical Society's secretary that 'Livingstone writes Kirk grieved at pain caused him explains utterly unintentional this consequent on Oswell's letter Kirk sees through villainy of the Zanzibar Conspire.'[8]

We must also note that Livingstone's old faith in the beneficial, hardly scrutable, workings of Providence, set him again reiterating the blind acceptance of God's purpose for him: 'I have been sorely let [down] & hindered in this journey, but it may have been all for the best. I will trust in Him to whom I commit my way.'[9] Livingstone's dislike for his 'quondam companion' in fact only died with him, but Kirk and Stanley were eventually reconciled. Six years after their quarrel Stanley said he was 'willing to make a thousand apologies' to heal the breach. Kirk, however, avoided him when he visited Zanzibar during 1877 (though Stanley was permitted to present medals to Livingstone's surviving companions of the last journey), and next year gleefully reported officially that Stanley had kicked a man to death, kept a black mistress, and sold captured Africans as slaves. But ten years later, Stanley could comment 'I have made my peace with Sir John Kirk and Horace Waller'.[10]

On some days at Unyanyembe Livingstone abandoned his megrims for strange irrelevancies from the past. Two examples will suffice. 'Dr Buckland', he confided to his diary, 'after becoming Dean of Westminster began to lose his reason, and showed it in outrageous abuse of his wife with his tongue', and he then went on at length to relate how two gaitered colleagues were brought in to remonstrate with the poor man for his unclerical behaviour.[11] On another day the deepest recesses of his mind reverted to his Directors' impudence in trying to make a 'public beggar' of him, and this led to a curious indictment that Waller was careful to suppress: 'the mendicant Friar as introduced by the saintly Neer do weel St Francis de Assisi was simply a sturdy beggar and his place is now a days taken up by the Begging Parson. . . . The London Missionary

Society tried to enlist me as one of the begging fraternity and offered to "send a man with me throughout the country" but I rebelled.'[12]

Livingstone's old interest in Nature revived at Unyanyembe, and erudite ornithological notes reappear in the Journal. Some of his most delightful descriptions were devoted to the Whydah birds in the town; and when describing a mother wagtail feeding its young, and perhaps remembering his own delight with baby Elizabeth at Kolobeng, he wrote, 'The first smile of an infant with its toothless gums is one of the pleasantest sights in nature. It is innocence claiming kinship, and asking to be loved in its helplessness'.

But most of all in the tembe Livingstone's labyrinthine mind dwelled on the deep intolerable evil of the African slave trade, and grasped once more the single thread of divine purpose spun for him. He wrote that 'the slaving scenes come back unbidden, and make me start up at dead of night horrified by their vividness'. Again he lamented that 'The power of the Prince of Darkness seems enormous'. But, contemplating the ultimate triumph over Satan, Livingstone rejoiced 'This will be something to have lived for, and the conviction has grown in my mind that it was *for this end* I have been detained so long'. It was a reiteration of what he had written during another euphoric mood six months earlier: 'What I have seen of this horrid system makes me feel that its suppression would be of infinitely more importance than all the fountains put together'.

So in the last year of his life Livingstone conceived that the only real advantage to be gained by demonstrating the origins of the Nile lay in the increased influence for good he would exert from the grave. Did he not tell Maclear 'If indeed my disclosures should lead to the suppression of the East Coast slave-trade, I would esteem that as a far greater feat than the discovery of all the sources together'. Another letter home contained a particularly arresting phrase: 'all I can add in my loneliness is, may Heaven's rich blessing come down on everyone—American, English, or Turk—who will help to heal this open sore of the world'. Written precisely a year before his death, it epitomised Livingstone's final aspirations, and it was inscribed on his grave in Westminster Abbey, although the word 'loneliness' was replaced, inaptly, by 'solitude'.

Once the pagazi arrived, Livingstone believed it would take but seven months to finish his task. There was no thought now of following the Lualaba down to the indentifiable Nile—the memory of Nyangwe prevented further association with the slavers, and without them he could never cross Manyema. Instead he intended to pass down the east side of Lake Tanganyika, skirt the southern shores of Bangweulu and identify its feeders which were surely the Nile origins. Afterwards he would visit the underground houses in Rua, and examine Lakes Lincoln and Kamalondo by boat, before passing on to the great unknown lake beyond. Then Livingstone would turn back towards Ujiji and comfortable retirement at home—or he would allow God to lead him farther into Africa to a 'lonely grave in a forest', and a martyr's influence for good. Providence without doubt would show him the proper path to take in due time.

*   *   *   *   *

An advance guard of Stanley's pagazi reached Unyanyembe on 9 August 1872. Six days later the remainder marched in. Together with his five 'faithfuls' Livingstone could now muster sixty-two reliable men, and on them he would bestow the ultimate praise in his power: they 'behaved as well as the Makololo'. The caravan marched out of Unyanyembe on 25 August 1872, with Dr Livingstone at its head and Majwara, the last human being to see him alive, beside him, beating a drum.

27

Chitambo

During the last stage of his pilgrimage which carried him from Unyanyembe to Chitambo, Livingstone's thoughts turned occasionally to home—as when he asked Waller to look for a suitable residence and to arrange 'a speedy fitting of artificial teeth'. But for the most part, he seemed to be driving himself along a hopelessly muddled course to deliberate death, concerned only with sacrificing his life for a cause.

The march began well. Livingstone, revitalised by rest and good food, felt 'more like a boy going home from school than the staid toothless old fogie which "the sources" have made me'. He led the caravan westward towards Lake Tanganyika, and saw its distant waters on 8 October 1872. Three days later they came to the lakeshore at Kalema where the White Fathers are today established. Too large to go south by canoe, the party for the next four weeks struggled slowly down the eastern coast.

The lake in 1872 was about nine feet deeper than it is today, for like Nyasa its level depends on the amount of sudd blocking its effluent river.* The watery inlets described by Livingstone are accordingly represented now by beaches sloping up to cultivated valleys, but his journal entries still allow us to identify precisely his camping sites and the villages, hills, rivers, and islands he passed.

It was the worst season of the year and the march down the lake was unbelievably arduous. This district of Ufipa was being ravaged by slavers and most of the people had fled to stockaded settlements in the uplands; the few remaining Africans lived in hidden villages.

They crossed the Ntembwe River on 29 October, and now the country became still more difficult. A line of clean high mountains rose precipitously from the lake, and the caravan only managed three or four miles a day as it struggled up the escarpment. To add to his difficulties, the old enemy dysentery returned; 'I am ill and losing much blood', he noted

* The lake is now rising again.

298

ominously on 9 November, as the column turned away from the lake. Unknowingly they then passed close to the magnificent Kalambo Falls, led by a guide who was determined that these strangers should not see this sacred place nor the holy, off-shore islands.[1]

The pace hardly quickened on the undulating plateau, for the caravan would stop for a day or two when one of the porters fell sick or Livingstone's dysentery grew worse. Fortunately he could obtain more nourishing food; near Mbala he is still remembered as 'the man who ate eggs'.

He was now on familiar ground, retracing the route that led him to Tanganyika during 1867. Passing the site of modern Kasama and the headwaters of the Chambezi, they changed course west on 3 December 1872, as though heading for Cazembe's. Sullen drops of rain had been falling for some days and now came down so persistently that it reminded Livingstone of the drenched journey to Luanda. He relied on goat's milk for nourishment and sometimes must have been very ill since some diary entries are so incoherent as to suggest delirium. On 20 December they turned again, this time to the south, to avoid extensive swamps ahead.

They were approaching Lake Bangweulu through water-logged country, and they were completely lost. Low cloud prevented Livingstone from making astronomical fixes, and his false readings and erroneous maps of 1868 added to his perplexity.

Anaemia by now seriously checked his activity; he had to be carried over a succession of rivers whose presence could only be identified in the swamps by their visible currents. Susi usually humped his master across while a man behind held his guns high up in the air. On one occasion the water reached up to Susi's mouth and the Doctor rather querulously noted that it 'wetted my seat and legs'. Waller later chose this incident as an illustration when he edited his friend's last journals. But Livingstone's incurable optimism yet set him writing that they were 'among the sponges of the Nile and near the northern shores of Bangweolo'. The lake in fact still lay many miles ahead.

For three more appalling months, at the height of the rainy season, the caravan floundered through the swamps. Livingstone's piles, irritated by dysentery, were bleeding continuously, but he was still able to walk without assistance. His mind remained clear, but as Stanley remarked he was 'like a blind and infirm man, aimlessly moving about'. They were victims of a geographical muddle, men caught up in navigational uncertainty.

Led—or often misled—by their guides, they pursued an erratic route through the swamps, which can still be traced from Livingstone's notes and sketch maps. Once they were led so far off course that they had to circle back, wasting two valuable weeks. And the downpour persisted: 'Rain, rain, rain as if it never tired', grumbled Livingstone towards the end of January. Early next month they reached the northern end of Bangweulu and turned south-east but on the 13th, the exhausted column halted where the Luenya River enters the lake. They were hopelessly lost. While Livingstone rested on a sandbank, Susi and Chuma went on to find the village of a chief named Matipa, for advice and canoes.

It was now that the relentless correspondent wrote his last letters. There were roguish messages for Waller and a recapitulation even in this extremity of his old grudge against Baines and the other enemies. A description of this latest journey was addressed to Maclear, 'Sir Paraffin' was reminded of some family bequests, a letter to his old friend Oswell admitted he felt 'forgotten and alone',* while a letter for Mrs Webb so distressed her that she destroyed it. The pen may have moved slowly now across the paper but it returned to the eternal rhythm of his life in the recognition of natural beauties, and sounded the same pure note of purpose regarding the suppression of the slave trade.

On 1 March 1873 he obtained canoes and punted slowly for three days through the 'flooded prairie' to Matipa's Island. But Matipa, suspecting Livingstone to be a slaver, procrastinated when asked for help. At last on the 19th (it was his sixtieth birthday), Livingstone's patience evaporated and he angrily fired his revolver through the roof of Matipa's hut. Thereupon three canoes were quickly produced, and on 24 March the expedition moved south again, towards the mouth of the Chambezi, distressed still by the pelting rain. Next day in his diary, Livingstone defied the elements in words which shouted out from the drenched pages: 'Nothing earthly will make me give up my work in despair'. And he was encouraged

---

* But he may not have been so lonely as he represented: during 1936 three old Africans, who remembered Livingstone, testified that he was accompanied by a half-caste son. Almost certainly their collective memory was at fault, and Stanley made no reference to the boy. Yet it is tantalising to consider the possibility of Livingstone fathering a son in Rovuma country during 1862, after Mary's death, and picking him up as he went up-river four years later. For this might explain Livingstone's 'fixation' for the Rovuma, his reluctance to return to the coast when hard pressed, and his 'thankfulness' at learning that Oswell would not join him at Unyanyembe.[2]

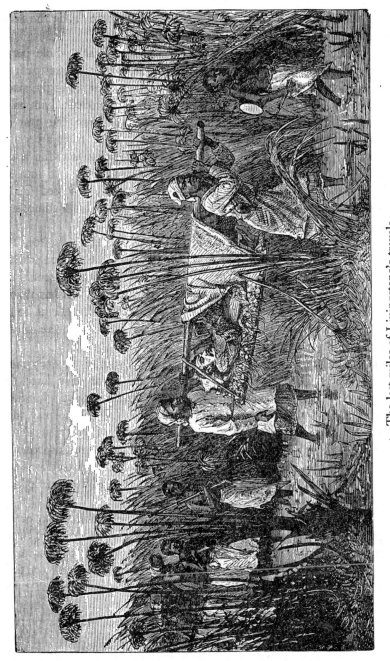

4　The last miles of Livingstone's travels

still by the thought that the 'water, water, everywhere . . . is the Nile apparently enacting its inundations, even at its sources'.

Beyond Lake Chaya he abandoned the canoe and the whole party took to the sodden land, with Livingstone treading the last bitter path to which his dream had led him. He was haemorrhaging increasingly, since the wall of the inferior haemorrhoidal artery had been eroded: 'I am pale, bloodless, and weak from bleeding profusely ever since the 31st of March last: an artery gives off a copious stream, and takes away my strength. Oh, how I long to be permitted by the Over Power to finish my work.' But by this time mounting decrepitude must have told him he could scarcely expect to live much longer. He gently accepted God's verdict. There could be no complete victory now during his lifetime; nor could there be defeat.

He became unable to walk and had to be propped up on a donkey. Yet even now Livingstone continued to determine latitudes and longitudes, and returned in his notes to his love for Nature. He recorded observations about the swamp fish, and in a curiously poignant phrase, that has almost a valedictory sound, described the silvery cry of the fish eagle as being 'pitched in a high falsetto key, very loud, and seems as if he were calling to someone in the other world'.

On 13 April 1873 after making a careful calculation of the daily rainfall, he crossed the wide Luitikila River and three days later the Lombwata. 'But for the donkey', he wrote, 'I could not move a hundred yards.' On the 18th Livingstone had to rest all day. Next morning they passed over the Lukulu, and on the following evening Livingstone jotted down the remarkable understatement: 'It is not all pleasure this exploration'. On the 21st the last formal entry was made after a fall from the donkey: 'Tried to ride, but was forced to lie down, and they carried me back to vil. exhausted'.

But he continued to scrawl rough notes in the pocket book, or on scraps of paper, sometimes newsprint laboriously sewn together. From these scribblings we learn that his men carried him in a Kitanda, a rough litter of woven reeds slung from a pole. Soon he could do no more than mark the stages of his journey with the date and length of march. On the 25th he roused himself sufficiently to enquire of a villager whether he knew of a hill from which four rivers rose, and dropped back disappointed when the man replied he did not. Next day he told Susi to purchase two tusks to buy food during the return journey to Zanzibar, perhaps

5 Evening at Ilala 29 April 1873

intended for the porters after his death. On the 27th the last pathetic words were set down in the small notebook: 'Knocked up quite, and remain—recover—sent to buy milch goats. We are on the banks of the Molilamo.'

His failing mind had distorted the name: they had come to the Lulimala River on the eleventh anniversary of Mary's death. For the events of the succeeding days we have to rely on the accounts given to Waller by Chuma and Susi, and the slightly different versions of Majwara and Carus Farrar. These say they spent the 28th quietly and only on the following day tackled the wide river crossing. Livingstone complained bitterly of lumbar pain when they gently transferred him on his bed to and from the canoe. Finally he implored the men carrying him to halt but they pointed to a group of huts ahead. It was Chitambo's village named Mwela Mwape or Kabende.*

The village stood in Ilala country, bordering the backwash of Lake Bangweulu. Livingstone had reached his journey's end.

It was drizzling that afternoon and they sheltered the litter under the eaves of a dripping hut while a banda of sticks and reeds was hastily erected. When they carried the dying man inside he complained of feeling cold, and at his request extra grass was piled on the roof.

Next morning Chitambo came to pay his respects to the white man whose reputation for goodness was known even in this remote place. But Livingstone was vomiting, his vision had become blurred and he felt too weak to receive him; Chitambo quietly withdrew. That day Livingstone dozed off repeatedly, and who knows what visions were floating through his tired mind.

Probably he no longer perceived the wide horizons of earlier days, but rather, in the humility of exhaustion, concerned himself with welcoming death as a transition rather than a crisis and with a feeling of great affection for the faithful Africans who had travelled with him thus far. According to one of them Livingstone occasionally wakened sufficiently to pray, and once looked up to murmur 'I am going home'.

As the last of the day declined, Majwara lit a candle and placed it on a box beside his master's bed. Livingstone was still anxious to fix his position; he motioned Susi to hold his watch while he reached up to wind

* Majwara said they marched on to the larger village of Ilala, but Chief Chitambo refused them permission to stay there and the caravan returned to Kabende, three miles back. This village, which was to acquire such enduring fame, was more usually called Chitambo or Chipundu. Farrar largely supports Majwara.

Chitambo

it. Majwara was now told to keep vigil at the door of the banda, and he crouched there alone in the strange subaqueous afterlight of the swamps. Some of the men went off to sleep in the village huts; others gathered round a camp fire to sing and sometimes to dance. About eleven that night raucous shouts in the distance disturbed the dying man, and Susi went in to tell him that the villagers had turned out to frighten away a herd of buffaloes from their gardens. 'Is this the Luapula?' Livingstone asked him in Ki-Swahili, and when Susi told him they were at Chitambo's village on the Lulimala, Livingstone went on, 'How many days to the Luapula?'. Susi replied, 'I think it is three days master', and heard a disappointed murmur of 'Oh dear, dear'. According to Majwara, Livingstone added that he felt sorry he would 'never see *his* river again'. At about midnight Majwara called Susi again to the banda, who, at Livingstone's request, placed a cup of boiled water beside the bed together with a dose of calomel. Livingstone's last words to him were 'All right, you can go now'.

Only a little later Livingstone must have sensed that a change was approaching and, with his remaining strength, eased himself off the rough bed and on to his knees, intent on ending his earthly life, as he had always wished, in communion with his Saviour. How long he prayed we do not know.

Sometime before four that morning Majwara started up from unmeant sleep and peered inside the banda. By the flickering light of the candle he saw his master kneeling beside the bed, his head cushioned between the hands. A little later he looked in again, saw no movement, and ran to call Susi. Susi silently entered the banda with Chuma, Matthew and one or two others. They drew back when they saw the bowed figure and waited a little, unsure of themselves. Then someone went up to touch the kneeling man's cheek. It was cold. David Livingstone had been dead for several hours. They reverently replaced his wasted body on the bed and went out into the night for anxious consultation.

* * * * *

Africans have an intense repugnance for a human corpse, which they associate with witchcraft. So now the instinct of Livingstone's followers was to abandon his body and make their way back to their separate homes as quickly and inconspicuously as possible.

Yet their master's death had not dimmed devotion. When Susi and

305

Chuma called them together in the growing light of early morning on 1 May 1873, the poverty of their loneliness weighed heavily upon them, and one among the party has told us that they 'cried a good deal'. Then they unanimously resolved to deliver Livingstone's body to his friends at Zanzibar, together with his papers. It is possible that in doing so they were carrying out their master's instructions, for we know that he had already told Susi that the documents left at Ujiji were important and must be retrieved. They may instead have been unwilling to bury the body without the approval of the dead man's relatives, but cynics have suggested that, remembering Musa's punishment, they wished to show that they had not deserted their master.

Following their custom, they hacked an opening in the wall of the banda, passed out the body and then, fearful that Chitambo would punish them for bewitching his village, bore it secretly across the Lulimala and hid it inside a newly built stockade. To keep away the curious they gave out that Livingstone was very ill, but Chitambo quickly discovered the truth, and to their relief acted with sense and generosity. So they beat their drums, fired off muskets and gave way to general wailing, their manner of showing respect to a dead man. Then Jacob Wainwright, the only one who could write a fair hand, made a careful inventory of Livingstone's possessions in the notebook, immediately below the entry dated 27 April.

Farrar and Farjallah Christie, who had been employed in a Doctor's house, knew the rudiments of anatomy and were appointed embalmers. Sometime during the next four days, they removed the contents of the chest and abdomen through a single incision, placed salt in the body cavities and poured brandy into the mouth and on to the hair.* The heart and viscera were next placed in a tin box which was reverently buried under a *Mpundu* tree† while Wainwright read out the burial service. That same day he carved on the tree 'Livingstone, May 4 1873', and added the names of the three N.C.O.s, whose names he spelled as Yazuza, Mniasere, and Uchopere.

The names could be distinguished in 1894 when a European visited the site, but by 1899 the tree was dying, so Robert Codrington cut it down

---

* Farrar described a large clot in the left part of the abdomen accepted by some authorities as evidence of a sudden fatal haemorrhage, but almost certainly it was a chronically enlarged malarial spleen.

† Some accounts give it as a *Mvula* or *Myonga* tree, but it is now accepted as *Parinari curatellifola*.

and carried away that part bearing the inscription, which the R.G.S. now displays in a place of honour. By then the inscription had become blurred and the names were recut, but making a curious error: assuming that the first 'a' of Yazuza was the end of a missing word, 'Chum' was prefixed to it, so that the name of Livingstone's second faithful servant fortuitously appears on the plaque. A memorial was erected at Chitambo in 1902, and likewise commemorates 'Chuma Souza Mniasere [and] Uchopere'. Wainwright's date of 4 May referred to the date of the heart's burial, but it was used on Livingstone's grave at Westminster, and so suggests that the Doctor died on that day.

The carcass was now allowed to dry in the sun for two or three more weeks, being turned over from time to time until it was mummified. Then most of the muscles were stripped away, and after the legs had been cut and flexed at the knees, the shortened trunk was clad in a shirt. A length of striped calico served as a winding sheet, and this in turn was wrapped in strips of bark taken from a *Myonga* tree. Sailcloth was then sewn round it to make a cylindrical bundle some four feet long, which was waterproofed with tar and lashed to a stout pole for carrying. It looked like an ordinary bundle of trade goods.

By the end of May their preparations were complete and Livingstone's servants set off with their burden through 1,500 miles of potentially hostile country. They were well aware that the tribesmen they encountered would resent the transport of a dead man through their village. Accordingly the cortège for this epic death march was deliberately made to look imposing rather than funereal. At its head went Majwara beating his drum; behind him came two men holding aloft the Union Jack and the scarlet banner of the Sultan of Zanzibar, while they carried their unusual burden unobtrusively in the middle. They marched west at first, as Livingstone would have done, towards the Luapula, but soon they were all struck by a mysterious disease which immobilised them for a month, and two of the women died.*

No thought of abandoning the corpse seems to have entered their minds. The march, when resumed, was steady and purposeful, as though commanded still by the sheer energy of Livingstone's goodness. They did not pass without bloodshed: on the western side of Bangweulu they

---

* Ten of the original members of the party were reported to have died in all; a few new men were engaged and a few deserted. Seventy-nine men and women eventually reached the coast. The donkey which carried Livingstone through the swamps was taken by a lion near Nsama's.

fought villagers who disputed their passage. But for the most part the column was accepted as an ordinary trading caravan, although Arabs near Nsama's guessed its secret and turned out to fire a salute in the white man's honour.

From the heel of Tanganyika the caravan struck northwards, and as they drew nearer to Unyanyembe, Chuma went on ahead carrying a report of Livingstone's death, laboriously written out by Wainwright. He found Cameron's relief expedition encamped in the town. Cameron advised Chuma to bury Livingstone's body at Unyanyembe, but after a hurried consultation with Susi, he refused. Regrettably the two men were unable to prevent Cameron appropriating some of the Doctor's astronomical instruments: he reported Livingstone's death in letters dated 16 and 20 October 1873.

On 9 November 1873, while Cameron went on to Ujiji, the strange procession continued the march to the coast, together with two of Cameron's staff who had resigned from the relief expedition. Their passage was by no means uneventful. At one village, tribesmen refused passage for a corpse, so the carriers removed the carcase from its shell and made a pretence of burying it, but in fact wrapped it in a cloth to look like a bale of calico and went on. Then one dreadful day Dr Dillon from Cameron's expedition shot himself in front of Chuma and Susi when delirious with fever.

Rumours of Livingstone's death reached the coast in December, while a messenger with more substantial news followed close behind. Chuma, going ahead with one of Cameron's letters, arrived in Zanzibar on 3 February 1874, where he was received by the acting British consul as Kirk was away.

The cortège reached Bagamoyo (which means 'lay down the burden of your heart') soon afterwards, to be welcomed by a group of Catholic missionaries. Here Livingstone's body was transferred to an inner shell of zinc enclosed in a rough wooden coffin which the priests stained black. The acting Consul came over to receive the body. He duly met Livingstone's 'faithfuls', and paid their wages before dismissing them and, by an oversight, they were allowed to retain the guns provided by Livingstone from Stanley's stores. Jacob Wainwright was recognised, unfairly, as the party's leader, and chosen to accompany the body to England.*

* Wainwright made a poor impression in England: he developed a taste for brandy, and boasted that his new affluence would enable him to buy several wives when he returned to

The coffin was placed on the first mailship from Zanzibar, and laid in a cabin fitted out as a mortuary chapel. It was guarded by Wainwright and an English merchant named Laing. Livingstone's papers, his clothes, consular caps, sword and the spear that nearly killed him during the flight from Nyangwe were also stowed on board; the rest of his possessions were auctioned off for £3.* Thomas Livingstone joined the ship at Alexandria. A guard of honour from the Hampshire Artillery Volunteers met the ship at Southampton on 15 April 1874. Then a special train carried the body to London where a small group of doctors led by Sir William Fergusson, Dr Moffat and a handful of Livingstone's old friends were assembled at the R.G.S. headquarters to open the coffin. They were startled to see the dead man's shrivelled body, and long hair and beard; W. C. Oswell thought the features were unchanged and Webb expressed surprise at finding the face perfectly preserved. An examination of the left arm revealed the false joint in the humerus and this was accepted as positive identification of the corpse. After a lock of hair, still dark brown though tinged with grey, was cut off, the body was placed in a more conventional coffin of English oak, and for two days lay in state in the Society's map room. Long afterwards an unpleasant character named Jennings offered to sell Agnes four of her father's teeth, which he said were extracted by Sir William Fergusson after the autopsy. Agnes declined to believe Sir William capable of such 'disgusting' conduct, and refused the offer.[3]

The arrival of Livingstone's body in England struck a note of high emotional intensity, unequalled since Nelson was brought home from Trafalgar. Florence Nightingale was speaking for many when she called him 'the greatest man of his generation'. The Government at once granted

---

Africa. But later he turned over a new leaf, and became an agent for the L.M.S. Susi and Chuma were brought to England a little later by James Young, and they provided Waller with most of his information about Livingstone's death and the funeral march. That June they were photographed with Thomas Livingstone, both wearing thick black reefer jackets. On returning to Zanzibar, Chuma joined the U.M.C.A. and accompanied the missionaries when they returned to central Africa by the Rovuma route. He served later with the explorer Joseph Thomson and revisited Lake Tanganyika during 1879. Chuma died of phthisis in 1882 when barely thirty years old. Susi took to drink on his return to Africa in 1874 and was destitute by 1879 when Stanley decided to employ him to assist in establishing the Congo Free State. During this period, Susi chose the site of modern Kinshasa. Between 1883 and 1891 Susi was a valued servant of the U.M.C.A., having been baptised David.

* Stanley was 'shocked and indignant' to discover this in 1874, and blamed the indignity on Kirk.

Livingstone a national funeral* in Westminster Abbey, the only missionary to be so honoured. The burial took place on 18 April, a 'bright and balmy day'. The number of mourners outside the Abbey testified to an intuitive knowledge that with Livingstone's death, something very fine had ended, that someone uniquely good had been removed from the scene. A long train of carriages, including one sent by the Queen, filled Broad Sanctuary.

The Abbey too was crowded; the Dean had reserved nine hundred seats. Not since the Prince Consort's funeral, Anna Mary told Hans Andersen, had the vergers seen so many people there.[4] The coffin was borne slowly down the nave while the congregation sang the 90th Psalm to Purcell's music. Before it walked Livingstone's two surviving sons with their grandfather, Robert Moffat. The pall bearers were Stanley and Jacob Wainwright in front, followed by Steele, W. C. Oswell, 'Gunner' Young, Webb, Waller and Kirk. Behind the coffin came an odd pair—Roger Price with Kalulu, Stanley's page. The Doctor's two sisters sat among the congregation—square solid women who spoke with a broad Scots accent. It was the first time they had ventured across the border. Near them was the Prime Minister.

Dean Stanley read the burial service, and Wainwright's thoughts no doubt turned back to the same words he had spoken over the grave of Livingstone's heart nearly a year earlier. A wreath of *immortelles* from the Queen was laid on the coffin. Then the congregation sang Doddridge's 'O God of Bethel, by whose hand' (with its appropriate last verse) to the tune of Tallis, and the hundreds of hymn sheets being turned over by the vast congregation sounded to one of those present like an involuntary sigh. Canon Conway preached a sermon in which he spoke of the last resting place into which they had lowered the remains of Dr Livingstone, and said with truth that it was also his first. The grave lay in the nave close to that of Field-Marshal Wade, the peacemaker of the Highlands, and Major Rennell, himself a noted African explorer. Nearby now rests the body of the Unknown Warrior.

The following Sunday pulpits throughout the land rang with eulogies of the dead man, and it seemed fitting that the lessons read in the regular course were Numbers XXI, describing the wanderings of Israel, and Ephesians III, relating the mission of St. Paul to the gentile world.

Before the funeral Canon Conway had asked William Cotton Oswell if he would send him some notes about his old friend which could be

* The undertaker's bill came to £487 6s 10d.[5]

incorporated in the sermon. Oswell wrote back: 'He was pre-eminently a man, patient, all-enduring under hardships, content to win his way by inches but never swerving from it; gentle, kindly, brotherly to the children of the land; absolutely calm and unruffled amidst danger and difficulty, and well satisfied to see but one step in advance. If ever a man carried out the Scriptural injunction to take no thought for the morrow—that was David Livingstone'.[6]

Stanley comforted Agnes with the assurance that 'no daughter was ever beloved so deeply. No daughter was ever blessed with a nobler father'.[7] But perhaps the most eloquent tribute came later from Lord Curzon when he said of Livingstone: 'As a missionary he was the sincere and zealous servant of God. As an explorer he was the indefatigable servant of Science. As a denouncer of the slave trade he was the fiery servant of humanity.'

Livingstone had often asserted that 'all will come right someday' and soon this promise would seem justified. Already it was paradoxical that he, the failed evangelist, should have inspired a reassessment of the missionary's role, and that this harsh critic of the Kuruman traders had come to believe the continent would be redeemed through commerce. So now, through a series of paradoxes, his last journey turned out to be the most triumphant of them all: Arab slavers, to whose destruction Livingstone was dedicated, had sustained him for this accomplishment; in seeking a river that existed only in his mind Livingstone had presented history with its noblest 'example of manly perseverance'; his horrified helplessness at Nyangwe resulted in a report which dealt the slave trade its mortal blow; and his lonely death, after seeming failure, so emphasised the totality of his life, that it spurred missionary circles in Britain to new endeavour. For Livingstone's valedictory message, 'it is [to be] hoped that on the African continent our deeds may in our children's days bear fruit worthy to be held in everlasting remembrance',[8] became true. Within a decade missionaries were established in Uganda; Lake Nyasa was encircled by their stations; they had reached that symbol of frustration and disappointment—Ujiji, and were pressing up the Congo; and because of his dream, a cathedral stood on the site of the great slave market at Zanzibar where he had watched little girls being made to show their 'paces' like animals. Instead of cursing the darkness of Africa, Livingstone had lit in it many candles of hope, which were shielded for nearly a century by his countrymen's conscience. This was Livingstone's achievement.

Abbreviations used in References

Agnes	Agnes Livingstone
BC	Burdett-Coutts papers
Blaikie	W. G. Blaikie, *The Personal Life of David Livingstone*, (1888)
BM	British Museum, additional manuscripts
CL	Charles Livingstone
DL	David Livingstone
FL	I. Schapera, *David Livingstone, Family Letters*, (1959)
HL	Mrs Harriette Livingstone
HMS	Henry Morton Stanley
JK	John Kirk
JL	John Livingstone
JM	John Murray III
JRGS	*Journal of the Royal Geographical Society*
JS	James Stewart
JSM	John Smith Moffat
JY	James Young
LMZ	Livingstone Museum, Zambia
Listowel	J. Listowel, *The Other Livingstone*, (1974)
Lloyd	B. W. Lloyd, *Livingstone, 1873–1973*
MC	I. Schapera, *Livingstone's Missionary Correspondence*, (1961)
MF	microfilm
ML	Mary Livingstone
MM	Mary Moffat
Monk	W. Monk, *Livingstone's Cambridge Lectures*, (1858)
MT	D. Livingstone, *Missionary Travels*, (1857)
Murray	Archives of John Murray, publisher, London
NAR	National Archives of Rhodesia
nd	no date
NLS	National Library of Scotland
Oswell	W. E. Oswell, *William Cotton Oswell*, (1900)
Pachai	B. Pachai (ed.), *Livingstone, Man of Africa*, (1973)
PGS	*Proceedings of the Royal Geographical Society*
RGS	Royal Geographical Society
RHL	Rhodes House Library, Oxford
RM	Robert Moffat
SA Papers	I. Schapera, *David Livingstone, South African Papers*, (1974)
SOAS	School of Oriental and African Studies, London, (late LMS Archives)
TB	Thomas Baines
Tidman	Rev. A. Tidman
USPG	The United Society for the Propagation of the Gospel; archives
Wellcome	Wellcome Institute, London

Abbreviations used in References

Wits University of the Witwatersrand, R.S.A.
ZE J. P. R. Wallis, (ed.), *The Zambesi Expedition of David Livingstone*, (1956)
ZJJS J. P. R. Wallis, (ed.), *The Zambesi Journal of James Stewart*, (1952)

The Brenthurst Papers are David Livingstone Papers etc. in possession of Mr H. Oppenheimer, Johannesburg.

References

This present work is a shortened version of a Ph.D thesis submitted to the University of Rhodesia. To avoid burdening its text with nearly 2,000 source references, only those relating to unpublished or particularly significant material are included here. A full list of sources, however, and Livingstone's detailed mood-graph may be consulted at the University of Rhodesia.

THE FORMATIVE YEARS

1 NAR, LI1/1/1, 1898, DL to Murchison, 27 Aug 64.
2 Information Dr Flora Macdonald, Salen, Mull, 9 Sept 1973.
3 NLS, 10767, 11, Janet Livingstone's advice to Rev. W. G. Blaikie.
4 Ibid., 15.
5 G. Moorhouse, *The Missionaries*, 41.
6 NLS, 10767, 9, Janet Livingstone's advice.
7 NAR, LI1/1/1, 449, draft of letter to Directors, n.d.
8 Myers's Autograph Letters Catalogue no. 82, Cecil to Rev. W. Ellis, 1838.

MABOTSA AND CHONWANE

1 NAR, MO5/1/1, 1775.
2 *FL*, I, 90.
3 NAR, MO5/1/1, 1745.
4 Ibid., 1759.
5 NAR, ST1/2, 2.
6 NAR, MO5/1/1, 1775.

KOLOBENG AND NGAMI

1 NAR, LI2/1/1, 29.
2 NAR, MO1/1/6, 9.
3 NAR, MO5/1/1, 1950.
4 NAR, MO1/1/6, 53.

THE ZAMBEZI

1 Oswell, 1, 214.
2 NAR, MO1/1/6, 89.
3 NAR, LI1/1/1, 57.
4 NAR, ST1/1/1, 174.
5 LMZ, G5, 47.
6 NAR, MO1/1/1, 101.
7 Ibid.

ON THE THRESHOLD

1 *MT*, 190.
2 *SA Papers*, 40-2.

References

3   *FL*, II, 200.
4   *SA Papers*, 158.
5   *FL*, II, 184.
6   NAR, LI1/1/1, 77a.
7   *PJ*, 107.
8   NAR, ST1/1/1, 174.
9   Ibid.
10 NAR, LI1/1/1, 77e.
11 Ibid., 77c.
12 Listowel, 74, 228.
13 NAR, LI1/1/1, 77l.
14 Brenthurst Papers, DL to J. G. Bennett, Feb 1872.
15 Shepperson, G. (1973), *The Geographical Journal*, CXXXIX, II, 212.
16 Simpson, D. H. (1971), 'The Exploration of Central Africa', Centre of African Studies, Univ. of Edinburgh, *Seminar*, 144.
17 NAR, MO1/1/6, 144; NLS, 10768, 4.
18 *FL*, II, 265.

'THE LITTLE BEGINNING'

1   NLS, 10767, 17.
2   NAR, LI1/1/1, 110.
3   Ibid., 106.
4   LMZ, Neil Livingston to CL, 5 Jan 55.
5   NAR, LI1/1/1, 162.
6   Ibid., 204.

THE DESIGNATED INSTRUMENT

1   NAR, LI1/1/1, 161.
2   Brenthurst Papers, DL to Sunley, 18 Nov 61.
3   NAR, LI1/1/1, 164.
4   Pachai, 137.
5   *The Atlantic Monthly*, CXXX, 217.
6   Lloyd, 62.
7   NAR, LI1/1/1, 150.
8   Monk, XVIII.
9   NLS, 10715, 59.
10 BC, DL to Miss Coutts, 14 Feb 58.
11 NLS, 10715, 59.
12 DL to J. Moore, Letter seen at Sawyers, London, dated 5 Aug 64.
13 Brenthurst Papers, DL to J. Frédoux, 26 Mar 56.
14 NAR, LI1/1/1, 456.
15 SOAS, 10, DL to Gabriel, 27 Jun 56.
16 Ibid., 4 Apr 56.
17 NAR, LI1/1/1, 449; 522.
18 Letter in possession A. O. Ransford.

'THE WONDER OF HIS AGE'

1   NAR, LI1/1/1, 584; *ZE* XXII.
2   *Bell's Weekly Messenger*, 22 Dec 56.
3   Ibid.
4   NAR, LI1/1/1, 658.
5   LMZ, G5/22.

6   Ibid.
7   NAR, MF 48, DL to MM, 8 Feb 62.
8   *The Times*, 23 Sep 57.
9   Murray, DL to JM, 18 Nov 57.
10 NAR LI1/1/1, 758.

'MISSIONARY TRAVELS'

1   NAR, LI1/1/1, 588.
2   *The Atlantic Monthly*, CXXX, 9.
3   NAR, ST1/1/1, 174.
4   Murray, DL to JM (draft).
5   NAR, LI1/1/1, 654.
6   Ibid., 714.
7   Lloyd, 11.
8   NAR, LI1/1/1, 776.

RETURN TO THE ZAMBEZI

1   BC, DL to Miss Coutts, 22 Mar 58.
2   NLS, 10715, 57.
3   Brenthurst Papers, C. Hardisty to wife, 13 Aug 62.
4   LMZ, G5/24.
5   Ibid., 10, 19, 23, 24, 27, 29, 30.
6   *ZJJS*, 19.
7   *PGS*, XVIII, 513.
8   LMZ, G5/24.
9   Ibid., 18.
10 Crépieux-Jamin, J., *ABC de la Graphologie* (1929), (BM. 7947. c. 8).
11 BC, DL to Miss Coutts, 6 May 58.
12 BM, 36525, 57–61.
13 LMZ, G5/11; ibid., 232; *ZE*, I, 82.
14 LMZ, DL to Oswell, 1 Nov 59.
15 NAR, BA7/1/1, 300.
16 Ibid.
17 Ibid., 126.
18 Ibid., 126.
19 NAR, LI1/1/1, 1109.
20 NLS, 10715, n.d.
21 Murray, DL to JM, 3 Mar 65.
22 RHL, DL to Waller, Nov 71–8 Mar 72.
23 NAR, LI1/1/1, 1099.

NYASA

1   Wits, A348.
2   BC, DL to Miss Coutts, 5 Jul 59.
3   NLS, 10768, 26.
4   BC, DL to Miss Coutts, 4 May 59.
5   NAR, LI3/1/1, CL to Mr F. Fitch, 14 Apr 59.
6   BC, DL to Miss Coutts, 10 Oct 59.
7   LMZ, G5/17, 19, 25, 27, 30, 31, 33, 36, 43, 47.
8   NAR, LI2/1/1, 69.
9   Ibid., DL to F. Fitch, 10 Dec 59.

References

THE LONG MARCH

1   NLS, 10715, 246; NAR, LI1/1/1, 1374; *ZE*, II, 391.
2   BC, DL to Miss Coutts, 4 Sep 60.
3   NAR, LI2/1/1, DL to F. Fitch, [3] Feb 62.
4   NAR, LI2/1/1, DL to F. Fitch, 19 Jan 61.
5   NAR, HE3/1/1, 142.
6   NAR, LI2/1/1, DL to F. Fitch, 25 Nov 61.
7   NAR, LI3/1/1, 104.
8   Ibid.
9   NLS, 10715, 239.
10 Ibid.
11 NAR, LI1/1/1, 1374.
12 NLS, 10715, 238.
13 NAR, ST1/2, 188.
14 NLS, 10759, 20.

THE U.M.C.A.

1   USPG, Miss A. Mackenzie to Dr H. Goodwin, 9 Apr 62.
2   NAR, LI3/1/1, 76.
3   NAR, ST1/1/1, 249.
4   LMZ, G5/13.
5   Ibid., 68.
6   BC, DL to Miss Coutts, 13 Mar 61.
7   NAR, LI3/1/1, 77.
8   Ibid., 76.
9   Ibid., 49.
10 Murray, DL to JM, 27 Nov 64.
11 NLS, 10715, 42.
12 Ibid., 13; NAR, LI3/1/1, 60.
13 Brenthurst Papers, C. Hardisty to wife, n.d.
14 NAR, LI3/1/1, 111.

THE 'HETTY ELLEN'

1   Brenthurst Papers, C. Hardisty to wife, n.d.
2   LMZ, G5/79.
3   LMZ, JK notebook.
4   NAR, ST1/1/1, 171.
5   NAR, ST1/2, 352.

TRAGEDY

1   NAR, ST1/2, 238.
2   NAR, LI1/1/1, 1351.
3   USPG, Miss Mackenzie, journal, 1 Apr 62.
4   Ibid., 30 Mar 62.
5   NAR, ST1/1/1, 172.
6   NAR, LI3/1/1, 88.
7   NAR, LI2/1/1, DL to Mrs Fitch, 29 Apr 62.
8   NLS, 10715, 172.

RIVER OF DEATH

1 LMZ, DL to G. Frere, 2 Dec 62.
2 NLS, 10715, 11.
3 Brenthurst Papers, C. Hardisty to wife, 13 Aug 62.
4 NAR, ST1/1/1, 64.
5 NAR, LI3/1/1, 122.
6 NAR, LI2/1/1, DL to J. Moore, 12 Jan 64.
7 NAR, ST1/1/1, 119.

RECALL

1 NLS, 10715, 187.
2 Ibid., 197.
3 NAR, MF 48; LI1/1/2, DL to RM, 10 Aug 63.
4 NAR, UN2/1/1, 176.
5 USPG, DL to Bishop Gray, 27 Feb 64; NAR, LI1/1/1, 1818.
6 USPG, A1(1).
7 NAR, UN2/1/1, 93.
8 NAR, UN2/1/1, 24–28.
9 NAR, BA7/1/1, 126.
10 NAR, ST1/2, 618.
11 NAR, LI2/1/1, DL to J. Moore, 12 Jan 64.
12 BM, 50184, 79.

NEWSTEAD

1 NAR, MF 48, DL to MM, 8 May 65.
2 Information from Dr H. Wilson, 7 Sept 1973.
3 NAR, LI1/1/1, 1788.
4 Ibid.
5 Ibid., 1779.
6 NAR, ST1/1/1, 120.
7 NAR, LI2/1, DL to F. Fitch, 3 Jul 64.
8 NAR, MF 48, DL to Agnes, 13 Mar 72.
9 NAR, TH1/1/1, 28.
10 Murray, DL to JM, 30 Jan 65.
11 Ibid., 23 Mar 65.
12 NAR, TH1/1/1, 28.
13 LMZ, DL journal, 18 Oct 64.
14 Murray, DL to JM, 8 Nov 64.
15 Ibid., 30 Jan 65.
16 Ibid., 3 Jan 65.
17 Ibid., 30 Jan 65.
18 Ibid., 27 Nov 65.
19 Ibid., 9 Jun 65; 1 Aug 65.
20 NAR, BA7/1/1, 404; 697.
21 NAR, MF 48, DL to Agnes, 19 Aug 65.
22 LMZ, G5/97.

THE LAST JOURNEY

1 NAR, TH1/1/1, 28.
2 NAR, LI1/1/1, 2074–7.
3 LMZ, DL to JY, 30 Nov 64.

4   Murray, DL to JM, 28 Sep 65.
5   NAR, LI1/1/1, 2257.
6   NLS, 10715, 15.
7   NAR, LI1/1/1, 2259.
8   Murray, Waller to JM, 25 Jan 75.
9   Information Prof. G. Shepperson, 5 Sep 1973.
10 Murray, DL to JM, 28 Sep 65.
11 Ibid., 17 Mar 66.
12 NAR, LI2/1/2, 54.

TANGANYIKA

1   Murray, Agnes to JM, 25 Apr 68.
2   Ibid.
3   Ibid.
4   Ibid., 10 Nov 69.
5   NAR, LI1/1/1, 2232.

LIVINGSTONE AND STANLEY

1   NLS, 10727, 23.
2   NLS, 10728, 64.
3   NAR, MF 48, DL to Agnes, 16 Dec 71.
4   NAR, LI1/1/1, 2303.
5   Murray, Agnes to JM, 4 Jan 73.

UNYANYEMBE

1   LMZ, G5/216.
2   NLS, 10728, 14.
3   Murray, Agnes to JM, 8 Aug 72.
4   NLS, 10728, 52.
5   Ibid., 59.
6   NAR, LI1/1/1, 2303.
7   NLS, 10728, 60.
8   RGS, Waller to Bates, 18 Oct 72.
9   NLS, 10732, 37.
10 NLS, 10705, HMS to A. Bruce, 7 Jan 87.
11 NLS, 10731, 18.
12 NLS, 10728, 74.

CHITAMBO

1   Information Mr D. D. Yonge, 27 Sept 1973.
2   NAR, PI1/2/1; RGS, DL 5/6/11.
3   RGS, Agnes to RGS, 2 Dec 1909.
4   Blantyre Memorial, Scotland.
5   *PGS*, XVIII, 449.
6   LMZ, Oswell to Canon Conway, 18 Apr 74.
7   NLS, 10705, 15.
8   NAR, LI1/1/1, 2009.

Bibliography

Adams, H. G., *David Livingstone*, Lond., 1892.
Agar-Hamilton, J. A. I., *The Native Policy of the Voortrekkers*, C. T., 1928.
Anderson-Morshead, A. E. M., *The History of the U.M.C.A.*, 5th ed., Lond, 1909.
Anstruther, I., *I Presume: Stanley's Triumph and Disaster*, Lond., 1956.
Bennett, N. R. (ed), *Stanley's Despatches to the New York Herald*, Boston 1970.
Bennett, N. R. and Ylvisaker, M., (eds), *The Central African Journal of Lovell L. Procter*, Boston, 1971.
Birkenshaw, P., *The Livingstone Touch*, C. T., 1973.
Blaikie, W. G., *The Personal Life of David Livingstone*, Lond., 1880.
Cairns, H. A. C., *Prelude to Imperialism*, Lond., 1965.
Cameron, V. L., *Across Africa*, (two vols.), Lond., 1877.
Campbell, R. J., *Livingstone*, Lond., 1929.
Chadwick, O., *Mackenzie's Grave*, Lond., 1959.
Chamberlain, D. (ed.), *Some Letters from Livingstone*, Lond., 1940.
Chambliss, J. E., *The Life and Labors of David Livingstone*, Philadelphia, 1875.
Chapman, J., *Travels in the Interior of Africa*, (ed. Tabler, E.C.), C. T., 1968.
Cole-King, P., 'Livingstone in Malawi', unpublished.
Coupland, R., *Kirk on the Zambesi*, Oxford, 1928.
Coupland, R., *The Exploitation of East Africa*, Lond., 1939.
Coupland, R., *Livingstone's Last Journey*, Lond., 1945.
Crawford, D., *Back to the Long Grass*, Lond.
Curtin, P. D., *The Image of Africa*, Lond., 1965.
Debenham, F., *The Way to Ilala*, Lond., 1955.
Devereux, W. C., *A Cruise in the Gorgon*, Lond., 1869.
Dolman, A., *In the Footsteps of Livingstone*, Lond., 1924.
Du Plessis, J., *A History of the Christian Missions in S.A.*, C. T., 1965.
Faulkner, H., *Elephant Haunts*, Lond., 1868.
Fletcher, I. M., 'David Livingstone', *Oc. Papers of the Rhodes-Livingstone Museum, No: 9*, Livingstone, Zambia.
Foskett, R., (ed.), *The Zambesi Doctors*, Ed., 1964.
Foskett, R., (ed.), *The Zambesi Journal and Letters of Dr John Kirk*, (two vols.) Lond., 1965.
Frazer, A. Z., *Livingstone and Newstead*, Lond., 1913.
Freeman, J. J., *A Tour in South Africa*, Lond., 1851.
Gelfand, M., *Livingstone the Doctor*, Oxford, 1957.
Goodall, N., *A History of the London Missionary Society*, Lond., 1954.
Goodwin, H., *Memoir of Bishop Mackenzie*, Camb., 1865.
Groves, C. P., *The Planting of Christianity in Africa*, (two vols.), Lond., 1964.
Hall, R., *Stanley, An Adventurer Explored*, Lond., 1974.
Huxley, E., *Livingstone and His African Journeys*, Lond., 1974.
Jeal, T., *Livingstone*, Lond., 1973.
Johnston, H. H., *Livingstone and the Exploration of Central Africa*, Lond., 1891.

Bibliography

Listowel, J., *The Other Livingstone*, C. T., 1974.
Livingstone, D., *Missionary Travels and Researches in South Africa*, Lond., 1857.
Livingstone, D., and C., *Narrative of an Expedition to the Zambesi and its Tributaries*, Lond., 1865.
Lloyd, B. W. (ed.), *Livingstone, 1873-1973*, C. T., 1973.
Lovett, R., *The History of the London Missionary Society* (two vols.), Lond., 1899.
Mackenzie, J., *Ten Years North of the Orange River*, Ed., 1871.
Macnair, J. I., *Livingstone the Liberator*, Lond., 1940.
Macnair, J. I., *Livingstone's Travels*, Lond., 1954.
Martelli, G., *Livingstone's River*, Lond., 1970.
Monk, W., (ed.), *Dr Livingstone's Cambridge Lectures*, Lond., 1858.
Moorhouse, G., *The Missionaries*, Lond., 1973.
Northcott, C., *Livingstone in Africa*, Lond., 1957.
Northcott, C., *Robert Moffat*, Lond., 1961.
Northcott, C., *David Livingstone*, Lond., 1973.
New, C., *Life, Wanderings and Labours in East Africa*, Lond., 1871.
Oliver, R., *The Missionary Factor in East Africa*, Lond., 1952.
Oswell, E., *William Cotton Oswell*, (two vols.), Lond., 1900.
Pachai, B., (ed.), *Livingstone, Man of Africa*, Lond., 1973.
Rampley, W. J., *Matthew Wellington*, London.
Ritchie, J. E., *Life and Discoveries of David Livingstone*, (six vols.), Lond.
Robertson, J. S., *The Life and Explorations of David Livingstone*, Accrington.
Rotberg, R. I., (ed.), *Africa and its Explorers*, Lond., 1970.
Rowley, H., *The Story of the Universities' Mission to Central Africa*, Lond., 1866.
Schapera, I., (ed.) *David Livingstone: Family Letters*, (two vols.), Lond., 1959.
Schapera, I., (ed.), *Livingstone's Private Journals*, Lond., 1960.
Schapera, I., (ed.), *Livingstone's Missionary Correspondence*, Lond., 1961.
Schapera, I., (ed.), *Livingstone's African Journal*, (two vols.), Lond., 1963.
Schapera, I., (ed.), *David Livingstone, South African Papers*, C. T., 1974.
Seaver, G., *David Livingstone: His Life and Letters*, Lond., 1957.
Shepperson, G., *David Livingstone and the Rovuma*, Ed., 1965.
Sillery, A., *Sechele*, Oxford, 1954.
Simmons, J., *Livingstone and Africa*, Lond., 1955.
Simpson, D., *Dark Companions*, Lond., 1975.
Smith, E. W., *Great Lion of Bechuanaland*, Lond., 1957.
Stanley, H. M., *How I Found Livingstone*, Lond., 1872.
Stanley, D., (ed.), *The Autobiography of Sir Henry Morton Stanley*, Lond., 1909.
Tabler, C. (ed.), *The Zambesi Papers of Richard Thornton*, (two vols.), Lond., 1963.
Waller, H. (ed.), *The Last Journals of David Livingstone in Central Africa*, (two vols.), Lond., 1874.
Wallis, J. P. R., *Thomas Baines of King's Lynn*, Lond., 1941.
Wallis, J. P. R., (ed.), *The Matabele Mission*, Lond., 1945.
Wallis, J. P. R., (ed.), *The Zambesi Journal of James Stewart*, Lond., 1953.
Wallis, J. P. R., (ed.), *The Zambesi Expedition of David Livingstone*, (two vols.), Lond., 1956.
Wells, J., *The Life of James Stewart*, Lond., 1898.
Young, E. D., *The Search after Livingstone*, Lond., 1868.

Index

Africa, 1, 70, 161, 235; debt to DL, 5, 65, 118, 134–5, 136, 223, 311; unknown interior, 7, 12, 14; fly-infestation, 55; malaria and European exploration, 56, 76, 77, 263; trading prospects, 66, 83, 86, 111, 125–7, 311; DL's deceptive dreams, 126–8; value of white settlement, 158–61; depopulation by slave trade, 241; see also Slave trade

African people, 20–1, 35, 103; DL's appreciation, 21, 26, 36, 81–3, 86, 118, 126; proposed use of as teachers, 23, 33, 39, 41, 42, 46; initiation rites (*boguera*), 25, 36, 137; and European arms, 25, 53, 55, 70, 72–3; DL and their sad condition, 209, 219, 241; memory of him, 238, 244; respect for Arabs, 242; practice of geophagy, 263; and DL's last days and death, 304–6

Afrikaners, 'thirstland trekkers', 76n; see Boers

Albert, Prince Consort, 15, 124, 128, 131

Ambaca, 96

American Civil War, 111, 225, 226, 227; Stanley and, 276

Amoda, porter, 239, 248, 256

Anderson, C., *Annalls of the English Bible*, 58

Angola, 81, 83, 85, 98, 130; Portuguese outposts, 95, 96; DL and, 98–9

Angola, Bishop of, 97, 98

Angoni (Mazitu), the, 190, 191, 244, 246, 248

Arabs, slave traders, 66, 81, 101, 185, 221, 241–2, 244, 253–4, 260; and African customs, 103–4; DL and, 242, 251–61 *passim*, 268, 270–2; legend of Moses, 268

Argyll, George Douglas, Duke of, 17, 159 and n; DL at Inveraray, 227–8

Arrowsmith, John, mapmaker, 138, 232

Bachokwe (Chiboque), the, predatory tribe, 91, 94–5, 101

Bagamoyo, 243, 275, 278, 279; S. and R. Expedition, 289

Baines, Thomas, 1n, 53, 177, 231; treatment by DL, 142, 151–5, 166, 207–8, 218, 233–4, 284; and Zambezi Expedition, 142, 144, 232

Bakaa, the, 30, 31

Baker, Sir Samuel, 141, 224, 235; Nile expedition, 273n, 274

Bakgalagadi, the, 27, 31

Bakgatla, 26–7, 30, 34; *and see* Bakhatla

Bakhatla, 37; L.M.S. station, 42

Bakwains, the, 39; *and see* Bakwena

Bakwena, the, 27, 30, 31, 32; DL and, 40, 41, 44–7, 54, 60, 68–9, 170; Ngami expedition, 48; status, 63; Boer attack, 71–2; fighting force, 72–3; at Battle of Dimawe, 73–4

Balaka, 220

Balobale, the, 91

Balonda, the, and DL's journey, 88–91; nudity, 89, 91

Bamangwato, the, 30, 48; status, 63

Bambarre, DL and, 261–70 *passim*, 273

Bantu language, 2, 30n

Bantu, the, 19, 20, 36, 51; the *Mfecane*, 24, 90; DL and their culture, 87, 90, 126

Baptist Missionary Society, 11

Barotse, the, 62, 170; helot class, 63

Barotseland, DL and, 80–1

Batawana, the, 52

Batoka, the, *see* Batonga

Batoka Highlands, 63, 113, 128; tribesmen, 106, 177

Batoka Plateau, 107, 129, 130, 169, 170

Batonga, the, 106, 169

Bechuana, the, 14; DL on, 25

Bechuanaland, 174

Bedingfeld, Lt. Commander Norman, 97, 100, 231; and Zambezi Expedition, 142, 144, 146, 151–2, 218; relations with DL, 146–7, 284

ben Habib, Syde, Arab slave trader, 81, 104, 220, 258; crosses Africa, 101, 103; distrusted by DL, 103–4

Bengo River, 99

Index

Index

324

Index

Index

Index

Index

Owen, Robert, 9, 19
Owen, Capt. W. F., 202

Palmerston, Lord, 160, 161, 224
Pambete, 252
Pascoal, African, 101
Pedro, King of Portugal, 106, 124, 130
Pereira, Portuguese traveller, 80
Philip, Rev. John, influence on DL, 19–20, 35; L.M.S. Superintendent, 20, 70; S. African policy, 20–1, 33; his Union Chapel dispute, 21
Pinkwe Hill, 177
H.M.S. *Pioneer*, 150, 178–84 *passim*, 198, 205, 221–2, 243; journey up lower Zambezi, 198; stranded at Shupanga, 205; and Shire River, 207–9; in Elephant Marsh, 209; at Mikorongo, 210
Pitsane, Makololo porter, 88
Port Elizabeth, DL's behaviour at, 21
Porto, Silva, Portuguese trader, 65, 253; and the Zambezi, 80, 81, 83
Portugal, 95–6, 98, 112; knowledge of the Zambezi, 64–5, 80, 148; slave traders, 66, 89, 107, 130, 136, 163, 185, 205, 209, 224; and DL, 113, 130–1, 151, 167–8, 178, 205, 219; relations with Britain, 124, 130, 215, 219; control of mouth of the Zambezi, 163, 167
Potgieter, Hendrik, Voortrekker leader, 46–7
Potgietersrus, 42
Prentice, Thomas, 14
Pretorius, Andries, Voortrekker leader, 46, 74n
Price, Roger, and Makololo mission, 171, 172, 173 and n; later career, 173–4, 310
Procter, Lovell James, senior priest of U.M.C.A., 179, 180, 183–4, 185, 192; on DL, 180
Ptolemy, *Geography*, 236, 237, 257, 259
Pungo Andongo, 100, 102
Pusey, Dr E. Bouverie, 179, 188, 209–10

Quango River, 95–6, 267
Quelimane, 207; and DL's journey, 71, 109, 114, 116, 121; his Consular appointment, 129 and nn; Portuguese custom house, 167

Rae, George, 202, 225, 231; character, 142, 208; and Zambezi Expedition, 144, 147, 148, 149, 152, 164, 166, 175, 207, 213; goes home, 167; and new steamer (*Lady Nyassa*), 182, 193, 194, 198, 207, 208, 222; opinion of Stewart, 195, 196; and *Pioneer*, 198, 199–200
Ramsay, Dr, of *Gorgon*, 199

Rhodes, Cecil, 25
Rhodesia, 24, 103; DL and, 177n
Rider, Alfred, artist, 56
Ridley, Catherine, 14 and n
Rivirivi valley, 220
Ross, Sir Ronald, and malaria, 79
Ross, Rev. William, 16, 21; and Kuruman station, 16; and DL, 18–19, 42
Rovuma River, exploration, 178, 181, 190, 191, 206–7, 211, 223, 300; route to Lake Nyasa, 209, 236, 242, 243
Rowley ('Parson'), Henry, priest with U.M.C.A., 179, 180, 183, 188, 201, 211, 218; on Shire River, 209
Royal Geographical Society, 54, 97, 275; and DL, 100, 119, 134, 224, 235; and Stanley, 291–2; and DL's death record, 306–7; opens his coffin, 309
Royal Navy, and DL's expeditions, 97, 100, 114–16, 148, 166, 167, 193–4, 201, 215, 216, 218, 243; and slave traders, 101, 242
Rua, cave dwellings, 264, 297
Rufiji River, 278
Russell, Lord John (Earl), 176, 178, 214, 218 and n, 223, 231; reception of DL, 224; and his last journey, 235, 236
Rustenburg, 41
Rutton, Richard and Benjamin, 290

Sabbath Schools, 9
Sabine, General, 126
St Columba, 6
St Moluag, 6
Salima, 220
Sand River Convention 1852, 72, 73
Sansureh River, 77
Sauko village, 165
Savuti Channel, 62
Scholtz, Commandant, 73, 74
Schuckmannsburg, 169
Scotland, 224–8, 233; prospects for lowly born, 7; Industrial Revolution, 8–9
Scudamore, Rev. Henry Carter, U.M.C.A. priest, 179–80, 185; death, 209, 249
Seamogoe, chief, 41
Search and Relief Expedition, 294; Oswell's behaviour, 289–90; composition, 290
Sebetwane, chief, 53, 55, 59, 61; and DL, 58, 62–3; death and succession, 63–4; slave trade, 66
Sechele, DL's sole convert, 27, 31, 39–45 *passim*, 48, 58, 68–9; baptism, 44; Boer attack on his tribe, 71–2, 73–4
Sedgwick, Prof. Alan, 159
Sehamy, DL and his death, 32, 35, 63

330

Index

Index

Tidman, Rev. Arthur, 40, 224; and L.M.S., 33, 71, 114–15, 121; DL's letters to, 46, 51, 52, 60, 68, 113; suspected 'animus', 122, 131; and DL's resignation, 122, 123; and Makololo mission, 171, 174

The Times, 100, 180, 219

Tippu Tip, 253

Tozer, Bishop William George, 261; successor to Mackenzie, 214–15; character and appearance, 215, 217–18; at Mikorongo, 215; and U.M.C.A., 215–16; and slave trade, 215; DL and, 216–17, 284; subsequent career, 217

Transvaal, 24, 25n, 40; Boer occupation, 19, 46; DL's journey to, 41–2; Government claim to Bakwena, 72, 74; and Boer Wars, 74

Tsaugara pan, 61

Tswana, the, 24, 41n, 173; Boer influence, 25

Ufipa district, 298

Ujiji, 308, 311; on caravan route to interior, 242–3; DL and, 251, 255–9, 272–3, 287; supply caravan, 269–70; Stanley/DL meeting, 274, 275, 280–1

Ulva, 6 and n, 228

Universities, response to DL's appeal, 128, 167, 178, 216

Universties Mission to Central Africa (U.M.C.A.), 128, 131, 166, 309n; arrival in *Pioneer*, 178–9; membership, 179–81; Anglican ethos, 179–80; reaction to conditions, 183; and a slave coffle, 185–6; Magomero station, 187, 205; conflict with Yao, 186–7, 188, 205; Durban contingent, 195; DL's animosity, 201, 205, 209–10; in low morale, 205, 206; withdrawal to Morumbala and Zanzibar, 216, 217; Nkhotakota compound, 220; return to the interior, 246

Unyanyembe, Arab colony, 243, 258, 259, 279–80, 283, 308; DL/Stanley journey, 287; arrival of Stanley's pagazi, 297

Urimba, 287

Vaal River, 34, 63

Victoria, Queen, 102 and n, 228, 233, 310; receives DL, 131; accepts *Missionary Travels*, 138; on Stanley, 277

Victoria Falls, 169, 231; DL and, 76, 104, 109, 177 and n; attempted measurement, 176; painted by DL, 176–7

Wainwright, Jacob and John, among Stanley's pagazi, 290 and n, 306, 308; later career, 308n, 310

Waller, Horace (lay member of U.M.C.A.), 181, 188, 231; friendship with DL, 181, 186, 202, 211, 234, 238, 243, 284, 295, 310; on Mackenzie, 200; resignation, 216; rescues slaves, 216; and DL's journals, 292 and n; and his last days, 304

Wamanyema, the, 261, 269, 272

Wankie coalfield, 177

Ward, Thomas, steward in *Pioneer*, 220

Wardlaw, Dr Ralph, abolitionist, 12

Washington, Capt. J., 128, 129, 161, 182; and Zambezi Expedition, 178, 218

Watt, Rev. D. G., 15, 38, 52

Webb, William, and Newstead Abbey, 228, 229, 233, 277, 310

Wellington, Matthew, Nasik boy, 290 and n

Whymper, Mr J. H., artist, 56n

Wikatani, and DL in *Lady Nyassa*, 222; and last journey, 239, 248

Wilson, Mr J. H., ivory trader, 48, 49, 54

Wilson, Capt., R.N., in *Gorgon*, 193, 195, 199, 200

Wilson, Dr Hubert, gs. of DL, 60

Yao, warlike tribe, 163, 184–5; encounter with, 186–7; U.M.C.A. and, 186–8 *passim*, 205, 239

Young, 'Gunner' E. D., 213, 222n, 310; African expedition in *The Search*, 249

Young, Sir James ('Sir Paraffin'), 12, 166, 202, 225 and n, 309n; and DL's last journey, 236

Zaire, 81, 255; Kiwakisi Caves, 264

Zambezi, the, 24, 59, 62, 71, 103; sacred ibis, 51; reached by DL and Oswell, 64–5; slave trade area, 65; and commerce, 66; character of its people, 81–2, 124; tsetse infestation, 81; geographical features, 88, 97, 145, 193, 266; DL's 1855 expedition, 104–15; his false presentation, 127, 136; Portuguese restrictions, 131; unnavigable at Kebrabasa, 149–150; closed to navigation, 156; emergence at Kaombo, 264; *see also* Zambezi Expedition *under* Livingstone, David

Zambia, 85, 248, 255

Zanzibar, 103, 104, 210, 212, 222, 277; Tozer's planned site for U.M.C.A., 216, 217; Kirk's appointment, 237, 285; and DL's last journey, 240, 241–3; slave markets, 241–2; inhabitants, 241

Zomba, 162–3, 166; Mountain, 164, 188

Zouga River (Botletle), 49 and n, 51–2

Zulus, the, 24, 190

Zumbo, Portuguese settlement, 112, 130, 169, 172, 175, 177

332